Sara Paretsky

McFarland Companions to Mystery Fiction

# Sara Paretsky

## A Companion to
## the Mystery Fiction

MARGARET KINSMAN

McFarland Companions to Mystery Fiction, 7
*Series Editor* Elizabeth Foxwell

McFarland & Company, Inc., Publishers
*Jefferson, North Carolina*

Margaret Kinsman is also a consulting editor of *Clues: A Journal of Detection* published by McFarland twice a year.

ISBN (print) 978-0-7864-7187-4
ISBN (ebook) 978-1-4766-2569-0

Library of Congress cataloguing data are available

British Library cataloguing data are available

Front cover: woman walking on a wet street © 2016 UygarGeographic/iStock

Printed in the United States of America

*McFarland & Company, Inc., Publishers*
*Box 611, Jefferson, North Carolina 28640*
*www.mcfarlandpub.com*

For V. I. and her community of readers:
"All books are either dreams or swords"—Amy Lowell

# Table of Contents

# Acknowledgments

This volume owes a great deal to Sara Paretsky herself, who generously opened her files and her home to me on many sociable occasions. In coming to know the author, I also gained insight into her famous character, V. I. Warshawski, and grew to understand the city of Chicago in new ways. It has been a privilege and a joy to have such rewarding subject matter; I was lucky to have the chance to write about what I know and love in a particularly vigorous period in the history of the crime and mystery genre. It would be hard to imagine a more satisfactory project to undertake. As a Midwesterner myself, although long located in London, I am proud to claim kinship with Chicago and two of her most loved daughters, V. I. and her creator.

The Newberry Library, where Paretsky's papers are held, was a wonderful place to work for short periods in November 2012 and September 2013. I am especially grateful to Martha Briggs, Lloyd Lewis Curator of Modern Manuscripts, who not only facilitated access to the Paretsky archive but also took a keen interest in the project; she offered the kind of support dreamt of by researchers. My own academic institution, London South Bank University, located a small bursary to fund a postdoc research assistant, Leon Betsworth, who worked diligently on bibliographic sources early in the project. Kathryn Hodson, department manager of the Special Collections and University Archives at the University of Iowa, could not have been more accommodating when I pitched up as an independent scholar. For several weeks in February 2014 I was a happy guest in her welcoming library environment, enriched by books, workspace, and conversation. Her colleagues Karen M. Mason and Janet Weaver at the Iowa Women's Archives provided another rich seam of inspiration. Avid mystery readers themselves and proud archivists of Iowa author Mildred Wirt Benson materials, including the typewriter on which some of the Nancy Drew novels were written, we found much in common as scholars and readers.

Series editor Elizabeth Foxwell and I are grateful to Yevgeniya Gribov, researcher/senior archivist at the National Historic Preservation Center, Girl Scouts of the USA, for her invaluable help in locating a copy of Paretsky's first published work, "The Tornado," in *American Girl* magazine. My thanks also go to Linda Erf Swift, whose photography skills and high standards enhanced many of the images in this volume; our long friendship and her welcoming Hyde Park household supported the work in countless other ways.

My sister, Suzanne Kinsman, read an early draft section; as one of V. I.'s fans, she gave some invaluable advice from a reader's perspective. Many friends and colleagues in London and the United States helped keep the project on the rails by supplying the comfort, confidence, and intellectual curiosity that attends upon deep, abiding friendships. Elizabeth Foxwell gave her characteristically beneficial advice and support. In the process of writing this Companion volume, I learned a valuable lesson from V. I. about house-work—namely, that life is too short.

Finally, the later period of researching and writing co-existed with an unexpectedly felicitous development in my own life involving the company of someone who is not only from the Midwest but also loves V. I. as much as I do. Jerry raided his law school library for copies of the Paretsky novels on which I was working deep in an Iowa winter, asked all of the right questions, steadied the boat more than once, and agreed with me on the important points.

# Preface

Sara N. Paretsky is the author of a body of work that changed the template of the American private-eye novel. Her pioneering work from the early 1980s onward opened doors for a legion of mystery readers and writers eager to push the boundaries of both canon and genre traditions not only in relation to representations of gender but also of race, class, ethnicities, sexualities, and place.

Her stories featuring the irascible, committed, and housework-shy detective V. I. "Vic" Warshawski gave many women readers a female character with whom they could identify in print. The use of Chicago as V. I.'s home turf also marked out new ground. The last four decades have proved to be an exciting and fruitful period for crime and mystery fiction: there is no doubt that Paretsky's influences on, and contributions to, the genre are seen as pivotal, and lasting. "Her novels," writes Liahna Babener, "are at the vanguard of feminist revisions of the hard-boiled mystery tradition" (400). Iowa born, Kansas raised, and resident in Chicago since the late 1960s, Paretsky and her Midwestern sensibilities (a vigorous idealism, a profound commitment to social justice, and the conviction that education is the key to an informed civic body) underpin the V. I. series, the first of which was published in 1982.

After more than thirty years, her influence on the world of crime and mystery fiction cannot be underestimated. Several generations of readers have embraced the V. I. Warshawski persona as inspirational and wished they had her for a friend in real life. The reading audience is international; the novels have been translated into more than thirty languages. The appeal of the V. I. series (seventeen novels and more than a dozen short stories to date) rests on three main features: the characterization of V. I. that deepens over time, the unexpected use of Chicago as a setting, and complex and sophisticated plots that are constructed around pressing contemporary social issues ranging from homelessness and domestic violence to the fallout from the war in Iraq. Details of V. I.'s personal life—her friends; family; lovers; aversion to domestic labor; eating habits; love of music and dogs; and most of all, doubts and anxieties—are made available to readers even as the intrepid detective races around Chicago following leads on her cases. It is an irresistible combination—a competent woman determined to do the right thing and frequently worried that she is not doing enough.

Although single and childless, V. I. is a far cry from the solitary figure of Philip Marlowe, playing chess against himself in a lonely room. V. I. is embedded in a range of kinship and friendship systems, and is as attentive as she can be to maintaining these. Like many women, V. I. is frequently pulled in too many directions; she takes on more commitments than she can reasonably manage and feels obliged to see them through. Often on overload, she gets bogged down in self-doubt; more than anything, she fears a state of helplessness and a dependence on others. She prefers to act alone, relying on her wits and physical fitness. When she faces down a condescending corporate executive with a quick verbal rejoinder or humiliates a would-be kidnaper by throwing up on his jacket, the reader momentarily steps into a scenario that reverses the usual order of things and cheers on Vic. Her parents, although long since deceased, continue to speak to her from beyond the grave, offering advice and good examples in the dreams and memories that V. I. reports back into the text; we have a clear understanding of the values and ethics that informed V. I.'s own upbringing and that continue to shape her as an adult.

The attraction of this detective figure is further enhanced by a strong circle of friends and the occasional lover. The likes of Dr. Lotty Herschel, Sal Barthele, Tessa Reynolds, Mary Louise Neely, and other repeating characters constitute a particular critical mass of accomplished professional women subject to the usual stresses and strains of everyday life just as V. I. is. The Chicago setting was innovative in the early 1980s when the definitive "mean city streets" locations in both fiction and film were New York, San Francisco, and Los Angeles. V. I. has an intimate relationship with her "briar patch"; we come to know her city through the detective's favorite restaurants, her love of Lake Michigan, her devotion to the Cubs baseball team, and her appreciation of the distinctive neighborhoods and ethnicities that make up the Chicago landscape. Beyond that, we understand V. I.'s weary engagement with the city's reputation for organized crime at all levels of the civic infrastructure, from the mafia and the church to the police and elected officials. With her own specialty in investigating financial crime, V. I. is no stranger to corporate and individual white-collar crimes such as fraud, asset stripping, and money laundering. Her affection for the flawed city is tempered with her desire that it should be a better place than it is. Informed by Paretsky's keen understanding of Chicago's industrial, social, and cultural histories, expressed through V. I.'s own sensitivities to her city, the Midwestern urban setting now occupies its own place in the lexicon of crime and mystery fiction.

Another important marker of the series is the complexity of the plots, a feature usually praised and sometimes criticized. Paretsky's own lifelong interest in issues of social justice is reflected in the plots that might focus on, for instance, the effects of poverty, institutional racism and sexism, low-paid work, prisoner rights, the for-profit medical sector, and the fraudulent use of pension funds. In the course of one novel, V. I. will often be running two or three seemingly unrelated investigations. As one thing leads to another and historical connections are uncovered, the cases usually come together in the revelation of something bigger than expected. Paretsky is adept at weaving together story lines from the past and the present, as in *Total Recall* and *Hardball*, using split timeframes and narrative points of view other than the detective's. Often V. I.'s cases will start with a family member needing help; in *Burn Marks*, V. I.'s reluctant offer of help to her indigent Aunt Elena escalates into an investigation of housing and construction scandals and complicities among a Chicago business consortium, providers of low-cost senior housing, and insurance companies. This pattern repeats throughout the series, with layers of entrenched political and financial privilege and power revealed in novel after novel; V. I. pursues cases because she is motivated by her own sense of outrage at the injustices that people on the margins suffer at the hands of bureaucratic and indifferent systems.

A sense of personal responsibility and a fierce desire to right wrongs also drive V. I. to plunge into cases where there are dark secrets at the heart of the family; V. I.'s actions and bravery help many a troubled youngster survive traumatic family situations. In the course of the cases, the private eye proves her mettle again and again—following obscure paper trails with patience and determination, breaking into offices in search of evidence, encountering dangerous situations, and sometimes suffering the consequences of physical violence in protecting victims from would-be attackers.

The pressure to continue a successful series is considerable—both publishers and readers want more of the same, and that can prove to be a trap. Paretsky has avoided some of the pitfalls by taking the occasional break to write other works and by bringing to the foreground some of the other series characters (such as Lotty Herschel in *Total Recall* and *Critical Mass*). She allows V. I. to age in real (although slowed) time and keeps her detective up to date in the world of technology. V. I. is a woman who moves with the times and will continue to delight new audiences. The movie *V. I. Warshawski* and several radio adaptations have brought the character to the attention of new audiences.

In addition to the popular V. I. series, Paretsky is the author of two standalone novels, *Ghost Country* (1998) and *Bleeding Kansas* (2008). She published a set of autobiographical essays under the title *Writing in an Age of Silence* (2007); the collection was based on a number of her public speeches on various platforms about her own journey as a writer. She has edited a series of anthologies for Sisters in Crime, the pioneering advocacy group for women writers, booksellers, librarians, agents, and editors working in the crime and mystery field that Paretsky was instrumental in cofounding. Her own short stories have appeared in many outlets, including edited anthologies and mystery magazines; a collection of V. I. short stories appears in *Windy City Blues* (aka *V. I. for Short*). The standalone short stories are characterized by a sly wit and a fondness for the macabre; the short form allows Paretsky to explore some of the themes that interest her (such as bullying parents, self-righteous religious fanatics, and body image) from a range of perspectives, including some clever parodies of earlier fictional detectives such as Miss Jane Marple, Race Williams, and Philip Marlowe. She publishes articles, essays, and reviews in newspapers, academic and professional journals, and periodicals on a range of subjects, including women's reproductive rights, the Patriot Act and its consequences for the public library system, the publishing world, and other contemporary matters. Much in demand as a public speaker, Paretsky continues to widen her audience. As an author who injected fresh air into the crime and mystery genre more than thirty years ago, Paretsky's work continues to engage readers who appreciate her varied dimensions as a writer and an advocate for social justice.

Needlepointed pillow, made by Mary Louise Wright, business manager of the *Journal of Applied Behavior Analysis*, University of Kansas, 1997, celebrates author and character. Gift to author. Photograph by author.

# Organization of the Companion

This companion is the first comprehensive reference work on Paretsky's influential series of mystery novels, as well as her other fiction and nonfiction work. It aims to provide readers with accurate biographical information on the author and her professional career as a writer and to document the significance of her impact on the popular genre of crime and mystery fiction from the 1980s onward. The companion is organized in such a way that readers of Paretsky's oeuvre, whether they are scholars, fans, or new readers of her work, will be able to access information about the V. I. novels, the short stories, the standalone novels and the memoir, media adaptations, the journalism, and the edited anthologies.

The reference work opens with lists of Paretsky's published works in both chronological and alphabetical order.

A brief biography and a career chronology, including reference to the many prizes and honors awarded to Paretsky since 1982, follow.

The bulk of the companion is composed of alphabetical entries that examine her novels and short stories; anthologies; autobiographical collection of essays; main characters in the V. I. series; typical themes, motifs, and symbols that crop up throughout the V. I. series; and many of her articles and essays written for newspapers and periodicals.

Attention is given to the main critical and theoretical debates focused on Paretsky's work, to the comments of reviewers and critics, and to media adaptations. Discussion of Paretsky's work in relation to the hard-boiled private-eye genre with its distinctive characteristics is included; and her work is considered in relation to a Chicago literary canon.

An annotated bibliography is provided that surveys the major articles, essays, interviews, and analyses—including a selection of PhD dissertations written about the author, her famous character, and their place in the history of the private-eye novel. Paretsky's work and the new subgenre of the feminist-inflected, hard-boiled detective novel has attracted considerable attention in popular forums and in the academy over the last thirty years. This wide body of commentary has been generated by an international community of graduate students, biographers, reviewers and critics, literary historians and theorists, journalists, librarians, fans, and others who have addressed and assessed the Paretsky oeuvre from a range of perspectives. What most of these perspectives share is the agreement that it is due to the work of Paretsky and others that the genre of crime and mystery fiction is now one where sustained adventure and female protagonists no longer seem to be mutually exclusive.

The companion offers a number of pathways into Paretsky's work; readers already familiar with the V. I. character may arrive at a deeper understanding of how themes and characters criss-cross and fertilize across the oeuvre. Lovers of her popular fiction may be interested in learning more about the non-fiction part of the body of work.

Some of the illustrations and reference materials quoted have been sourced from Paretsky's private papers and from the Paretsky Papers archive located at the Newberry Library in Chicago. These materials appear for the first time in a published work.

As Paretsky is still writing and publishing, and as critical and theoretical work on her continues to emerge, this companion is necessarily not complete. Any omissions, oversights, or errors are my own.

# Paretsky's Works in Chronological Order

The list of Paretsky's works was gathered from a number of sources, including *Current Biography Yearbook* (1992); *Reference Guide to American Literature,* 3rd ed. (1994); *Contemporary Popular Writers* (1997); *St. James Guide to Crime and Mystery Writers* (1996); *Mystery and Suspense Writers,* Vol. 2 (1998); *Bulletin of Bibliography* (1999); *Contemporary Literary Criticism,* Vol. 135 (2001); *Dictionary of Literary Biography,* Vol. 306 (2005); and *Contemporary Authors,* Vol. 129 (1990, updated 2011). The chronological list starts with the 1959 piece "The Tornado" and includes all of Paretsky's subsequent fiction and nonfiction to date. A few of her titles differ in the British and American editions. British titles different from their American counterparts follow American titles in the alphabetical and chronological listings, so both titles are listed under the American title. Articles "The," "A," and "An" are ignored for alphabetization. Titles such as "Mr." or "Dr." used in fictional characters' names are ignored for alphabetization. A number of Paretsky's short stories have been published in more than one periodical and/or anthology—where possible, the bibliographical history of the short stories has been included. In this list and the alphabetical list, the novels and short stories that feature V. I. Warshawski are marked with an asterisk. Dates given are the dates of first publication of that title. Foreign editions of her work are not included here due to length considerations; however, it should be noted that the extent of her work in translation is impressive.

*Novels/short stories featuring V. I. Warshawski

"The Tornado." *American Girl* magazine Aug. 1959: 77–78. Print.

"This Is for You, Jeannie." *Women: A Journal of Liberation* 3.3 (1972): 46–51. Print.

"The Breakdown of Moral Philosophy in New England Before the Civil War." PhD diss., University of Chicago, 1977.

*Indemnity Only.* New York: Dial; London: Gollancz, 1982. New York: Dell, 1991. Delacorte pb edition 1990. Dell 1991 pb reissued as 30th anniversary edition with new author introduction November 2011.

"Mysteries." *Chicago Tribune Book World* 8 May 1983, sec.7: 5. Print.

*"The Takamoku Joseki." *Alfred Hitchcock's Mystery Magazine,* Nov. 1983. 33–42. *Women of Mystery.* Ed. Cynthia Manson. New York: Berkley, 1993. 227–39. Paretsky, *Windy City Blues* 246–58. Paretsky, *V. I. for Short* 1–12.

*First Cases: First Appearances of Classic Private Eyes.* Ed. Robert J. Randisi. New York: Dutton, 1996. 159–70. *Win, Lose or Die.* Ed. Cynthia Manson and Constance Scarborough. New York: Carroll, 1996. 38  46. Landrigan 213–22.

*Deadlock.* New York: Dial; London: Gollancz, 1984. New York: Ballantine, 1984. Pleasantville, NY: IMPress Mystery, 2004.

*"Three-Dot Po." Randisi, *The Eyes Have It* 227–44. *Ms. Murder.* Ed. Marie Smith. London: Xanadu Publ., 1989. 32–43. Paretsky, *Windy City Blues* 226–45. Paretsky, *V. I. for Short* 13–32. *The Big Book of Christmas Mysteries.* Ed. Otto Penzler. New York: Vintage Crime/Black Lizard, 2013. 452–61.

*Killing Orders.* New York: Morrow, 1985. London: Gollancz, 1986. London: Penguin, 1987. Print.

*"At the Old Swimming Hole." Hopkins and Potter 32–43. *Lady on the Case*. Ed. Marcia Muller, Bill Pronzini, and Martin H. Greenberg. New York: Bonanza, 1988. 277–94. Print. *Murder and Mystery in Chicago*. Ed. Carol-Lynn Rossel Waugh, Frank D. McSherry Jr., and Martin H. Greenberg. New York: Dembner, 1987. 1–20. Print. Paretsky *Windy City Blues* 124–49. Paretsky, *V. I. for Short* 133–58. Randisi, *Mean Streets* 171–95.

*_Bitter Medicine_. New York: Morrow; London: Gollancz, 1987. New York: Ballantine, 1987. Print.

*"Skin Deep." *The New Black Mask*, no. 8 (1987): 102–20. *Homicidal Acts*. Ed. Bill Pronzini and Martin H. Greenberg. New York: Ballantine, 1988. 151–64. *City Sleuths and Tough Guys*. Ed. D. W. McCullough. Boston: Houghton, 1989. 461–73. *P.I. Files*. Ed. Loren Estelman and Martin Greenberg. New York: Ballantine, 1990. 57–69. *A Modern Treasury of Great Detective and Murder Mysteries*. Ed. Ed Gorman. New York: Carroll, 1994. 197–208. Paretsky, *Windy City Blues* 209–25. Paretsky, *V. I. for Short* 59–75. Halligan 99–112. Mansfield–Kelley and Marchino 308–19. *Chicago Noir: The Classics*. Ed. Joe Meno. Akashic Books, 2015. 177–193.

"A Poignant Tribute to Cicero." *Chicago Sun-Times* 20 Dec. 1987: 19. Print.

*_Blood Shot_. New York: Delacorte, 1988. Published as *Toxic Shock* in UK. London: Gollancz, 1988. Print.

*"The Case of the Pietro Andromache." *Alfred Hitchcock's Mystery Magazine* Dec. 1988. *The Year's Best Mystery and Suspense Stories*. Ed. Edward D. Hoch. New York: Walker, 1989. *New Crimes* [1]. Ed. Maxim Jakubowski. New York: Carroll, 1990. Wallace, *Sisters in Crime* 113–35. Greenberg 15–49. Paretsky, *Windy City Blues* 61–91. Paretsky, *V. I. for Short* 76–105. George, *Moment on the Edge* 279–307. *Great TV and Film Detectives*. Ed. Maxim Jakubowski. New York: Reader's Digest Assn., 2005. 474–91. Print.

"Dealer's Choice." *Raymond Chandler's Philip Marlowe: A Centennial Celebration*. Ed. Byron Preiss. New York: Knopf, 1988. 119–33. New York: Simon & Schuster ibooks, 1999. 119–33. *The New Mystery*. Ed. J.

Charyn. New York: Dutton, 1993. 80–95. Paretsky, *A Taste of Life and Other Stories* 11–40. Print.

"Chicago." *Savvy* Sept. 1988: 48–51. Print.

"Private Eyes, Public Spheres." *The Women's Review of Books* Nov. 1988: 12–13. Print.

"Let's Have a Big Smile, Now." *Naming the Daytime Moon*. Ed. Julie Parson et al. Chicago: Another Chicago P, 1988. 46–48. Print.

"Wheezie and Juts Are Still Going at It." *Chicago Sun-Times* 11 Dec. 1988: 18. Print.

*Beastly Tales: The Mystery Writers of America Anthology*. Ed. Sara Paretsky. New York: Wynwood, 1989. Introd. Paretsky, 9–13.

"A Taste of Life." *Reader, I Murdered Him: An Anthology of Original Crime Stories*. Ed. Jen Green. London: The Women's P, 1989. 172–76. Paretsky, *A Taste of Life and Other Stories* 1–10. Block 237–45.

"Wild Women out of Control." *Family Portraits*. Ed. Carolyn Anthony. New York: Doubleday, 1989. 165–79. Print.

"A Note from the Author." *Indemnity Only*. New York: Delacorte, 1990 reissue. vii–ix.

*_Burn Marks_. New York: Delacorte: London: Chatto, 1990. Print.

"The Man Who Loved Life." Gardaphe 163–74. Osborne 159–69. Paretsky, *A Taste of Life and Other Stories* 41–55. Windrath 85–93.

*"The Maltese Cat." Wallace, *Sisters in Crime #3*. 169–97. *The Year's 25 Finest Crime and Mystery Stories: First Annual Edition*. Ed. Jon L. Breen. New York: Carroll, 1992. 231–94. *Bad Behavior*. Ed. Mary Higgins Clark. San Diego: Harcourt, 1995. 197–225. Paretsky, *Windy City Blues* 150–85. Paretsky, *V. I. for Short* 106–41. Wallace, *Best of Sisters in Crime* 197–227.

"Scouting Out the Best that Baseball Has to Offer." *USA Today* 6 July 1990: 4D. Print.

"Lily and the Sockeyes." *The Third Womansleuth Anthology*. Ed. Irene Zahava. Freedom, CA: Crossing P, 1990. 187–99. Print. Robinson, *Penguin Book* 152–72.

"Chills and Charm." *Entertainment Weekly* June/July 1991: 54 + 56. Print.

"Hooker Malone Is Missing: A Serial Mystery." Short story coauthored by Paretsky, Stephen Dobyns, Loren D. Estelman, Walter Mosley, and David Stout. *New York Times Book Review* 20 Oct. 1991: 44. Print.

*A Woman's Eye*. Ed. Paretsky. New York: Delacorte, 1991; London: Virago, 1991. Print.

*"Settled Score." Paretsky, *A Woman's Eye* 400–22. *The Year's 25 Finest Crime and Mystery Stories: Second Annual Edition*. Ed. Jon L. Breen. New York: Carroll, 1993. Paretsky, *Windy City Blues* 186–208. Paretsky, *V. I. for Short* 142–64.

"Eye of A Woman: An introduction by Sara Paretsky." Paretsky, *A Woman's Eye* vii–xiv.

"Keeping Nancy Drew Alive." *The Secret of the Old Clock*. By Carolyn Keene. Facsimile ed. Bedford, MA: Applewood, 1991. n.pag. Print.

"Introduction to the 30th Anniversary Edition of *Indemnity Only*." (2011 reissue of 1991 Dell pb). vii–xii. Print.

"Soft Spot for Serial Murder." *New York Times*. 28 Apr. 1991: E17. Print.

*Guardian Angel*. New York: Delacorte; London: Hamilton, 1992. Print.

*"Strung Out." Randisi and Wallace 216–38. Paretsky, *Windy City Blues* 92–123. Paretsky, *V. I. for Short* 165–96.

"Freud at Thirty Paces." Cody and Lewin 150–67. *The Armchair Detective* Summer 1993: 26–33. *The Year's Best Fantasy and Horror: Seventh Annual Collection*. Ed. Ellen Datlow and Terri Windling. New York: St. Martin's, 1994. Print.

"Independent Sleuth." Herbert et al. 233–34. Print.

"Sara Paretsky: What I'm Reading." *Entertainment Weekly* 27 Aug. 1993: 105. Print.

"Making Sense of the Senseless." *Sisters in Crime Newsletter*, no. 7 (Summer 1994). 1+7. Print.

*Tunnel Vision*. New York: Delacorte; London: Hamilton, 1994.

"The Hidden War at Home." *New York Times* 7 July 1994: A13. Print.

"Protocols of the Elders of Feminism." *Law/Text/Culture* 1 (1994): 14–27. Print.

"The Naked City." *Great Chicago Stories*. Ed. Tom Maday and Sam Landers. Chicago: TwoPress Publ., 1994. Chapter 45, n.pag. Print.

"The Great Tetsuji." Liza Cody et al. 109–15.

*"Grace Notes." Paretsky, *Windy City Blues* 11–60. Paretsky, *V. I. for Short* 197–246. *The Year's 25 Finest Crime and Mystery Stories*. Ed. Jon L. Breen. New York: Carroll, 1996. Breen and Gorman 543–79. Collins and Spillane 417–48. Print.

*Windy City Blues* [short story collection]. New York: Delacorte, 1995. Published in the UK as *V. I. for Short*. London: Hamilton, 1995. Print.

*A Taste of Life and Other Stories* [short story collection]. London: Penguin Sixty, 1995. Print.

*Three Complete Novels* [contains *Indemnity Only*, *Blood Shot* and *Burn Marks*]. New York: Wings, 1995. Print.

"Introduction: A Walk on the Wild Side: Touring Chicago with V. I. Warshawski." Paretsky, *Windy City Blues* 1–10. Plus "Author's Note," n.pag. Paretsky, *V. I. for Short* "Author's Note," n.pag.

"It's No Trial to Watch 'Murder One.'" *Cape Cod Times* 16 Sept. 1995: C7. Print.

"One Trial, Many Angles to Investigate." *New York Times* 10 Sept. 1995: 49. Print.

*Women on the Case: Twenty-Six Original Stories by the Best Women Crime Writers of Our Time*. Ed. Paretsky. New York: Delacorte; London: Virago, 1996. Print.

*"Publicity Stunts." *Women on the Case*. Ed. Sara Paretsky. New York: Delacorte, 1996. 392–414. London: Virago, 1996. 374–95. New York: Dell, 1997. 392–414. Matthews and Randisi 17–43. Paretsky, *V. I. x 3* 15–28. Hellman 111–40.

"Heartbreak House." Penzler, *Murder* 279–95. *Mary Higgins Clark Mystery Magazine*, Summer/Fall 1997:15–21. *A Century of Great Suspense Stories*. Ed. Jeffery Deaver. New York: Berkley, 2001. 432–44. Print.

Introduction. *Women on the Case*. Ed. Sara Paretsky. New York: Delacorte, 1996. vii–xiii London: Virago, 1996. vii–xiii. Dell pb edition 1997. vii–xiv.

"Property Rites: Women, Poverty, and Public Policy." *Illinois Issues* (Springfield, IL) June 1996: 30–34. Print.

"Baptism in the Bungalow Belt." *Chicago Tribune* 29 Aug. 1996: 1A9. Print.

"The Man Who Loved Life." Gardaphe 163–74. Osborne 159–69. Paretsky, *A Taste of Life and Other Stories* 41–55. Windrath 85–93.

"Sexy, Moral and Packing a Pistol." *The Independent* (London) 18 June 1997: 22. Print.

*Ghost Country*. New York: Delacorte; London: Hamilton, 1998. Print.

"MJ Must Remain Larger than life." *Chicago Sun-Times* 4 May 1998: 12. Print.

*\*Hard Time*. New York: Delacorte; London: Hamilton, 1999.

"The Rough Landing We Give Refugees." *New York Times* 26 June 1999: A13. Print.

"Damned by Dollars." *American Scholar* 68.1 (1999): 160. Print.

"A Gun of One's Own." *Publishers Weekly* 25 Oct. 1999: 44–45. Print.

"The Long Shadow of the Falcon." *Guardian* (London) 6 May 2000, rev. sec.: 1–3. Print.

"Sweet Home Chicago." *Publishers Weekly* 8 May 2000: 57. Print.

"Writers on Writing: A Storyteller Stands Where Justice Confronts Basic Human Needs." *New York Times* 25 Sept. 2000: B1–2. Print.

"Evil Yankees, Awful Mets." *Newsweek* 30 Oct. 2000: 68. Print.

"This Was My Destiny: Housework, Babysitting, Marriage." *Guardian* (London). 21 Dec. 2000: 10–11. Print.

Introduction. *The Maltese Falcon*. By Dashiell Hammett. 1930. London: The Folio Society, 2000. 9–19. Print.

*\*"Photo Finish." Mary Higgins Clark Mystery Magazine*, June 2001: 37–52. Print. Hillerman and Herbert 282–99. Paretsky, *V. I. x 3* 1–14.

*\*Total Recall*. New York: Delacorte; London: Hamilton, 2001. Print.

"Diversions." *Chicago Tribune Magazine* 11 Nov. 2001: 13. Print.

*\*Blacklist*. New York: Putnam; London: Hamilton, 2003.

"At the 'Century of Progress.'" *Mysterious Pleasures*. Ed. Martin Edwards. London: Little, 2003. 253–77. Print.

"The New Censorship." *New Statesman* (London) 2 June 2003: 18+. Print.

"Margery Allingham: An Appreciation." *Margery Allingham: 100 Years of a Great Mystery Writer*. Ed. Marianne Van Hoeven. Aylsham, UK: Lucas Books, 2004. xi–xiii. Print.

Preface. *Chicago Apartments*. By Neil Harris. New York: Acanthus P, 2004. 11–12. Print.

"A Letter to My Grandmother on Coming Home from Europe." *The Illinois Brief* Winter 2004: 2. Repr. as "Grannie, Look What We're Doing to the Land of Freedom." *Guardian* (London) 3 Jan. 2005:14. Print.

*\*Fire Sale*. New York: Putnam; London: Hodder, 2005. Print.

"Remarks in Honor of Carolyn Heilbrun." *Tulsa Studies in Women's Literature* 24.2 (2005): 241–45. Print.

"Acid Test." *Deadly Housewives*. Ed. Christine Matthews. New York: Harper, 2006. 122–55. Print.

*Writing in an Age of Silence* [essays]. New York: Verso, 2007. Print.

Introduction. Paretsky, *Writing in an Age of Silence* xi–xx.

*\*"A Family Sunday in the Park." [orig. publ. as "Marquette Park"]. Paretsky, *V. I. x 3* 29–41. Paretsky, *Sisters on the Case* 248–70.

*\*V. I.x 3* [short stories]. Chicago: Sara and Two C-Dogs P, 2007. Print.

*Sisters on the Case*. Ed. Paretsky. New York: Obsidian Mysteries, 2007.

"Afterword to *The Brothers Karamazov*." *The Brothers Karamazov*. By Fyodor Dostoyevsky [sic]. New York: Signet, 2007. 899–906. Print.

"Sisters on the Case: Introduction." Paretsky, *Sisters on the Case* ix–xiii.

"Bush's Pick a Reminder of What's Not Right." *Chicago Tribune* 7 Jan. 2007. Web. http://articles.chicagotribune.com/2007-01-07/news/0701070087_1_contraception-eric-keroack-pregnancy

"Refusing to Allow Pressure to Silence a Critical Voice." *Chicago Tribune* 1 Apr. 2007: 1–2. Print.

"Sara Paretsky Replies." *Library Journal* 1 June 2007: 10. Print.

"Mean Streets." *Guardian* (London) 23 June 2007: 22. Print.

*Bleeding Kansas*. New York: Putnam; London: Hodder, 2008. Print.

"In Chicago, We've Fought to Stand Together." *Washington Post* 24 Aug. 2008: BO1. Print.

"Why I Support Barack Obama." *Huffington Post* 18 Oct. 2008. Web. www.huffingtonpost.com/sara-paretsky/why-I-support-barack-obam_b_126953.html

"Ode to the Season: When Your Landlord Is

a Precinct Captain." *Chicago Tribune* 18 Dec. 2008. Web. http://articles.chicagotrib une.com/2007-12-18/features/07121404 50_1_precinct-captain-building-depart ment-coal

"What Book?" *Daily Mail* (UK) 17 Apr. 2009: 61. Print.

*Hardball*. New York: Putnam; London: Hod-der, 2009. Print.

"Terror in the Name of Jesus." *Guardian* (London) 2 June 2009: 26. Print.

"Imagining Edgar Allan Poe." Connelly 325–29.

"Lives: Le Treatment." *New York Times Magazine* 16 Aug. 2009: 50. Print.

*Body Work*. New York: Putnam; London: Hodder, 2010. Print.

"My Hero: Elizabeth Barrett Browning." *Guardian* (London) 10 Apr. 2010, rev. sec.: 6. Print.

"Poster Child." *Send My Love and a Molotov Cocktail*. Ed. Gary Phillips and Andrea Gibbons. Oakland: PM P, 2011. 49–67. Print.

"Portrait of a City: Chicago." *British Airways Highlife* June 2011. Web. http://www.bahi ghlife.com/News-And-Blogs/Culture-Blog/portrait-of-a-city-chicago.html

"Art History." *Kansas State Collegian* 11 Mar. 2011: 4. Print.

"Sara Paretsky on Liza Cody." *Guardian* (London) 15 Sept. 2011: 23. Print.

"Why I Write." *Publishers Weekly* 21 Nov. 2011: 27. Print.

*Breakdown*. New York: Putnam; London: Hodder, 2012. Print.

"The Written Word." *Booklist* 1 May 2012: 14. Print.

"Our Bodies, Our Fertility." *Chicago Tribune* 22 Jan. 2012: 15. Print.

"Another Turn of the Screw." 16th Annual McCusker Lecture. Dominican University/Freedom to Read Foundation, Amer. Lib. Assn. 24 Oct. 2012. Repr. *World Libraries* 20.2 (2010 [sic]). Web. http://ojsserv. dom.edu/ojs/index.php/worldlib/article/ view/543/465

"Flying Da Coach." TimeOutChicago.com Nov. 1–14: 2012. Web.

*Critical Mass*. New York: Putnam; London: Hodder, 2013. Print.

"Books—Five Best: A Personal Choice: Sara Paretsky—on Bearing Witness to the Unspeakable." *Wall Street Journal* 16 Nov. 2013: C10. Print.

"Miss Bianca." *Ice Cold*. Ed. Jeffery Deaver and Raymond Benson. New York: Grand Central, 2014: 93–118. Print.

"Sara Paretsky: My First Car." *Chicago Tribune* 7 Feb. 2014. Video. Web. http://www. chicagotribune.com/chi-sara-paretsky-on-her-first-car-20140207-story.html

"The Inventory: Sara Paretsky." *Financial Times* magazine (London) 9–10 Aug. 2014: 8. Print.

"George Eliot's *The Mill on the Floss*: Book of a Lifetime by Sara Paretsky." *The Independent* (London). 23 Aug. 2014: 26–27. Print.

"By the Book." *New York Times Book Review* 14 Sept. 2014: 8. Print.

"The Dollus Syndrome: Diversity in Crime Fiction." *Booklist* 1 May 2015: 10–11. Print.

*Brush Back*. New York: Putnam; London: Hodder, 2015. Print.

"The Detective as Speech." *Out of Deadlock*. Ed. Enrico Minardi and Jennifer Byron. Newcastle upon Tyne (UK): Cambridge Scholars Publishing, 2015. 11–18. Print.

# Paretsky's Works in Alphabetical Order

"Acid Test." *Deadly Housewives*. Ed. Christine Matthews. New York: Harper, 2006. 122–55. Print.

"Afterword to *The Brothers Karamazov*." *The Brothers Karamazov*. By Fyodor Dostoyevsky [*sic*]. New York: Signet, 2007. 899–906. Print.

"Another Turn of the Screw." 16th Annual McCusker Lecture. Dominican University/Freedom to Read Foundation, Amer. Lib. Assn. 24 Oct. 2012. Repr. *World Libraries* 20.2 (2010 [*sic*]). Web. http://ojs serv.dom.edu/ojs/index.php/worldlib/article/view/543/465

"Art History." *Kansas State Collegian* 11 Mar. 2011: 4. Print.

"At the 'Century of Progress.'" *Mysterious Pleasures*. Ed. Martin Edwards. London: Little, 2003. 253–77. Print.

*"At the Old Swimming Hole." Hopkins and Potter 32–43. *Lady on the Case*. Ed. Marcia Muller, Bill Pronzini, and Martin H. Greenberg. New York: Bonanza, 1988. 277–94. Print. *Murder and Mystery in Chicago*. Ed. Carol-Lynn Rossel Waugh, Frank D. McSherry Jr., and Martin H. Greenberg. New York: Dembner, 1987. 1–20 Print. Paretsky, *Windy City Blues* 124–49. Paretsky, *V. I. for Short* 133–58. Randisi, *Mean Streets* 171–95.

"Baptism in the Bungalow Belt." *Chicago Tribune* 29 Aug. 1996: 1A9. Print.

*Beastly Tales: The Mystery Writers of America Anthology*. Ed. Sara Paretsky. New York: Wynwood P, 1989. Introd. Paretsky, 9–13. Print.

*Bitter Medicine*. New York: Morrow; London: Gollancz, 1987. New York: Ballantine, 1987. Print.

*Blacklist*. New York: Putnam; London: Hamilton, 2003. Print.

*Bleeding Kansas*. New York: Putnam; London: Hodder, 2008. Print.

*Blood Shot*. New York: Delacorte, 1988. Published as *Toxic Shock* in UK. London: Gollancz, 1988. Print.

*Body Work*. New York: Putnam; London: Hodder, 2010. Print.

"Books—Five Best: A Personal Choice: Sara Paretsky—On bearing witness to the unspeakable." *Wall Street Journal* 16 Nov. 2013: C10. Print.

"The Breakdown of Moral Philosophy in New England Before the Civil War." PhD dissertation, University of Chicago, 1977. Print.

*Breakdown*. New York: Putnam; London: Hodder, 2012. Print.

*Brush Back*. New York: Putnam; London: Hodder, 2015. Print.

*Burn Marks*. New York: Delacorte; London: Chatto, 1990. Print.

"Bush's Pick a Reminder of What's Not Right." *Chicago Tribune*. 7 Jan. 2007. Web. http://articles.chicagotribune.com/2007-01-07/news/0701070087_1_contraception-eric-keroack-pregnancy

"By the Book." *New York Times Book Review* 14 Sept. 2014: 8. Print.

*"The Case of the Pietro Andromache." *Alfred Hitchcock's Mystery Magazine* Dec. 1988. *The Year's Best Mystery and Suspense Stories*. Ed. Edward D. Hoch. New York: Walker, 1989. *New Crimes* [1]. Ed. Maxim

Jakubowski. New York: Carroll, 1990. Wallace, *Sisters in Crime* 113–135. Greenberg 15–49. Paretsky, *Windy City Blues* 61–91. Paretsky, *V. I. for Short* 76–105. George, *Moment on the Edge* 279–307. *Great TV and Film Detectives.* Ed. Maxim Jakubowski. New York: Reader's Digest Assn., 2005. 474–91. Print.

"Chicago." *Savvy* Sept. 1988: 48–51. Print.

"Chills and Charm." *Entertainment Weekly* June/July 1991: 54, 56. Print.

*Critical Mass.* New York: Putnam; London: Hodder, 2013. Print.

"Damned by Dollars." *American Scholar* 68.1 (1999): 160. Print.

*Deadlock.* New York: Dial; London: Gollancz, 1984. New York: Ballantine, 1984. Pleasantville, New York: IMPress Mystery, 2004. Print.

"Dealer's Choice." *Raymond Chandler's Philip Marlowe: A Centennial Celebration.* Ed. Byron Preiss. New York: Knopf, 1988. 119–33. New York: Simon & Schuster ibooks, 1999. 119–33. *The New Mystery.* Ed. J. Charyn. New York: Dutton, 1993. 80–95. Paretsky, *A Taste of Life and Other Stories* 11–40. Print.

"The Detective as Speech." Minardi and Byron 11–18. Print.

"Diversions." *Chicago Tribune Magazine* 11 Nov. 2001:13. Print.

"The Dollus Syndrome: Diversity in Crime Fiction." *Booklist* 1 May 2015: 10–11. Print.

"Evil Yankees, Awful Mets." *Newsweek* 30 Oct. 2000: 68. Print.

"Eye of a Woman—An Introduction by Sara Paretsky." Paretsky, *A Woman's Eye* vii–xiv.

*"A Family Sunday in the Park"* [orig. publ. as "Marquette Park"]. Paretsky, *V. I. x 3* 29–41. Paretsky, *Sisters on the Case* 248–70.

*Fire Sale.* New York: Putnam; London: Hodder, 2005. Print.

"Flying Da Coach." TimeOutChicago.com 1–14 Nov. 2012. Web.

"Freud at Thirty Paces." Cody and Lewin 150–67. *The Armchair Detective* Summer 1993: 26–33. *The Year's Best Fantasy and Horror: Seventh Annual Collection.* Ed. Ellen Datlow and Terri Windling. New York: St. Martin's, 1994. Print.

"George Eliot's *The Mill on the Floss*: Book

of a Lifetime by Sara Paretsky." *The Independent* (London) 23 Aug. 2014: 26–27. Print.

*Ghost Country.* New York: Delacorte; London: Hamilton, 1998. Print.

*"Grace Notes."* Paretsky, *Windy City Blues* 11–60. Paretsky, *V. I. for Short* 197–246. *The Year's 25 Finest Crime and Mystery Stories.* Ed. Jon L. Breen. New York: Carroll, 1996. Breen and Gorman 543–79. Collins and Spillane 417–48. Print.

"The Great Tetsuji." Cody et al. 109–15. Print.

*Guardian Angel.* New York: Delacorte; London: Hamilton, 1992. Print.

"A Gun of One's Own." *Publishers Weekly* 25 Oct. 1999: 44–45. Print.

*Hard Time.* New York: Delacorte;. London: Hamilton, 1999. Print.

*Hardball.* New York: Putnam; London: Hodder, 2009. Print.

"Heartbreak House." Penzler, *Murder* 279–95. *Mary Higgins Clark Mystery Magazine,* Summer/Fall 1997: 15–21. *A Century of Great Suspense Stories.* Ed. Jeffery Deaver. New York: Berkley, 2001. 432–44. Print.

"The Hidden War at Home." *New York Times* 7 July 1994: A13. Print.

"Hooker Malone Is Missing: A Serial Mystery." Short story coauthored by Paretsky, Stephen Dobyns, Loren D. Estelman, Walter Mosley, and David Stout. *New York Times Book Review* 20 Oct. 1991: 44. Print.

"Imagining Edgar Allan Poe." Connelly 325–29.

"In Chicago, We've Fought to Stand Together." *Washington Post* 24 Aug. 2008: B01. Print.

*Indemnity Only.* New York: Dial; London: Gollancz, 1982. New York: Delacorte pb edition, 1990. New York: Dell, 1991. 30th Anniversary reissue edition of 1991 Dell pb with new author introduction November 2011.

"Independent Sleuth." Herbert et al. 233–34.

Introduction. Paretsky, *Beastly Tales* 9–13.

Introduction. *The Maltese Falcon.* By Dashiell Hammett. 1930. London: The Folio Society, 2000. 9–19. Print.

Introduction. *Women on the Case.* Ed. Sara Paretsky. New York: Delacorte, 1996. vii–xiii London: Virago, 1996. vii–xiii. Dell pb ed. 1997. vii–xiv.

"Introduction: A Walk on the Wild Side: Touring Chicago with V. I. Warshawski" Paretsky, *Windy City Blues* 1–10. Plus "Author's Note," n.pag. Paretsky, *V. I. for Short*. "Author's Note," n.pag.

"Introduction to the 30th Anniversary Edition of *Indemnity Only*." (2011 reissue of 1991 Dell pb). *Indemnity Only*. New York: Dell, 1991. vii–xii.

Introduction. Paretsky, *Writing in an Age of Silence* xi–xx.

"The Inventory: Sara Paretsky." *Financial Times* Magazine (London) 9/10 Aug. 2014: 8. Print.

"It's No Trial to Watch 'Murder One.'" *Cape Cod Times* 16 Sept. 1995: C7. Print.

"Keeping Nancy Drew Alive." *The Secret of the Old Clock*. By Carolyn Keene. Facsimile ed. Bedford, MA: Applewood, 1991. n.pag. Print.

*Killing Orders*. New York: Morrow, 1985. London: Gollancz, 1986. London: Penguin, 1987. Print.

"Let's Have a Big Smile, Now." Parson et al. 46–48.

"A Letter to My Grandmother on Coming Home from Europe." *The Illinois Brief*. Winter 2004: 2. Repr. as "Grannie, Look What We're Doing to the Land of Freedom." *Guardian* (London) 3 Jan. 2005:14. Print.

"Lily and the Sockeyes." *The Third Womansleuth Anthology*. Ed. Irene Zahava. Freedom, CA: Crossing P, 1990.187–99. Print. Robinson, *Penguin Book* 152–72.

"Lives: Le Treatment." *New York Times Magazine* 16 Aug. 2009: 50. Print.

"The Long Shadow of the Falcon." *Guardian* (London) 6 May 2000, rev.sec.: 1–3. Print.

"Making Sense of the Senseless." *Sisters in Crime Newsletter* Summer 1994: 1+7. Print.

*"The Maltese Cat." Wallace, *Sisters in Crime #3* 169–97. *The Year's Finest Crime and Mystery Stories: First Annual Edition*. Ed. Jon L. Breen, New York: Carroll, 1992. 231–54. *Bad Behavior*. Ed. Mary Higgins Clark. San Diego: Harcourt, 1995. 197–225. Paretsky, *Windy City Blues* 150–85. Paretsky, *V. I. for Short* 106–41. Wallace, *Best of Sisters in Crime* 197–227.

"The Man Who Loved Life." Gardaphe 163–74. Osborne 159–69. Paretsky, *A Taste of Life and Other Stories* 41–55. Windrath 85–93.

"Margery Allingham: An Appreciation." *Margery Allingham: 100 Years of a Great Mystery Writer*. Ed. Marianne Van Hoeven. Aylsham, UK: Lucas Books, 2004. xi–xiii. Print.

"Mean Streets." *Guardian* (London) 23 June 2007: 22. Print.

"Miss Bianca." *Ice Cold*. Ed. Jeffery Deaver and Raymond Benson. New York: Grand Central Publishing, 2014: 93–118. Print.

"MJ Must Remain Larger than Life." *Chicago Sun-Times* 4 May 1998: 12. Print.

"My Hero: Elizabeth Barrett Browning." *Guardian* (London) 10 Apr. 2010, rev. sec.: 6. Print.

"Mysteries." *Chicago Tribune Book World* 8 May 1983, sec. 7: 5. Print.

"The Naked City." *Great Chicago Stories*. Ed. Tom Maday and Sam Landers. Chicago: TwoPress Publ., 1994. Chapter 45, n.pag. Print.

"The New Censorship." *New Statesman* (London) 2 June 2003: 18+. Print.

"A Note from the Author." *Indemnity Only*. New York: Delacorte pb ed, 1990. vii–ix. Print.

"Ode to the Season: When Your Landlord Is a Precinct Captain." *Chicago Tribune* 18 Dec. 2008. Web. http://articles.chicagotribune.com/2007-12-18/features/0712140450_1_precinct-captain-building-department-coal

"One Trial, Many Angles to Investigate." *New York Times* 10 Sept. 1995: 49. Print.

"Our Bodies, Our Fertility." *Chicago Tribune* 22 Jan. 2012: 15. Print.

*"Photo Finish." *Mary Higgins Clark Mystery Magazine*, June 2001: 37–52. Print. Hillerman and Herbert 282–99. Paretsky, *V. I. x 3* 1–14.

"A Poignant Tribute to Cicero." *Chicago Sun-Times* 20 Dec. 1987: 19. Print.

"Portrait of a City: Chicago." *British Airways Highlife* June 2011. Web. http://www.bahighlife.com/News-And-Blogs/Culture-Blog/portrait-of-a-city-chicago.html

"Poster Child." *Send My Love and a Molotov Cocktail*. Ed. Gary Phillips & Andrea Gibbons. Oakland: PM P, 2011. 49–67. Print.

Preface. *Chicago Apartments.* By Neil Harris. New York: Acanthus P, 2004. 11–12. Print.

"Private Eyes, Public Spheres." *Women's Review of Books* Nov. 1988: 12–13. Print.

"Property Rites: Women, Poverty, and Public Policy." *Illinois Issues* (Springfield, IL). June 1996: 30–34. Print.

"Protocols of the Elders of Feminism." *Law/Text/Culture* 1 (1994): 14–27. Print.

*"Publicity Stunts." *Women on the Case.* Ed. Sara Paretsky. New York: Delacorte, 1996. 392–414. London: Virago, 1996. 374–95. New York: Dell 1997. 392–414. Matthews and Randisi 17–43. Paretsky, *V. I. x 3* 15–28. Hellman 111–40.

"Refusing to Allow Pressure to Silence a Critical Voice." *Chicago Tribune* 1 Apr. 2007: 1–2. Print.

"Remarks in Honor of Carolyn Heilbrun." *Tulsa Studies in Women's Literature* 24.2 (2005): 241–45. Print.

"The Rough Landing We Give Refugees." *New York Times* 26 June 1999: A13. Print.

"Sara Paretsky: My First Car." *Chicago Tribune* 7 Feb. 2014. Video. Web. http://www.chicagotribune.com/chi-sara-paretsky-on-her-first-car-20140207-story.html

"Sara Paretsky on Liza Cody." *Guardian* (London) 15 Sept. 2011:23. Print.

"Sara Paretsky Replies." *Library Journal* 1 June 2007: 10. Print.

"Sara Paretsky: What I'm Reading." *Entertainment Weekly* 27 Aug. 1993: 105. Print.

"Scouting Out the Best that Baseball Has to Offer." *USA Today* 6 July 1990: 4D. Print.

*"Settled Score." Paretsky, *A Woman's Eye* 400–22. *The Year's 25 Finest Crime and Mystery Stories: Second Annual Edition.* Ed. Jon L. Breen. New York: Carroll, 1993. Paretsky, *Windy City Blues* 186–208. Paretsky, *V. I. for Short* 142–64.

"Sexy, Moral and Packing a Pistol." *The Independent* (London) 18 June 1997: 22. Print.

*Sisters on the Case.* Ed. Sara Paretsky. New York: Obsidian Mysteries, 2007. Print.

"Sisters on the Case: Introduction." Paretsky, *Sisters on the Case* ix–xiii.

*"Skin Deep." *The New Black Mask,* no.8 (1987): 102–20. *Homicidal Acts.* Ed. B. Pronzini and M. H. Greenberg. New York: Ballantine, 1988. 151–64. *City Sleuths and Tough Guys.* Ed. D. W. McCullough. Boston: Houghton, 1989. 461–73. *P.I. Files.* Ed. Loren Estleman and Martin Greenberg. New York: Ballantine, 1990. 57–69. *A Modern Treasury of Great Detective and Murder Mysteries.* Ed. Ed Gorman. New York: Carroll, 1994. 197–208. Paretsky, *Windy City Blues* 209–25. Paretsky, *V. I. for Short* 59–75. Halligan 99–112. Mansfield-Kelley and Marchino 308–19.

"Soft Spot for Serial Murder." *New York Times* 28 Apr. 1991: E17. Print.

*"Strung Out." Randisi and Wallace 216–38. Paretsky, *Windy City Blues* 92–123. Paretsky, *V. I. for Short* 165–96.

"Sweet Home Chicago." *Publishers Weekly* 8 May 2000: 57. Print.

*"The Takamoku Joseki." *Alfred Hitchcock's Mystery Magazine* Nov. 1983. 33–42. *Women of Mystery.* Ed. Cynthia Manson. New York: Berkley, 1993. 227–39. Paretsky, *Windy City Blues.* 246–58. Paretsky, *V. I. for Short* 1–12. *First Cases: First Appearances of Classic Private Eyes.* Ed. R. J. Randisi. New York: Dutton, 1996. 159–70. *Win, Lose or Die.* Ed. Cynthia Manson and Constance Scarborough. New York: Carroll, 1996. 38–46. Landrigan 213–22.

"A Taste of Life." *Reader, I Murdered Him: An Anthology of Original Crime Stories.* Ed. Jen Green. London: The Women's P, 1989. 172–76. Paretsky, *A Taste of Life and Other Stories* 1–10. Block 237–45.

*A Taste of Life and Other Stories.* London: Penguin Sixty, 1995. Print.

"Terror in the Name of Jesus." *Guardian* (London) 2 June 2009: 26. Print.

"This Is for You, Jeannie." *Women: A Journal of Liberation* 3. 3 (1972): 46–51.

"This Was My Destiny: Housework, Babysitting, Marriage." *Guardian* (London). 21 Dec. 2000:10–11.

*Three Complete Novels* [contains *Indemnity Only, Blood Shot* and *Burn Marks*]. New York: Wings, 1995. Print.

*"Three-Dot Po." Randisi, *The Eyes Have It* 227–44. *Ms. Murder.* Ed. Marie Smith. London: Xanadu Publ., 1989. 32–43. Paretsky, *Windy City Blues* 226–45. Paretsky, *V. I.*

*for Short* 13–32. *The Big Book of Christmas Mysteries.* Ed. Otto Penzler. New York: Vintage Crime/Black Lizard, 2013. 452–61.

"The Tornado." *American Girl* magazine Aug. 1959: 77–78. Print.

*Total Recall.* New York: Delacorte; London: Hamilton, 2001. Print.

*Tunnel Vision.* New York: Delacorte; London: Hamilton, 1994. Print.

*V. I.x 3* [short stories]. Chicago: Sara and Two C-Dogs P, 2007. Print.

"What Book?" *Daily Mail* (UK) 17 Apr. 2009: 61. Print.

"Wheezie and Juts Are Still Going at It." *Chicago Sun-Times* 11 Dec. 1988: 18. Print.

"Why I Support Barack Obama." *Huffington Post* 18 Oct. 2008. Web. www.huffington post.com/sara-paretsky/why-I-support-barack-obam_b_126953.html

"Why I Write." *Publishers Weekly* 21 Nov. 2011: 27. Print.

"Wild Women out of Control." *Family Portraits.* Ed. Carolyn Anthony. New York: Doubleday, 1989. 165–79. Print.

*Windy City Blues* [short stories]. New York: Delacorte, 1995. Published in the UK as *V. I. for Short.* London: Hamilton, 1995. Print.

*A Woman's Eye.* Ed. Sara Paretsky. New York: Delacorte, 1991; London, Virago, 1991. Print.

*Women on the Case: Twenty-Six Original Stories by the Best Women Crime Writers of Our Time.* Ed. Sara Paretsky. New York: Delacorte, 1996; London: Virago, 1996. Print.

"Writers on Writing: A Storyteller Stands Where Justice Confronts Basic Human Needs." *New York Times* 25 Sept. 2000: B1–2. Print.

*Writing in an Age of Silence* [essays]. New York: Verso, 2007. Print.

"The Written Word." *Booklist* 1 May 2012: 14. Print.

# A Brief Biography

Sara Nancy Paretsky was born on 8 June 1947 in Ames, Iowa, the second child and sole sister to four brothers. Her parents, Mary Edwards and David Paretsky, met there as graduate students in the 1940s and married. Paretsky describes herself as "the descendant of immigrants … [who] on both sides of my family, came here to escape religious persecution" (WIAAOS xvii). Her paternal grandparents, who worked in the garment industry in New York City, met "walking a picket line for the International Ladies Garment Workers Union" (ibid., 33). This grandmother had come to New York as a refugee from the pogroms in Eastern Europe; most of her family later perished in the Holocaust. Paretsky's mother grew up in small-town Illinois where her father was the local doctor, and her mother died giving birth to her (WIAAOS 32). Mary Edwards was accepted into medical school in 1941; although she did not take up the place at the time, she eventually went to Iowa State College to study science. Both parents were well educated and widely read. Paretsky's father could "read Greek, as well as German and Yiddish" (ibid., 31).

After her father completed his PhD in bacteriology at Iowa State College, the expanding family moved to Lawrence, Kansas, where Dr. Paretsky took up a faculty appointment at the University of Kansas. Sara and her four brothers (Jeremy, Daniel, Jonathan, and Nicholas) grew up in a farmhouse outside Lawrence in the 1950s and 1960s as some of the few Jewish students in the school system. It was an era in which America was "obsessed by the threat of Communism" (WIAAOS xvi), and Paretsky remembers that her parents—progressive in matters such as supporting anti-segregation initiatives in housing and education—were cautious about what they said and to whom. Her father's Jewish identity and his activities in the small Jewish community of Lawrence as an organizer of the regular Friday night services added another layer to what Paretsky describes as the family's marginalization in the conservative milieu of the Kansas town (2002 letter to fan in author's private papers accessed November 2012).

As well as lessons in difference, Paretsky's upbringing gave her a love of books, a respect for education, and a keen interest in issues of social justice. An abiding interest in the written word, and high ideals of service for the public good, particularly in relation to women's issues, have subsequently informed the whole of Paretsky's life and her achievements. Another legacy from her childhood is Paretsky's passion for baseball, a devotion she passed on to her fictional detective; at the two-room country school she attended she played third base for the school team. At age 11, Paretsky saw her first piece of writing in print. A short account of a tornado she experienced with her schoolmates, "The Tornado," won a nonfiction award and appeared in *The American Girl* magazine in 1959.

Her childhood, however, was also marked by her parents' conservative views on gender roles and sexual politics, as well as their lack of support for her writing aspirations.

Laura Shapiro's *Ms Magazine* profile of the author relates Paretsky's memory of growing up "in a family where girls became secretaries and wives, and boys became professionals. I wasn't expected to have talents" (67). Paretsky's memoir *Writing in an Age of Silence* further attests, "as the only girl in my family, I was constrained from the age of nine to give up my own childhood in becoming the caretaker of my young brothers" (39). Although she was a National Merit Scholar at Lawrence High School in 1964, this was a difficult period in Paretsky's life; she told journalist Susan Ferraro that "her parents required her to take the high school secretarial course, though she was in college-track courses" (43). Cheryl Reed's review of Paretsky's memoir records: "[H]er parents refused to pay for her college education or let her attend anywhere other than the University of Kansas, where her father taught" (12B). In the meantime, money was being found to send her brothers to "expensive schools far from home" (Paretsky, WIAAOS 31). Much later, Paretsky's mother, after many years of working in the home, became the children's librarian in Lawrence, where a reading room was named posthumously in her honor. But Paretsky writes that she suffered low self-esteem and little sense of her own worth because of the criticisms and neglect that emanated from her parents. She also remembers the encouragement of three teachers who valued her stories and provided sparks of confidence in her writing. Paretsky dedicates her sixth V. I. novel *Burn Marks* to the fourth-grade teacher and two high-school teachers "who believed in my writing before I did" (*Burn* 1990).

Her time at the University of Kansas was fruitful; Paretsky was awarded a Watkins Scholarship, named "for Elizabeth Watkins, who had to quit school at thirteen to look after her siblings and her father, and who left the fortune she later acquired to support women students" (Paretsky, WIAAOS 25). The dean of women, Emily Taylor, "played a strong role in starting me on the road to rethinking where I belonged on the planet" (ibid., 24–25). As an undergraduate, Paretsky chaired the first University of Kansas Commission on the Status of Women and produced its report. She earned scholarships that enabled her to spend her first college summer in Vienna studying German and the second summer in Chicago working as a volunteer in a day-care center (1966 was the summer of Dr. Martin Luther King's open-housing initiatives in the segregated city, and it proved to be a seminal experience for the young college student). In 1967, she graduated from the University of Kansas after three years, earning a BA in political science, summa cum laude.

Returning to Chicago in the late sixties, she furthered her studies with an MA in 1969 from the Division of the Social Sciences at the University of Chicago with a master's thesis on "the abolitionists and their connection to the religious movements of the 1840s" (ibid., 36). She also started a PhD in the university's U.S. history program. Paretsky supported herself during this period working as a secretary in the university's political science department. In summer 1970, with a stake of $200, the 23-year-old Paretsky went to New York City in the hopes of becoming a writer. When the money ran out, she worked as a secretary for four months before returning to Chicago. Her decision to live, study, and work in Chicago was influenced by the memorable summer in 1966 when she worked as a community service volunteer on a project in the white, working-class, Gage Park neighborhood. The local community was hostile to the integrated housing movement spearheaded by King. Racial politics dominated events that summer in Chicago, and the atmosphere was volatile. The experience had a profound effect on Paretsky, who writes: "I came away from my summer filled with the sense that change for good was possible, that if I and my peers put enough energy and good will into the struggle, we could transform America" (ibid., 36). She told interviewer Sam Phipps: "It changed my life forever, that summer … it had such an impact on me in terms of seeing how helpless ordinary people were" (4).

She has also testified to how the women's movement of the 1960s influenced her: "[I]t let me see that the doubts I had about my ability to occupy public space weren't necessarily the result of my own defects, but of socialization" (Rozan 44). By 1971, Paretsky was continuing her doctoral research and had found work running affirmative action conferences for the Urban Research Corporation in Chicago. She was now involved in reproductive politics and active in the women's movement; a long-time believer in equality, she writes that "in the winter of 1971, I became a feminist" (WIAAOS 77). In 1972, she published the short story "This Is for You, Jeannie" in *Women: A Journal of Liberation*. The story describes the disintegrating marriage of a couple who seem to have it all and the terrible consequences of the wife's mental deterioration. Thematically, as K Edgington points out, the story "reflects the pressing issues of liberal feminists of the day" (57).

When the Urban Research company went bankrupt in 1974, Paretsky worked for the next three years as a freelance business writer while continuing work on her dissertation. In 1976, she married University of Chicago physics professor Courtenay Wright, a widower with three teenage sons. She and Wright have made their home ever since in the Hyde Park neighborhood of Chicago in a three-story house built in 1883. The following year, 1977, Paretsky was awarded an MBA from the Graduate School of Business and a PhD from the Department of History, both at the University of Chicago. Her dissertation, "The Breakdown of Moral Philosophy in New England Before the Civil War," discussed the "nineteenth-century roots of American Christian fundamentalism" (WIAAOS 53). In the same year, she joined CNA (Continental National America) Insurance as a manager responsible for advertising and direct-mail marketing programs; she remained there from 1977 to 1986. Paretsky's nine years with CNA gave her an insider's knowledge of the insurance industry and its potential for financial skulduggery that she put to use in her subsequent career as a mystery writer.

In 1979, Paretsky attended a Northwestern University extension course on "Writing Detective Fiction for Publication" taught by crime writer Stuart Kaminsky. As the 2011 introduction to the 30th anniversary edition of *Indemnity Only* explains, Paretsky was determined to write a mystery in the style of the noir private-eye novels of Dashiell Hammett and Raymond Chandler, but that would portray women "like me and my friends, doing work that hadn't existed for women when we were growing up" (Paretsky, 2011 "Indemnity" Dell edition, x). She imagined a detective figure who "didn't care what people thought of her, and [who] didn't worry about getting fired" (ibid., x), an antidote to the more stereotypical femme fatale or faithful secretary models of earlier hard-boiled fiction. Paretsky says in *Writing in an Age of Silence*, "I wanted to create a woman who would turn the tables on the dominant views of women in fiction and in society" and that "I also wanted … VI to be a sexual person and a moral being at the same time" (80, 81–82). And so V. I. came to life in *Indemnity Only*, a novel begun in the late 1970s and published in 1982. Kaminsky took an interest in Paretsky's manuscript and sent it to his own agent, Dominick Abel, who agreed to represent her. Paretsky writes that it took him "a year to find someone in New York willing to take a chance on a woman private eye in the Midwest, but the Dial Press finally did so" (ibid. xi). Victor Gollancz bought the book for UK publication, and noir fiction specialist Hayakawa Publishers bought it for translation into Japanese. The critical reception was enthusiastic, and sales figures rose.

The second V. I. outing, *Deadlock*, won a Friends of American Writers award in 1985. The character of V. I. and the vividly realized Chicago location injected fresh air into a genre with a historic bias toward male loner detectives based in New York, Los

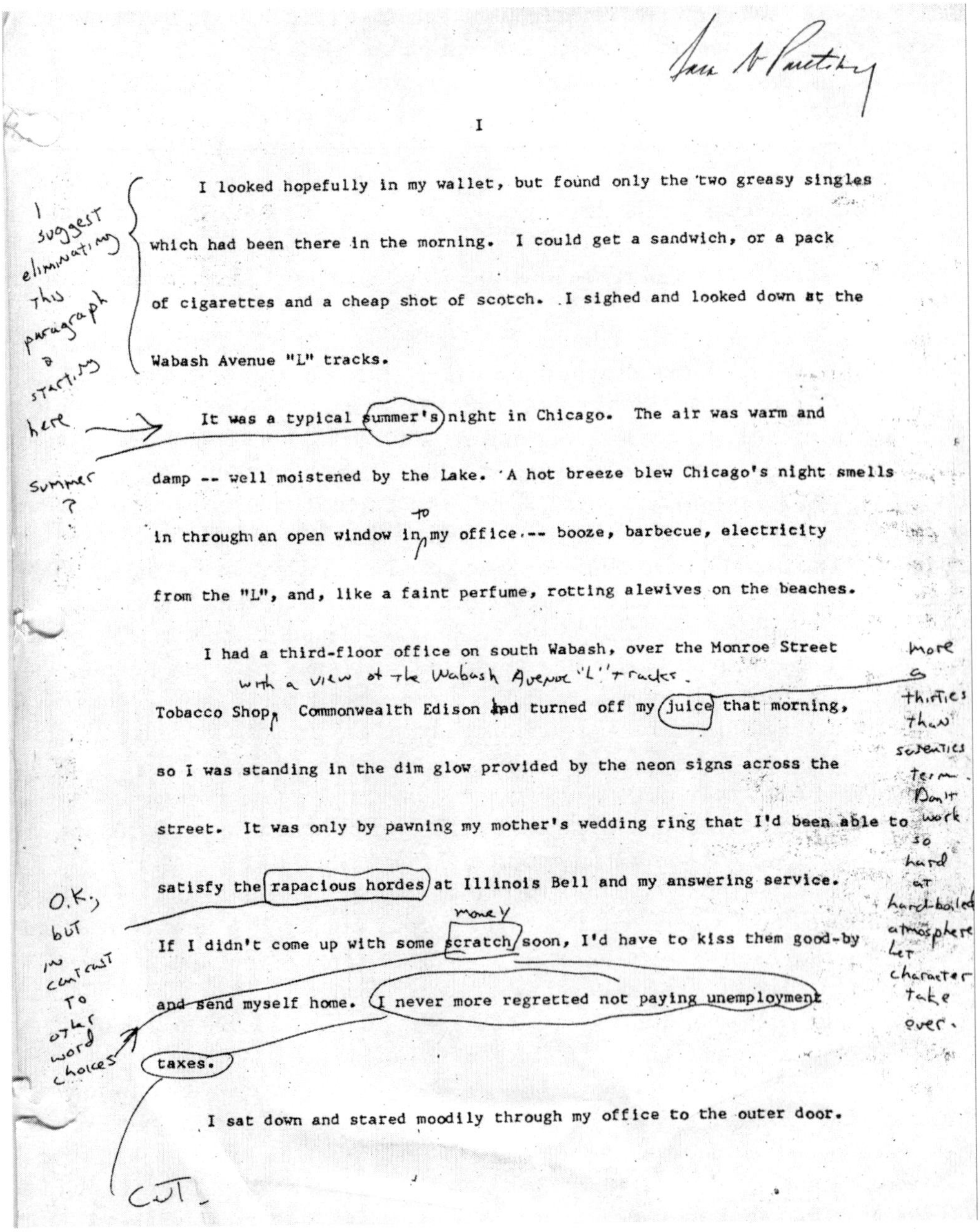

*[Photograph of the first typewritten manuscript page with handwritten edits. Typewritten text reads:]*

I

I looked hopefully in my wallet, but found only the two greasy singles which had been there in the morning. I could get a sandwich, or a pack of cigarettes and a cheap shot of scotch. I sighed and looked down at the Wabash Avenue "L" tracks.

It was a typical summer's night in Chicago. The air was warm and damp -- well moistened by the Lake. A hot breeze blew Chicago's night smells in through an open window in my office.-- booze, barbecue, electricity from the "L", and, like a faint perfume, rotting alewives on the beaches.

I had a third-floor office on south Wabash, over the Monroe Street Tobacco Shop. Commonwealth Edison had turned off my juice that morning, so I was standing in the dim glow provided by the neon signs across the street. It was only by pawning my mother's wedding ring that I'd been able to satisfy the rapacious hordes at Illinois Bell and my answering service. If I didn't come up with some scratch soon, I'd have to kiss them good-by and send myself home. I never more regretted not paying unemployment taxes.

I sat down and stared moodily through my office to the outer door.

*[Handwritten marginal notes: "I suggest eliminating this paragraph & starting here"; "summer?"; "with a view of the Wabash Avenue 'L' tracks."; "to"; "money"; "O.K., but in contrast to other word choices"; "more thirties than seventies term. Don't work so hard at hard-boiled atmosphere. Let character take over."; "CUT"]*

**The first page of the original typewritten manuscript of *Indemnity Only* dated 3 December 1980 with handwritten edits from Stuart Kaminsky. From author's private papers. Photograph by Linda Erf Swift.**

Angeles, or San Francisco. After publishing the first three V. I. novels (the third, *Killing Orders*, was issued in 1985), Paretsky sold the movie rights to the Warshawski character to TriStar Pictures in Hollywood, giving her sufficient financial leeway to leave CNA in 1986 and work full time as a writer. This was the same year in which she cofounded Sisters in Crime at the annual Bouchercon gathering of mystery fans and writers. For the first year, the author led the advocacy organization, established to promote and connect women writers, editors, reviewers, publishers, booksellers, librarians, and readers in the crime and mystery field.

Recognition of her importance as a mystery writer and activist gathered pace through the late 1980s. She was named a *Ms Magazine* Woman of the Year in 1987 "[f]or bringing a woman detective and feminist themes to murder mysteries, and for championing women writers in this mostly male genre" (award parchment in author's private papers accessed November 2012). In 1988 she was named to the University of Kansas Hall of Fame; that same year she was awarded the Silver Dagger from the British Crime Writers Association (CWA) for *Blood Shot* (UK title *Toxic Shock*). *Blood Shot*, the fifth V. I. novel, was also awarded the Private Eye Writers of America Shamus Award for the best hardcover P.I. novel of 1988. In 1989, Paretsky served as vice-president of Mystery Writers of America. The 1991 film *V. I. Warshawski*, starring Kathleen Turner, brought the character to a wider audience, although the film did not achieve an ideal level of commercial success. Throughout the late 1980s and early 1990s Paretsky was also publishing occasional short stories and editing anthologies of women's writing for Mystery Writers of America and Sisters in Crime.

After publishing the eighth V. I. novel *Tunnel Vision* in 1994, Paretsky took a break from the Warshawski series to explore other literary horizons. A collection of V. I.-centered short stories, *Windy City Blues* (published in the United Kingdom as *V. I. for Short*), came out in 1995, followed in 1998 by *Ghost Country*, a standalone novel set in Chicago and centered on four characters whose lives are transformed by a mysterious woman named Starr. Paretsky returned to the V. I. character with *Hard Time* in 1999; readers, critics, and reviewers welcomed her back with enthusiasm.

Throughout the 1990s and the subsequent two decades, more awards and critical acclaim followed: in 1993 *Guardian Angel* was given the German Crime Writers Association Marlowe Award, and in 1996 Paretsky received the Mark Twain Award for Distinguished Contribution to Midwest Literature. In 1997, she was the Author Guest of Honor at the annual Bouchercon in Monterey, California; earlier in the year she had spent a period as an invited visiting fellow at Wolfson College in Oxford, United Kingdom. In fall 1998 she was a visiting professor at the Center for Creative Writing at Northwestern University in Evanston, Illinois.

She delivered the 2001 Judith Austin Memorial Lecture at the Library of Congress, and in 2002 the National Organization for Women Chicago chapter presented her with the "Women Who Dared Excellence in Media Award." By this time, Paretsky had published 10 V. I. Warshawski novels, one standalone novel, and more than a dozen short stories. She had also edited three anthologies and was contributing articles and op-ed pieces to newspapers such as the *New York Times* and the *Guardian* (London). In 2002, she traveled to London to receive the British Crime Writers Association Cartier Diamond Dagger for Lifetime Achievement. Closer to home, the Chicago Historical Society gave her the Richard Wright History Maker Award for Distinction in Literature, in recognition of "the achievements of people linked in sustained and significant ways to Chicago" (letter dated 24 October 2001 in author's private papers accessed November 2012). Paretsky's 12th novel, *Blacklist*, published in 2003, was awarded the Gold Dagger by the British Crime Writers Association in 2004. Maureen Corrigan's review of this award-winning mystery noted, "[W]hat's particularly amazing about the Warshawski books is that, unlike other long-running series that eventually begin to run on empty, these mysteries have grown richer and more ambitious with age" (T6).

The University of Kansas honored Paretsky in 2006 with an Alumni Distinguished Achievement Award "[i]n recognition of her outstanding contribution to The Arts, and to her Country" (inscription on award in author's private collection accessed November 2013). In 2007, to mark the 25th anniversary of V. I.'s debut, Paretsky was invited to speak at the Library of Congress Center for the Book, and a theme issue of *Clues: A Journal of Detection* (Vol. 25.2, Winter 2007) was published. In addition, Paretsky's collection of autobiographical essays *Writing in an Age of Silence* was published. The state library of Kansas selected *Writing in an Age of Silence* as a 2008 Kansas Notable Book. Her second standalone novel, *Bleeding Kansas*, came out in 2008. This was also the year in which Paretsky, along with Marcia Muller and Sue Grafton, featured in Pamela Beere Briggs's documentary film *Women of Mystery: Three Writers Who Forever Changed Detective Fiction*.

In 2010 Paretsky was invited to deliver one of the keynote addresses at the 76th PEN International Congress held in Tokyo in 2010 on the subject of women and silence. In 2011, the Mystery Writers of America gave her the Grand Master Award, Bouchercon honored her with a Lifetime Achievement Award, and the Private Eye Writers of America presented her with the Hammer Award (a prize celebrating a memorable private-eye character). Paretsky was a featured speaker at the 2011 Library of Congress National Book Festival and, in that same year, recorded several video public service announcements about the value of libraries for the American Library Association's campaign to defend public libraries. Chicago organized a "Sara Paretsky Day of Celebration" on 14 March 2012 to mark the 30th anniversary of V. I.'s debut; the Chicago Public Libraries gave the author the Harold Washington Literary Award for that year. In 2014, she was one of the featured speakers at the Key West Literary Festival that was celebrating mystery, crime, and the literary thriller. She was the International Guest of Honor at the 12th annual Theakston's Old Peculiar Crime Writing Festival, Harrogate, UK, in July 2015. In May 2015, Paretsky was the commencement speaker at the University of Kansas; in the same month she received the Lifetime Achievement Award from the Malice Domestic conference in Washington, D.C. Paretsky became the 2015 president of the Mystery Writers of America, charged with leading the organization to respond to issues of the marginal-

**Sara Paretsky received the Paul Engle prize during the Iowa City Book Festival, October 2015. Courtesy Iowa City UNESCO City of Literature Organization.**

ization of African American, GLBT, and women writers. In October 2015, Paretsky received the Paul Engle Award at the Iowa City Literary Festival organized by the Iowa City UNESCO International City of Literature with other sponsors. Paretsky has received the honorary degree of Doctor of Letters from several universities, including DePaul University and Elmhurst College. Her alma mater, the University of Kansas, recognized her in 2015 with the honorary degree of Doctor of Letters.

Her work as a mystery writer has attracted the attention of the academy in other ways. Paretsky's novels feature on college-level courses in popular culture, women's studies and genre fiction. Her oeuvre is regularly the subject of critical and theoretical debate and publication, both within the academy and in more popular fora such as online magazines, discussion groups, and blogs. Her work continues to be the focus of dissertations and theses by MA and PhD students from the United States and further afield. Two scholarly discussions of her work were published in 2015: a monograph by Cynthia S. Hamilton and a collection of essays edited by Enrico Minardi and Jennifer Byron. Paretsky's papers are lodged at the Newberry Library in Chicago, an important Midwest independent research library with a public adult education program that was key to the author's early development as a writer. On the dedication page of the 15th novel, *Breakdown*, Paretsky names "Bill" Towner, president of the Newberry from 1962 to 1986, as one of the librarians "who've helped me navigate the great sea of learning."

Her activism extends beyond the world of publishing; Paretsky has served on the board of Chicago NARAL (National Abortion Rights Action League); Thresholds, a foundation that serves Chicago's mentally-ill homeless; and Literature for All of Us, a literacy group for teenage mothers. Reproductive rights is "the most fundamental freedom," she told Laura Shapiro in 1988 (67). Paretsky worked for many years with NARAL, speaking at national and regional events, and it is not surprising that the complex issue of reproductive rights and choice has turned up in several of her novels and short stories (see, for example, *Killing Orders, Bitter Medicine, Blood Shot,* "Poster Child," and "The Man Who Loved Life"). In the early 2000s, Paretsky lent her support to the American Civil Liberties Union challenges to the Patriot Act by posing in national ads, taking "her commentary on the road … and set[ting] up links on her Website" (Long, 2005 D2). She has endowed a number of scholarships at her Kansas alma mater and in Chicago in support of young female students who demonstrate leadership, creativity and originality. In addition, she gives funds to a range of local Chicago institutions including the Newberry Library, the Chicago Community Trust, Planned Parenthood of Chicago, Chicago Chamber Musicians, Three Arts Club, sports programs for girls, and a scholarship fund for DuSable High School graduates attending college. Paretsky donated the profits from the book launch sales of *Critical Mass* (2013) to Sisters4Science, a Chicago afterschool program that introduces junior and high-school girls to science through hands-on activities; girls in the program were invited to give presentations at the launch event held at the Swedish American Museum in Chicago and co-hosted by Women and Children First bookstore. Similarly, the 2015 *Brush Back* launch held at Seminary Co-op Bookstore in Chicago included guests from Girls in the Game, a sports program for girls. A 2004 article on women and philanthropy described Paretsky's decision to set up a private foundation in 2001; the author told Joanna Krotz, "I try to make grants of $5,000 to $15,000 each to support organizations ranging from sports camps for innercity girls to a nonprofit publisher of books by and about women" (238). The interviewer reveals that "[a]fter once donating money to a group that aided girls but first lectured them against using contraception, Paretsky now requires that grantees be pro-choice" (ibid.).

On a more personal note, Paretsky involves herself in the annual University of Chicago Revels "a beloved Hyde Park tradition [in which] faculty and community members … join together" to write and perform a musical lampooning life on and off campus (Allen 2011). Paretsky regularly contributes as a scriptwriter and performer. She and her husband share V. I.'s love of golden retrievers and have had three consecutive dogs in residence. Paretsky was writer-in-residence at Northwestern University Center for Creative Writing during fall 1998. Her support of public libraries is linked to her interests in educational opportunities for youngsters and reaches from her own city of Chicago to national librarians' professional associations and publications. Much in demand as a public speaker, she has occupied platforms in support of organizations such as the National Abortion Rights Action League, the Authors Guild, the national Library Association, Sisters in Crime, the ACLU, and Amnesty International.

She regularly appears on national and international stages, and on radio and TV, speaking as a writer, an activist, and a citizen promoting reading, libraries, literacy, and authorship to audiences both local and international. Her writing career extends beyond fiction to essays and articles for the print media, including newspapers, magazines, and journals. She has edited a number of anthologies of short stories by women crime writers as well as a collection of her V. I. short stories. The Paretsky oeuvre demonstrates a continuing integrity in the presentation of the self-identified feminist detective with a richness of character and her beloved, if flawed, city, along with the author's consistent engagement with issues of social justice and the lives of people on the margins. Paretsky's lasting contribution to the world of letters is in the creation of her iconic female private-eye, an individual who gives voice to female experience and validity to female agency.

# A Career Chronology

| | |
|---|---|
| **1947** | Sara Nancy Paretsky born on 8 June to Dr. David Paretsky (research scientist) and Mary Edwards Paretsky (librarian) in Ames, Iowa. The second in a family of five children and the only daughter. |
| **1951** | Paretsky family moves to Lawrence, Kansas, where Dr. Paretsky takes up an appointment in the Bacteriology Department at the University of Kansas. Sara and her brothers attend local schools, including a "two-room country school" (WIAAOS 26), one of the few Jewish families in the school system. |
| **1959** | Paretsky's first publication, an account of surviving a tornado, appears in *American Girl* magazine. |
| **1964** | Graduates from Lawrence High School as a National Merit Scholar. Matriculates at the University of Kansas; designated a Watkins Scholar, which allows her to live in the innovative Watkins Hall of residence (kuhistory.com). |
| **1965** | Earns scholarship to spend summer in Vienna, Austria, studying German. |
| **1966** | Spends summer in Chicago's Gage Park neighborhood as a community service volunteer in a children's day-camp program organized by the Presbyterian church. Later writes "that summer changed my life forever" (op. cit., 55). |
| **1967** | Graduates from University of Kansas, summa cum laude, with a BA in political science. As an undergraduate, Paretsky chaired the first University of Kansas Commission on the Status of Women. |
| **1968** | Moves to Chicago and begins graduate studies at the University of Chicago. Works as secretary in the political science department at the university. |
| **1969** | Receives MA from the Division of the Social Sciences, University of Chicago. Master's thesis is on "the abolitionists and their connection to the religious movements of the 1840s" (op. cit., 56). |
| **1970** | Spends summer in New York City hoping to find work in the magazine world. Works briefly as a secretary before returning to Chicago in the autumn. Becomes involved in the women's movement and begins PhD in U.S. history at the University of Chicago. |
| **1971–74** | Works for Chicago's Urban Research Corporation as publications and conference manager. |
| **1972** | Publishes short story "This Is for You, Jeannie" in *Women: A Journal of Liberation*. |
| **1974–77** | Works as freelance business writer and continues work on PhD dissertation. |
| **1976** | Marries Courtenay Wright, a physicist at the University of Chicago and a widower with three teenaged sons. Takes up residence in his Hyde Park home. |

**1977**   Is awarded MBA from the Graduate School of Business, University of Chicago; is awarded PhD from the University of Chicago History Department (dissertation title is "The Breakdown of Moral Philosophy in New England Before the Civil War"). Joins Continental National America (CNA) Insurance as manager responsible for advertising and direct mail marketing programs.

**1979**   Makes New Year's resolution to "write a novel in 1979 or send that fantasy packing" (Delacorte Press 1991 edition of *Indemnity Only*, vii). Attends Northwestern University extension course "Writing Detective Fiction for Publication" taught by crime writer Stuart Kaminsky.

**1980**   Finishes manuscript of *Indemnity Only* with central character V. I. Warshawski. Kaminsky sends it to his agent, Dominick Abel, in New York.

**1981**   Abel finds publisher Dial Press for *Indemnity Only*.

**1982**   *Indemnity Only* is published by Dial Press in the United States, Victor Gollancz in the United Kingdom, and Hayakawa Press in Japan; received with enthusiasm by reviewers.

**1984**   Short story "The Takamoku Joseki," featuring V. I. Warshawski, is published in *Alfred Hitchcock's Mystery Magazine*. Second V. I. novel *Deadlock* is published in the United States by Dial and in the United Kingdom by Gollancz.

**1985**   Short story "Three-Dot Po" featuring V. I. Warshawski is published in *The Eyes Have It* anthology. Third V. I. novel *Killing Orders* is published in the United States by Morrow and in UK by Gollancz. Receives Friends of American Writers award for *Deadlock*.

**1986**   Leaves CNA to work full time as writer. Sells rights to V. I. character to Tri-Star Pictures in Hollywood. At annual Bouchercon in Baltimore, cofounds Sisters in Crime (an advocacy organization to promote women writers, editors, reviewers, librarians, and booksellers in the crime and mystery field). Publishes short story "At the Old Swimming Hole" featuring V. I. in the second Private Eye Writers of America anthology.

**1987**   Receives the 1987 Ms. Magazine Ms Woman of the Year Award "[f]or bringing a woman detective and feminist themes to murder mysteries, and for championing women writers in this mostly male genre" (from award parchment in author's private papers accessed November 2012). Fourth V. I. novel *Bitter Medicine* published in the United States by Morrow and in the United Kingdom by Gollancz. Short story "Skin Deep" featuring V. I. is published in the *New Black Mask*.

**1988**   Is named to the University of Kansas Hall of Fame. Fifth V. I. novel *Blood Shot* is published by Delacorte in the United States and as *Toxic Shock* by Gollancz in the United Kingdom. Receives British Crime Writers Association Silver Dagger Award for *Blood Shot*. Receives Private Eye Writers of America Shamus Award for *Blood Shot* "Best Hardcover P.I. Novel of 1988." Short story "The Case of the Pietro Andromache" featuring V. I. is published in *Alfred Hitchcock's Mystery Magazine*. Short story "Dealer's Choice" published in *Raymond Chandler's Philip Marlowe: A Centennial Celebration*. Short story "Let's Have a Big Smile, Now" published in anthology of stories and poems by Chicago women.

**1989**   Receives YWCA Outstanding Achievement Award. Serves as vice-president of Mystery Writers of America. Edits *Beastly Tales* anthology of mystery stories. Publishes short story "A Taste of Life" in *Reader, I Murdered Him* anthology.

**1990**   Delivers Friends of American Writers lecture at Roosevelt University, Chicago. Publishes sixth V. I. novel *Burn Marks* with Delacorte in the United States and

Chatto & Windus in the United Kingdom. Short stories "Lily and the Sockeyes," "The Man Who Loved Life," and the V. I. story "The Maltese Cat" are published.

**1991**    Edits *A Woman's Eye*, an anthology of original short stories by women writers. Is nominated for and subsequently receives 1992 Anthony Award for Best Collection or Anthology for *A Woman's Eye*. Publishes short story "Settled Score" featuring signature detective. Short story "Hooker Malone Is Missing: A Serial Mystery" is coauthored by Paretsky, Dobyns, Estelman, Mosley, and Stout, and published in the *New York Times Book Review*. Appears at Edinburgh International Book Festival in August.

**1992**    Seventh V. I. mystery *Guardian Angel* is published by Delacorte in the United States and Hamilton in the United Kingdom. Publishes V. I. short story "Strung Out" in collaborative Private Eye Writers/Sisters in Crime anthology. Short story "Freud at Thirty Paces" published in British Crime Writers Association annual anthology.

**1993**    Receives German Crime Writers Association Marlowe Award for *Guardian Angel*. Awarded Honorary Doctor of Humane Letters degree from MacMurray College, Illinois.

**1994**    Eighth V. I. novel *Tunnel Vision* is published by Delacorte in the United States and Hamilton in the United Kingdom. Short story "The Great Tetsuji" published in third British Crime Writers Association annual anthology edited by Liza Cody et al.

**1995**    Publishes *Windy City Blues*, a collection of nine V. I. short stories, including previously unpublished "Grace Notes." U.S. Delacorte edition includes author's introduction and a guide to V. I.'s Chicago locations. The UK Hamilton edition published as *V. I. for Short*. Penguin publishes three Paretsky short stories in Penguin Sixty edition *A Taste of Life and Other Stories*.

**1996**    Receives Mark Twain Award for Distinguished Contribution to Midwest Literature. Named to the Lawrence Lions Alumni Association Hall of Honor at Lawrence High School, Kansas. Edits *Women on the Case*, an anthology of 26 original stories by women crime writers published by Delacorte in the United States and Virago in the United Kingdom. Collection includes Paretsky's story "Publicity Stunts." Short story "Heartbreak House" published in anthology *Murder for Love*.

**In 1996 Sara Paretsky was recognized for her "distinguished contribution" to Midwestern literature by the Society for the Study of Midwestern Literature. From author's private papers. Photograph by Linda Erf Swift.**

**1997**    Spends three months in England as visiting fellow at Wolfson College, Oxford. Attends the Bouchercon in Monterey, California, as author guest of honor. Publishes short story "The Man Who Loved Life" in Women's Press anthology.

**1998**    Paretsky's first standalone novel *Ghost Country* is published by Delacorte (in the United States) and Hamilton (in the United Kingdom). Is visiting professor at Northwestern University as writer-in-residence at the Center for Creative Writing in Evanston, Illinois.

**1999**    Receives Honorary Doctor of Humane Letters from Columbia College, Chicago. After a gap of five years, the ninth V. I. novel *Hard Time* is published by Delacorte (in the United States) and Hamilton (in the United Kingdom). It makes the *New York Times* bestseller list.

**2000**    Receives Illinois Coalition for Immigrant and Refugee Rights Professional Achievement Award for her demonstrated belief "in the necessity of a pro-immigrant agenda" (from letter dated 3 April 2000 in author's private papers accessed November 2013). Appears at Edinburgh International Book Festival in August.

**2001**    Delivers Judith Austin Memorial Lecture at Library of Congress on 3 April. Short story "Photo Finish" featuring V. I. is published in *Mary Higgins Clark Mystery Magazine*. The 10th V. I. novel *Total Recall* is published by Delacorte (in the United States) and Hamilton (in the United Kingdom).

**2002**    Receives a number of prestigious awards, including National Organization for Women Chicago chapter "Women Who Dared Excellence in Media Award"; the British Crime Writers Association Cartier Diamond Dagger for Lifetime Achievement; an Honorary Degree of Doctor of Humane Letters from Elmhurst College, Illinois; and the Richard Wright History Maker Award for Distinction in Literature from the Chicago Historical Society Making History Awards that recognize "the achievements of people linked in sustained and significant ways to Chicago" (letter dated 24 October 2001 in author's private papers accessed November 2012).

**2003**    *Blacklist*, the 11th in the V. I. series, is published in the United States by Putnam and in the United Kingdom by Hamilton. Short story "At the 'Century of Progress'" published in anthology *Mysterious Pleasures*.

**2004**    Another year of honors for Paretsky who receives the British Crime Writers Association Gold Dagger Award for *Blacklist* (£3000); an Honorary Doctor of Humane Letters degree from the College of Liberal Arts and Sciences at DePaul University, Chicago; she is named on *Crain's* list of 100 most influential women in Chicago.

**2005**    Paretsky publishes the 12th V. I. mystery *Fire Sale* (Putnam in the United States and Hodder in the United Kingdom). She receives the 2005 Susan B. Anthony Legacy Award to a Leader in Arts & Letters and the Shamus Lifetime Achievement Award from the Private Eye Writers of America. Barnes and Noble Booksellers recognize Paretsky as the 2005 Focus on Illinois Award winner for her contributions to the Illinois Writing and Publishing Community.

**2006**    Publishes short story "Acid Test" in *Deadly Housewives* anthology. Receives the Ridley Award for *Blood Shot* from Murder in the Grove in Boise, Idaho. Receives the Tenth Annual Alumni Distinguished Achievement Award from the College of Liberal Arts and Sciences at the University of Kansas "[i]n recognition of her outstanding contribution to The Arts, and to her Country."

**2007**   Publishes collection of autobiographical essays *Writing in an Age of Silence* with Verso Press in the United States. Publishes short story "A Family Sunday in the Park" (featuring V. I.) in *Sisters on the Case*, an anthology celebrating 20 years of Sisters in Crime and edited by Paretsky. She receives the ACLU of Illinois Harry Kalven Freedom of Expression Award in honor of "outspoken defence of the first amendment through your published opinion pieces, particularly your inspiring new book, *Writing in an Age of Silence* ... and your courageous voice in defence of reproductive freedom, expressed through V. I. Warshawski" (in letter from ACLU, 26 June 2007, in author's private papers accessed November 2012). Discusses *Fire Sale* in program at Library of Congress Center for the Book in commemoration of V. I.'s 25th anniversary, 27 February. Academic journal *Clues: A Journal of Detection* publishes special edition of scholarly essays in honor of V. I.'s 25th birthday.

**2008**   Named as National Book Critics Circle Finalist for publishing year 2007 for *Writing in an Age of Silence;* volume of essays also selected as a 2008 Kansas Notable Book by the State Library of Kansas. *Bleeding Kansas*, Paretsky's second standalone novel, is published by Putnam (in the United States) and by Hodder (in the United Kingdom).

**2009**   The 13th V. I. novel, *Hardball*, is published by Putnam (in the United States) and Hodder (in the United Kingdom).

**2010**   *Body Work*, the 14th in the series, is published by Putnam (in the United States) and Hodder (in the United Kingdom). Paretsky is invited as keynote speaker at the 76th PEN International Congress, Tokyo, where she talks about her memoir *Writing in an Age of Silence*.

**2011**   Receives Grand Master award at Mystery Writers of America Edgar Awards, New York. Publishes short story "Poster Child" in *Send My Love and a Molotov Cocktail* anthology. Receives Distinguished Arts Award from the Kansas Governor's Arts Awards. Receives Bouchercon Lifetime Achievement Award in St. Louis, Missouri. Receives the Hammer Award for Best P.I. Series Character from the Private Eye Writers of America. Appears at the 2011 National Book Festival.

**2012**   Publishes 15th V. I. novel *Breakdown* with Putnam in the United States and Hodder in the United Kingdom. Receives Harold Washington Literary Award from Chicago Public Libraries. The city declares "Sara Paretsky Day" on 14 March in honor of 30th anniversary of publication of *Indemnity Only*. Receives award from Giving Matters, Literature for All of Us, a Chicago Literacy program for teenage mothers. Plaque reads, "Let our laughter and joy, our voices, thoughts and actions weave beauty around the land" (in author's private papers accessed November 2013).

**2013**   Publishes 16th V. I. mystery *Critical Mass* (Putnam in the United States and Hodder in the United Kingdom). Receives the 2012 Freedom from Religion Foundation Freethought Heroine Award in Madison, Wisconsin. Invited to talk on *Critical Mass* at the Library of Congress on 15 November.

**2014**   Gives John Hersey Memorial Address "My Quest for Heroes" to kick off the 32nd annual Key West Literary Festival on 9 January. Appears at Edinburgh International Book Festival in August. Publishes short story "Miss Bianca" in anthology *Ice Cold*.

**2015**   Paretsky becomes president of the Mystery Writers of America. University of Kansas awards Paretsky with honorary degree of Doctor of Letters "for outstanding contributions to the mystery writing field and American literature" (news.ku.edu. 22 Oct. 2014). Delivers commencement address at University of Kansas in May. Receives Lifetime Achievement Award from the Malice Domestic convention in Bethesda, Maryland. Serves as International Guest of Honor at the annual Theakston's Old Peculiar Crime Writing Festival in Harrogate, UK, in July. In October, received the Paul Engle Award at the Iowa City Literary Festival. Publishes 17th V. I. novel *Brush Back*.

Between 1989 and 1996 Paretsky established a number of scholarships, including the Sara Paretsky Scholarship Fund and the Mary Edwards & Sara Paretsky Scholarship at the University of Kansas, as well as the Geraldine-Lute-Paretsky Fund at the Chicago Community Trust. The funds are usually designated to support high-school and college women students with interests in the arts, science, or sports.

# The Companion

### "Acid Test" (2006)

This short story explores the mother-daughter relationship between Karin and Temple. It was published in the *Deadly House-wives* anthology edited by Christine Matthews. Temple saves her own and her mother's lives, earning her mother's praise for not being weak and scared. Temple's friend, Lettice, thinks Temple has a cool mother.

### "Afterword to *The Brothers Karamazov*" (2007)

Paretsky's afterword to a Signet Classics edition of Fyodor Dostoevsky's novel is a thoughtful and detailed appreciation of both author and novel, arguing "in the writer's prejudices and in his deep empathy for the downtrodden, Dostoevsky has created the most fully human work imaginable" (899).

### Ajax Insurance Company

Ajax—a fictional insurance company based in the south Loop "at the northwestern corner of Michigan and Adams" (KO 99)—and its employees play a part in several of V. I.'s investigations, starting with the debut novel *Indemnity Only*. In this first case, V. I. goes to the Ajax building, a "sixty-story skyscraper" (DL 187), in search of information about a young employee whose disappearance she is investigating. Bluffing her way past the gatekeepers, V. I. meets Ralph Devereux, an associate at the company who knows the missing person. When they later compare notes about the case over drinks and dinner, Ralph makes his romantic intentions clear, and they have a brief affair. It turns out that Ralph's boss, an Ajax executive officer, is implicated in the scam discovered by V. I.

Throughout the series, further Ajax associates enter the picture as investigative colleagues and romantic interests, and the company itself is frequently involved in her cases. In *Deadlock*, V. I. meets Ajax's visiting British associate Roger Ferrant "probably the most knowledgeable man in the world about Great Lakes shipping" (DL 188); he hires her to find crucial information about some sabotage done to a ship insured by Ajax and now the subject of a major claim. Toward the end of the case they embark on a short romance before Ferrant returns to London. Ferrant turns up again in *Killing Orders*, when Ajax shares become the object of an illegal takeover that V. I. helps to resolve. Ferrant and V. I. resume their romance and are nearly killed one night when her apartment is targeted in an arson attack. At the close of the novel, Roger helps her find a new apartment and again returns to London. In *Burn Marks*, Robin Bessinger is an Ajax assessor working on the burnt-out single-resident-occupancy hotel where V. I.'s indigent Aunt Elena used to live. They work together on the arson case and have a short-lived romantic liaison. Ralph Devereux reappears in *Total Recall*; and once again the company, now owned by a multinational conglomerate, is implicated in a major set of insurance claim scandals that V. I. reveals. As Ralph explains to V. I., there have been some shake-ups at Ajax in the last few years since "Hurricane Andrew overwhelmed us.... Edelweiss snapped up a chunk of our depressed stock" (TR 40). The Edelweiss acquisition was initiated as the move of a "hostile suitor," as Ralph tells V. I., "but they certainly haven't been a hostile master" (TR 40). However, all is not well in the now international insurance company, and V. I. discovers shenanigans that Ralph does not see or understand until too late. Ajax Insurance Company is possibly inspired by the CNA Insurance Company where Paretsky worked as a marketing manager from 1977 to 1986. The distinctive CNA building—a rust-red, iron-cladded, and boxlike structure in the South Loop—overlooks Grant Park and is close to the corner of Wabash and Monroe where Paretsky positions V. I.'s office building, the fictional Pulteney. Paretsky's imagined Ajax Building is, according to V. I., a "glass-and-steel skyscraper [which] occupies sixty of the ugliest stories in Chicago" (KO 99). Goodkin's discussion of *Killing Orders* speculates on how the name Ajax resonates with suggestions of the heroic order, catharsis, and cleansing. He writes that Paretsky told him the name "was meant to suggest an association with 'the hero of the Trojan wars,'" and he further notes that Ajax is "also the name of a popular household cleanser" (83, 85).

## Allingham, Margery

An English writer (1904–66) of Golden Age detective fiction best known for her stories featuring Albert Campion, an upper-class sleuth in the tradition of Sherlock Holmes. In a 2015 London Times Crime Club interview posted on her Web site, Paretsky cites Allingham as one of her favorite crime writers. Westminster Council (London) invited Parestky as guest of honor at the May 2004 ceremonial unveiling of a Green Plaque commemorating an Allingham address near Paddington. Paretsky contributed the introductory "Margery Allingham: An Appreciation" to the festschrift *Margery Allingham: 100 Years of a Great Mystery Writer* published in 2004. The character of V. I. arguably shares something with that of Albert Campion, who says, in the 1934 *Death of a Ghost*, "If one cannot command attention by one's admirable qualities, at least one can be a nuisance."

## Alvarado Family

[Note: Alvarez in *Blood Shot / Toxic Shock*]. Carol first appears in *Indemnity Only* as "Lotty's nurse, a young Puerto Rican woman" (138). Later in the novel, her brother Paul, "an architecture student at Circle" (174), is enlisted to help look after the young Jill Thayer who Lotty and V. I. are sheltering for a few days. In this first novel, Carol and her brother do not have a last name. In *Killing Orders*, the third in the series, she is mentioned as "Carol Alvarado, the nurse at Lotty's North Side clinic" (189). In the fourth V. I. mystery, *Bitter Medicine*, the family comes briefly to the fore when events are kicked off by Carol's request to V. I. for some help with her younger sister Consuelo (sic). In this novel the Alvarado family consists of Carol, Consuelo, Paul, and Mrs. Alvarado, the mother who "raised six children working as a cafeteria attendant in one of the big downtown banks" (Bitter 12). She has high expectations for her children. Two more brothers, Herman and Diego, make occasional appearances in the V. I. series. In the 1984 short story "Three-Dot Po," Lotty leaves V. I. on Christmas Day "at seven to eat dinner with her nurse Carol Alvarado, and her family" (WCB 230). In the 1988 *Toxic Shock* (*Blood Shot*), the family's last name is changed when "Carol Alvarez, the nurse and chief backup at Lotty's clinic, arrived ... [and] greeted me warmly" (191). By the following *Burn Marks*, the family name has reverted to Alvarado when V. I. leaves a message for Lotty via "Carol Alvarado, the clinic nurse" (65). Next, in *Guardian Angel* (1992) Carol tells V. I. she is burned out and wants a change: "The truth is, V. I., I'm sick of that clinic. I've been doing it day in and out for eight years and I need a change" (33). She plans to nurse her mother's cousin who has AIDS, although she knows both V.I. and Lotty think "that at thirty-four I should divorce my mother and make a life for myself" (GA 33). Carol makes a painful transition away from Lotty's clinic, but is satisfied she has done the right thing combining work at County Hospital's AIDS ward with a job on the night trauma unit where, as she tells V. I., "[Y]ou can do real nursing here" (203). At the end of *Guardian Angel,* V. I. tells Carol, "[M]aybe you leaving the clinic was good for me as well as you. It's time I stopped turning to you and Lotty every time I scrape my knee" (359).

**See also** *Indemnity Only, Bitter Medicine, Tunnel Vision*

### "Another Turn of the Screw" (2012)

Paretsky delivered the 16th Annual Mc-Cusker Lecture on 24 Oct 2012 at Dominican University in River Forest, IL, an event co-sponsored by the Freedom to Read Foundation of the American Library Association. Reprinted in the journal *World Libraries*, "Another Turn of the Screw" may have some origins in a 30 Mar. 2004 event with Paretsky at the University of Arkansas's Mullins Library. In the lecture, Paretsky discusses the struggle for writers to balance life, art, and the demands of the marketplace that have occurred at least since the nineteenth century: "I am a person at war with myself on many fronts. I want to be a moral, courageous person, but I too often take the soft, risk–free option. I want to be an artist who puts my work first, but I was brought up under the evil wings of the Angel in the House."

### "Art History" (2011)

Paretsky's speech as recipient of 2011 Kansas Governor's Distinguished Artist Award was printed in the *Kansas State Collegian*. In her remarks, she said the award "is a shorthand for every writer, every storyteller, poet, painter, singer, whose art has helped another person endure the dark night of the soul" (4).

### Ashford, Leydon

Lawyer Leydon Ashford is a former law school classmate of V. I. who is bipolar. She appears in "Poster Child" to represent Dr. Adair, who is accused of killing a pro-life advocate. Estranged from her family due to her mental health issues, Leydon dies in *Breakdown* after making a cryptic utterance that V. I. must decipher.

### "At the 'Century of Progress'" (2003)

This short story was published in the *Mysterious Pleasures* anthology edited by Martin Edwards. Paretsky imagines Agatha Christie's Miss Marple and her nephew visiting Chicago in 1933 to see the World's Fair, named the Century of Progress. The Jane Marple character remembers a previous visit to Chicago when she was 23—"such a rough city compared to London, yet charged with excitement" (255). Paretsky adds another famous literary detective: Carroll John Daly's Race Williams, who comes from the early days of *Black Mask* magazine and also is visiting the Century of Progress exhibition. Paretsky achieves the "voice" of each of the legendary characters from the two main twentieth-century strands of crime and mystery fiction: the genteel world of upper middle-class England as exemplified in the Christie mysteries and the mean American city-streets milieu depicted in the action-filled stories of *Black Mask* magazine in the 1920s.

### "At the Old Swimming Hole" (1986)

This V. I. short story was published first in Randisi's anthology *Mean Streets*. Subsequently it appeared in Smith's anthology *Ms Murder* and then in *Windy City Blues* (aka *V. I. for Short*) in 1995. In 1998, it was included in Hopkins and Potter's anthology *Crime Story Collection*. In another return to her past, V. I. agrees to sponsor her old high school friend Alicia in a swimming competition raising money for the American Cancer Society because "both Alicia's mother and mine had died of cancer" (WCB 124). Turning up at the event to watch Alicia's race, V. I. finds herself diving into the pool to help a swimmer who "was having trouble righting herself, couldn't seem to make headway in the lane" (WCB 126). The swimmer, bank employee Louise Carmody, dies from a gunshot wound; the police are called; the hunt for the killer begins. V. I. begins to suspect that it was Alicia who was the target, perhaps because she is in debt, but Alicia won't talk and subsequently goes missing. The FBI also seems to be interested in Alicia; they suspect her of "selling Defense Department secrets to the Chinese" (WCB 139). V. I. eventually tracks her friend down to the pool at their old high school in South Chicago, where Alicia has volunteered as a swimming coach. She gets the truth out of Alicia; her younger brother, Tom, has run up huge gambling debts, and Alicia has borrowed money to help him. But it looks as if Tom also stole her top-secret computer discs in the hopes of selling them to raise more money. In a dramatic shootout at the pool Alicia is wounded, but lives "long enough to tell the truth to the FBI" (WCB 149). The story ends on a gloomy note; the police are "sore that they'd let Alicia get shot. [S]o they dumped some charges on me.... I spent several days in jail" (WCB 149). This ambivalent ending, with the detective unjustly incarcerated and the police behaving badly, is characteristic of the way in which Paretsky often concludes V. I.'s cases, pointing to the problematic relationships between justice and truth, and accuser and accused.

## "Baptism in the Bungalow Belt" (1996)

This guest essay for the *Chicago Tribune*'s series on the city's political landscape recalls Paretsky's experiences during summer 1966 when she was working as a volunteer on a community day-care program in a white, working-class neighborhood of Chicago. She particularly remembers the explosive events of 5 August 1966 in Marquette Park, where "Martin Luther King Jr. was leading a rally [there] to support open housing and fair employment in Chicago." The blue-collar neighborhood turned out to attack the demonstrators as they filed into the park, and the police, unprepared and disorganized, were unable to protect the marchers. The summer left a lasting impression on Paretsky, whose dedication to social justice was confirmed.

## Barthele, Sal

Owner of the Golden Glow bar, on Adams Street in the South Loop, where V. I. and journalist Murray Ryerson frequently meet for refreshment, and to discuss their current investigation. A shrewd businesswoman and property owner, Sal is part of V. I.'s support network and her circle of activist female friends and colleagues. Sal features in most of the novels, primarily as the proprietor of the Golden Glow; however, her wider role in the community is signaled such as in *Tunnel Vision*, where she appears as the chair of the board of directors for Arcadia House, a non-

profit battered women's shelter. She belongs "to an organization of women restaurateurs ... a small group in Chicago" (BW 66). Sal's lesbian-identified sexuality is hinted when she turns up at V. I.'s surprise 40th birthday party "with her current love, a young actress" (TV 431). Sal's bar is located in the financial district of Chicago and attracts stock-market traders as well as "business travellers [who] mingle with regulars from the high-rises and converted lofts along Printers Row" (BW 65). The Golden Glow is "a tiny saloon dating back to the last century ... [with] a mahogany horseshoe-shaped bar ... and a couple of real Tiffany lamps" (IO 22). Sal herself "is tall, majestic in build, and her wardrobe doubles her impact.... [H]er Afro was cropped close to her head" (BW 65). In the short story "Skin Deep," Sal is described as "very black, and statuesque. Close to six feet tall, with majestic carriage, she can break up a crowd in her bar with a look and a gesture" (VIFS 60). Sal's sister, Evangeline, is charged with murder in this story, and Sal calls on V. I. for help. In the early V. I. novels, the detective keeps a tab at the Golden Glow, where Sal stocks a supply of the detective's favorite Johnnie Walker Black Label. However, by the 14th novel, *Body Work* (2010), times have changed: "I handed Sal my AmEx card. She used to run a tab for me when she and I first opened our businesses twenty years ago, but those days have disappeared with the rest of the economy" (68). The ninth novel, *Hard Time*, opens with V. I.; Ryerson, who now works for Global Entertainment Network; and a mob of "Chicago glitterati" (HT 1) attending a GEN media event at the Golden Glow. As the crowd "draped themselves around executives from Global Studios" (HT 2), Sal asks V. I., "what got into me, to let [Murray] turn my bar into this backslapping media circus?" (HT 1).

**See also *Tunnel Vision, Hard Time, Body Work,* "Skin Deep"**

## Bessinger, Robin

V. I. meets arson specialist Robin Bessinger in *Burn Marks* when she visits the burnt-out remains of her Aunt Elena's single residency hotel. Bessinger is "with Ajax's arson and fraud division" (11). Convinced that the hotel has been deliberately set on fire and knowing something of V. I.'s reputation, he persuades her to "go back into the Ajax trenches once again" (96) as an independent investigator in the hopes she will track down the suspected arsonist. She reminds him that Ajax Insurance "didn't know if it loved or hated me for fingering their claims vice president as the mastermind of a worker's comp fraud scam" (96) in a reference to her first case in *Indemnity Only*. Robin and V. I. slowly embark on a close personal relationship; after a restaurant dinner one evening, "one thing kind of led to another, but I left before they drifted too far" (84). A few nights later, they are on their way back to V. I.'s apartment when Lt. Bobby Mallory (accompanied by Sergeant Michael Furey, another of V. I.'s admirers) interrupts them on the doorstep: "I could feel my cheeks flame in the dark—no matter how cool you are, it unsettles you when your father's oldest friend surprises you in a passionate embrace" (97). They argue over the investigation, and things cool between them when Robin does not trust her professional judgment. At the close of *Burn Marks*, he tries to make amends, but she hedges her bets about seeing him again, realizing that "I was going to have to build up my strength and get over a lot of wounds before I was in the humor for much et cetera" (332).

### Bitter Medicine (1987)

"I don't have such grand ideals as a detective ... I'm just the garbage collector, cleaning up little trash piles here and there" (281–82).

Originally titled *Malpractice*, the fourth V. I. mystery is dedicated to Kathleen (a friend who died of lupus) with a quote from John Donne's "A Valediction: Forbidding Mourning." The punning title, in characteristic Paretsky style, works on several levels, hinting at the medical theme and more abstractly pointing to the harms and "life" lessons in store for V. I.

The novel opens during a hot Chicago summer, plunging V. I. into a case focused on the medical professions and medical insurance underwriters. T. J. Binyon, in a *TLS* review,

says it "lifts Sara Paretsky immediately into a different league" (1987). New supporting characters Mr. Contreras, police detective Conrad Rawlings, Tessa Reynolds, and Peppy the golden retriever make their debuts in *Bitter Medicine* and continue throughout the subsequent novels. The story begins because of V. I.'s long history with the Alvarado family. Carol Alvarado, the nurse at Dr. Lotty Herschel's clinic, has, more than once, helped Lotty get V. I. back on her feet: "a year ago Christmas, Carol sacrificed the day to look after me when I took an unplanned bath in Lake Michigan" (13). Then "there was the time Paul Alvarado [Carol's brother] babysat for Jill Thayer [a character in *Indemnity Only*] when her life was in danger" (13). So, on a sweltering July day, V. I. feels she "had no choice" (13) when she is asked by the family to drive the pregnant Consuelo Alvarado and her unemployed husband, Fabiano Hernandez, to the northwest suburbs for Fabiano's job interview at a factory. Setting off in her un-air-conditioned Chevy Citation for the long, hot drive, V. I. delivers Fabiano to the factory; moments later, Consuelo, age 16 and diabetic, appears to go into early labor, and V. I. rushes her to the nearby Friendship Five Hospital for emergency care. V. I. contacts Carol, and plans are made to send obstetrician Malcolm Tregiere, one of Dr. Lotty Herschel's associates at the Chicago Beth Israel hospital, out to Friendship Five to supervise Consuelo's case. V. I. skirmishes with the admitting staff at Friendship, who assume that because of Consuelo's Hispanic name, she is poor and unable to pay hospital bills; they threaten to move her to a public hospital. The furious detective reminds them about Illinois public health law that "says you cannot deny emergency treatment because you think the person can't pay ... every hospital in this state is required by law to look after a woman giving birth" (22). The attending Friendship obstetrician Peter Burgoyne, together with Tregiere, are unable to save Consuelo's baby, and later that night Consuelo dies of complications. More deaths, violent events, and complications follow in rapid succession. Tregiere is brutally murdered before he can complete his autopsy re-

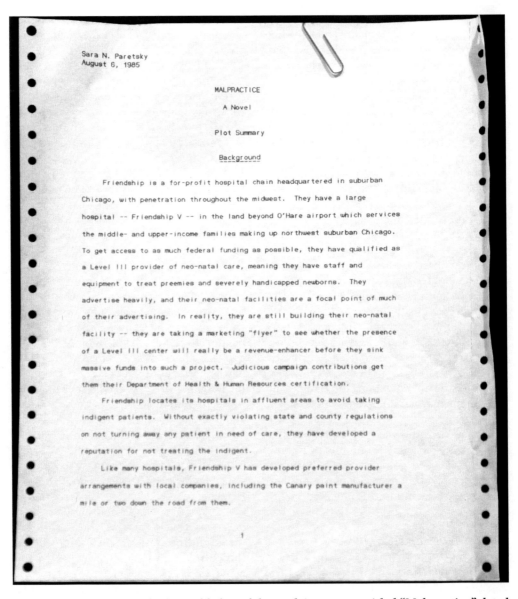

Paretsky's plot summary for her publisher of the work in progress titled "Malpractice," dated 1985, later published as *Bitter Medicine*. From Paretsky Papers Newberry archive (Box VI of 9, 1992 gift). Photograph by Linda Erf Swift.

port on Consuelo. The police believe it is a gang killing related to Fabiano, who is suspected of a gang affiliation and has threatened to sue Lotty over the deaths of his wife and child. Malcolm's lover, the sculptor Tessa Reynolds, and Lotty herself are convinced otherwise and pressure Vic to investigate Tregiere's death. V. I. receives unwanted attention from some vengeful Chicago gang members; she starts a brief fling with the appealing Burgoyne; her ex-husband, Richard Yarborough, turns up as the legal counsel for one of Friendship Hospital's management executives; and downstairs neighbor Mr. Contreras becomes a staunch ally. Lotty's clinic is the focus of an anti-abortion protest that escalates into a near-riot; her office is vandalized, and patient files that include

Consuelo's are destroyed or stolen. Mr. Contreras is badly injured when he attempts to thwart a break-in at V. I.'s apartment and ends up in intensive care. The red Venetian goblets that are so precious to V. I. survive this break-in as the detective discovers to her relief: "the only things I really care about—my mother's wineglasses—were still standing in the dining-room cupboard" (191). Burgoyne refuses to release the hospital records relating to Consuelo's case. Then Fabiano is found shot dead, and the police put V. I. on their list of possible suspects. Vic figures out that events at Friendship Hospital are key—the deaths of Consuelo and her baby, the death of Tregiere, the neatly timed riot at Lotty's clinic, Fabiano's threatened lawsuit against Lotty, and Fabiano's murder. Needing to collect the evidence that will prove her suspicions, V. I. burgles her way into Burgoyne's office at Friendship Hospital and steals Consuelo's file. Lotty and Max help her decode the medical notes, and together with reporter Murray Ryerson, they piece together the story of how Friendship Hospital's profit motives led to Consuelo's death and a subsequent cover-up, which in turn necessitated the murders of Tregiere and Fabiano. In a tense confrontation with Burgoyne, Vic and the police learn the truth about the extent of Burgoyne's involvement with the crimes of his boss, the unscrupulous executive director Alan Humphries. In shame and despair, Burgoyne takes his own life; the killers of Tregiere and Fabiano are tracked down in a final chase by V. I. and police detective Conrad Rawlings, and disappear into the machinations of the criminal justice system. In a poignant closing chapter, V. I. and Mr. Contreras are in a Michigan lakeside town on a late summer weekend retreat, both of them still recovering from the previous events, and in reflective moods. Mr. Contreras reminds Vic of the good that has come out of this case: she has acquired Peppy, the golden retriever that belonged to Burgoyne and will prove to be a faithful companion to both V. I. and Mr. Contreras in the rest of the series. At the end of *Bitter Medicine*, it is Peppy who restores V. I. to the here and now: "I pushed myself up to standing. While the dog danced

herself into a crescendo of ecstasy, I picked up the stick and hurled it into the setting sun" (321).

Paretsky, when asked by reviewer Lisa Bergland about her interest in health care and the theme of corruption in the health industry, responded, "I'm interested in writing about large organizations, rather than people simply driven by poverty, rage and so on. In large institutions you don't really see murder, but you see a lot of soul-negating behaviour that's too easy to take for granted" (1). David Everson's astute review observes how well the novel works through a series of "nice ironies," which contrast "the impersonal, seeming bureaucratic efficiency ... of McHospital with the human values embodied in the storefront clinic run by V. I.'s close friend, Dr. Lotty Herschel"; and juxtapose "the disorder and near-the-surface violence of the city with the superficial order and hidden corruption of the suburbs" (46). His review also praises Paretsky as "particularly gifted at drawing sympathetic portraits of V. I.'s friends—male and female" (ibid.).

**See also Alvarado family, Mr. Contreras, Lotty Herschel, Peppy, Tessa Reynolds, Richard Yarborough**

## Blacklist (2003)

"I'm going to sic Murray Ryerson on it" (397).

The 11th novel in the V. I. series opens with V. I. "stumbling on tree roots and chunks of brick," trying to find her way, late at night in the first week of March, across unfamiliar ground; "in the dark everything is different," she reflects (1). She is in the gardens of "Larchmont Hall ... its pale brick making it loom like a ghostly galleon in the moonlight" (18). The gothic imagery and an explanation of why V. I. is "anxious, and feeling alone.... After the Trade Center, I'd been as numbed and fearful as everyone else in America" (1) signal the start of a complex political thriller that deals with the McCarthy witch hunts of the 1950s and disturbing comparisons with post–9/11 America. *Blacklist* (the title references the infamous practice during the 1940s and 1950s of barring artists and entertainers from work on the basis of their alleged sympathies with progressive political causes and refusal to cooperate with official investigations into Communist Party activities) was awarded the Gold Dagger for Best Crime Novel of the Year by the British Crime Writers Association in 2004. Set, as usual, in Chicago and with excursions into the affluent northwest suburbs, the plot revolves around the suspicious death of African American journalist Marcus Whitby. V. I. stumbles on his body in the course of a routine nighttime stakeout on behalf of her regular client, the wealthy Chicagoan Darraugh Graham, "CEO of Continental United Group" (201). When the suburban cops treat the reporter's death as suicide (they construe it as a drunken drowning), the Whitby family hires V. I. to look into what they are certain is a suspicious death. Her investigations on their behalf proceed alongside her original assignment (looking into the complaint of Graham's nonagenarian mother about noticing, from her retirement home window, lights in the nearby empty mansion that once belonged to her family). V. I. discovers that Whitby was working on a story about the 1930s Federal Negro Theater project, a New Deal agency set up to provide jobs for theater people now unemployed. Whitby's focus is on some key members who were subsequently investigated during the communist witch hunts of the 1950s. In the meantime, she finds out that, rather than the squatters feared by Geraldine Graham, the vacant Graham mansion is being used by 16-year-old Catherine Bayard (whose publisher grandfather had famously stood up to McCarthy's HUAC hearings in the early 1950s and was thus one of V. I.'s heroes). She is sheltering Benji Sadawi, a terrified young Egyptian dishwasher at her elite Gold Coast high school, who is being targeted as having alleged terrorist connections. Before long, the two cases are tangled together, leading the detective into a web of complicated and dangerous secrets linking two powerful families and reaching back to the depression and the McCarthy era. V. I. is stumbling in the dark, literally and figuratively, suffering from "exhaustion of the spirit" (3). She struggles not only with her cases but also to come to terms with the aftermath of the

events of 9/11 and with the continuing absence of her lover, foreign correspondent Morrell, on a dangerous assignment in Afghanistan. Lonely, anxious about Morrell's safety, worried about the powers of the hastily legislated Patriot Act, and concerned about Benji's welfare, Vic's principles, skills, and loyalties are put to extreme tests. V. I. is also suffering from the recent resignation of her assistant, Mary Louise Neely; the paperwork is building up in her office, "filing so far in arrears I wasn't sure I could bring myself to start on it" (49). Mr. Contreras is in turn worried about V. I., who has "lost ten pounds in the six months after the Trade Center," and he takes to "frying up French toast and bacon" (3) when the detective returns from her daily runs. Paretsky's parallel story lines and timelines, which involve old and new secrets of discrimination, bigotry, political betrayals, sexual scandals, and the use of power and money by the privileged, are skillfully used to evoke the obsessions of the earlier Red Scare period and link them to the post–9/11 climate of right-wing paranoia in the United States. In a tense scene on Vic's doorstep, she demands that the federal agent who has been sent to search her apartment show his warrant; he reminds her that under the Patriot Act he is "permitted to bypass the warrant process" (237). During a subsequent interrogation with more authorities at the Chicago Police Department HQ, V. I. is threatened with the charge of "aiding our enemies," because "America is at war" (247), as they remind her. Incandescent with fury at the erosion of civil liberties and in despair at the intimidating climate, the detective explains her feelings: "I think this is the most serious thing that has happened in my lifetime … the fear we've unleashed on ourselves since [9/11], so we can say that the Bill of Rights doesn't matter anymore … if the Bill of Rights is dead my life, my faith in America, will break" (248). Beverly G. Six's theoretical essay on the novel suggests this speech highlights a key concern of both author and character: "[W]hile the dominant cultural ideologies assert that the threat to America is from without, our detective pinpoints the more urgent threat, the threat from within

... not in the presence of a frightened, Egyptian boy but in a frightened populace" (155). Maureen Corrigan's review for the *Washington Post Book World* praises the novel for "the intelligence it brings to bear on the once again urgent issues of political dissent and national security" (2003: T6). *Blacklist* provides a set of compelling mysteries for Vic to unravel at the same time that it explores contemporary political and social issues, alongside more timeless questions about approaching life passively or as an active participant. The epigraph to the novel—"I cannot rest from travel: I will drink/Life to the lees"—is taken from Tennyson's 1842 dramatic monologue "Ulysses" and signals the preoccupations displayed by several of the characters such as questions of restlessness, the human longing for adventure and experience, aging, and the role of the responsible social individual. The regular cast of recurring characters (Dr. Lotty Herschel, Max Loewenthal, Mr. Contreras, Sal Barthele, Murray Ryerson, and Bobby Mallory) variously support her, scold her, patch her up, and help her. There is a touching cameo appearance of the activist priest Father Lou from the earlier *Hard Time*, whose quiet help with the young Egyptian boy helps steady V. I.'s purpose, and again manages to put her in touch with relatively unexplored aspects of her own spirituality. Also in evidence are the familiar motifs of dreams, music, food and restaurants, clothes, urban regeneration, the Cubs, family frictions, the dogs Peppy and Mitch, the formidable older woman and the spunky young girl figures (Geraldine Graham and Catherine Bayard respectively) with whom Vic forges unlikely alliances, V. I.'s deceased parents Tony and Gabriella, and the detective's famously non-negotiable desire for autonomy. Fretting over the lack of communication from Morrell, she lectures herself: "Ulysses chose his path, Penelope: don't let that control you, I adjured myself sternly: 'Don't weep over yourself,' my mother had told me [aged eight or nine].... 'Do something'" (103). And so, as in the rest of the series, V. I. characteristically chooses to engage rather than retreat, even though "every attempt that Warshawski makes to 'expose' the Patriot Act's corruption ... is illegal" (Six, op. cit., 144). Six further points out that in this novel, "it is the law that threatens to destroy the "fundamental social stability" that readers have come to expect in the resolution of the hard-boiled detective's case" (ibid.). Lorna Gibb's review in the *Times Literary Supplement* concludes that "the novel's great achievement is its ability to work on many levels, as a puzzle, a thriller, a thoughtful, comparative study of two periods of political turmoil and a portrait of a brave, highly principled but vulnerable woman" (24). The novel is dedicated to Paretsky's mother-in-law, Geraldine Courtney Wright, who is further commemorated in the character Geraldine Graham, an independent 91-year-old woman whose "precise speech made her sound even more formidable than her commanding manner" (14).

**See also Chicago, Mr. Contreras, dreams, families, food, Darraugh Graham, Bobby Mallory, music, Tony and Gabriella Warshawski, Lotty Herschel, Morrell, Murray Ryerson**

## Bleeding Kansas (2007)

*Bleeding Kansas* is Paretsky's second stand-alone novel. The book is set in contemporary Kansas, and the title references the term coined by Horace Greeley of the *New York Tribune* who was describing 1850s Kansas with its violent clashes between the pro-slavery Missouri border gangs and the anti-slavery settlers who wanted Kansas to enter the Union as a free state.

The novel is structured around three present-day Kansas families (the Grelliers, Freemantles, and Schapens) living in the farming community of Douglas County in the harsh landscape of the Kaw River Valley. The families, who were allies long ago in the antislavery struggles, are increasingly divided over a range of contemporary issues—homosexuality, the war in Iraq, and fundamentalist Christianity. When a Freemantle niece returns to the area from New York, her activities as a lesbian, a practicing Wiccan, and an antiwar activist polarize the small farm community and have a dramatic effect on both the Grellier family and the fundamentalist

Two families have been farming in the Kaw River Valley for over a hundred and fifty years, their lives connected through generations by history and geography.
Then Gina Haring, bringing with her the liberal air of the big city, moves into a dilapidated house near both farms. Almost every one of the Grelliers is drawn to her, but it is Susan, a woman of ephemeral passions, whose involvement stirs up the wrath of the Schapen clan. The results for her own family will be cataclysmic.
'SHE IS WRITING WITH THE KIND OF PASSION FOR SOCIAL JUSTICE THAT INSPIRED CHANDLER AND HAMMETT'
JOAN SMITH, THE SUNDAY TIMES
www.saraparetsky.com
Fiction
£6.99
SARA PARETSKY
BLEEDING KANSAS
Trouble in America's heartland
SARA PARETSKY
BLEEDING KANSAS

**The original cover for the Hodder paperback UK edition of *Bleeding Kansas* features a landscape photograph.**

Schapen family. Religious intolerance, antiwar activism, old grudges and family secrets, ties of love, and greed and hypocrisy divide these contemporary families into various camps of young and old, male and female, lovers and friends. Paretsky's strong sense of place is at work in this novel as she explores a still-turbulent Kansas through the lens of a small town community trying to come to terms with changing religious and sexual mores, and in-comers with different values and ideas. The novel explores the ways in which bigotry, biblical fundamentalism, and fear and ignorance all ignite zealotry in a place still divided ideologically (for instance, the state's twenty-first-century struggle over creationism in the public school curriculum). The novel is written in the third person and is told in multiple voices like the earlier standalone book *Ghost Country*. Amy Gutman's review of *Bleeding Kansas* notices that "Paretsky's preoccupations remain very much the same in this work as in her Warshawski novels: how greed and hypocrisy hide behind socially sanctioned institutions and beliefs, including big business and organized religion; and how the antidote to hatred and violence is kindness and common sense" (3). *Bleeding Kansas* made the *New York Times* bestseller list at no. 15 in January 2008. The novel is dedicated to her four brothers—"Fellow refugees from our own patch of bleeding Kansas." The epigraph is taken from the 1856 book *Kansas* written by writer and historian Sara Robinson.

## *Blood Shot* (published in the United Kingdom as *Toxic Shock*) (1988)

"If I lived past next week, I'd vacuum" (150).

The fifth V. I. mystery won the Private Eye Writers of America Shamus Award for the Best Hardcover P.I. Novel of 1988 and the British Crime Writers Association Silver Dagger Award. These prizes, coming in the year after *Ms* Magazine named Paretsky as one of their women of the year, demonstrate a growing recognition for the author, the character, and the series. Marilyn Stasio's review for the *New York Times* describes the novel as the author's "best and boldest work to date in creating a criminal investigation that is a genuine heroic quest" (22).

The action gets underway at a February reunion of V. I.'s championship high-school basketball team in a run-down part of South Chicago. Reluctantly back in the old and once-prosperous blue-collar neighborhood of her youth, V. I. notices "decaying bungalows" (1) and remembers "when each piece of trim was painted fresh every second spring and new Buicks or Oldsmobiles were an autumn commonplace ... in a different life, for me as well as South Chicago" (1–2). This reflective note underpins the rest of the novel as details of V. I.'s childhood and youth are revealed in tandem with the story of what starts as a routine investigation into a missing person. Caroline Dijak, a childhood friend who is now a local community activist, has planned a publicity event (with the champs from 20 years ago and the current high-school winning team) to support her organization SCRAP (South Chicago Reawakening Project). When V. I. agrees to visit Caroline's sick mother, Louisa, on Houston Street where the Dijaks and Warshawskis had been neighbors, the detective is plunged into past memories and torn loyalties. V. I.'s mother, Gabriella, and Louisa Dijak, a pregnant unmarried teenager thrown out by her parents, always stood up for each other; the 11-year-old V. I. was often enlisted as a babysitter for the infant Caroline so that her mother could do shift work at the local Xerxes Solvent plant. Shocked to discover Louisa bedridden and gaunt, and feeling somewhat guilty about her own recent neglect of the Dijak mother and daughter—"South Chicago hovered too uneasily at the base of my mind for me to willingly court its return to my life, and it had been over two years since I'd spoken to Louisa" (13)—Vic agrees to Caroline's unexpected request to find out the identity of her father. "If I hadn't known her all my life, it would have been easier to say no.... I didn't want to, but I couldn't keep from responding" (18). As Katrine Ames's review notes, "what begins as a relatively routine missing-person case quickly evolves into an investigation of environmental skull-duggery, cover-

ups, insurance scams, incest and murder" (75). Soon the body of V. I.'s old friend and basketball teammate Nancy Cleghorn, who was the environmental affairs director for Caroline's community action group, is found in Dead Stick Pond, once "Illinois's last wetland for migratory birds ... [but] now so full of PCBs that little could survive there" (82). Trying to learn who would want Nancy dead and determine the connection between the search for Caroline's father and Nancy's death, V. I. finds herself in murky waters. In another closely plotted novel that links corporate greed, corrupt Chicago politicians, medical malpractice, long-hidden family secrets, and suppressed knowledge, "[t]he streets and waterways of South Chicago, as well as its citizens, come alive," according to Jane Bakerman's review (15). The determined private eye uncovers some unpleasant truths about the identity of the father Caroline has never known; at the same time, her criminal investigation into the circumstances of Nancy's death reveals, as Bakerman says, "a long history of calculated, profitable endangerment of the blue-collar workers who inhabit a district itself victimized by pollution and economic exploitation" (ibid.). Vic begins to piece together the complicated story of the corporate and medical cover-up of chemical hazards that link Louisa's illness and Nancy's murder. As she gets closer to the truth, her own life is threatened; kidnapped on her morning run by hired thugs who leave her to drown in the lethal waters of Dead Stick Pond, she is found by her resourceful neighbor Mr. Contreras and the dog Peppy. Ames's review points out that V. I.'s near death and the dramatic rescue are dealt with in "a masterly scene of almost unendurable claustrophobia [when] V. I. is wrapped in a blanket and left to drown in a polluted swamp" (op. cit.). Dr. Lotty Herschel, who patches up Vic, and Lt. Bobby Mallory, who is annoyed when she disobeys his orders, both go head to head with the detective over what they perceive as her recklessness. Other people's concerns about her personal safety irritate V.I., who characteristically snaps in response to Bobby: "I'm self-employed just so I don't have to take orders from anyone" (180). Soon back on the case, V. I. and the unlikely heroine Ms. Chigwell (the 79-year-old sister of the disgraced Dr. Chigwell) take a midnight dinghy trip up the Calumet River in an attempt to rescue Louisa from the Xerxes Chemical plant where she is held hostage. After another dramatic showdown with some company owners and their henchmen intent on murder, the connections among the Ajax Insurance Company, Humboldt Chemicals, and the Xerxes factory become clear—occupational health hazards for factory workers, the hazardous disposal of chemical waste, the unethical handling of medical data, and the collusion of local South Chicago aldermen. Enraged and energized by the cynical profit-seeking motives of the corporate world, V. I. does not let go of the case until she gets to the bottom of the environmental conditions and the cover-up, which led to Louisa's death. Reporter Murray Ryerson, one of the repeating characters in V. I.'s world, provides her with help in chasing down some of the early leads in the case in exchange for an eventual exclusive from V. I. for his newspaper. Officer Mary Louise Neely makes her entrance in this novel as the young policewoman who, later in the series, leaves the force and becomes V. I.'s partner as private investigator. At the end of the case, with none of the big sharks in jail or even in the dock and estranged from Caroline after Louisa's death, V. I. is drained and full of self-doubt. When Caroline finally turns up at V. I.'s house to tell V. I. she hopes they will always be sisters, V. I. replies, in the final line of the novel, "Till death do us part, kid" (328)—playing with the traditions of both hard-boiled wisecracks and wedding vows. Maureen Reddy's essay notes that this "double parody ... underscores the novel's theme of the centrality of women's friendships and also implies that such friendships take precedence over heterosexual marriage or romance in V.I.'s life" ("Female Detective" 1057). Their reconciliation and V. I.'s struggle for a better understanding of her own family background in South Chicago suggests the detective's strength can be applied to personal change when necessary. Bakerman's review applauds "this capacity for growth" as something that "distin-

guishes her from most male counterparts and improves the formula" (op. cit.). Another review by Mary Lowry notices the way in which V. I. and Caroline "both struggle to forge a new relationship as grown-up friends" (41). V. I.'s vulnerability is signaled—Henry Kisor, in a *Sun-Times* review, notes that the detective's "sandpapery tenderness just gets better with each novel Sara Paretsky turns out."

The novel's epigraph, "For Dominick," refers to Paretsky's agent Dominick Abel in New York City. Another close associate of Paretsky's is referenced in the character Dr. Ann Christophersen, who Lotty consults for assistance in untangling the medical notation system used by Dr. Chigwell to track the employee illness rate at the Xerxes Solvent factory. The real Ann Christophersen cofounded Women and Children First bookstore in Chicago, where most of Paretsky's U.S. book launches are held.

**See also dreams, Lotty Herschel, Murray Ryerson, Women and Children First bookstore**

## Bochco, Steven *see* "One Trial, Many Angles to Investigate"

### Body Work (2010)

"It makes me cranky when people don't listen to me" (6).

The 14th V. I. novel's title is, characteristically, a play on words—hinting at Body (of) Work, working out, and the work a body can do. Claire Black's interview with Paretsky describes how the author "uses performance art, Iraq, and, of course, VI's physical spills (at 50, she is still not one to walk away from a fight), to explore the notion of the body" (8). This interview also describes the genesis of the novel; on a drive out of an airport visual images of the female body on advertising posters juxtaposed with a billboard bearing the message "abortion is a sin" provoked the author's imagination. Looking for a story that would allow her to explore issues related to representations and ownership of the female body, Paretsky had the idea of a female Body Artist who invited people to paint on her body and who kept her own background, including her name, secret. In a culture where we are used to images of sexualized women's bodies as objects of desire, where there is pressure on women and girls to fit in with such images of modern femininity, and where reproductive rights are a contested arena, Paretsky's exploration of body policing issues and gender roles is salient. This novel engages with the cultural and social reality that, by and large, women can expect to be judged as a body first and as a person second.

The events in *Body Work* follow on seven months after the end of *Hardball*. As Christmas approaches, Chicago is in the grip of severe snow and ice storms; the city landscape is frozen and hazardous. The novel opens on a scene of violent death in the icy parking lot outside the hip and edgy Club Gouge, where V. I.'s young cousin, Petra, waits tables. Late one winter night, V. I. is on her way home from a visit to Petra; "Seconds after I left Club Gouge, I heard gunshots, screams, squealing tires, from the alley behind the building," and moments later, "Nadia Guaman died in my arms" (1). No one sees the shooter, but the Chicago police suspect unstable Iraq vet Chad Vishinski, who frequents the nightclub and who has created disturbances there on earlier occasions when Nadia has also been at the venue. The main attraction at the club is a controversial act billed as the Body Artist, a performance artist who invites people on stage to paint her naked body; the images people paint onto her skin are then projected onto a screen and offered as prints for sale. The mysterious and apparently troubled Nadia often visits Club Gouge and paints the same portrait over and over on the Body Artist's torso. Marine vet Chad, who is also a regular member of the audience, reacts violently to the images painted by Nadia, and his friends have often had to restrain him from charging the stage. Chad's friend, Rodney, paints numbers regularly on the artist. The police accuse Chad of Nadia's murder; his family, who accept that his drunken and agitated behavior is problematic but who are adamant he would not have shot Nadia, hire V. I. to prove his innocence. In the course of investigating Nadia's death,

V. I. discovers that her family has lost another daughter to the war in Iraq, and a son has been brain-damaged following a motorcycle accident. The portrait Nadia was painting on the Body Artist is of her older sister, Alexandra, who was killed in Iraq where she was working for the defense contractor Tintrey. The Guaman family also includes a high school student Clara and her brother, Ernest, whose "brain injuries left him unable to work" (70). Clara turns to Vic for support and solace when her parents implode under the burden of too many losses; Clara is another one of Paretsky's typically resilient and plucky young female characters who is helped by V. I. to move forward in her life. In the meantime, Club Gouge's owner/manager, the abrasive Olympia, seems to be involved with a Ukrainian mob with interests in the drug trade and money-laundering. V. I. also uncovers a scandal about faulty military equipment supplied by private contractors doing business in Iraq and Afghanistan. In this respect, the novel echoes Arthur Miller's 1947 play, *All My Sons*, about a family that disintegrates when the businessman father's acts of corrupt profiteering and moral abdication come to light (he has allowed defective parts to be installed in military aircraft and let his partner take the rap). V. I. discovers that the contractors supplying protective gear to the U.S. military in Iraq have "substituted sand for gallium in their body armor" (421), and the death of Alexandra can be attributed to this. Personal honor is always at stake for V. I., as is the question of the individual and social responsibility.

The novel also explores the questions of whether provocatively erotic art leads to violence against women and whether the Body Artist is exploiting her audience or being exploited. In the lengthy second chapter, the Body Artist performs her act in the club; watching her are V. I. and her party (Jake and some of his musician pals, Mr. Contreras, Petra, Lotty, and Max). Here Paretsky raises a number of questions about conceptual art, artistic expression, and boundaries, and registers a complex range of responses from the people at the club. V. I. notices whispering and laughing, which suggest to her that "it was the audience that was disturbed" (10). Mr. Contreras is vehement: "It just ain't right!" (11). Jake and Petra both think "it was awesome," although Jake also acknowledges that he is "uncomfortable at a public display of nudity" (16). V. I., too, is disturbed, pointing out to Jake, "whether we like it or not, we live in a world where the exposed female body is a turn-on" (16). In parallel with questions about the eroticized female body and the double-standards attached to the idea of the female artist's body, the novel also explores how men's bodies are exploited; for example, in sending young men like Chad to war in Iraq, where their bodies and minds are on the line. Chad has been awarded a Bronze Star for his military service in Iraq; but the hero has become a casualty of war suffering from PTSD. Images of male and female bodies defined in ads, film, sports are invoked. The stripping away of illusion and pretense—symbolized by the Body Artist and her naked performances—raises the question of what is under the skin. The novel also explores homophobia (Alexandra had kept her sexuality a secret, fearing her family's reaction) and domestic violence close to home; further afield, the financial and political misbehavior resulting from the Iraq War is discussed. In a rare moment of self-reflection, V. I. writes in an email to Jake, her musician lover who has embarked on a tour in Europe, "I think I'm driven more by despair, even, than confidence.... I wish that my life had followed a calmer path" (441–42). The novel ends on a personal note as Lotty, Max, and V. I. listen to a BBC Radio 3 broadcast from London featuring Jake's High Plainsong group. Jake speaks to V. I. across the airwaves, explaining that he put the music together for the first song "as a salute to a lady of my acquaintance ... a woman of high courage.... V. I. Warshawski, I hope you're listening" (443).

The London *Sunday Times* review describes the novel as Paretsky's "heartfelt commentary on her country's involvement in the Iraq war ... veterans struggle with their demons and avant-garde art has taken a decadent turn" (52). Jacobsen's review finds "the use of body art is an inspired plot device that weaves all the way through to a clever, whirlwind finish" (2010). The detective's rates are now "a hundred fifty an hour" (32), and she is benefiting from the computer age: "I used to write my notes on scraps of paper and lose them ... [n]ow everything's tidily laid out in my Investigator's Casebook spreadsheets, which automatically updates my handheld" (58–59). Although she may be using a more sophisticated range of today's technological devices, the detective's methods of tracking down the people she wants to question have not changed much. In a comic scene of door-stepping, V. I. leads the troops (including Mr. Contreras and the dogs) to an apartment building where she hopes to flush out a suspect. The dog fights with a cat; the noise brings out the neighbors; mayhem ensues. A violent encounter between V. I. and a group of thugs is derailed momentarily when V. I. throws up: "[Rodney] lost his footing, slipped in my vomit, fell hard, head bouncing against the ice" (276). Paretsky mentions V. I.'s "Antonella Mason painting" (28) in her office, an example of the author's habit of referencing a range of nonfictional women whose achievements merit attention. In this case, Antonella Mason is an Italian-born, NYC-based independent artist who exhibits paintings and videos in venues that host live performances, poetry reading, and jazz events thus linking her to the fictional Body Artist in the novel. Stasio's review is concerned about a "dense and weighty plot" but concludes that even the "subplots are loaded with provocative ideas" (2). Wisniewski's review finds "the pleasures of this story are in ... the wry observations about greed and sexism, the gripping misery of the Chicago winter, the flaky cousin who won't stay out of trouble, and the loving loyalty of Warshawski's neighbor." The novel is dedicated to three young women who have worked as personal assistants to Paretsky.

## Breakdown (2012)

"If I'd known I'd be barefoot in paradise, I would have washed my feet" (55)

The year after Paretsky was named the 2011 Grand Master by the Mystery Writers of America and received the 2011 Bouchercon

Lifetime Achievement award, she published her 15th V. I. novel. *Breakdown* is dedicated to three named Chicago librarians "and the many other librarians who've helped me navigate the great sea of learning—including my mother, Mary E. Paretsky." The detective is now 50-something, but, according to reviewer Connie Ogle, "she's still not afraid to go toe-to-toe with sleazeballs, bureaucrats or the rich and powerful (and she still looks great in a slinky dress)" (H1). The tightly plotted novel explores right-wing politics of hate and racism, as well as the attack mentality and tactics of contemporary news corporations that privilege entertainment over facts, and the shortcomings of the public mental health system. It also references the contemporary popularity with younger readers of the vampire romance genre. At the heart of the story is an anxiety about the loss of independent investigative journalism and the attendant threat to democracy.

The first chapter opens in a style characteristic of the gothic novel; on a dark and rainy summer night, V. I. is prowling through an overgrown and abandoned cemetery at the panicky request of her cousin, Petra, who is now resident in Chicago and working on youth programs for the "Malina Foundation, which serves immigrants and refugees" (3). Petra is worried about the teenage members of her book group who appear to be out past curfew; one of them, Kira Dudek, has left her seven-year old sister, Lucy, alone in the family apartment. Petra has asked Vic to track them down and convey them home safely. Earlier in the evening, V. I. had been arrayed in a party frock for a gala event at the Valhalla ballground on the arm of her old pal, Murray Ryerson, now working in the news division of the Global Entertainment Network (a cable media outfit not unlike Fox News). Wade Lawlor hosts GEN's lead news show, and the party is being held in his honor. V. I. has some forthright views about Lawlor: "I hate his politics, I hate his molassied voice, and I hate his pretense of being a working-class boy" (31). But as Murray's job is not secure, he cannot afford to have V. I. insulting Lawlor. He also hopes to bring V. I. on board as "the resident expert on eval-uating criminal evidence" (34) for a series of stories on public medical care of the mentally ill homeless and criminally insane. The GEN staff, more concerned with ratings than facts, are not buying Murray's pitch, so when Petra's call comes, V. I. is glad to leave the party and head for the cemetery; the girls have met there, inspired by the supernatural romance novels featuring Carmilla, Queen of the Knight and a shape-shifting raven. Shrieking, they are enacting a mysterious ceremonial ritual next to a crumbling mausoleum as V. I. approaches. Realizing with horror that what she thought was a statue on the nearby tombstone is the body of a man with a metal rod in his chest, V. I. hustles the girls out of the cemetery's back entrance and faces the police. At the police station, V. I. is questioned by officers who assume she is involved because the victim, Miles Wuchnik, is a private investigator. V. I. insists that he is a stranger to her. Petra's book club includes girls from immigrant families as well as the daughter of Dr. Sophy Durango, who is running for the U.S. Senate on a liberal platform; and Arielle Zitter, whose stunningly wealthy grandfather Chaim Salanter (a Holocaust survivor), is bank-rolling Durango's campaign and the Malina Foundation where Petra works. Durango, as president of the University of Illinois, has "refused to allow incoming freshmen to substitute Creation 'science' for evolutionary biology" (39), thus inviting the wrath, amongst others, of her opponent in the contest for the U.S. Senate seat, creationist Helen Kendrick. Lawlor, who is backing Kendrick, tries to implicate both Salanter and Warshawski in the murder of Wuchnik so that Durango's campaign can be discredited. Through the actions and libelous claims of the bigoted Lawlor in respect of Salanter, Durango, and V. I. herself—and his TV rants, in the name of patriotism, against illegal aliens—Paretsky explores the campaign party politics of the Republicans and their media helpers. Durango's belief in evolution comes under fire by a media already hostile to her because she is female and African American; Chaim Salanter is smeared as someone whose fortune was acquired by dubious means after World War II.

In the meantime, Leydon Ashford, an old law school colleague of V. I. who is bipolar, has fallen from the top of Rockefeller Chapel on the University of Chicago campus. Near death, she leaves the cryptic message "I saw him on the catafalque" (95)—a reference to James Joyce, as the chapel dean points out to V. I. The quote from *Portrait of the Artist as a Young Man*—"the child Stephen Dedalus is overhearing adults talk about the death of Parnell" (102)—later proves to be an important clue in unraveling what happened to Leydon, whose wealthy brother has cut off her family funds because he has tired of his sister's mental health issues. Leydon's story of suffering from bipolar disorder provides a major theme in the novel—the shortcomings of the public mental-health system on which the uninsured Leydon has to rely. Long-buried family secrets, as well as old sibling bonds and rivalries, play a part in the unfolding stories of both Leydon and Lawlor. In chapter 50, close to the end of the novel, V. I.'s narrative voice is suspended, and she is presumed drowned in a suburban lake. Chapter 51, also in the voice of a third-person omniscient narrator, takes place in a TV studio at Global's headquarters, where Murray fronts the live broadcast *Chicago's Own Nancy Drew* in front of a studio audience. He summarizes V. I.'s career, promising the audience that "after a break, we'll uncover the events that led her to that suburban lake in the middle of the night" (412). What Murray reveals puts the spotlight on Lawlor who protests his innocence until a mystery woman wearing a "large hat [which] shrouded her eyes and nose" comes on set to tell the audience that Lawlor had already told her the truth "after he'd shot me full of haloperidol ... but before he dumped me into Tampier Lake to die" (419). V. I. is back from the dead; she and Murray take advantage of contemporary media technology by airing the show live, knowing the footage will go "viral across the Web" (428) and into the blogosphere. Murray pays a price for his big scoop; GEN fires him, but he takes "a job with Sophy Durango, as her campaign's media adviser" (428). In addition to the sophisticated use of TV systems, V. I. is keeping up with the times with an iPad and Facebook. Bass player Jake Thibaut, V. I.'s lover, conducts the music for Leydon's funeral in Rockefeller Chapel; the novel closes on the somber note of the dean's eulogy with its reminder from 1 John 4:18 that "perfect love casts out fear" (431). Donna Seaman's review for *Booklist* praises both author and character; "V. I. reigns as crime fiction's spiky, headstrong warrior woman of conscience, and Paretsky, classy champion of the powerless, has never been more imaginative, rueful, transfixing, and righteous."

**See also Petra Warshawski, Jake Thibaut, GEN**

## Browning, Elizabeth Barrett *see* "My Hero: Elizabeth Barrett Browning"

### *Brush Back* (2015)

"I was beginning to wonder if I had 'sucker' embroidered on my forehead, or maybe in my brain" (201).

The 17th V. I. novel returns the sleuth to her roots in South Chicago. Not for the first time [see entries on *Fire Sale, Blood Shot,* and *Deadlock*], V. I. reluctantly responds to a request for help that pulls her back into past memories and places she has no wish to revisit. Using a tighter landscape than the previous *Critical Mass*, which worked forward and backward in time across both Europe and the United States, the story's focus is on V. I., her family of origin, some long-forgotten high-school acquaintances, and city/state politics.

The plot kicks off over an unexpected visit from an old high-school boyfriend. Truck-driver Frank Guzzo wants V. I.'s help concerning his mother's claim that she was framed for the murder of her daughter, Annie, 25 years ago, a crime for which Stella Guzzo was tried, convicted, and sent to prison. Recently released after serving her sentence, the 80-year-old Stella is seeking exoneration. V. I. remembers the case well: she and Frank had a short but intense romantic relationship shortly after V. I.'s mother, Gabriella, died from cancer when V. I. was 16. His sister, Annie, took piano lessons from V. I.'s mother and adored Gabriella. Stella was known in the neighborhood for her volatile temper and for beating her daughter. Furthermore, Stella hated the Warshawski family, blaming Gabriella for "enticing" the affections of both her daughter and her husband, and holding V. I.'s cousin, Boom-Boom, responsible for ruining the teenage Frank's chance to play baseball with the Cubs. In typical V. I. fashion, she agrees to give Frank one hour's worth of ferreting around on Stella's behalf in the hopes that it will lead to nothing so she can turn her back on the problem. When Stella attacks the Warshawski family (including the long-dead Boom-Boom) through the media, Vic throws herself into the challenge of uncovering the murky circumstances around Annie's death.

The investigation leads her to a complex set of financial dealings between city haulage and construction businesses, including the pet coke mountains of hazardous waste that now occupy South Chicago's landscape; Chicago sports moguls; and Illinois politicians and lawyers whose positions owe more to their tight connections than their expertise. V. I.'s legendary skills in uncovering financial crime serve her well once again as she assembles the story behind Annie's death and gathers the crucial information to back her suspicion that the local "*Say, Yes! Foundation* [was using] funds to bankroll elections" (408). Wrigley Field, home of V. I.'s beloved Cubs and a Chicago landmark, provides a distinctive backdrop to the action when the teenage Bernie is abducted, and Vic tracks her down to a tunnel under the baseball park. The sports theme is further elaborated through this new series character, Bernadine (Bernie) Fouchard, a skilled hockey player like her godfather Boom-Boom; and in the punning chapter titles such as "Out at the Plate," "The Umpire Strikes Back," and "Pinch Hitter." Bernie is an idealistic and impetuous teenager not unlike V. I.'s young cousin Petra Warshawski who appeared in recent novels and then "joined the Peace Corps in El Salvador" (14). The youth of these characters contrasts with the otherwise aging set of regular characters, including V. I. herself, hovering around 50 but aware of her "tired, middle-aged legs" (377). Mr. Contr-

eras is holding at 90, and Lotty Herschel and Max Loewenthal are both somewhere in their late 60s. V. I. says of Bernie, "[S]he approached the world around her with the confidence bordering on recklessness that reminded me of my cousin, or perhaps myself when I was a teenager, when I didn't feel the anguish of people whose lives had come uncoupled from their dreams" (14). *Brush Back* also includes a striking number of minor characters in their 80s and 90s: the lawyer Ira Previn and his wife, Eunice; Melba and Harold Minsky; retired Judge Grigsby; and ex-Cubs manager Mr. Villard are all portrayed as elderly but still active and functioning. Marilyn Stasio's review notes that "Paretsky's unsentimental character studies [are] truthfully drawn and mercilessly insightful without being judgmental" ("Flight" 25). Jake Thibaut, V. I.'s musician lover, remains in the picture; his music group, High Plainsong, has fallen victim to cutbacks in arts funding and gives its last concert— "Swan Song, they'd billed it" (458). Conrad Rawlings, the Chicago policeman who was once V. I.'s lover; Murray Ryerson, the journalist who is always looking for a scoop on V. I.'s most recent investigation; and Freeman Carter, V. I.'s attorney, all play their parts. *Brush Back* returns not only to V. I.'s old neighborhood but to territory from earlier in the V. I. oeuvre, which now has a history of its own. In the second novel, *Deadlock*, V. I. rushes to the defense of Boom-Boom's reputation when he is killed in a shipping accident and is suspected of company theft. Now, 25 years later, Boom-Boom's namesake, the 17-year-old Bernadine is staying with V. I. for a few weeks before her summer hockey training camp. When Stella makes a case that Boom-Boom murdered Annie "in a fit of jealous rage and framed [Stella] for the murder" (44), Bernie and V. I. go to work to clear his name, just as V. I. did many years before. The freighter *Lucella Wieser* [see *Deadlock* entry] makes a brief appearance in this novel. Dead Stick Pond, a location that featured in *Blood Shot* [see entry], is used in *Brush Back* for another chilling showdown; this time it is Bernie who is dumped into the toxic mud and left for dead until Mr. Contreras, V. I., and the dogs come to her rescue. The Pulteney Building in the Loop, once the rundown location of V. I.'s first office, has been turned "into high-end condos" (139) as Vic discovers when she calls on a retired judge who now lives on the 17th floor. A local business empire in *Fire Sale* [see entry] is referenced when a lawyer involved in the detective's current case remembers "a class-action case involving the women at the local By-Smart [*sic*] warehouse" (230). The conclusion of *Brush Back* echoes that of the earlier *Killing Orders* [see entry]. In both novels, Vic receives unsolicited gifts of cash from wealthy sources sympathetic to her efforts to expose corruption: In *Killing Orders,* this enables her to buy an apartment to replace the one that was destroyed in an arson attack; the two checks she is given in *Brush Back* are for the purposes of getting herself "a nice little car" after her Mazda is wrecked and for Jake and "his musician friends" (458). The novel is dedicated to the author's older brother, Jeremy Paretsky, with an epitaph from the prologue of Chaucer's *Canterbury Tales*, referencing the Clerk—"gladly would he learn and gladly teach."

The *Washington Post* selected *Brush Back* as one of the best mystery novels of 2015, and the *St. Louis Post-Dispatch* chose Brush Back as one of the best novels of 2015 ("Monstrous Moms" E-8; Henderson).

## Burn Marks (1990)

"the one thing you must never forget in Chicago is to look out for your own" (336).

The sixth V. I. Warshawski book includes an epigraph naming three of Paretsky's school teachers "who believed in my writing before I did." Familiar themes are explored such as financial corruption (in this case, in the construction industry and low-cost housing agencies) and political shenanigans at both city and county levels. At the same time, the novel celebrates the strength of neighborhood and family connections in Chicago, filling in details of the family of V. I.'s father, Tony. Tony Warshawski and Bobby Mallory come from the same Chicago streets and later work as cops together on the beat. At the end of the novel, V. I. returns to Nor-

wood Park for Bobby's birthday party, the area "where my father and uncles and Aunt Elena grew up ... a place of tidy tiny bungalows on minuscule well-tended lots ... a mirage of a neighbourhood—it seems to have nothing to do with the sprawling, graffiti-laden, garbage-ridden city to the southeast" (336). The ties and loyalties formed in childhood in neighborhoods such as this still count for a great deal in Chicago; as V. I. discovers in the course of this case, such strong personal and professional connections, combined with greed and ambition, can lead to terrible betrayals and consequences.

The novel opens with Elena, Tony's renegade sister, waking V. I. in the middle of the night from a dream about her mother, Gabriella. Elena needs shelter after her Single Resident Occupancy hotel, the Indiana Arms, has burned to the ground and expects V. I., in the name of family loyalty, to welcome her. V. I. unwillingly takes her in, torn between pity for Elena's evident distressed state (dirty, drunk, homeless, and destitute) and fury at Elena's assumption that her niece will look after her, as well as Cerise, a young and strung-out friend who turns up a couple of days later. V. I. feels "the tired old tentacles of responsibility drape themselves around me" (47). Elena, V. I. remembers, "had always been the family Problem" (2), outstaying her welcome with more than one relative during V. I.'s childhood. With characteristic focus, V. I. realizes her best option is to find replacement housing for Elena as soon as possible. Setting about the task "with an easy optimism bred of ignorance" (12), V. I. visits an emergency housing bureau and pounds the streets looking for vacant SRO rooms, only to conclude there "just wasn't housing available for people with Elena's limited means" (14). She contacts Peter, Elena's remaining sibling now resident in Kansas City and "the first member of [V. I.'s] family to make something substantial of his life" (15). When he refuses to help, V. I. finally pulls in a personal political contact who secures an SRO room for Elena in return for the detective's financial support for Roz Fuentes, an up-and-coming Democrat running for local election. Vic's efforts are complicated by her

**The Chatto & Windus cover for the UK edition with photograph of V.I. (credited to Koo Stark) and Chicago grid graphic in background. Photograph by Linda Erf Swift.**

Cerise disappears from the clinic, along with V. I.'s cash, credit card, and driver's license. When Cerise's body and V. I.'s wallet are found at a major construction site in downtown Chicago, things heat up. Meanwhile, Roz, running as the first Hispanic female candidate for local election in Cook County, wants V. I.'s financial and moral support. Turning up at the Democratic Party fund-raiser hosted by major Chicago developer Boots Meagher, Vic guesses that Roz is running her campaign on dirty money donated from various prominent Chicago developers and construction companies that V. I. suspects are involved in the SRO fire she is investigating for Ajax Insurance. When Roz tells V. I. to abandon the case, V. I.'s suspicions are further aroused; then she finds dynamite attached to the ignition coil in her car and narrowly escapes a fatal explosion. Determined to get to the bottom of the fire at the Indiana Arms, V. I. eventually discovers that a property management firm associated with Boots Meagher and some other Chicago high-rollers "had been buying up property in the triangle behind McCormick Place and the Dan Ryan for several years … positioning themselves for a bid on the stadium" (303). But they had been unable to acquire the still-occupied Indiana Arms building. No longer sure who is friend or foe, V. I. begins to suspect that her would-be boyfriend Michael is doing "favors for the pals because they were all good old boys from the neighbourhood" (285) and that he could be involved in putting the bomb in her car. The wary V. I. decides to find proof before giving his name to Murray for his story on a redevelopment

less than cooperative houseguests. When Cerise insists that her baby died in the fire, V. I. reports this to Robin Bessinger, the Ajax Insurance Company investigator handling the inquiry into the fire; already suspecting arson, Bessinger requests Vic's assistance at his firm's meeting with the Chicago Office of Fire Investigation. He expresses a romantic interest in V. I., who is juggling an on-again, off-again relationship with Chicago policeman Michael Furey (a godson of Bobby Mallory). With an official fraud inquiry underway, Elena delivered to her new SRO, and the very ill Cerise under the care of Lotty's clinic, it looks as if V. I. can return to her usual business of conducting financial investigations on behalf of her regular clients. But swindle involving the stadium bid and a group of Chicago businessmen. Uncertainties about which old friends are hiding what beset V. I. throughout the novel; explaining her decision to go public over Roz's campaign funding after Roz refuses to discuss the matter with V. I., the detective tells a colleague, "I won't take it, to be spun around … especially not by someone like Roz, trading on old loyalties and asking us to countenance—well, worms" (334). Michael is finally flushed out as the enemy when he shoots Mr. Contreras in the shoulder and tries to kill Vic and Elena because Elena can "tie him to the fire at the Indiana Arms" (338). Michael, desperate to cover his tracks, takes V. I. prisoner with the intention of forcing her to "kiss your aunt good-bye and then have a farewell party yourself" (314). The final showdown involving Michael, his henchmen, the handcuffed V. I., and Elena takes place at night at the top of a building under construction. V. I. wounds Michael and one of his accomplices and then moves into top gear when she sees the third murderer, Ron Grasso, "dragging Elena toward the edge of the platform…. I forced myself to follow him, to fight down the spinning in my head, to place the muzzle in his back and pull the trigger…. I had never killed a man before, but I knew from the way his body lay … that he was dead" (323). V. I., Elena, and Mr. Contreras all recover from their ordeal; Michael, to V. I.'s satisfaction, is "suspended without pay, out on $100,000 bond for felonious assault on me, Elena, and Mr. Contreras" (332). In uncharacteristically acquisitive mode, toward the end of the novel, V. I. buys herself a new car "a bright red Trans Am … with twin exhausts and 180 horsepower…. It seemed like the car I'd been waiting for all my life" (335). Officer Mary Louise Neely, now a member of Bobby Mallory's team at the 11th Street downtown station, plays a small part in this novel. V. I.'s attempts to express some sisterly solidarity with her fall on stony ground. Lieutenant Bobby Mallory learns some hard truths about his protégé Michael and his fiercely protective feelings about V. I. In a tender final scene at his 60th birthday party, he and V. I. seem to ar-

rive at a new understanding of each other and the conflicted relationship between them. Accepting their differences, and in honor of his birthday, V. I. gives him the present she has brought: "When he looked inside and saw Tony's shield lying in the cotton, he didn't say anything, but for the second time that week I saw him cry" (340). When the detective is knocked unconscious by an unknown assailant, Paretsky borrows a phrase from Auden's poem "September 1, 1939" to describe the sensation experienced by V. I.: "Before I could get to my feet the night around me broke into a thousand points of light and I fell into blackness" (177). Another literary reference surfaces in Paretsky's use of the title to a Hemingway short story when V. I. decides that "a clean well-lighted place and a glass of whiskey" (98) is what is needed.

Anthony Quinn's review in the *Sunday Times* notes that the detective is "haunted by an existential melancholy quite the equal of Marlowe's" (1990), quoting a moment when V. I. retreats to her car and sits "hunched over the steering wheel. Sometimes life seems so painful it hurts even to move my arms" (Burn 340). Her "courage and moral rectitude are beyond reproach" Quinn adds.

**See also Peter Warshawski, Ajax Insurance Company, Robin Bessinger, Mary Louise Neely**

## "Bush's Pick a Reminder of What's Not Right" (2007)

This op-ed piece for the *Chicago Tribune* critiques President George W. Bush's recent "appointee to head the Office of Population" on the grounds that Eric Keroack "is someone who thinks women are too immature to make fundamental decisions about their own bodies." Paretsky writes that she is "tired of … these same old men, telling me, my nieces, my goddaughters and my granddaughter what to do with our bodies." The subject of women's reproductive rights is an important one to Paretsky. She is an advocate of a woman's right to choose and spent many years on the board of the Chicago NARAL (National Abortion Rights Action League). The issue of reproductive rights surfaces in

Paretsky's novels and short stories (see, for example, *Killing Orders, Bitter Medicine, Tunnel Vision*, "The Man Who Loved Life," and "Poster Child") and in nonfiction (see "Terror in the Name of Jesus").

### "By the Book" (2014)

The author responds to the *New York Times Book Review's* set of questions about books in a regular column featuring contemporary writers. She names "the Victorians, Barbara Pym and Jane Austen" as two of her favorite novelists, and Margery Allingham and Dorothy Salisbury Davis as two of her favorite writers of detective fiction. Her childhood reading included "books about girls doing active things," and a book she was unable to finish was Eleanor Catton's *The Luminaries* because she "couldn't get engaged by any of the characters" (8).

### Cain, James M.  see  *Indemnity Only*

### Carter, Freeman

V. I.'s long-suffering attorney Freeman Carter advises her, bails her out of jail, and tries to keep her off thin ice in matters of the law. As "Crawford, Mead's token criminal lawyer" (GA 18), Carter belongs to the same law firm as V. I.'s ex-husband Richard Yarborough when V. I. first retains his services. Crawford, Mead's clients include "two former governors and the heads of most of Chicago's contributions to the Fortune 500" (GA 15). V. I. credits him with being "the only partner who ever talked to the womenfolk without showing what a big favor he was doing us" (GA 18). In *Killing Orders*, his 13-year-old daughter takes a phone message for V. I. who reports "she sounded like a poised and competent child" (180). In the later *Guardian Angel*, he learns some unpleasant truths about the Crawford, Mead law firm's practices; decides to cut his ties to the firm; and sets up the law offices of Carter, Halsey & Weinberg. The relationship between him and V. I. suffers from considerable strain in this novel, when Freeman misunderstands some action taken by V. I. in relation to her ex-husband, who is involved in a shady deal.

He is exceptionally adept at extricating V. I. out of hot legal spots when required; as Carter himself says to the detective: "I'm used to the odd alignment you make between the law and facts" (BW 63). On a visit to the lawyer's office in the financial district of the Loop in *Hard Time* to discuss a trumped-up police charge against her, V. I. reminds herself, "[H]e makes a good impression in court, which I like, and has the brains to back it up, which I like even more" (52). One of V. I.'s biggest headaches is her running tab with Carter's firm, which can get out of control. In *Total Recall* (2001), V. I. is reminded by Carter that she's "gotten the balance down to thirteen thousand" (285). In the 2010 *Body Work*, the 14th novel in the series, V. I. calls on Freeman for some urgent legal help for a client: "Even though my outstanding balance right now was close to sixty thousand, I assured Freeman that if the client couldn't pay him, I'd take care of it" (64). He gives her legal advice in *Hard Time* that she ignores. In the 2015 *Brush Back*, the lawyer has a hard time convincing V. I. to stay away from an annoying client: "I want the words spelled out, Warshawski. I know you" (49).

See also ***Total Recall, Hard Time, Body Work, Hardball, Brush Back***

### Chandler, Raymond

An American-born and British-educated novelist and screenwriter, Raymond Chandler (1888–1959) created legendary private-eye Philip Marlowe, who wisecracked his way through a series of novels and films from the 1940s to the 1970s as well as more recent forays on television. Chandler's work, alongside that of Dashiell Hammett and other *Black Mask* writers of the 1930s and 1940s, helped define the genre style that came to be known as the hard-boiled school of detective fiction. [See Hard-Boiled entry]. Paretsky explains in many print and broadcast interviews that V. I. was inspired in part by her desire to create a female character that could occupy the Marlowe role in her own right and that might also overturn some of the more stereotyped roles of villain and/or femme fatale found in Chandler's novels. Paretsky's short story "Dealer's Choice" was commissioned for a 1988 centennial celebration publication; written in homage to Chandler, it is a witty imitation of his characteristic hard-boiled stylistics. In 1999 Paretsky contributed to an NPR *Talk of the Nation* roundtable discussion of Chandler's books and his style of writing.

**See also "Dealer's Choice"; Media Events**

## Chicago

It can be argued that the subject matter of the private-eye genre *is* the city. When American authors such as Dashiell Hammett and Raymond Chandler took the mystery novel out of Agatha Christie's English country houses and drawing rooms, placing it in the alleyways of Los Angeles and San Francisco, the focus changed to mean city streets and the figure of the cynical, wise-cracking private investigator, rootless in his own city landscape. Paretsky's use of Chicago, rather than the more traditional literary and film settings of New York or the California cities, initially was seen as risky in the early 1980s. In her introduction to the 30th anniversary edition of *Indemnity Only*, Paretsky remembers that it took her agent "a year to find someone in New York willing to take a chance on a woman private eye in the Midwest" (xi). However, her use of the Chicago urban landscape and the portrayal of the self-motivated female detective at home in her city streets, proved a winning combination.

The city is famously and traditionally stereotyped in terms of three power bases: the mob gangster (often tied to city and state offices of justice), the police (with a reputation for corruption and stupidity), and the press (with a reputation for tabloid sensationalism). Machine guns, police brutality,

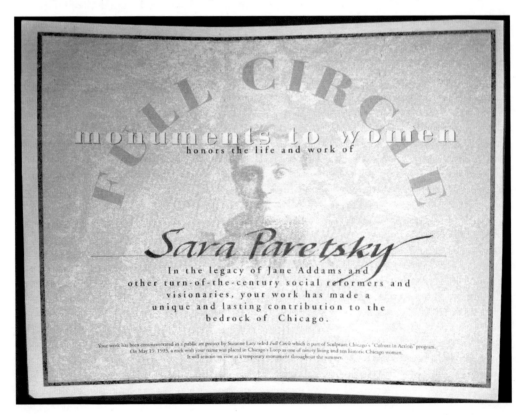

This certificate from Full Circle Monuments to Women honors Paretsky's work as a visionary and social reformer in the tradition of Jane Addams, the famous Chicago social worker whose work made a unique and lasting contribution to the bedrock of Chicago. From author's private papers. Photograph by Linda Erf Swift.

and newspaper scoops seem to be Chicago's weapons of choice for assassinating people and reputations. This offered rich territory to a young writer interested in a setting where she could explore the close connection of powerful civic institutions with crime. In a 1988 article for *Savvy*, Paretsky explains: "I began my life in Chicago in the neighborhoods; it's to them I turn when I want to understand the city. The violence of politics, the poetry of marshes, the loyalty that makes a little bank carry its neighbors long past default. That's Chicago" (51). Arguably, in a genre that historically favors the mean streets of New York, San Francisco, and Los Angeles, Paretsky's use of the Midwest Chicago setting is as innovative a gesture as is the construction of the pioneering female detective figure. Chicago comes alive under Paretsky's pen, not only in the geographical specificity of the streets, the lake, the Loop, and the neighborhoods but also in the embedded stories of V. I.'s network of friends, relatives, and colleagues who represent a wide variety of individual and community histories in the Chicago cityscape. Richard Nason's review of *Bitter Medicine* for *Medical Tribune* appreciates how the author's "language ... dashes off quick sketches of the rust, dust, noise, grit and glow of Chicago" (21). Carolyn Heilbrun's review of the same novel praises Paretsky as "wonderfully readable, and an excellent evoker of the Chicago streets" (78). The detective is located, in contrast to the loner Philip Marlowe tradition, in relation to an extended family of Chicago residents who share her values, who become exasperated with her, who would defend her to the death, and who (in the case of her parents) continue to speak to her from beyond the grave. This mitigates the stereotype of the isolated single woman lost in the city; the extended kinship network also gives V. I. an understanding of and connection to Chicago's industrial, social, and political histories. It is, above all, the backgrounds and experiences of her working-class immigrant parents and her childhood in blue-collar South Chicago that root V. I. in her city. The novels, more often than not, include story lines that reference the lives of young people, of the working poor, of street gang members, of women, the elderly, the indigent—lives that largely go undocumented in both official and fictional accounts of the city. In *Fire Sale*, for example, there is the story of the embattled, poverty-stricken, high-school basketball team girls who manage significant achievements despite the limiting labels of *teenage single parent* or *the Hispanic kid*. Such imagined stories pay testimony to real and largely unrecorded stories of suffering and accomplishment in the ethnically diverse city of Chicago. Jean White's 1988 review of *Blood Shot* notes that "[o]nly Chicago could have produced a V. I. Warshawski, and Paretsky beautifully captures the polyglot diversity of the city, no longer hog butcher to the world but still full of vitality and energy" (6). The debut novel *Indemnity Only* opens with V. I. at the wheel of her car on a hot summer evening; "As I drove south along Lake Michigan, I could smell rotting alewives like a faint perfume on the heavy air ... traffic was heavy, the city moving restlessly, trying to breathe" (1). Later in the same novel, on a drive down to Hyde Park, V. I. describes "a lazy evening with a lot of people out cooling off. [T]his was my favourite time of day in the summer" (181). The city seems to be as much a character as the detective, as Marcel Berlins's 1990 review of *Burn Marks* noted: "Chicago is proving to have layers of decadence and corruption that not even Los Angeles can match. The city is an essential character in all Paretsky's novels" (Berlins 1990).

The mystery series put Chicago on the popular culture literary map, much as the TV series *ER* put the city on television screens in the 1990s. Paretsky's choice of the Chicago setting helped open the door for other mystery writers interested in using a variety of regional settings, both rural and urban. The fictional detective's relationship with her city is a complicated one. Chicago has a reputation as a brash, tough, no-nonsense city, immortalized in the masculine images of Carl Sandburg's poem characterizing the "coarse and strong city" as having "big shoulders" commensurate with its role as "player with railroads" and "stacker of wheat" (3). Nelson Algren's prose-poem homage *Chicago, City on the Make*, describes the city as the "town of the hard and bitter strikes and the trigger-happy cops" (64). As written about by novelists, poets, sociologists, and philanthropists in the late-nineteenth and early-twentieth centuries, the city, birthplace of the skyscraper, was characterized as energetic, raw, unfinished, industrial, and full of hustlers. Paradoxically, the growing city is also characterized by the reforming energies of women such as Jane Addams, Bertha Palmer, and Dr. Sarah Haskell Stevenson, who all undertook pioneering work with immigrant families crowded into slum housing near the stockyards in the early 1900s. Addams's Hull-House on Halsted became an international symbol of the settlement movement. The city's reputation for violence as well as for progressive reform makes it an apt choice for a writer interested in crime and mystery fiction and with the idea of creating a female protagonist. Paretsky's detective, then, is located in both a genre and a city that are marked as "masculinist" and with important resisting aspects to those tough traditions. Perhaps this gives Paretsky's character a harder edge—she will not stand for any nonsense in a city renowned for political shenanigans at all levels. Born, bred, and educated in Chicago, the detective is loyal to her roots in the ethics and values of the hard-working South Chicago neighborhood where she grew up; she is also wise to the city's reputation for civic and political malfeasance, having seen and experienced it herself. Laura Ryan's 2006 interview with Paretsky reports that the author "wanted to make her character represent her adopted city, and Chicagoans have a strong sense of ethnic and racial identity. Because her own grandfather was Polish, Paretsky settled on a Polish-American heroine" (6). The detective character's affection for her city is well-tempered with exasperation and dismay at its apparently never-ending capacity for criminal activity. As she traverses the length and breadth of the city (with occasional ventures into the suburbs) in her car and on public transport (she is not above taking the bus or the El), she displays detailed knowledge of the landscape, whether she is railing about some of Chicago's famous skyscrapers or appreciating the Chagall mosaic. Paretsky gives her detective an appreciation and knowledge of the city's artchitectural and industrial landscape; on the same day, she can be driving "down Congress toward Louis Sullivan's masterpiece" (GA 14) in the morning and later find herself near the Sanitary and Ship Canal, a "thirty-mile stretch of water, crisscrossed by rail beds" where "grain and cement elevators hover over heaps of scrap metal" (GA 59). James Kaufman's review of the early *Bitter Medicine* notices that the detective "talks a lot about the city, about its customs, its traffic, its neighborhoods, and about the Cubs" (6). Sarah Bryan Miller's review of the later *Total Recall* adds to the theme: "Paretsky once again demonstrates her perfect pitch when it comes to Chicago, its people and its neighborhoods, putting both her characters and her traffic jams in exactly the right places" (F8). The detective's cases often take her into the heart of established Chicago structures (such as the Roman Catholic Church, the mob, the police force, the medical profession, the shipping industry, the entertainment world); her abilities to sniff out corporate and institutional malpractice in her various quests are nearly always fueled by a rage that those in her beloved city could act this way. She wants Chicago to be better than it is. The lake is a constant motif signaling the paradoxical beauty of Chicago as well as its capacity for wickedness: "The polished mirror surface was streaked with a light and color that would have inspired Monet. It looked at once peaceful and inviting. But its cold depths could kill you with merciless impersonality" (*Bitter* 57). In *Deadlock*, at her cousin Boom Boom's lakeside condo, V. I. stops to admire the view and draw courage: "[T]he wind whipped whitecaps up on the green water. A tiny red sliver moved on the horizon, a freighter on its journey to the other side of the lakes. I stared for a long time before bracing my shoulders" (DL 47). On her way back to Chicago from Wisconsin, V. I. drives "east all the way to the big lake before starting south … the breeze off Lake Michigan was cool, and it was easier to think…. [T]he water was a purply gray in the summer twilight" (HB 148). In the January temporal setting of *Killing Orders* the detective hears "the sullen roar of Lake Michigan.... [T]he regular, angry slapping of wave against cliff made me shiver violently" (KO 282). In the early spring setting of *Brush Back*, V. I. admires "sunlight glinting on little waves on Lake Michigan, the sky the soft clear blue that makes you imagine you could take up painting" (15). In *Tunnel Vision*, as V. I. drives back into the city from the suburbs, she has a wistful moment of truth: "I saw the city for a moment as an outsider. Compared to the outsize malls and massive roads I'd left behind, Chicago looked decrepit, even useless. I wondered if my beloved briar patch was as tired as I was, and what would keep either of us going" (TV 211). V. I.'s exasperated fondness for her city is regularly contrasted with her equally exasperated relationship to suburban landscapes: driving to Morrell's Evanston home in *Total Recall*, V. I. passes through "the disturbing vistas of the western suburbs: no center, no landmarks, just endless sameness … all punctuated with malls showing identical megastores" (TR 179). *Bitter Medicine* opens on a hot summer day with V. I. at the wheel driving to the north suburbs: "The heat and the tawdry sameness of the road drugged everyone to silence. The July sun shimmered around McDonald's, Video King, Computerland, Arby's, Burger King, the Colonel, a car dealership, and then McDonald's again" (*Bitter* 11). In this same novel, after driving in circles in the anonymous suburban streets, the detective heads back into the city, reflecting, "I never get lost driving in Chicago. If I can't find the lake or the Sears Tower, the L tracks orient me, and if all else fails, the x-y street coordinates keep me on target" (*Bitter* 39). Chicago in the winter is evoked in *Body Work*: on a drive south along Lake Shore Drive, the detective is "close enough to see the desolate, ice-covered surface stretch to the horizon under the pale starlight" (285). One of Paretsky's running Chicago motifs throughout the series is V. I.'s love of the Cubs, a loyalty the detective shares with her creator, who explained in an interview with Donald Evans, "the summer of '66, when I first came to

Chicago, I worked in a community youth program in Gage Park. The Sox would not return my phone calls, but the Cubs gave our kids free tickets every Thursday. As you know, in Chicago the definition of an honest politician is one who stays bought. The Cubs bought my loyalty 40-plus years ago, and they've been breaking my heart ever since" (78). The Cubs, famous for disappointing their stalwart fans by consistently appearing at the bottom of the league, symbolize V. I.'s instinctive support of the underdog and her empathy for people who are on the margins of society. She does not judge those living on the edge but demonstrates compassion for their plight, much as she extends endless patience in relation to the Cubs' ups and downs. In the debut novel *Indemnity Only* V. I. drives south along the lake tuning into the game "in the bottom of the third, [when Dave] Kingman struck out: 2–0 St. Louis. The Cubs had bad days, too—in fact, more than I did, probably" (149). Later, listening to the evening news, she hears that the team "had pulled it out in the eighth inning.... I knew how the Cubs were feeling tonight, and sang a little Figaro on the way home to show it" (153). In *Total Recall*, she checks the sports section of the newspaper on her way to a concert at Orchestra Hall (Chicago's citizens have a reputation for simultaneously embracing both highbrow and lowbrow culture), only to find that "the Cubs had gone so far into free fall that they'd have to send the space shuttle to haul them back to the National League" (TR 120–21). Her dedication to the Cubs—as a South Chicagoan would more typically be a Sox fan—also signifies her instinctively defiant nature as well as loyalty to her policeman father, Tony. As Vic explains in *Hardball*: "South Side still means White Sox [and] Comiskey Park … a few blocks from the stockyards where my dad grew up. His high school buddies were all Sox fans. Only Tony Warshawski and his brother Bernie, sick of the stench of blood and burning carcasses, decided to risk their lives by taking the El up to Wrigley Field" (HB 179). The detective's characteristic loyalty and stubbornness are "what makes V. I. lovable and what makes her a Cubs fan"

(Evans 82). Her staunch support of the Cubs through thick and thin is symbolic of her approach to her work—if she thinks a cause is just, she will throw herself into the investigation against almost any odds. Finally, the Cubs motif affords Paretsky a way of sketching in some of Chicago's deep-seated cultural characteristics and features—such as the geographical north/south divide and the city's obsession with and pride in its famous sports teams and athletes. In *Bitter Medicine*, V. I. takes a break from her current case to watch "the Cubs lose an aggravating game against New York" (*Bitter* 74). Later in the same novel, she listens to a game covered by the excitable real-life broadcaster Harry Caray, whose screaming delivery style was loved and hated by Chicagoans in equal measures.

Chicago is a coded landscape in Paretsky's oeuvre, described in terms of V. I.'s knowledge of what is signified in a location, a neighborhood, a monument, a group of people, a building, or a restaurant. Both author and character are particularly sensitive to the divisions between rich and poor people, and between black people and white people. These sensitivities are signaled, for instance, by V. I.'s loathing of the wealthy northern suburbs and by the author's treatment, in *Hardball*, of Chicago's historical racism. The

detective says, "[T]he fault lines of race in the city, they run through my family, along with the rest of the South Side" (HB 169). Ruth Morse's review of this novel for the *Times Literary Supplement* notices how "Paretsky has evoked—and celebrated—the multiplicity of Chicago's neighbourhoods, its old and new immigrants and its tragic history of race relations" (21). The author uses a combination of fictional and nonfictional Chicago locations throughout the novels. Her geographical references are accurate as V. I. cruises up and down Lake Shore Drive, navigates the grid system of the Loop and the near north side, sits in traffic jams on the Eisenhower and Dan Ryan expressways, and searches for parking in crowded areas. Ever observant, the detective often offers a running commentary on what she sees as she drives through Chicago. In *Blacklist*, as V. I. drives "south and west toward my office, all I could see was old six-flats like mine coming down and new town houses going up. Strip malls with identical arrays of Starbucks, wireless companies and home renovation chains were replacing factories and storefronts" (41). V. I.'s apartment at Racine and Halsted is located west of Belmont Harbor, where V. I. often runs the dogs. Her childhood home on Houston in South Chicago is in the neighborhood where Chicago's steelworkers used to live. Parestky makes frequent use of the Hyde Park area, where the University of Chicago is located (and where the author has lived since the 1970s). The university's Rockefeller Chapel features in *Breakdown*; the coffee shop in Seminary and another one in the Divinity School Library basement (both now long gone) are used as locations in the early novels. Fictional locations include the Golden Glow bar on Federal and Adams deep in the financial part of the west Loop and the Ajax Insurance Company building in the same part of the Loop (probably inspired by the distinctive red CNA building where Paretsky

**A Cubs hat for the fans. Paretsky's website notes that the author, like her fictional detective, "lives and dies with the Cubs." Photograph by Margaret Kinsman.**

worked). The bar is owned by a female friend of V. I.'s, Sal Barthele. The newspaper reporter Murray Ryerson and V. I. often meet at the Golden Glow. Another fictional location is V. I.'s office in the rundown Pulteney Building in the Loop, on "the southwest corner of Wabash and Monroe" (TV 11); her fourth-floor office faces east (toward Lake Michigan) above the Wabash El line. From the other side of the street, the neon sign of Arnie's Steak Joynt, where V. I. often eats in the early novels, flashes into her office window (this fictional location probably references the popular Arnie Morton chain of steakhouses started on State Street in the late 1970s). She occupies this office from the first novel (*Indemnity Only*) through the eighth (*Tunnel Vision*), when the decaying building is sold to a developer. The premises were never a salubrious location, as V. I. frequently reminds herself: "The lobby of the Pulteney building on South Wabash gave up its usual fetid smell of moldy tile and stale urine … [but] I couldn't afford a better building and having an office close to the financial center because its crime was my speciality" (*Bitter* 59) is reason enough for a while to overlook its deteriorating state. The office is sparsely furnished in typical Raymond Chandler style, but with reminders of her deceased parents in the big wooden desk obtained from a police auction and "[t]he little Olivetti portable [which] had been my mother's, as well as a reproduction of the Uffizi hanging over my green filing cabinet" (IO 2). When the Uffizi print is damaged in the chaotic move out of the flooded building in *Tunnel Vision*, Mr. Contreras sees to its repair; at V. I.'s 40th birthday party, he returns it to her, with "the walnut frame so expertly restored that only my most anxious searching could find the nicks in it" (TV 432). She sets up a new office in the gentrifying area of Bucktown north and west of the Loop, in a warehouse she shares with her sculptor friend Tessa Reynolds. Located on Leavitt near where it intersects with Milwaukee, the area is largely residential with a predominantly Hispanic population when V. I. and Tessa acquire the warehouse premises and rehab it for their purposes. Inevitably, the area begins to gentrify, and

eventually the "taquerias within half a block of my front door serv[ing] fresh tortillas past midnight … are a memory" (BL 41). V. I. has a number of fictional Chicago watering holes, including the Dortmunder hotel where V. I. and Lotty often repair for dinner in the early novels; the Belmont Diner that was "the last vestige of the shops and eateries of Lakeview's old working-class neighbourhood" (TR 260–61), where V. I. breakfasts occasionally; and Sonny's Bar in South Chicago (*Windy City Blues*). With its reputation for dark streets, violence, reliable crime rates, and corruption at every political level, Chicago lends itself as a fruitful setting to crime and mystery fiction. It "supplies a powerful sense of place [with] rich histories and rooted families—all of which can be slapped away in an instant by a sinister creep" (Keller S20). Its identity as a city with a grimy underbelly goes back most famously to the days of Prohibition and Al Capone's organized mob activities. Earlier than that era, the city struggled with violent labor disputes. The Chicago police force is often remembered for its heavy-handed approach to issues of public order going back to those early labor confrontations, continuing through the civil rights era and the 1968 Democratic Party Convention. These aspects of Chicago might limit its characterization to a set of clichés and stereotypes, but Paretsky's great knowledge and understanding of the city emerges time and again in the novels, where she makes Chicago's complex history and politics integral to her stories. The 13th novel *Hardball* takes a close look at the Chicago Police Department's long-standing reputation for the brutal treatment of African American suspects in their custody. In a case that reaches back to the 1960s, V. I. discovers that her father, Tony, is probably implicated in the cover-up of a police beating of a black youth arrested during a civil rights march. The city represented by Paretsky in the novels is faithful to the real city, peopled with rich and poor, immigrant and indigenous, young and old, family groups and people on their own, honest and corrupt. In a 2010 interview, Paretsky told fellow Chicago author David Heinzmann about her early struggle to get published: "my biggest obstacle were publishers who said not enough people read in the Midwest to make it profitable to sell a book set here.... I think that coastal arrogance kept people from looking at Chicago" (C12). As Heinzmann notes, "Paretsky's success is part of what began to thaw that ice ... more writers began to see their books published, and [now] there [is] an emerging crop" of Chicago-based genre authors. Paret-

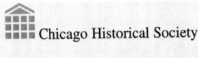

**Original poster advertising Paretsky's appearance in June 1998 for the Sunday in the Park with Studs series of talks with eminent Chicagoans.**

sky explains to Heinzmann, "our politics is a three-ring circus [and] we do have this huge well of corruption [which] is good for our crime writers" (ibid.). Paretsky's city of residence has appreciated her achievements, and V. I.'s fame, in a number of ways. The author has been broadcast-interviewed by Studs Terkel, the famous Chicago chronicler of the lives of ordinary and extraordinary people (Chicago History Museum/WFMT 1992). In 2002, the Chicago Historical Society gave her the Richard Wright History Maker Award for Distinction in Literature, an award that recognizes "the achievements of people linked in sustained and significant ways to Chicago." (letter dated 24 October 2001 in author's private papers accessed November 2012). In 2012, she was given Chicago's Harold Washington Literary Award; a mayor's proclamation designated 14 March 2012 to be "Sara Paretsky Day" in formal acknowledgment of the contributions she has made to the city and in honor of V. I.'s 30th anniversary. Paretsky contributed to a feature article on Chicago for *Savvy* magazine in 1988; in her testimonial, she remembers, "[W]hen I first moved here, I was startled by how strongly people identified both with their neighborhoods and with whatever foreign country their ancestors came from" ("Chicago" 48). Those early impressions of the significant role played by ethnicity in the Chicago landscape found expression in the V. I. series; V. I. herself is the daughter of a Polish-American father and an Italian mother, half-Jewish, who fled Mussolini's Italy as a teenager. V. I.'s friends and associates represent a broad range of backgrounds and cultural/ethnic identities. For instance, the elderly Mr. Contreras is proud to claim his roots in Italy. Max Loewenthal and Dr. Lotty Herschel were both born into affluent Austrian Jewish families who, as World War II loomed, managed to move some of their children out of Vienna and into England on the Kinderstransport. Max and Lotty both subsequently established lives and successful careers in Chicago; they, like Mr. Contreras, are part of V. I.'s inner circle. Lotty's clinic nurse, Carol Alvarado, is part of a large family with links to Puerto Rico. Chicagoans Sal Barthele, Tessa Reynolds, and Conrad Rawlings are African Americans from different economic backgrounds: Sal is a self-made, successful businesswoman; Tessa comes from a wealthy professional family; Conrad's is a hard-working blue-collar family. One of V. I.'s lovers, the journalist Morrell, is the son of Hungarian émigrés who spent his childhood in Cuba. Paretsky's adopted city provides her with a distinctive urban landscape to which the V. I. oeuvre does justice.

**See also the Web site "V. I. Warshawski's Chicago"**

## Chicago Literary Traditions

Although Paretsky is primarily identified as a mystery writer, and her work most often discussed within those parameters, it is worth looking at the ways in which she can also be located within distinctive Chicago literary traditions that date back to the period following the Great Fire of Chicago in 1871. A powerful relationship between the city and its writers over the last 150 years or more can be traced through a variety of schools and periods. Although the Chicago tradition encompasses authors of all kinds, it is possible to generalize and identify some qualities they share. The city is their subject, and in the works of some writers (such as Carl Sandburg's famous poem "Chicago"), it becomes a personified presence. Many Chicago writers pay attention to the ethnicity and heterogeneous voices of the city, focusing on specific neighborhoods and groups, such as James T. Farrell's stories of the South Side Irish, Sandra Cisneros's tales of the Latin American population around Humboldt Park, Saul Bellow's attention to the Jewish community around Hyde Park, and Richard Wright's and Lorraine Hansberry's portrayals of African American families struggling in a racist city. Writers often reflect a populist, middle-American, and rather anti-establishment outlook in which energy is valued over elegance and street smarts over intellectual effete pretension. The crooked and rigged nature of power and authority is often taken as a given. The literature of Chicago tends to emphasize the vigor of the city and the steadfastness of its blue-collar working people, as well as its many vernaculars of speech, architecture, industry, finance, and cultural expression. Paretsky's oeuvre reflects all of these characteristics; and her work is, at the same time, carving out new spaces in terms of both genre tradition and a Chicago tradition. Despite the participation of women in written and oral debate and in civic and cultural life from the 1870s onward, the Chicago writer and voice is perceived as unabashedly male and virile, perhaps most famously exemplified in Sandburg's description of Chicago as "a tall bold slugger set vivid against the little soft cities" (3). Literary expression emanating from Chicago is often identified with the schools of realism and naturalism as in the late-nineteenth century and early-twentieth century work of Theodore Dreiser, Sherwood Anderson, and Hamlin Garland. These schools—as well as their themes of urban industrial labor, grinding poverty, the migration from small towns to cities, and the paradoxical nature of the flawed metropolis—overlapped with a vigorous tradition of journalism, and writers often migrated from one type of writing to the other. A contemporary of famous social reformer Jane Addams, Ida B. Wells was a turn-of-the-century activist in the causes of women's suffrage and civil rights. Both women wrote essays, speeches, pamphlets, articles, and memoirs, and both demonstrated powerful literary imaginations. Paretsky's literary production demonstrates this versatility—she moves easily between fiction (novels and short stories) and journalism, scholarly essays, memoir writing, and public speaking, and she engages with a range of social issues at both civic and national levels. Another parallel type of literary expression can be identified in the emerging early-twentieth-century school of sociology at the University of Chicago, with its ethnographic mappings and descriptions of youth, poverty, and ganglands. Poetic expression has flourished in Chicago, beginning with Harriet Monroe's early-twentieth-century *Poetry: A Magazine of Verse* and peaking perhaps with Gwendolyn Brooks, the African American poet of the urban poor and recipient of the Pulitzer Prize. Paretsky

participated in the city's public commemoration service for Brooks after her death in December 2000.

Theater has a long history in Chicago; Lorraine Hansberry's work is an example, as is the later David Mamet's. The thriving literary scene in Chicago has been accompanied by lively editors, critics, publishers, and booksellers, as well as a host of journals, magazines, and societies such as the Little Room salon offering platforms and outlets for the work of writers. Sidney H. Bremer, Barbara Berg, and other scholars such as Lisa Woolley and Carla Capetti, influenced by emerging feminist theoretical perspectives and the new disciplines of women's studies and cultural studies from the 1970s on, turned their attention to widening the received story of the Chicago canon in particular and teasing out some of the complex relationships among gender, genre, and the city. Bremer's work explores turn-of-the-century writers such as Edith Wyatt, Elia Peattie, and Susan Glaspell; she points to how their novels and short stories present Chicago as "informed by communal concerns, interfused with organic nature, and enmeshed in familial continuities" (210). She sees these writers reflecting and presenting the city as an infinitely rich environment of cultural diversity, in which female characters are given the right to wander and explore their city while aware of, but not hindered by, the historical injunction for unaccompanied women that there lies danger— either the loss of personal safety or the loss of respectability. Paretsky's fictional works of later twentieth-century and early-twenty-first century Chicago can certainly be described in such terms. Susan Merrill Squier, in her introduction to *Women Writers and the City*, wrote: "women writers respond to the urban environment in a significantly different way from men writers" (8). Liz Heron's introduction to *Streets of Desire* (1993) describes the city "as the site of women's most transgressive and subversive fictions throughout the century, as a place where family constraints can be cast off and new freedoms explored" (2). Paretsky then can be located in what Bremer describes as the "lost continuities" of a counter-tradition of Chicago writing that takes as its starting point an insistence on the autonomous status of female experience. Paretsky's V. I. Warshawski novels are as much narratives of female self-discovery as they are mystery stories. The structures and inequities of gender, and themes of social justice, are never far from the surface in Paretsky's work; the challenges of locating female agency and voice in literary traditions and settings where agency is associated with maleness cannot be underestimated. The crime and mystery fiction genre is one that historically stereotypes male characters as active and independent, and female characters as passive, sexually dangerous, and untrustworthy; likewise, the Chicago literary canon is one that is identified with the masculine imperatives of the big, brawling city. Chicago fiction is as tied to its mean city streets as is the private-eye novel. In Paretsky's fiction, V. I. Warshawski's city is experienced in terms of the communal concerns and familial continuities that Bremer outlines. V. I.'s extended family of affiliation mitigates the stereotype of the isolated single woman in danger on the city streets, and the lonely existential hotel room of Philip Marlowe with a whiskey bottle in the drawer.

Finally, it is interesting to consider the extent to which Paretsky's novels fit within or extend a "tradition of urban writing" (Cappetti 2) identified with Chicago writers such as Algren, Farrell, and Wright whose work is arguably "inspired by social and sociological themes" (ibid., 4). Cappetti suggests that by the 1930s, Chicago was "the mecca of modern journalism and newspaper humor, the home of a great deal of early American literary realism, and arguably the birthplace of American urban literature ... [where] the living speech and the stories of the city, of migrants and immigrants and of modern industrial America were first given literary form" (ibid., ). It is not difficult to see how Paretsky's stories, often focused on Chicago's marginalized populations and informed by V. I.'s profound sense of her own family's background as refugees and immigrants, also map onto such an anthropological strand of literary production.

## Clues: A Journal of Detection

Currently published biannually by McFarland & Co., *Clues* is a peer-reviewed journal publishing scholarly articles on all aspects of mystery and detective material in print, television, and film. The publication was started in the 1970s by Pat Browne at Bowling Green State University's Popular Culture center. Under her stewardship the journal was published by Bowling Green's Popular Press for 22 years. After a short gap, the academic journal was acquired by Heldref Publications and relaunched in 2004 with an issue on the work of Margery Allingham. Volumes 23–25 appeared quarterly under the imprint of Heldref; in 2008, the journal was acquired by McFarland. It is the only U.S. scholarly periodical devoted to mystery fiction; its readers include literature and film students and researchers; popular culture aficionados; librarians; and mystery authors, fans, and readers. The journal has published a number of articles on Paretsky's works, several of them collected in a Sara Paretsky theme issue (Vol. 25.2) celebrating the 25th anniversary of V. I.'s debut in *Indemnity Only.*

## Cody, Liza  *see*  "Sara Paretsky on Liza Cody"

## Contreras, Mr. Salvatore

V. I.'s neighbor and self-appointed guardian, Mr. Salvatore Contreras is a widower "in his late seventies" (66) when he debuts in *Bitter Medicine* (1987), the fourth novel in the series: "Mr. Contreras had been a machinist for a small tool-and-die operation until he retired five years ago. He thought listening to my cases was better than watching *Cagney and Lacey*. In turn he regaled me with tales of Ruthie and her husband" (67). His daughter, Ruthie, has two children and regularly urges her father to move in with her family in the suburbs. James Kaufman's 1987 review of *Bitter Medicine* notes the introduction of new supporting characters, "in particular her delightful 70-year-old downstairs neighbor, Mr. Contreras" (6).

Mr. Contreras, as independent and nearly as grumpy as V. I., lives in a ground-floor apartment underneath V. I.'s third-floor flat in the "little co-op on Racine north of Bel-mont" (40), where he grows tomatoes in the backyard and reminisces about his beloved wife, Clara, and his time in the military during World War II. In the next novel, *Blood Shot*, he and V. I. jockey around each other's personal and psychic spaces; she is wary of his tendency to "talk indefinitely ... the dog, his cooking, and I make up the bulk of his entertainment" (24). V. I. finds herself brushing off some of his offers of dinner and company, not wanting "my downstairs neighbor feeling he had the right to hover over me" (164). However, their fundamental devotion to each other surfaces again and again through the somewhat comic squabbles and misunderstandings over issues of privacy and personal autonomy. He and the dog Peppy effect a dramatic rescue of V. I. in *Blood Shot* when she is left to drown in a dangerously polluted pond in South Chicago; at the hospital the next day, Lotty tells V. I. that he and the dog have stayed all night against hospital policy: "the two of you are well matched—stubborn, pigheaded, with only one allowable way to do things—your own" (178). He grew up "down in McKinley Park," where his "folks lived on Twenty-fourth, off Oakley. Part of Little Tuscany" (GA 27, 66). He is eager to participate in V. I.'s adventures and, more than once, rescues her from a tight spot. "[T]anned, healthy, and strong for a man his age" (BM 66) when he is first introduced, he holds his own in the stamina department for several novels. He ages slowly through the series; in *Guardian Angel* (1992), which opens with he and V. I. attending to Peppy's impending litter of pups, he is 77. He and V. I. often bicker over their different approaches. In *Burn Marks* V. I. says that "he's attached himself to my life like an adoptive uncle—or maybe a barnacle" (Burn 8), and in the subsequent *Guardian Angel* she complains that "his incessant burrowing into my love life sometimes brought me to the screaming point" (GA 25). In turn, he lets her know that "[s]ometimes you're a little bit fresh" (GA 26). They have a bitter argument in *Guardian Angel* over V. I.'s affair with policeman Conrad Rawlings. Mr. Contreras admits his anxiety that a romance with the African Amer-

ican Conrad will bring her pain is rooted in his own lifelong prejudices about race: "I grew up in a different time" (356). V. I., in turn, worries that their difference of opinion might be insurmountable and tells him, "Please don't cut me out of your life, or take yourself out of mine.... You and I have been friends a lot longer than I've known Conrad. It would bring me great pain to lose you" (356). They come to an uneasy truce over the matter. Always eager to be involved in V. I.'s cases, he is delighted when, in the 1999 *Hard Time*, V. I. enlists his assistance in finding a new car after her Trans Am is sidelined: watching him search the newspaper ads, V. I. notices "his eyes [are] bright with interest ... he doesn't really have enough stimulation in his life –it's why he gets overinvolved in my affairs" (HT 26). In *Blacklist*, his concern over V. I.'s bad cold offers her some temporary "comfort, giving back an illusion of childhood with a mother whose scolding conceals affection and the promise of protection" (BL 52). But an hour later, they disagree over a TV report on a young Egyptian immigrant who has disappeared; she notes, "[W]e'd had the same disagreement a few dozen times, ever since the FBI and INS started rounding up Middle Easterners on suspicion of terrorism" (BL 53). In this same novel Mr. Contreras extends his care and concern to the adolescent Catherine Bayard who has been recovering from a broken arm and the loss of her friend, Benji: "It was Mr. Contrereas who brought Catherine the consolation she needed ... she convalesced on his couch and watched horse races on television with him and the dogs (BL 408). In *Hardball* (2009), although by now "close to ninety," he is still "ready to fling himself into battle" (9). In this same novel, he becomes an ally of V. I.'s impetuous young cousin, Petra, who claims him as "my newest honorary uncle" (118) and who provides him with further opportunities for adventure and new experiences. Through Petra's volunteer work with a senator's campaign, "Uncle Sal" and V. I. are invited to a VIP fund-raising event, which Mr. Contreras attends "in his one good suit" with his "battle medals and ribbons" (115) prominently displayed. By the

2010 novel *Body Work*, he is slowing down, and V. I. notices that he hates "knowing he wasn't fit enough or fast enough anymore to keep up with me, let alone look after me" (431). His devotion to his detective neighbor surfaces in a number of ways, providing a pattern for his appearances throughout the series. He often feeds her and keeps her company; he scolds her for taking risks even as he begs to be included in the activity; he accompanies Vic periodically on snooping trips and finds himself in the firing line. From his ground-floor vantage point, he monitors visitors to her apartment (sometimes intercepting genuine bad guys and often just irritating V. I.'s current romantic interest). He saves her from near death, fishing her out of the toxic waters of Dead Stick Pond in *Blood Shot*, for example. He offers her counsel, some of it misguided, but always well-intended. In the concluding chapter of *Bitter Medicine,* he steers her away from self-pity with the caution: "You gotta be able to laugh at yourself. I mean, if I laid down and cried for every mistake I ever made, I'd a drowned to death by now" (259). In the later *Hardball*, he takes a sterner line when he discovers she may have endangered Petra: "no one except you ever knows right from wrong. The rest of us are too ignorant to have opinions" (13). Another layer to the neighbors' relationship is established when Mr. Contreras becomes the part-time guardian of V. I.'s beloved dogs, first Peppy in *Bitter Medicine*, and then her half-lab offspring Mitch in *Guardian Angel*. Fiercely protective of V. I.'s well-being, Mr. Contreras himself displays the very qualities he values in her—the questing spirit, loyalty, courage, bravery, persistence—even though he does not always approve of the way she goes about things or of her choices of romantic partners. His ability to intrude into V. I.'s affairs, invited or not, mirrors the detective's own penchant for sticking her nose in, even when she is warned off by people worried that she is getting too close to the truth. He is prone to the occasional flare of jealousy if he feels neglected by V. I. In the 2010 *Body Work*, V. I. accepts his offer of French toast for breakfast because "he'd been a little hurt that I'd spent Sunday with Jake—it's his job

to fuss over me when I've been involved in violent crime" (50).

In genre terms, Mr. Contreras and Lotty Herschel serve similar functions: the sidekick figure who provides a sounding board and whose loyalty, while often tested, is never totally withdrawn. They are the embodiment of a moral compass similar to that of the detective figure; the source of humor and lighter moments; and finally, in Paretsky's twist on genre, provide a "family" structure of sorts, thereby mitigating the celebrated "lone" Philip Marlowe type of detective. Sal Contreras's own Italian parentage—referred to in a conversation with V. I. in *Breakdown*: "My ma came from Messina and my dad was from Naples, and they neither of them could understand the other's dialect" (50)—further establishes his symbolic kinship with V. I. He does not share V. I.'s passion for the Cubs or for their Wrigleyville neighborhood during baseball season; as someone who had "grown up west of old Comiskey" (BW 22), he is a Sox fan. By the time of *Blacklist*, the 11th novel in the series, Mr. Contreras "has keys to my place, with strict orders to save them for emergencies—which he and I define very differently" (BL 34–35).

**See also Lotty Herschel; Peppy and Mitch**

## *Critical Mass* (2013)

The 16th V. I. mystery opens in 1913 Vienna with a third-person narrative voice introducing the reader to two six-year-olds playing in a nursery: Martina Saginor and Sophie Herschel. By the 1930s, Martina is a teacher and physicist with a small stipend at the Radium Institute in Vienna, conducting ground-breaking research into atomic particles based on Enrico Fermi's earlier work on uranium decay. Her daughter, Kathe (later known as Kitty), and Sophie Herschel's daughter, Charlotte (later known as Lotty), play together, not harmoniously, at the Herschel apartment in the ghetto in Vienna. Both families worry about the worsening conditions and legal restrictions on the Jewish population in Austria under the Nazi annexation. In June 1939, the Herschel family sends Lotty and her brother, Hugo, on the Kindertransport to London, where they spend the rest of the war. Kitty makes it safely to England the following year where a Jewish family in Birmingham takes her in. What happened in Kitty's and Lotty's lives during and after the war, and what brings them back into contact in twenty-first century Chicago, is the subject of *Critical Mass*. The novel is structured with a split timeframe, which moves back and forth between pre- and post–World War II Europe and the United States; the characteristic first-person voice of V. I. in present time alternates with that of the omniscient narrator filling in the past history from the point of view of Martina. *Critical Mass* shares both structural and thematic features with the earlier *Total Recall*, in which Lotty's story as a Holocaust survivor emerges in her own voice.

The novel's present-day events kick off with V. I. deep in Illinois farm territory looking for Judy Binder, the troubled and strung-out daughter of Kitty Saginor Binder. Judy has made frequent use of Lotty's clinic over many years with attempts to kick her drug habit; Judy's recent phone call to Lotty reporting that someone is trying to kill her has prompted Lotty to enlist V. I.'s help. At the rundown farmhouse where Judy lives with her meths cooker friend, Ricky Schlafly, V. I. finds Ricky dead in a cornfield, along with two mastiffs— one dead and the other badly wounded. There is no sign of Judy. A visit to Kitty Binder in Skokie elicits the information that Kitty's grandson, Martin (a computer whiz kid working at the cutting-edge Metargon computer design lab who seems to have inherited "his great-grandmother's powerful gifts" [CM 459] as a scientist) has been missing for 10 days. The Metargon CEO is concerned about Martin's absence on two fronts—worried that Martin might be taking top-secret technological information from the lab and unhappy over the developing friendship between his daughter, Alison, and Martin.

The multigenerational strands of the story come together when Max, Lotty, V. I., Jake, Alison, and a reappeared Martin journey to Vienna to visit the "Leopoldstadt, the section of Vienna that Hitler had turned into a ghetto" (CM 450) where they find the missing link in Martina's story. Questions of na-

tional security and intellectual property/ patent law come up in the present-day story, as well as in the earlier period of Martina's physics research at the Vienna Institute where some of her Austrian scientist colleagues were members of the Nazi party and where Martina struggled over the dilemma of knowing the research might be aiding Hitler in the race for the atomic bomb. Martina is betrayed by a Nazi student; she and her daughter, Kitty, are deserted by the fellow physicist who fathered the child; she loses her job at the Research Institute and is sent to a concentration camp. This is the last anyone knows of Martina until more of her postwar story, including her work on the Manhattan Project, emerges in the parallel third-person narratives told from Martina's point of view and spliced into the present-day story related in the more characteristic first-person voice of V. I.

Marilyn Stasio's review sees Martina as "the serene center" of the fractured narrative timeline and split locations that frame the story; it is fragments from Martina's remembered childhood in Vienna and her solitary old age in the United States that open and close the novel. Stasio writes, "Parestky makes us feel both her own love for science and her fury at the way women like Martina have been denied the pursuit of their passion" ("Without a Trace" 23). Joan Smith's review for the London *Sunday Times* describes the novel as "a daring departure for Paretsky, combining her interests in women's history, science and the Holocaust" ("Daring" 46). The novel was named in the June 2014 *Sunday Times* (London) list of the best 50 mysteries published in the previous five years. The epigraph to *Critical Mass* names Paretsky's physicist husband "Courtenay, who taught me to seek the beauty of Nature's secrets."

The fictional Martina was inspired by the real-life Marietta Blau, an Austrian physicist who "was a member of the Institut fur Radiumforschung (IRF) in Vienna" (CM 463) in the 1930s, as Paretsky explains in a historical note at the end of the book. Paretsky's portrayal of a dedicated and accomplished woman scientist also inspired the unusual book launch held in October 2013; the independent Chicago bookstore Women and Children First organized an event featuring the author and student guests from Sisters4 Science, an afterschool program that introduces middle and high-school girls to experimental science through hands-on activities. Along with the author reading from her novel, the event featured presentations from S4S youngsters; and profits from the book sales that day were donated to the Science program. The author was also invited to discuss *Critical Mass* at the Library of Congress; in November 2013 she gave a lecture about her research for the book in Washington, D.C. Sponsorship by the Library's Humanities and Social Sciences Division enabled a free, open-to-the-public event. A press release announcing the event describes Paretsky's skills in "developing compelling characters … as she weaves together Lotty's childhood in Vienna, missing persons, meth labs, Chicago history and the race for the atomic bomb during World War II" (*States News Service* 2013).

## Critical Reception/Overview

From the start Paretsky's work met with enthusiastic reviews in quality newspapers and journals in the United States and further afield. Her novels attracted readers from a wide background of age, gender, ethnicities, and nationalities. She was published from the beginning on both sides of the Atlantic and in translation by Japanese and Scandinavian publishing houses. Her first five novels were published in the 1980s, the decade in which "[f]eminist literary criticism, feminism as a social movement, and feminist crime novels [grew] up together," according to Maureen Reddy's 1990 essay that identifies an emerging feminist counter-tradition in the mystery genre (174). That decade also saw the birth of a range of alternative publishing presses. Eager to promote women's writing and reading were Virago, Pandora, the Women's Press, and Pluto Press in the United Kingdom, and Black Lizard Books and Naiad Press in the United States. Independent bookstores also played a part: for instance, Silver Moon and Sisterwrite in London, England; Kate's Mystery Books in Boston, MA; and Prairie Lights in Iowa City, IA. Popular culture, gender studies, and women's studies were moving into the academy as areas of study and as subjects for critical/theoretical debate. Publications such as *Belles Lettres, Women's Review of Books*, the *Journal of Popular Culture, Clues,* and other scholarly journals were also part of the picture in the 1980s. Early critical responses to Paretsky's books began with scholars such as Kathleen Gregory Klein, Victoria Nichols and Susan Thompson, and Michele Slung who chronicled the history of the female detective figure from the nineteenth century onward; all of their work acknowledged the impact of the first several V. I. Warshawski novels. Klein notes "the tensions between the demands of the detective novel and the feminist ideology require a careful balancing act" (*Woman Detective* 1988, 216); her initial contention that the mystery genre and feminism were incompatible gave way to a more nuanced position re feminism(s)' impact on genre traditions in her afterword to the 1995 edition of *The Woman Detective: Gender and Genre.* Maureen Reddy's early critical/theoretical discussions made a strong case for identifying the critical mass of new work by writers such as Sara Paretsky, Marcia Muller, and Sue Grafton as constituting a "counter-tradition" with shared features ("Feminist Counter-Tradition"; *Sisters in Crime*). Feminist readers and scholars such as Anne Cranny-Francis, Lynn Pykett, and Maggie Humm, starting from a variety of positions within the broad spectrum of feminism(s), initiated discussions about what characterized a "feminist" intervention in the genre, recognizing that the complicated project could not be reduced to a single or universalized perspective. All of these critiques make reference to the Paretsky novels of the 1980s and early 1990s, although feminist criticism of feminist detective fiction was relatively slow to establish itself as a debate. Arguments over the conservative ideology of the genre dominated. By the 1990s, crime and mystery fiction was becoming "the subject of increasingly intense and varied theoretical inquiry" (188), as David R. Anderson notes; he further recognized the new directions taken by feminist "critical practice that lays bare the political and gendered ideologies embedded in detective fiction" (190). Assumptions that a strong female protagonist makes a text feminist were increasingly interrogated and refined. The critical debate was progressively inflected by theories of "difference" in terms of the race, gender, sexuality, and class of the detective figure. Perhaps because of Paretsky's early and continuing commercial success (the series entered the bestseller lists in the early 1990s), and her popularity with generations of readers, she is a particularly disputed figure in critical debate. Sally Munt's *Murder by the Book?* (1994) discusses feminism and the crime novel of the 1980s, describing some of the new women detective figures as "sheep in wolves' clothing" (30). She assesses Paretsky's novels as arising out of the liberal humanist strand of feminism historically identified with Mary Wollstonecraft and John Stuart Mill. Munt finds that in Paretsky's novels "the threat to the family is always removed by Warshawski, the enigma resolved, and order restored … [thus] perpetuat[ing] a mildly revisionist status quo, so that Warshawski is complicit with its continuing hegemony" (45). Munt's discussion on feminism and the crime novel also comments on the performativity of gender roles in private-eye fiction; she is somewhat critical of Paretsky's construction of the female subject, describing the emphasis on V. I.'s expensive clothes and shoes as "fetishization" (47). Walton and Jones's 1999 discussion of the hard-boiled mode points to its "potential for both identification and difference" (92), making it an attractive site for writers interested in playing with genre conventions. They credit Paretsky's creation of the V. I. character with playing a major part in the development of the late-twentieth-century female private eye, a figure now "solidly entrenched in the genre" (39). Walton and Jones's *Detective Agency* offers a sophisticated analysis of the contemporary, mainstream hard-boiled tradition at the end of the twentieth century. Informed by cultural studies, they reject the view that the genre is inherently conservative, arguing that it is

audience-led and potentially subversive. They further argue that the hard-boiled feminist narrative voice constructs a resistant speaking subject that has proved particularly accessible to different racial and ethnic configurations. They conclude that the feminist hard-boiled sub-genre successfully allows a wide audience to explore and re-configure the established borders of gender and genre. Gill Plain's 2001 book takes a similar position to that of Munt, suggesting that Paretsky's attempt to mold the hard-boiled mode into a feminist narrative that still pays homage to tough-guy fiction is a project "riven with contradictions" (142). Plain understands Paretsky's novels to have much in common with fairy tales that "have traditionally been narratives of reassurance and reward" (164). Commentators have noted that the detective is, for a hard-boiled private investigator, "unusually concerned with forms of loss—of parents, individuality, and personal autonomy" (Dempsey 307). A public academic symposium on the Nancy Drew mysteries took place in April 1993 at the University of Iowa. The event, and the subsequent publication of the proceedings, placed the spotlight on the important part played by Iowa writer Mildred Wirt Benson as the original author of many of the Nancy Drew mysteries, and on the impact the mystery stories have had on generations of readers and writers. Columbia professor Carolyn G. Heilbrun (aka Amanda Cross, author of the Kate Fansler mystery series) gave the keynote address; other contributions came from a range of scholars working in the areas of women's history, literature, and popular culture as well as from contemporary mystery writers such as Linda Barnes and Nancy Pickard, who acknowledge the debt they owe not only to the Nancy Drew mysteries but also to the V. I. Warshawski works as an early example of what could be done with a modern female detective. Lee Horsley's 2010 essay looks back to "[t]he female detectives of the 1980s and 1990s [who] both imitate and subvert the stereotypical qualities of hard-boiled fiction, imbuing the male role with character traits that foster communal bonds and a socially responsible ethos, while retaining the instrumental "male" qualities of physical prowess, tenacity, and confident agency" (37). Andrew Pepper's contributions on the developing counter-traditions within the hard-boiled genre looks at how the newer writers are raising questions about the nature of justice; about the instability of identity; and about power relations between rich and poor, black and white, men and women. He suggests that "the hard-boiled is best understood in terms of an ambivalent political outlook rather than a singular ideological orientation" ("Hard-Boiled" 151), making it a flexible locus. Critical reception has kept pace with the increasing emphasis on diversity (of race, class, gender, and sexual orientation) found in the genre, acknowledging, as Pepper does, that it is a type of popular fiction open to the representation of difference and to the unsettling of power relations (*Contemporary* 174–75). Genre theory, gender theory, and feminist literary theory overlap and intersect—common threads are found in their understandings of the suppleness and flexibility of "formula" and popular fiction, the construction and performativities of masculinities and femininities, and the ways with which readers' expectations can be played. Virago Press founder Carmen Callil observed that historically women writers "have used popular fiction to take by the scruff of the neck the rules and regulations of the society which governs them and to shake the life out of [them].... [I]n that way, popular women's fiction has always been a way of encouraging women to behave badly" (6). Commentators on Paretsky's work have approached aspects of the writer's career and her oeuvre from a number of perspectives. The commonest shared starting points are identification of Paretsky as an author working in the hard-boiled mode and bringing feminist sensibilities to bear on those genre traditions. Lengthy biographical/critical profiles are included in reference series such as the *Dictionary of Literary Biography*, the two-volume Scribner *Mystery and Suspense Writers,* and the *St James Guide to Crime and Mystery Writers.* More detailed theoretical genre approaches inform the discussion by Walton and Jones on the private-eye figure and Paretsky's/Warshawski's places

in that landscape. A number of theoretical/critical essays, published in a range of scholarly journals, have contributed detailed analyses of individual novels in the V. I. series. Beverly Six's discussion of *Blacklist* locates Paretsky in an American tradition of "protest literature" (144) and highlights the ways in which Paretsky's characteristic concerns with corruption and corporate crime are, in this novel, "tied specifically to post–9/11 federal-government incursions on American civil liberties" (ibid.). Donna Bickford focuses on the ways in which the 1994 *Tunnel Vision* deals with aspects of homelessness, particularly as it affects women, arguing that "Paretsky's portrayal of a homeless woman and her children and the limited and problematic resources available to help them highlights that the available options are undesireable" is "vitally important cultural work" (50). Richard Goodkin's 1989 essay in *Yale French Studies* explored the role of the Iphigenia myth in *Killing Orders.* The standalone *Ghost Country* is discussed by Joe R. Christopher in a scholarly article tracing the novel's parallels to Christianity, Judaism, and Babylonian and Assyrian myths. Andrew Pepper focuses on *Blacklist* as an example of crime fiction which is "responding, often in critical and imaginative ways, to the security environment in the wake of the 9/11 attacks" ("Policing" 404) and "the contentious issue of state sovereignty" (ibid., 22). In comparison, however, to recent fiction by John le Carré and Don Winslow, Pepper is disappointed by the Paretsky novel which "insists on finding resolution to the messy, open ended questions it raises about repression and global security within the boundaries of the state" (ibid., 21). In more general terms, Guy Szuberla's 1991 article and Thomas Gladsky's 1995 essay both discuss the significance of ethnicity in the construction of V. I.'s cultural identity as the daughter of immigrants and the friend of Chicagoans from a wide range of backgrounds. A number of PhD and MA dissertations, from U.S. and other institutions of higher learning, have focused on Paretsky's work. The year 2015 saw the publication of two full-length critical works on Paretsky; see Christine Hamilton's

*Sara Paretsky: Detective Fiction as Trauma Literature* and Enrico Minardi and Jennifer Byron's *Out of Deadlock*. The critical/theoretical response to Paretsky's work gains strength and depth over the course of the last 30 years, much as the series itself develops complexity and longevity.

## Cross, Amanda *see* Heilbrun, Carolyn G; "Remarks in Honor of Carolyn Heilbrun"

## "Damned by Dollars"

"Damned by Dollars" is an extract from a speech delivered by Paretsky on 19 September 1998 at the Upper Midwest Booksellers Association Trade Show in St. Paul, MN. Published in the *American Scholar* on the "Podium" page, Paretsky discusses the dollar pressures of today on writers, saying "[T]he forces of silence can come as readily from the market as from a totalitarian state" (160). She takes her title from a letter written by Herman Melville to Nathaniel Hawthorne lamenting the pressure he felt: "I am so pulled hither and thither by circumstances. The calm, the coolness, the silent grass-growing mood in which a man ought always to compose—that I fear, can seldom be mine. Dollars damn me" (ibid.).

## *Deadlock* (1984)

> "The refrigerator didn't have much of interest in it" (46).

The second V. I. mystery takes V. I. deep into the world of cargo shipping on the Great Lakes and the rivalries between two shipping industry magnates. The detective's own backstory is amplified as more is revealed about her family history.

The story opens with Vic attending the large Polish funeral of her favorite cousin, Boom-Boom, a local Chicago sports hero and a former member of the celebrated Black Hawks hockey team. An injury caused his retirement from the team, and he went to work for the busy Eudora Grain Company. His death is attributed to a tragic accident on a slippery wooden dock. At the post-funeral reception, family gossip circulates that Boom-Boom might have stolen some papers from his employers and jumped to his death because he was in trouble. As Boom-Boom's executor, V. I. must wind up his legal affairs. This innocent task takes the unwary detective into the murky waters of the shipping industry and the world of the wealthy, ruthless Chicago families who own the grain elevators, the freighters, and the docks. Once again, she discovers fraud, extortion, and blackmailing activities at the highest levels of corporate management, this time on the Chicago waterfront. Eager to clear any doubts about how her cousin died and initially incredulous that "someone might kill Boom-Boom to keep him from talking" (45), she meets Eudora regional V.P. Clayton Phillips who takes her to the dock where Boom-Boom died in a fall under the *Bertha Krupnik*, a freighter leased by his employer's company. At the Port of Chicago's private club for owners and officers, she also meets Niels Grafalk; the Grafalk Steamship Line owns the freighters used by Eudora

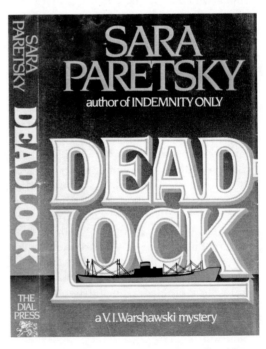

**The original Dial Press cover for the U.S. edition of *Deadlock*. The design incorporates a Great Lakes cargo ship into the title graphics.**

Grain to ship goods. In talking to her cousin's fellow workers, Vic learns of Boom-Boom's recent argument with Philips over some office papers. Visiting Boom-Boom's office at the Eudora headquarters, V. I. discovers from her cousin's secretary that Boom-Boom had, against office policy, pulled a set of shipping contracts from the files and taken them home. The paperwork in question, she learns, covers several months' worth of Eudora Grain's various shipping contracts with the Grafalk Steamship company and the smaller Pole Star Line, which is owned by Martin Bledsoe and has experienced vandalism of its freighter, the *Lucella Weiser*. Soon security guard Henry Kelvin, who had been watching Boom-Boom's gold-coast condo at V. I.'s request, is killed by an intruder. V. I.'s suspicions that Boom-Boom's death is not accidental are deepened by the strange behavior of his lover, the celebrity ballet dancer Paige Carrington, whose expensive tastes in clothes and cars seem to be at odds with her income. The energetic detective's search for her cousin's murderer and the intruder who killed Kelvin eventually imperils her own life. After one of her visits to Eudora Grain, the brakes and steering on her car fail, and there is a catastrophic collision as she tries to exit the freeway. She survives the accident with a dislocated shoulder but will not allow her injuries to slow down her inquiries. She flies up to Thunder Bay in an effort to talk to the captain and chief engineer of the *Lucella Wieser;* frustrated by their stonewalling, she ends up stowing away on the ship in a last-ditch attempt to discover what Boom-Boom had found out and why two people have been killed in the attempt to keep the information quiet. When the sabotaged cargo ship blows up, V. I. has another narrow escape. Back at the Port of Chicago, she tracks down Martin in search of more information; in another dramatic scene, she finds him at a dock where Phillips's crushed body is discovered in the self-loading mechanism of a freighter leased by Martin to cover the loss of the damaged *Lucella*. The mysterious circumstances of Phillips's death on the ship further puzzle V. I. Convinced there must be a link between Boom-Boom's death at Eudora Grain and the sabotaged freighters, V. I. goes on a fishing trip to the Ajax Insurance Company, as its Special Risks Department is handling the shipping losses. She and Roger Ferrant "from the London firm of Scupperfield, Plouder, the lead underwriters on the *Lucella*'s hull and cargo insurance" (188) exchange theories about how and why the sabotage took place. Vic discovers Paige's treachery, whose longstanding affair with the wealthy Grafalk provides a chilling background to the dancer's more recent relationship with Boom-Boom. Once Vic has put the pieces together that link Grafalk's systematic cargo shipping fraud to the deaths of Boom-Boom and Phillips but needs forensic evidence to prove murder, V. I. visits Grafalk's yacht. She reveals her knowledge that he "stands to gain a lot" (216) from the disarray to the shipping industry caused by the bombing of the *Lucella* in Poe Lock that has had to close for repairs, and her awareness of the state of his business. In a dramatic confrontation on the boat, the desperate shipping tycoon attempts to kill her; she survives by setting the yacht on fire, diving into a freezing Lake Michigan, and swimming away while Grafalk goes down with the ship. In the final chapter—titled "The Long Good-bye" in a nod to Raymond Chandler—V. I. puts the whole story together for Grafalk's wife, Claire, who asks for the truth after telling the detective, "Mr Ferrant says you and he discovered that Neils was running Grafalk Steamship at a loss and had cause to suspect him of blowing up Martin's ship" (250). V. I. explains to her that with the main players (Grafalk and Phillips) and the key witnesses all dead, "there's no one left to prosecute … the investigation will go on quite a while, but they're never going to be able to fix blame for blowing up the *Lucella*" (251–52). The novel concludes on a personal note with the two women expressing their private griefs over the ways in which the duplicitous Paige betrayed both V. I.'s beloved cousin Boom-Boom and Claire's "once loved" husband (252). Paige, like Grafalk and Phillips, never will be held accountable for her actions. After V. I.'s dramatic escape from the burning yacht, she spends "two days in the hospital recovering from the shock of my near drowning" (251) and subsequently has a brief romantic encounter with Bledsoe whose "lovemaking matched his kissing. That had helped, but I knew the nightmares would last a long time" (252).

Emily O'Leary's review notes that "Vic keeps things jumping.... Miss Paretsky never really lets you relax" (18G). More equivocal, T. J. Binyon praises the novel for being "well told...; but Warshawski herself is just a little bit too good to be true" ("Criminal" 1984, 1391). The title, a play on words referencing the canal water locks that boats pass through, also signals the various impasses encountered by V. I. on her way to the truth about Boom-Boom's death.

The novel is dedicated to Lucella Wieser, "a lady who sailed these seas with wit and great courage for over a hundred and six years," the epigraph notes. "Lute" Wieser, Paretsky's great-aunt who died in 1982, is further commemorated in the giant freighter named after her in the book. Her remarkable life is also celebrated in Aunt Lute Books, the multicultural women's press cofounded by another family member in 1982 that is still running a nonprofit publishing program. *Deadlock* was chosen as one of the 100 best mysteries of the 20th century by the Independent Mystery Booksellers Association and was given a Friends of American Writers award in 1985. The late Boom-Boom and his goddaughter, Bernie Fouchard, turn up in the 2015 *Brush Back*.

## "Dealer's Choice" (1988)

This short story is written in the first-person voice of Raymond Chandler's famous private-eye Philip Marlowe and is set in 1942 in Los Angeles. Paretsky wrote it for inclusion in Knopf's *Raymond Chandler's Philip Marlowe: A Centennial Celebration*, a collection of 23 Marlowe stories by modern crime writers. In this publication Paretsky's author note states, "[I]t was Chandler who really framed the relationship of the PI to justice, law, and society, and my detective, V. I. Warshawski, certainly operates according to the values Chandler outlined in 'The Simple Art of Murder'" (132). The story is included in *The New Mystery* (1993) and the 1995 Penguin 60 edition titled *A Taste of Life and Other Stories*. References to World War II, including the internment of Japanese Americans, provide an unsettling background to the events that unfold.

The story opens in classic Chandler style, with a "woman waiting in the outer office when I came in.... [S]he was all in red.... [H]er voice was soft and husky" (*Taste of Life* 11). Paretsky catches Marlowe's laconic speech and thought patterns; when the visitor in red tells the detective she needs "some help with a man," Marlowe responds, "You look as though you do just fine without help" (ibid., 3). The story also demonstrates Paretsky's grasp of the famous Chandler metaphor and simile: "[S]he gave me a shrug that moved like a whisper through the shantung" (14); "my words carried a lot of weight with him, about as much as maggots listening to protests from a dead body" (16). In a nod to genre traditions and to Marlowe in particular, Paretsky's Marlowe puts his "bottle of rye neatly in the middle of the drawer," then the author twists the tradition by including the private-eye's reflective commentary on himself: "[O]h, yes, Marlowe's a very methodical guy.... [H]e always tidies up his whisky bottle when he's been drinking.... [Y]ou can tell he came from a good home" (21).

Marlowe's visitor, who introduces herself as "Naomi Felstein," wants the detective to approach well-known gambler Dominick Bognavich and have him drop "the markers" of her brother who is in debt to him. Marlowe falls into "the sweetest sucker trap I've ever seen" (33); he discovers two dead bodies, is knocked out and concussed, and is nearly dumped over a cliff before he finally discovers that the secret to the case lies in Naomi's real identity as Kathleen Akiko Moloney. Ichuro Kimura, her grandfather who "came here from Japan in 1879" (36), has been denounced as a Japanese spy by a neighboring landowner who has long wanted to acquire Kimura's ranch. In the climate of anti–Japanese sentiment and the real possibility of internment at the infamous Manzanar camp, Kathleen gave the title to the land to Dominick for safekeeping and helped her grandfather go into hiding. Kathleen and

Marlowe recover the stolen property title and smuggle Kimura back into the "little place she owned in Beverly Hills, just ten rooms and a pool in the back" (39). Marlowe turns down Kathleen's invitation for a drink; the solitary and cynical hero returns "through the canyons back to the city. The concrete looked good to me" (39–40).

Reviewer Anthony Quinn, writing for the *Sunday Times* (London), notes that Paretsky's story "caught the original rhythms and inflections precisely and managed to retain a sly signature of [her] own" (H7a). The characters of Dominick and Kathleen likely are nods to Paretsky's agent, Dominick Abel, and his wife, Kathleen Moloney.

## Devereux, Ralph

A minor character who makes several appearances in the V. I. series, Ralph Devereux is "a man in his thirties who didn't have to be told how good-looking he was" (*Indemnity Only* 21). Introduced in *Indemnity Only*, he is a budget manager at Ajax Insurance Company in the department where V. I. is investigating the disappearance of Peter Thayer. V. I. takes him to the Golden Glow bar where they compare notes about the Thayer boy and where she learns "he had only recently moved to the city, following a divorce that left his wife in possession of their Downers Grove house" (22). He and V. I. have a short romance, but his tendency to overprotect V. I. does not work for her, and they part. He appears again in *Total Recall*, now an executive as claims vice president at Ajax. In this novel V. I. remembers meeting him "early in my life as an investigator ... at the time I was the first woman in Chicago, maybe even the country, with a PI license. It was a struggle to get clients or witnesses to treat me seriously" (TR 39). When she encounters him at Ajax in conjunction with her current case, she finds herself "trying to hide a twinge of sadness ... he had jowls now, and while he wasn't exactly fat, those slim hips had disappeared into the same past as our brief affair" (TR 39). The Ajax company is implicated in V. I.'s cases in both of these novels, although Ralph is not a guilty party.

## "Diversions" (2001)

In a short Q & A with the author published in *Chicago Tribune Magazine*, Paretsky responds to a set of questions regarding people with whom she would like to dine: "John and Abigail [Adams].... [S]he had qualities I admire ... loyal and intelligent" (13). Paretsky's selection of Abigail Adams, wife of the second president of the United States and an accomplished woman in her own right, as a dinner companion is characteristic of the author's habit of referencing historical female role models. She has endowed her own detective character with the qualities of loyalty and intelligence she values in Abigail Adams.

## Dostoyevsky, Fyodor *see* "Afterword to the Brothers Karamazov"

## Dreams

Dreams feature regularly in the Paretsky oeuvre. Several of the V. I. novels begin with the detective surfacing from a dream, woken by the dogs, a doorbell, or a ringing telephone. *Burn Marks* opens in the middle of the night with V. I. dreaming that she and her mother are trapped in the upstairs bedroom of their "old house on Houston" (*Burn* 1). When she wakes to the urgent sound of her doorbell, she remembers "all the times in my childhood the phone or doorbell had roused my father to some police emergency.... [M]y mother refused to admit her fear, although it stared at me through her fierce dark eyes" (1). In the opening paragraph of *Guardian Angel*, V. I., awakened by the dog Peppy, "groaned and slid deeper under the covers, hoping to sink back into the well of dreams" (GA 1). That novel ends with V. I. unable to sleep, kept awake by "unbearable phantoms" (370)—the recurring nightmares about losing Lotty. In the middle of the night she tells Conrad, her lover of less than a month, "I'm so scared—scared she's going to leave me the way my mother did" (370). Paretsky's use of the dream motif emphasizes uncharted spaces between waking and sleeping, and between reason and intuition where an alternative reality is registered on the part of the dreamer. The dreams seem, in V. I.'s case, to create room for memories (particularly of her mother, Gabriella), regrets about not having children, and losing Lotty. V. I.'s dreams often foreground visions of Gabriella when she was still alive, sometimes taking place during her last illness. Dreams allow people to come back from the dead across both spatial and temporal boundaries—the dreamer can rewrite the script of the past or imagine a yet unwritten future. The connection with her mother is strong in the dreams—V. I. sees her, hears her, and sometimes touches her. The dream motif also underscores the essential loner status of the detective—dreaming is something done in the singularity of the self. From the earliest literary expression, the world of dreams is represented as part of the human experience; dreams often function as messages, as signs and premonitions, as a doorway into other kinds of understanding and imagining. This is not the expected rational cognitive space of the cynical private-eye figure in the crime and mystery canon as epitomized by Sam Spade or Philip Marlowe. In genre terms, it has been unusual historically for a female character to occupy the authoritative position of the private investigator. The dream motif may function as one way for V. I. to lay claim to her own truth as a woman operating in a man's world. The flickering perspective of her dreams certainly gives her, and the reader, food for thought. When Vic reports her dreams and her understanding of them in the narrative, the reader is inclined to accept them as authentic renderings of the detective's subconscious realities much as we accept such phenomena in our own lives and as we have experienced them for centuries in art. Accounts of visions and dreams emanating from Shakespeare's witches and spirits, and from historical figures such as Ss. Hildegarde and Julian of Norwich, are embedded in our literature and have lives of their own as warnings, comfort, and transcendent images. Thus an alternative authority is established.

V. I.'s dreams seem to run the full gamut from comforting to dark and troubling. Paretsky allows V. I.'s subconscious free rein, through dreams and interior monologues. Some of her dreams are close to nightmares; others are repeating (such as the ones she

has of her mother during her last illness); others seem to signal warnings or offer revelations about her current case. The manifestations of Gabriella in V. I.'s dream landscape serve a number of purposes: she speaks or appears from beyond the grave to exhort her daughter, to warn her of danger, to comfort her, and to remind her of the values and ethics in which they both believe. Often the dreams give us a glimpse of Gabriella's past as remembered by her daughter; the vivid dream in *Burn Marks* brings Gabriella's past into V. I.'s childhood present when V. I. envisions herself trapped with her mother while "the dogs barked and snapped as they hunted us. Gabriella had fled the fascists of her native Italy but they tracked her all the way to South Chicago" (*Burn* 1). Sometimes V. I.'s dream suggests a way of working out some aspect of the case or reveals a more personal aspect of the detective—her terrors, fears, and regrets. In *Bitter Medicine*, Vic dreams repeatedly of babies: "I slept restlessly, haunted again by Consuelo's baby" (*Bitter* 49). The detective is approaching her 40th birthday in *Tunnel Vision* and suffers through a painful break-up with her policeman lover Conrad Rawlings; involved in parallel cases with children at risk, she again dreams of babies. In *Total Recall*, haunted by Lotty's temporary disappearance, V. I.'s "dreams woke me in the grey light of predawn. Nightmares of Lotty lost, my mother dying, faceless figures chasing me through tunnels.... I lay sweating, my heart pounding" (TR 153). Her father and his early police career feature in the case investigated by V. I. in *Hardball*; he, too, makes his way into V. I.'s dreams: "'Papa!' I tried to shout, but, dreamlike, I had no voice. I sat up, sweating and weeping" (HB 123). In this same novel, a dream offers V. I. a different version of the "truth" she has been struggling to understand in a complicated case. Dreaming seems to be linked to voice, the struggle to express herself, and a way of figuring out how she fits into the world. In *Blacklist* V. I. takes temporary refuge in Father Lou's rectory at St. Remigio's church; in an unfamiliar bed in strange circumstances, she wakes "from my most familiar nightmare. My mother had disappeared. I was looking for her, panic-stricken, because the only reason she would leave was that she didn't love me any more" (BL 219). In this novel, her deepest fear is that her lover Morrell will not return safely from Afghanistan; after the nightmare about her mother V. I. sits "blear-eyed, wanting just to lie back down and sleep for a hundred years. Until I felt well. Until Morrell came home. Until these times of fear and brutality passed" (BL 219). Earlier in the novel, she dreams she "was in a cave, looking for Morrell. Someone had handed me a wailing infant; I was hunched over, trying to get out of the way.... Far away I could hear planes whining overhead" (BL 34). The dream motif adds unusual layers to the V. I. character and to the modern mystery novel.

## Drew, Nancy, and Carolyn Keene

The fictional girl detective Nancy Drew first appeared in 1930 when publisher Edward Stratemeyer hired Mildred Wirt Benson to ghostwrite the early volumes for what became a best-selling series of mystery novels. Benson (an Iowa-born writer like Paretsky, with papers in the Iowa Women's Archives, University of Iowa Libraries) can be credited with the creation of Nancy as a distinctively strong-willed and competent young woman with a mind of her own who is not afraid to jump into action. The Nancy Drew books flourished under a number of ghostwriters, whose names were subsumed under the collective pseudonym Carolyn Keene. Generations of women readers and writers have paid tribute to the way in which the Nancy Drew character inspired them as an outspoken young woman who could have adventures and think and act for herself.

The first Nancy Drew conference was held at the University of Iowa in 1993; the proceedings were published by the University of Iowa Press under the title *Rediscovering Nancy Drew*, edited by Carolyn Steward Dyer and Nancy Tillman Romalov. Paretsky wrote "Keeping Nancy Drew Alive" [see entry] for the introduction to a facsimile edition of *The Secret of the Old Clock* published by Applewood Books in 1991.

KEEPING NANCY DREW ALIVE

By

SARA PARETSKY

AUTHOR OF

THE V.I. WARSHAWSKI MYSTERY SERIES: BURN MARKS
THE V.I. WARSHAWSKI MYSTERY SERIES: BLOOD SHOT
THE V.I. WARSHAWSKI MYSTERY SERIES: GUARDIAN ANGEL
& OTHERS

MENTION NANCY DREW to any woman between the ages of twenty-five and seventy, and chances are her face will turn dreamy and she'll say, "Nancy Drew! I haven't thought about her for years, but I used to love her." Nancy Drew and her blue roadster have been symbols of freedom for little girls since Grosset & Dunlap first published *The Secret of the Old Clock*, in 1930. With almost two hundred titles in the series, and new adventures arriving at the rate of eighteen a year, it's clear that Nancy's appeal is as strong as ever.

Hardcover sales of Nancy Drew adventures have surpassed Agatha Christie's phenomenal record. Publications from the *Journal of Popular Culture* to the *Wall Street Journal* have pondered the series' popularity without presenting a convincing explanation. At the same time, scholars complain about the pell-mell pace of the adventures and the protected environment in which Nancy lives.

**The title page of Nancy Drew facsimile edition with a foreword by Sara Paretsky. Photograph by Margaret Kinsman, University of Iowa Library Special Collections, 2014.**

## Eliot, George  *see*  "George Eliot's *The Mill on the Floss*: Book of a Lifetime by Sara Paretsky."

## "Evil Yankees, Awful Mets" (2000)

Paretsky's short article for *Newsweek* is headlined "A Cubs Fan Vents About New York, Its Inhabitants—and a Lifetime of Rooting for the Losers." The author confesses, "this year's World Series has me in a dilemma" (68). The subject matter of baseball is a favorite of the author who is a lifelong Chicago Cubs fan, as is her fictional detective V. I. Warshawski.

## Families

Families, in all their manifestations, feature throughout the V. I. Warshawski novels and in Paretsky's standalone work. The family structure is portrayed as a place of refuge and strength, as well as a place of danger. Unusually in terms of the hard-boiled mode, V. I.'s own family background emerges as a strong and continuing influence on the central detective character, even though she is on her own (deceased parents, an ex-husband, no siblings or children) when the reader first meets her. As the detective says to policeman and friend Conrad Rawlings, "your childhood home dogs you your whole life" (*Fire Sale* 8). Over the course of the series, the reader learns a great deal about V. I.'s parents and their backstories, V. I.'s childhood in South Chicago, relatives on both sides of the family whose troubles involve the reluctant V. I., and V. I.'s ex-husband Dick Yarborough, a yuppie lawyer who continues to cross V. I.'s path. In genre terms, V. I. on the surface is the classic "lone-wolf" detective figure, answerable only to herself and living and working alone. However, Paretsky bends genre tradition by constructing V. I.'s own birth family and the family of "affiliation" she has assembled as an adult as significant factors in the detective's day-to-day life. V. I.'s dead parents (Gabriella and Tony) become familiar to readers as their back stories emerge, sometimes when a case takes V. I. back to real events of her childhood as in *Hardball* or the case she investigates in the short story "Grace Notes" that reveals things she did not know about Gabriella's past. More often, snip-pets of Tony and Gabriella's own histories are recounted through V. I.'s memories of her upbringing in blue-collar South Chicago and in her dreams, where V. I. can hear her mother's voice. Their values and ethics inform V. I.'s approach to life—like them, she is frugal, loyal, courageous, and attached to the notion of public service. The "surrogate family" with whom the detective identifies in her current life is a group of like-minded friends and colleagues who often come with their own family attachments. For instance, the elderly downstairs neighbor Salvatore Contreras, with whom V. I. shares the dogs Peppy and Mitch, has a daughter, Ruthie, and two grandchildren who live in the suburbs. A retired machinist and a proud World War II vet, Mr. Contreras prefers sharing the excitement of V. I.'s life to spending time with his dull daughter and her family. Dr. Lotty Herschel, V. I.'s beloved friend and mentor, is a single professional woman like V. I. Most of Lotty's family perished in the Holocaust; Lotty's closest relationship, next to her friendship with V. I., is with hospital administrator Max Loewenthal, another refugee from 1930s Austria. Lotty and Max play important roles in V. I.'s life as stalwart friends and protectors. More important, neither is afraid of holding V. I. to account when they believe she is behaving recklessly or irresponsibly. They quarrel, as family members do, over such matters. V. I.'s former lover, policeman Conrad Rawlings, has a sister, Camilla (who appears in *Tunnel Vision*), and a possessive mother who does not approve of his relationship with V. I. Sal Barthele, owner of the Golden Glow bar, has a sister who needs Vic's help when she is accused of murder in the short story "Skin Deep." The investigative reporter Murray Ryerson, V. I.'s friend and occasional lover, plays an important and continuing role in V. I.'s professional life. Another Chicago policeman, Lt. Bobby Mallory, also occupies a significant place in V. I.'s life. He and his wife, Eileen, were friends of V. I.'s parents and in some ways consider themselves *in loco parentis* after Gabriella's and Tony's deaths. Mallory and Mr. Contreras both construct themselves as protective surrogate father figures to V. I. and thus feel free to interfere with and criticize aspects of V. I.'s lifestyle and professional choices. Although Mallory and V. I. have many a professional conflict over the detective's investigating methods and misadventures, in the long run, Bobby can no more let V. I. down than can Mr. Contreras. This "alternative community of her own choosing ... provides her with emotional and intellectual support. In [one] sense, the novels are the story of the growth and development of this community and the toll V. I.'s dangerous occupation takes upon it," Dempsey notes (306). One of V. I.'s regular clients Darraugh Graham, a wealthy Chicagoan, comes with family members (nonagenarian mother Geraldine in *Blacklist* and son Ken in *Tunnel Vision*); he is a close associate of V. I.'s and stays loyal to her for his business requirements. While these families have their ups and downs and often suffer through demanding situations, on the whole they function as a robust counterpoint to some of the more dysfunctional family groups that V. I. encounters on case after case. A characteristic Paretsky theme is that of the endangered child at the mercy of unscrupulous and self-serving adult members of the family—for instance, in *Tunnel Vision*, the teenaged Emily Messenger is trying to protect her younger siblings, please her mother, and avoid her father's rages and sexual demands on her. The Messenger family—privileged and ruthless—is portrayed alongside the homeless family of Tamar Hawking, who has run away from an abusive husband and is determined to keep her children with her. The themes of domestic abuse and incest, hidden inside the family structure, not only unite the stories of these two families but also include the repeating character of police officer Mary Louise Neely who reveals to V. I. that she suffered sexual abuse as a child. Incest emerges again in *Blood Shot* when the long-buried secret of Caroline Dijak's anonymous father is uncovered—Caroline's mother was molested by her uncle and the family subsequently turned their back on the teenage mother and her baby. Another troubled child features in *Hard Time*—Robbie Baladine who is mocked by his mother and siblings for being chubby and no good at athletics. Sim-

ilarly, Jill Thayer in *Indemnity Only* is the younger sister of the murdered Peter Thayer whose parents are too busy worrying about appearances and their own grievances with each other to see Jill's suffering. More troubled, but valiant, teenager figures would include Catherine Bayard and Benji Sadawi in *Blacklist*. Family frictions are a feature of this novel—between Darraugh Graham and his 91-year-old mother, Mrs. Whitby and her daughter Harriet, between V. I. and Morrell. Hard-working families struggling to make ends meet against the odds provide another strand in the Paretsky oeuvre—for instance, teenager Josie Dorrado's family in *Fire Sale*. Josie's mother Rose works for "Fly the Flag, a little company on 88th Street that made banners and flags" (FS 58), but is worried that it might go out of business explaining to V. I. "I need this job: I got four children to feed, plus now Julia's baby" (FS 59). The circumstances of the Dorrados are contrasted to those of Josie's boyfriend, Billy Bysen, whose wealthy family owns a number of minimum-wage paying businesses in Chicago. *Body Work* features the Guaman family, struggling to make sense of the death of a daughter working in Iraq, the aftermath of their son's motorcycle accident, and the murder of a second daughter at a Chicago nightclub. The later novel *Breakdown* includes a story line based on a group of teenage girls who share an interest in vampire novels. The teenagers come from strikingly different backgrounds: Lucy and Kira Dudek are sisters in a single-parent immigrant family whose "mom works a night shift as a hotel maid" (BD 3); Kira's friend Nia Durango is the daughter of Sophy Durango who is "president of the University of Illinois ... [and] also a candidate for the United States Senate" (BD 39). Such contrasting circumstances of family life allow Paretsky to explore, over and over, the hidden secrets and potential for violence at the heart of family life, no matter how privileged the family. A recurring feature in the V. I. oeuvre is "[r]estoring lost children or patching broken family relationships," writes Christine Jackson (131), which often is undertaken in the spirit of a heroic quest, Jackson suggests. V. I.'s attempts at patching and restoring the families she becomes involved with often prove to be an exhausting and enervating aspect of the detective's professional life. Her own contradictory feelings about "family" are expressed in, for example, *Burn Marks*, when her Aunt Elena makes demands on her that pull the detective in two. Although V. I. sometimes expresses a wistful yearning to be part of the sort of family other people appear to have, deep down she seems to cherish her life choices as a single woman answerable only to herself.

## "A Family Sunday in the Park" (2007)

The short story, subtitled "V. I. Warshawski's First Case" and also known under the title "Marquette Park," was first published in Paretsky's paperback *V. I. x 3*. Set in the summer of 1966, the story features Tori (the young V. I.) and her cousin Boom-Boom, who are under instructions to "remain close to home today" (29). Tori is worried; she knows "Martin Luther King was leading a march with Al Raby and other Negroes to protest housing segregation in Chicago" and she knows her father "Officer [Tony] Warshawski had been assigned to Marquette Park" (29) in the middle of the white working-class neighborhood which has gone on the warpath over King's activities. The Warshawski family itself is deeply divided over the impending march and how to respond to it. Gabriella, Tori's mother, makes Tori promise to stay out of harm's way for the day at Boom-Boom's house. When Tori overhears her Uncle Tomas threaten to kill Tony over some issue she doesn't understand, she decides she must go to Marquette Park to warn him. She gets caught up in the mayhem at the Park that day—the people on King's non-violent march, the local residents who turn out in violent protest at the marchers, and the Chicago police who are not successful in protecting King and his followers from the attack. She unwittingly helps uncover what has happened when one demonstrator is killed.

## Ferrant, Roger

British insurance executive Roger Ferrant has a romance with V. I. in *Deadlock* while he is on loan to Ajax because of his expertise in shipping insurance. He returns to Britain at the end of the novel and makes another appearance in the subsequent *Killing Orders*, where he and V. I. renew their affair while they work together on a case that again involves Ajax Insurance Company. Ferrant and V. I. nearly lose their lives when her apartment is set on fire in the middle of the night by hired arsonists in an attempt to scare her off the case. Although they survive the fire, the relationship itself is too fragile; once the case is resolved, they part amicably. Before returning to England, Roger helps her find a new apartment—a "co-op on Racine near Lincoln, in a clean quiet little building, with four other units and a well-cared for lobby" (285).

## Financial Crime

One of the hallmarks of the V. I. mystery series is V. I.'s expertise in investigating white-collar financial crime at every level of the city's political, business, and social institutions. This is also an area her investigative journalist friend Murray Ryerson specializes in, and together they make a good team. Murray likes to follow the money and write the story. V. I. is always willing to burgle or bluff her way into offices searching for the paper trail that provides Murray with evidence. The human potential for individual greed and acquisitiveness where money and power is concerned seems to provide V. I. with an endless stream of cases in which she deals with the resulting corruption, betrayal, violence, and murder and which Ryerson can expose in the press, thereby effecting a justice of sorts. Helen Dudar's profile of the author notes that both character and author are "faithful readers of the Wall Street Journal, whose reports of white-collar malefactions have inspired the central plots of many of the mysteries" (73). The debut novel *Indemnity Only*, with the title's nod to the insurance clause, establishes a pattern of complex financial fraud—in this case, collusion between managers of a bank and a trade union over the union's pension fund—which V. I. investigates with diligence and mounting fury. The next novel *Deadlock* has a massive insurance fraud in the world of Great Lakes shipping as its centerpiece. *Killing Orders* investigates financial fraud and corruption at the heart of the powerful Catholic church in collusion with the Mafia. In *Bitter Medicine*, the for-profit sector of the medical profession is spotlighted. Another pension fraud—this time between a manufacturing factory that previously employed Mr. Contreras and the up-market law firm in which V. I.'s ex-husband is a partner—provides one of the story lines in *Guardian Angel*. More financial shenanigans involving the insurance world, local politicians and community leaders frame some of the events of *Total Recall*. V. I.'s expertise in financial crime, plus her studies at the University of Chicago law school and her subsequent stint in the public defender's office, provide her with a set of useful connections to law firms, politicians, business moguls, bankers, insurance employees, legal professionals, and public servants. The cases in which V. I. becomes embroiled are more often than not inspired by events in the public domain. Susan Corrigan's interview with the author described Paretsky's oeuvre to date as "ten volumes of impeccable news-driven detective novels" (12). Like the author, Corrigan continues, "V. I.'s caseload and social conscience follows the news of the day" (ibid.). S.J. Rozan's interview suggests that "because of [Paretsky's] years in corporate America, she is one of the few crime writers who can make the reader care about 'the people on the margins' while simultaneously explaining with complete clarity the workings of a complicated white-collar financial scam" (45). A review by Marilyn Stasio notes that Paretsky's "expertise in financial crime is tightly linked to her convictions on human rights" (2001:23); most of her detective's cases are driven by a combination of V. I.'s fury at corporate and institutional misbehavior, and her willingness to untangle the complicated hidden webs of white-collar crime.

## Finchley, Terry

Nicknamed "the Finch," Terry Finchley is a Chicago police detective who works with Lt. Bobby Mallory, Detective Conrad Rawlings, and McGonnigal. They are all repeating characters. First introduced in *Killing Orders*, Finchley is "a young black cop who'd been in uniform when I first met him" (KO 182). He subsequently makes regular appearances throughout the series. The Finch and Conrad Rawlings are close buddies. In *Body Work* (2010), the Finch is now "on the personal staff of my dad's old protégé, Captain Bobby Mallory" and still holding it against Vic that "Rawlings got shot while he was involved with me.... Conrad survived, but our affair didn't, and I've never been sure which the Finch blames me for more—the breakup or the shooting" (5, 41–42). He is also the commanding officer of Mary Louise Neely, who leaves the force at the end of *Tunnel Vision* (1994) and becomes V. I.'s assistant. "The Finch" is described as "a rising star in the violent crimes unit" in the subsequent *Hard Time* when Neely seeks his help after V. I. is threatened with arrest; as the book notes, "When Mary Louise resigned, she was careful to do it in a way that left him on her side" (HT 24).

**See also *Body Work*; *Hardball*; Mary Louise Neely; *Tunnel Vision***

## Fire Sale (2005)

"My family motto is never skip a meal" (49).

The 12th novel in the V. I. series was the first for UK publisher Hodder after Paretsky's move from Penguin. It is dedicated to five young women in Paretsky's family (nieces, granddaughter) who, the epigraph notes, are "my own hope for change in the world." The *Publishers Weekly* review praises the themes and energy in the book, noting that the novel "shows why Paretsky and her heroine are such enduring figures in American detective fiction" (36). One theme explored by Paretsky is the question of how people can make things change for each other and for the better of society in the challenging circumstances of today's world. In the final chapter, Dr. Lotty Herschel reminds the discouraged and tired V. I. that work like hers—getting "Rose Dorrado a job so she can support her children"—makes a difference "in this hard world" (402). Paretsky told one interviewer about her struggle to "come out with a manageable story" in the current economic climate that allows "companies [to] do things such as paying their employees so badly that they have to go on welfare to eat…. [I]t becomes very hard to define a crime in a way that matters" (Page, "Anger" 30).

The story opens in the fall as the nights are drawing in. V. I. has returned to her South Chicago roots once again when Mary Ann McFarlane, Vic's high-school basketball coach who is now suffering from cancer, asks her former pupil to step in as temporary coach of the girls' team. Vic returns to the rundown Bertha Palmer High School (named after one of Chicago's famous nineteenth-century female philanthropists) located in an "abandoned neighborhood on the city's southeast edge" (9) to run practice sessions for 16 aspiring players, who have more to deal with than the lack of good practice equipment. In this neglected and largely immigrant part of the city, families are often on the breadline; drugs, gang rivalries, teenage pregnancy, and poverty mark the lives of many high-school students. Sancia Valdez, the 16-year-old single mom who plays center position on the team, brings her toddler and baby to practice sessions. Another team member, Celine Jackman, is "a leader in the South Side Pentas, and Theresa's one of her followers" (15). As V. I. notes to glamorous British reporter Marcena Love, who is interviewing the team members for a newspaper feature, "It's going to take way more than basketball to keep these kids off drugs, out of childbirth, and in school" (15). V. I. searches for corporate money so that a replacement coach can be hired. She approaches the wealthy Bysen family who own the giant discount retail firm By-Smart, which employs many local workers at minimum wage. The family rebuff the sponsorship request but later hire Vic to find Billy, the idealistic youngest son, who is missing after an argument between his bigoted evangelical Christian grandfather and Pastor Andres, a local community activist. Billy's instincts and sympathies are with the company's underpaid and underprotected work force, which puts him on a collision course with the other members of his family who are protecting their own interests and

affluent lifestyles. In the meantime, Rose, mother of basketball team member Josie Dorrado, needs V. I.'s help in finding out who is sabotaging the Fly the Flag factory where she works (at minimum wage) and why. The small factory has been struggling to stay in the flag-making business. Rose is worried about losing her job and wants V. I. to investigate suspicious things such as superglue in the locks. On an early November evening when V. I. drives by the factory, the building is fire-bombed; the owner/manager Frank Zamar is killed, and V. I. is injured by flying debris. In the aftermath of the fire, appearing on the scene is V. I.'s ex-lover: policeman Conrad Rawlings, who has been promoted to watch commander at a South Chicago station. There are still personal tensions between them, which are mirrored in the antagonisms bubbling up among V. I., her current lover Morrell, and Marcena Love who is staying at Morrell's home. The Romeo-and-Juliet romance between Josie Dorrado and Billy Bysen provides a contrast to the somewhat darker relationships of the adults. Further plot complications include the city dump where some secrets about waste disposal contracts are hidden, small fundamentalist churches and pastors with dubious motives, and a basketball player who goes missing. V. I. struggles to make sense of the explosion at the Fly the Flag factory. Billy and Josie run away together. The Bysen family—bigoted, rich, and powerful—are fighting amongst themselves about company and personal issues. Throughout the novel, V. I.'s own insecurities about herself are in play, giving the story an interesting emotional depth. She finds herself, much to her astonishment, telling Morrell, "I've been jealous of Marcena," and that she is "tired of people counting on me" (398). She struggles to accept his assurance that her spirit "keeps a lot of people on their toes" (399) as a compliment. It is easier for her to take some comfort from Lotty's reminder of what V. I. has accomplished with the high school students: "you took three girls who never thought about the future and made them want to have a future, made them want to get a college education" (402). At the close, she and

Lotty linger over dinner, considering the injunction of Lotty's grandfather that one must "live in hope, the hope that your work can make a difference in the world" (402).

The *London Times* review states, "there's nothing feel-good about *Fire Sale*, which doesn't stop it being among her best" (Berlins, "Still" 16). Bill Ott's *Booklist* review notes that "Paretsky has never been better than she is here at evoking a sense of place—abandoned and rusting steel mills casting long shadows over the difficult lives of largely immigrant families." ("Fire Sale" 1712). Joan Smith's review in the *Sunday Times* praises Paretsky for writing "about the world of recent immigrants, desperately trying to hang on to low-paid factory jobs" ("Mean Streets" 54). Smith further notes that the novel plays to Paretsky's "strong suit, the ruthless world of big business, which has fascinated her since Warshawski's first outing in *Indemnity Only*" (ibid.). The *Guardian*'s review notes that V. I.'s "abrupt way with words … has not deserted her" (O'Grady 17).

## Food

Food is important to V. I.; her life is punctuated, particularly in the early novels, by making stops at restaurants, eating on the run, throwing together the occasional meal at home when she remembers to stock the refrigerator, or eating at the homes of friends such as Mr. Contreras and Lotty. In the debut novel, she meets reporter Murray Ryerson for a working lunch and signals her dual priorities when the waiter slaps their food down: "I snatched the pictures back just in time to save them from spaghetti sauce and started sprinkling cheese on my pasta: I love it really cheesy" (IO 148). In search of a snack en route to policeman Bobby Mallory, she wisecracks about the Warshawski family motto: "'Never skip a meal,' perhaps in Old Church Slavonic, wreathed around a dinner plate with knife and fork rampant" (KO 93). As she says in the sixth novel, "It's hard to think when you're hungry—the demands of the stomach become paramount" (*Burn* 124). In *Guardian Angel* Paretsky gestures toward genre tradition when V. I. insists: "Before we did anything else I needed a glass of water

and something to eat—other bodily needs that never seemed to afflict the great detectives" (357). The motif of food serves structural functions: to pause the breakneck action of the investigation, giving the detective and the reader a breather; to demonstrate the detective's legendary knowledge of Chicago neighborhoods (she can always find a place to eat); to develop V. I.'s personal relationships when she talks to friends over a meal or to provide information about the case when she compares notes with people such as Murray or Lotty; to offer some comic relief when food and wine are spilled on V. I.'s smart clothes or when supercilious waiters antagonize her. Finally, and more metaphorically, V. I.'s desire for and appreciation of good food expresses a pleasure in being alive in the face of the death she confronts in every case. The theme of eating and drinking contributes to the realism of the novel by locating the unusual detective figure in a semblance of "normal" domestic routine, demonstrating V. I.'s somewhat erratic ability to look after herself. Her chronically empty refrigerator is a running gag that is a frequent source for her commentary; arriving home late and hungry one night, she tells the reader, "[I]t was only when I got upstairs that I remembered giving the servants the day off, so there was no dinner ready. I sent out for a pizza and watched a *Magnum* rerun" (*Burn* 130). In the earlier novels, Mr. Contreras often feeds V. I. as a way of being included in her adventures; in *Blood Shot* he "frie[s] up tall mounds of bacon and gargantuan stacks of French toast…. [I] repaid him by telling the tale of my midnight trip up the Calumet" (306). She and Murray continue to eat together when they compare notes over the current investigation: "we were in Ethel's, a Lithuanian restaurant on the northwest side, filling Murray's six-four frame with a few dozen sweet-and-sour cabbage rolls" (TS 126). Eating keeps her energized and is also a source of comfort to her. Rejecting the offer of dinner with a friend who "believed eating was just a duty you owed your body to keep it alive" (KO 109), V. I. heads home in her car, fantasizing about comfort food and making a list: "pasta, potato chips, pretzels, peanut butter, pastrami pizza, pastry" (KO 109). After a violent quarrel with Lt. Bobby Mallory in *Burn Marks*, V. I. is ejected from his office and wanders "into the first coffee shop I came to.... I ordered a b.l.t. with fries. Grease is so much more comforting than greens" (*Burn* 298). Her appreciation of good cooking comes from her mother, Gabriella, from whom V. I. learned to make her famous frittata suppers and how to put together a pasta. But Gabriella's exacting standards regarding Italian food are hard for V. I. to meet. On a grocery shopping trip V. I. admits, "I even bought domestic Parmesan. Gabriella would have upbraided me sharply—but then she wouldn't have approved of my buying pasta in a store to begin with" (*Burn* 33). When she offers to make a frittata for Lotty and young Jill Thayer, Lotty warns Jill, "Vic is a good cook, but a messy one ... you and I will spend the night cleaning the kitchen" (IO 168). V. I., Lotty, and Mr. Contreras often feed each other in their own homes. Lotty is renowned for her strong Viennese coffee, and Mr. Contreras relies on his barbecuing skills, his home-grown tomatoes, and his ability to rustle up a pasta dish. Out on the road, V. I. never seems to be at a loss when looking for a place to eat: "I stopped at a diner for scrambled eggs, stopped at a coffee bar for a double espresso, and reached my office by ten" (FS 49). From Arnie's Steak Joynt (across from her first office building, the Pulteney in the Loop) to the Belmont Diner in her own neighborhood to the restaurants in Greek Town, she knows where to find sustenance, although she mourns the changing landscape in Chicago streets full of "trendy cappuccino bars to gratify yuppifed palates such as my own (TV 171). *Body Work*, the 14th novel in the series, takes place during an icy Chicago winter; V. I. eats on the run stopping "at La Llorona for tortilla-chicken soup which I ate at traffic lights.... I spilled a lot of it and got to Mona's building looking like a toddler who'd just been introduced to solid food" (BW 254). She is as comfortable in the rapidly disappearing "mom-and-pop delis" (TV 171) she favors as at more up-market establishments such as "Grillon's, an old Chicago tradition" where she and Roger Fer-

rant dine on rare beef, a Stilton cheese "flown in from Melton Mowbray just for the restaurant" (KO 268), and a '64 port. Another favorite place is the Dortmunder in the basement of the Chesterton Hotel at Belmont and Sheridan where she and Lotty often meet for supper. She is appreciative of good food and fine wine that she is most likely to enjoy in the company of Lotty and Max, who has a legendary wine cellar. She also enjoys accidentally coming across restaurants such as the High Corral in *Indemnity Only* that she describes as "small, clean, and full of good food smells.... [N]o one would ever write it up for *Chicago* magazine, but it was a simple, well-prepared meal and mellowed my spirits considerably" (IO 175). In *Hardball* V. I. stops on the road back to Chicago "at one of the old Italian restaurants, where you got a straightforward pasta and the chef was called a cook" (HB 150); in conversation with the owner, she "described a memorable meal I'd eaten in Orvieto, across the square from the cathedral, roast pigeon with fig terrine" (150). This encounter gives her respite from her anxieties about her current case. In *Blood Shot* the detective is back in her old neighborhood in South Chicago and finds that "Fratesi's Restaurant was still where I remembered it...; [I ate] a frittata that was surprisingly light and carefully seasoned" (51–52). V. I. is allowed the traditional private-eye fondness for a shot of whiskey, although it is expressed differently. Rather than resorting to a quart bottle of rye in the bottom desk drawer, the detective drinks Johnnie Walker Black Label at Sal Barthele's Golden Glow Bar in the south Loop, usually in the company of Murray while they hash over a case. V. I. also likes the red wines of Italy and often serves drinks to visitors in the wineglasses that belonged to her mother, Gabriella; these social drinking occasions serve to distance her from the hard-drinking solitude of earlier private-eye detectives such as Philip Marlowe. Now and again, however, there is a nod to this model when V. I. overindulges and lives to regret it. After an evening drinking champagne with her neighbor, Vinnie, and his partner, she wakes up the next morning with no "clear memory of getting back to my own apartment.... [S]omeone was running an artificial surf machine inside my head.... [M]y shoulders felt as though I'd spent the night on a circular saw" (*Burn* 255). Such episodes are less frequent as the series progresses.

### "Freud at Thirty Paces" (1992)

The short story "Freud at Thirty Paces" was first published in an anthology of the British Crime Writers Association (CWA); it subsequently appeared in a 1993 issue of the *Armchair Detective*. The *Publishers Weekly* review of the CWA anthology praises the collection as one that showcases "humor, suspense, intricate puzzles and deft innuendo" (72).

Paretsky's story "brings together two New York City psychiatrists for a witty duel" (ibid.). The rivalry between Drs. von Hutten and Pfefferkorn begins with their different consulting room practices: "Dr. von Hutten belonged to that strict class of analysts who believe they must say as little as possible to the patient" (*Armchair* 27). Dr. Pfefferkorn "saw patients in an untidy room ... across the hall [from] a waiting area, where novels and magazines were jumbled in a stack on a side table" (ibid.). Each thinks the other "makes a mockery of the teachings of Freud" (ibid., 3). They are both fond of literary psychoanalysis—"analysing the personalities of writers based on their work" (ibid.) and "in 1980 both settled on the same writer as the passionate object of their research" (op. cit., 28), the twelfth-century mystic St. Juliet of Cardiff. The dispute is conducted via scholarly essays, letters to the editor, pamphlets, and debates at the annual meeting of the Psychoanalytical Association at which an array of professional colleagues take sides and positions. When matters escalate, Pfefferkorn challenges von Hutten to a duel in Central Park. The weapons—"two sets of the *Complete Works of Sigmund Freud*"—are laid out "on the grass in front of them" (ibid., 1); the combatants hurl books as well as professional and personal insults at each other. Mrs. von Hutten and Mrs. Pfefferkorn arrive on the scene in time to announce they "have discovered that St. Juliet never existed" and to instruct their husbands "go back to analy-sis—about which you both know something, even if it is something different—and leave St. Juliet to the experts" (ibid., 3). The background story Paretsky constructs around St. Juliet reflects the author's own academic training as a history scholar, as the two warring analysts trace elusive sources and argue about interpretations. The story also reflects Paretsky's own sophisticated understanding of the breadth and depth of debates around Freudian analysis and training, especially Freud's views on women.

### Friendship

The motif of friendship, particularly female friendships and alliances, runs throughout the V. I. series, signaling that this detective is positioned in a social milieu defined by her friendship and kinship systems rather than an imitation of the traditional private-eye figure with a whiskey bottle or a chessboard for company. The emphasis on V. I.'s friends and colleagues suggest that such relationships matter for the well-being of the individual as well as for society as a whole; who one chooses to have as friends is important. Whereas V. I.'s friendships locate her in a reality familiar to many readers, the motif also positions female friendships as mirroring/reflecting western feminist experience of the last 40 years. Historically, long before the 1960s, female cooperative endeavor played an important part in identifying, challenging, and subverting the oppressions suffered by women at home, in the workplace, and in the public sphere. Several of V. I.'s friendships such as those with Lotty and fellow law school students are rooted in shared experiences of the women's movement of the 1970s. V. I.'s friendship network includes male friends and ranges across a plurality of ages, ethnicities, sexualities, class identities, and nationalities. Early in the series, V. I. tells British insurance expert Roger Ferrant that she tries to be careful in her investigations because "I think you owe taking care of yourself to the friends who love you, and I don't want to cause my friends any grief" (KO 103). However, this is a position that V. I. cannot always sustain; her determination to do things alone and her way often leads her into direct conflict with friends. Reconciliation after fractures with people such as Mr. Contreras and Lotty often takes a while. Friendship is thus portrayed both as enabling and as a potential source of anxiety. The series includes friendships that are variously embedded in shared ethical and political belief systems. There also is an emotional depth to many of V. I.'s friendships such as the deep esteem and affection she expresses for her closest friend Dr. Lotty Herschel, an older woman of great personal and professional stature. The two met during V. I.'s law school days when they were both active in the underground abortion network. An article by Barbara Zheutlin notes that V. I. and Lotty "accept each other as they are. They may fight, they may wish that the other were somehow less stubborn and wilful, but neither asks that the other change who she is" (18). Other close friends of V. I.'s have their origins in shared professional interests; for instance, her slightly irascible and very useful relationship with investigative reporter Murray Ryerson; her association with Sal Barthele, an astute businesswoman and owner of the Golden Glow Bar, V. I.'s favorite watering hole in the Loop; and the friendship/colleague relationship with Mary Louise Neely, a young policewoman who leaves the force to work as V. I.'s assistant. Sal Contreras, V. I.'s elderly downstairs neighbor, becomes a valued friend who joins in her adventures whenever she will let him. There is great affection and great irritation between them, signaling the relationship as familial, as is V. I.'s prickly connection to police lieutenant Bobby Mallory and his wife, Eileen. The Mallorys are family friends from V. I.'s childhood when Bobby and her father, Tony, were policemen together in the same precinct. V. I.'s adult relationship with Bobby and Eileen has marks of friendship, as well as some "in loco parentis" conflict. Tessa Reynolds, the upper middle-class sculptor who shares V. I.'s warehouse office building on Leavitt Street, is a friend as well as co-tenant. V. I.'s cousin Petra comes to live in Chicago when she finishes college; in *Hardball*, she and V. I. get off to a rocky start but forge a stronger relationship during the subsequent *Body Work* and *Breakdown*. Petra becomes a favorite of Mr. Contreras. The detective's affair with the blue-collar policeman Conrad Rawlings, which comes to an end in *Tunnel Vision*, survives as a friendship of sorts through the rest of the series. Her lawyer, Freeman Carter, is a professional friend. Her ex-husband, Dick Yarborough, surfaces throughout the series, more often as an antagonist and obstruction than as a friend. Max Loewenthal, Lotty's friend and lover, also becomes a friend of V. I.'s. In *Killing Orders* V. I. says, "The older I get the less politics means to me. The only thing that seems to matter is friendship." In *Bitter Medicine* Lotty invokes the spirit of friendship in urging the reluctant V. I. to apply herself to solving the murder of Lotty's colleague, Malcolm Tregiere: "I am asking you, friend to friend, for a friend" (*Bitter* 57). It is hard for V. I. to refuse this when friendship and loyalty are central to her belief system. V. I.'s habit of going it alone and ignoring offers of help or advice from people who are concerned about her (she always knows best) puts enormous strains on her friendships. Passionately protective of her desire to depend only on herself and also fiercely loyal to friends, she often carelessly endangers both herself and others. In *Blood Shot*, Lotty suggests that V. I.'s courage might be other than heroic: "I would ask that you not be reckless, Victoria … except that you seem to be in love with danger and death. You make life very hard for those who love you" (BS 190). This is a theme to which Lotty returns throughout the series, calling attention to the contradictions in V. I.'s apparent commitment to the idea of friendships as nurturing and intimate, and her singular pursuit of her goals, often at the expense of her loved ones. V. I. knows, from her own undergraduate days, the value of female solidarity with its implication of collective action and the importance of give and take in any individual relationship. But she is often too impatient for cooperative endeavors and prone to taking risks that others will not. Asking for help from others is something that "just drives me wild" (BS 221), as Vic explains to Lotty who has issued an ultimatum and told V. I., "if you want to be friends, you cannot behave with such careless disregard for my feelings for you" (ibid.). However, now and again she finds herself depending on assistance from unlikely sources, including the 79-year-old Ms. Chigwell, with whom she takes a harrowing nighttime boat trip up the deserted Calumet canal in *Blood Shot*; and Lotty's equally elderly Uncle Stefan, who helps her out with his engraving skills in *Killing Orders*. Vic enlists the aid of Mr. Contreras in the earlier novels; he proves to be a worthy sidekick even in the most challenging of circumstances such as the horrific encounter with a rat when he and V. I. are wading through flooded tunnels in search of a homeless family in *Tunnel Vision*. All of these courageous older characters nearly lose their lives as a result of helping V. I., but they recover from the physical wounds and subsequently express a great deal of satisfaction and pride in their own efforts to be of use. V. I. in turn can find herself influenced and inspired by people who have touched her life. It could be argued that, as the series develops, she becomes more open to understanding the importance of strong connections with people. At the conclusion of *Tunnel Vision* V. I. is still melancholy from the breakup of her affair with Conrad Rawlings and uncertain of her capacity for intimacy; a surprise 40th birthday party thrown by Mr. Contreras and others reminds V. I. of the close bonds she has. "What else can I say, except that good friends are a balm to a bruised spirit?" the detective asks herself as the novel closes (TV 432). Friendships throughout the series are portrayed realistically in all their ups and down. V. I. and her friends argue, laugh, and cry together; socialize at dinner tables, concerts, and baseball games; have misunderstandings and temporary rifts; show compassion, tenderness, and anger; offer practical help and attention; and often go the extra mile for each other. The friendships cut across age differences, racial boundaries, cultural backgrounds, and professional/political divides. V. I.'s cases frequently begin with a problem brought to her by a friend (or a relative or current client), thus emphasizing the ways in which her personal and professional lives are enmeshed; V. I.'s loyalty to friends and her sense of obligation to family

and clients often lead her into situations not of her own choosing. The investigation in *Deadlock* is kickstarted when V. I. attends her beloved cousin Boom-Boom's funeral and begins to suspect that he did not die of natural causes. In the opening of *Killing Orders,* V. I. reluctantly responds to her embittered Great-Aunt Rosa's request for help; the detective seeks relevant financial information from her old friend, Agnes Paciorek, who is later found murdered. V. I.'s motivation for revenge on behalf of her friend propels her into a confrontation with a Mob boss. In *Blood Shot*, V. I.'s childhood friend Caroline Dijak begs V. I. to find out the identity of her father; what should have been a relatively simple missing-persons inquiry spirals into something much bigger involving Chicago aldermen, insurance fraud, and the suppression of medical hazards at a chemical factory. V. I.'s abiding love and respect for Lotty is seen when the detective helps to exonerate Lotty when she is charged with murder in the short story "The Case of the Pietro Andromache"; in *Total Recall*, V. I.'s loyalty to her friend is tested to the limits when Lotty disappears and V. I. tracks her to Europe. Conversely in *Guardian Angel*, Lotty's affection and regard for V. I. is severely strained when they swap cars at V. I.'s request with the result that Lotty suffers a beating when she is mistaken for her friend. Vic and Lotty suffer a great emotional rift in this novel when Lotty draws away from her friend for some time after the physical injuries heal. More of Lotty's back story emerges in the 2013 *Critical Mass*; the bond between V. I. and Lotty deepens when they journey to Vienna to discover a crucial document that was hidden near Lotty's childhood apartment just before the war. Aunt Elena's problems with housing, money, and alcohol dominate the proceedings in *Burn Marks*; V. I. is both repelled by and feels compassion for her indigent relative. V. I. is usually emotionally involved, for better or worse, in most of the cases she undertakes. In this sense, both families and friendships can prove dangerous. When Murray betrays her in *Hard Time* by writing negatively about her in the press, V. I. is distraught.

## GEN (Global Entertainment Network)

V. I.'s friend and sometime lover Murray Ryerson ends up working for the media conglomerate GEN, which bears a passing resemblance to the Fox media corporation, after his newspaper is purchased by GEN and his career as an investigative journalist takes a downturn in *Hard Time*. The Global Cable section of GEN offers an avenue for Murray to reinvent himself as a TV reporter on its national cable news show with its scroll across the top of the screen "*GENuine News, No Substitutes Allowed!*" (BD 39, emphasis in original). It is a painful process, chronicled in *Hard Time* and referred to again in the later *Breakdown*. By the time of the events in *Breakdown*, the lead cable news show is hosted by Wade Lawlor, a "local boy made national superstar" (27) whose visible right-wing politics and self-regard make V. I. suspicious of him and worried for Murray; he tells her his job is not "so secure that I can dis the network's golden goose" (31). Later in the novel Murray has the scoop of a lifetime when he goes on air with a program titled *Chicago's Own Nancy Drew* in which he and V. I. expose Lawlor for his part in a past murder. Murray's reward for the scoop—"one that gave Global the best viewer rating they'd ever had" (428)—is an email from a GEN executive firing him, unable to "forgive Murray for killing his golden-egg layer" (428).

## "George Eliot's *The Mill on the Floss*: Book of a Lifetime by Sara Paretsky" (2014)

This personal memoir, written for the *Independent* (London) newspaper, discusses George Eliot's portrayal of the sibling bond in her famous novel; Paretsky writes that Eliot "understood that relationship in a way no other writer ever has" and confesses that her own older brother's "judgment of me and my work still matters more to me than that of most people."

## *Ghost Country* (1998)

Paretsky's 13th book and her first venture away from the successful V. I. private-eye series is set in Chicago, uses multiple narrative voices, and has affinities with the mode of magical realism. The background is a contemporary Chicago, with locations ranging from Gold Coast housing to psychiatric hospitals to street-living in the subterranean depths under Wacker Drive. The story unfolds around four characters who are in various ways marginalized from mainstream society. Each of them—the troubled adolescent from a privileged family, the aging alcoholic opera diva, the homeless woman living on the streets, and the hard-pressed psychiatry resident—is struggling with self-doubt. They all long for a miracle that will change their personal circumstances and the social/economic/familial structures that constrain them. They are drawn together by some transformative experiences set in motion by another homeless (and mute) woman named Starr, who is an enigmatic, silent, and charismatic presence in the novel. In a message to readers, published on her Web site, Paretsky explains how, in this book, she imagines "the sacred and the dispossessed, meeting on the streets … real people whose lives have unravelled" and whose lives are changed by the mysterious, and possibly magical, Starr." Variously described as belonging to the school of magical realism or "a feminist parable" (L. Wilson 115), the novel is episodic in structure, with the story narrated through the different points of view of the teenage Mara, the singer Louisa, and the idealistic young medic Hector. The contrasting Chicago locations include a shelter for homeless women; the luxury apartment of a wealthy doctor and his two daughters; the hospital where Hector tries to balance budget constraints with needy patients; and the Wall, a site underneath a Michigan Avenue hotel where crowds gather to see visions of the Virgin Mary in the reddish liquid staining the bricks. Hector and Mara, as well as Mara's sister, Harriet, regain a sense of self and inner strength by the end of the novel, each of them having to re-evaluate their ideas about family, love, faith, duty, and compassion in the modern world. In a larger sense, the women's stories suggest the theme Paretsky often visits in her mystery fiction, and refers to in *Writing in an Age of Silence*; that is, the struggle to express female identity and voice. In the epigraph, Paretsky dedicates the novel to "Enheduanna [a Sumerian poet], and All Poets Missing in Action."

Emily Melton's *Booklist* review describes the novel as "rich, astonishing, and affecting," noting that "Paretsky deserves rave reviews for taking a huge risk and doing so with amazing success" (1045). Writing for the *Chicago Tribune*, Dick Adler praised Paretsky for an "imaginative and intensely moving non-mystery novel that courageously takes her into Willa Cather territory" ("Non-Mystery Novel"). However, reviewer Helen Benedict, in the *Women's Review of Books*, was disappointed that the fable-like story did not work (28). *Publishers Weekly* concurred, describing it as a "fable that ... defies credibility" (Rev. of *Ghost Country* 67). In an interview with Nicholas Basbanes, Paretsky acknowledged the risk she took in "stepping away from her bread-and-butter character," telling him, "[I]t's always pretty frightening to leave something that has been so successful for you, but I felt I needed some time away from V. I. for awhile" (3B).

### "Grace Notes" (1995)

The short story "Grace Notes," which features V. I., was written for the *Windy City Blues* collection (published as *V. I. for Short* in the United Kingdom). The plot develops around V. I.'s discovery of previously unknown Italian relatives and a search for a long-lost music score that may have been written by her great-grandmother and that was possibly in the possession of V. I.'s mother, Gabriella. V. I.'s vulnerable spot has always been Gabriella, "who died of cancer in 1968 at the age of forty-six" (WCB 11). The adult V. I. is still grieving for her mother, so when a long-lost Italian cousin from Gabriella's family turns up in Chicago eager to make family connections and to trace the libretto, V. I. welcomes the debonair and convincing Vico. In the course of discovering Vico's mercenary motives and the real story behind the missing score written by "Marianne Martines ... an eighteenth-century Viennese composer" (ibid., 8) and annotated by

Mozart, V. I. comes across a letter from her mother. Dated "the 30th of October 1967, her last birthday" (ibid., 9), the letter to V. I. has been hidden in an olivewood box that she inherited when her mother died. The letter outlines the provenance of the music score and Gabriella's wishes about what should be done with it. Her closing words to V. I. echo the guidelines by which she has raised her only child: "Always strive for justice, never accept the second-rate in yourself, my darling" (ibid., 0). In a review for the *New York Times*, Josh Rubins notes that although the story "begins promisingly ... the bittersweet family material gives way to routine showdowns with cartoonish bad guys" (24). The story fills in details of Gabriella's family history in the Tuscan village Pitigliano, where Gabriella was born "on October 30, 1921" (VIFS ed. 202). V. I. learns that her Italian grandmother, Nonna Laura, "converted to Judaism" so she could marry "Gabriella's father, Grandpa Matthias" (VIFS ed. 204). Further she discovers that her "grandmother died in Auschwitz when the Italian Jews were rounded up in 1944. Then, my grandfather ... was liberated ... and was sent to a Jewish-run sanatorium in Turin" (ibid., 04). The story includes a character named "Isabel Thompson, an authority on rare music from the Newberry Library" (WCB ed. 58) in honor of Paretsky's long-standing friend of the same name from their time together as University of Chicago students.

### Graham, Darraugh

A wealthy Chicagoan who "has been with me almost since the day I opened my agency" (BL 4), Darraugh Graham is one of V. I.'s steady clients. His company, Continental United, has premises in the Loop; V. I. describes him as "a wintry, distant man" (BL 4). Because he provides her with regular work doing financial background checks for his business interests, V. I. usually goes along with his sometimes imperious calls on her to help with various family issues. Bumping into Darraugh in a Loop office building, V. I. reminds herself, "I was lucky that Darraugh continued to come to me, instead of turning all his business over to one of the big outfits

... it behoves me to pay attention to his private chitchat" (HT 34). Darraugh is a widower with a son, Ken, who features as a minor character in *Tunnel Vision*; Darraugh prevails on V. I. to find Ken a community service placement to offset his computer hacking activities that have resulted in a temporary suspension from his studies at Harvard—"where our family has gone for two hundred years" (TV 17), as Darraugh reminds his son. V. I. reluctantly agrees to take Ken on as a computer assistant. His skills prove useful in one of her cases; and when he develops an unwelcome crush on her, the subsequent sparring between them adds a new dimension to V. I.'s sharp tongue. Darraugh's nonagenarian mother, Geraldine, appears in *Blacklist* when Darraugh summons V. I. to look into the mysterious lights seen by Geraldine in the abandoned family mansion next door to her gated senior residence. Darraugh comes from a family with position, privilege, and power. A tragic episode in his family history comes to light in *Blacklist* when V. I.'s investigations turns up secrets that Darraugh does not want revealed; he threatens V. I. "in a way that left me wondering whether I would or could ever work for you again," she tells him (BL 405). They come dangerously close to an affair at the end of this novel, but V. I. realizes "it was only loneliness, mine as well as his, that was drawing us together.... I think he understood.... I think we parted on good terms" (406).

**See also *Blacklist*; *Tunnel Vision***

## "The Great Tetsuji" (1994)

This short story was first published in an anthology from the British Crime Writers Association; the collection was published the following year by St. Martin's Press in the United States. It takes the form of a parable about rational philosopher Marcus Aurelius whose desire to become a first-rank Go player (the ancient Chinese board game) becomes an obsession and causes him to lose his job, his friends, and his home. When his friend, Sara, beseeches him to seek help from "a diviner or a seer, who can help cure you of this obsession" (111), Marcus consults the magician Johannes Michaelensis. The magician helps Marcus realize his wish to "commune with the great Tetsuji ... to speak to his spirit beyond the grave ... [to know] the secret from him of how to become sho-dan [a master of Go]" (113). Marcus learns to look beyond the moves and the strategies "he had studied so diligently" to see "the shape of the game which lay behind it" (114). After the encounter with the magician, Marcus's obsession vanishes, and he calls "on Sara on his way home and ask[s] her to eat lunch with him" (115). The next time he plays Go, he "was seized with a great joy ... and played to the shape of the game" (115).

This is the second of two published short stories by Paretsky that focus on the game Go; it is likely they were inspired by her professor husband's love of the game.

**See also "The Takamoku Joseki"**

## *Guardian Angel* (1992)

"I'm a sore loser" (161).

Seventh in the V. I. Warshawski series, *Guardian Angel* involves debt-financing, shady banking, pension funds, and junk bonds. Mary Beard's TLS review describes the book as "a typical tale of the 1990s, an account of rottenness at the heart of the new elite" (21). The novel raises questions about guardianship of the elderly and how city and county emergency services respond to the needs of an aging population; the theme of friendship also runs through the story with V. I. reflecting on and elaborating her code of friendship. There are major fractures with her friend, Dr. Lotty Herschel, and her lawyer, Freeman Carter, as well as a minor fracas with her journalist pal Murray Ryerson. She and policeman Conrad Rawlings begin a tentative affair, to the consternation of neighbor Mr. Contreras and Conrad's family who disapprove of relationships that cross racial boundaries. V. I.'s ex-husband, Dick Yarborough, also features in the novel; he and his law firm have a great deal to hide.

In a subtle genre twist, the novel opens not with death but with birth. Peppy, the golden retriever shared by V. I. with her downstairs neighbor, gives birth to eight pups in Mr.

**New York Times**
WEDNESDAY, MARCH 11, 1992

**CLINTON TAKES FLORIDA E
SURVEYS SHOW SWEEP OF
PROTEST VOTES STILL D**

Gov. Bill Clinton and his wife, Hillary, arriving yesterday in Chicago to carry his campaign to the Midwest.

*Super Tuesday Transforms Campaign*

*A Surge by Clinton
Endangers Tsongas*

**Presidential candidate Bill Clinton on the primary campaign trail with a copy of Paretsky's *Guardian Angel*. *New York Times*, March 11, 1992. Clipping from Paretsky Papers Newberry archive (Box V1 of 7, 5.2000 Addition). Photograph by Linda Erf Swift.**

Contreras's living room. It is Peppy, and not a lover, whose "hot kisses" drag V. I. from "deep sleep to the edge of consciousness" (1) at 5:30 a.m. on the June day that she has the litter. On the eve of a book tour to promote *Guardian Angel*, Paretsky commented to interviewer Susan Ferraro, "I think that's the closest V. I. will get to motherhood" (23). The litter is the result of an accidental mating between the golden retriever Peppy and black labrador Bruce; the latter belongs to neighbor Hattie Frizell, an irascible woman in her 80s who lives on her own with five large dogs. When she is hospitalized after a

fall, her yuppie lawyer neighbors—determined to gentrify the neighborhood and critical of her ramshackle house and lifestyle—contrive an appointment as Mrs. Frizell's legal guardians and have her five noisy dogs euthanized. V. I. is puzzled about their interest in the old woman's affairs. Mr. Contreras, meanwhile, is worried about the disappearance of his old comrade Mitch Kruger, who has hinted that there is something suspicious about the engine-making company Diamond Head, where he and Mr. Contreras once worked. He prevails on Vic to investigate. When Mitch's body is pulled out of the Sanitary Canal near Diamond Head, V. I. and Mr. Contreras are convinced it is more than an accident involving an elderly drunk. Vic's investigations into Mitch's death and her concerns about the frail Mrs. Frizzel's affairs lead her into some murky connections between her ex-husband's law firm, Dick Yarborough's current father-in-law, and the shady uses of Diamond Head's pension fund. In an attempt to avoid the guns-for-hire who are tailing her, V. I. asks Lotty to swap cars for a day. The result is catastrophic: Lotty is attacked and badly beaten when she is mistaken for V. I. Lotty is slow to recover from the physical and mental trauma, and a deep rift develops between the two close friends. In the meantime, V. I.'s life is endangered when she visits the Diamond Head factory seeking information—about to be crushed by a factory crane, she ends up in the Sanitary Canal. A subsequent attempt on her life occurs when she is nearly run down by a warehouse truck near the Stevenson expressway; she survives by jumping from her car, but her pursuer is not so lucky. From a pylon underneath the exit ramp, she watches as "a starburst the color of blood decorated the truck's windshield" and reflects, "it seemed so queer that people were rushing to and fro above me, utterly oblivious of the violence down here. The world should have paused a moment to catch its breath, make some acknowledgment" (349).

The novel is infused with a sense of weariness and loss; there is an emphasis on V. I.'s status as a loner and on her fear of abandonment by her loved ones. Mr. Contreras is suffering over the unexplained death of his old friend Mitch who "kind of outdrank his [pension]" and who did not have Mr. Contreras's "luck at the track" (26, 27). V. I. and another neighbor feel guilty that they were unable to prevent the deaths of Mrs. Frizell's beloved dogs. The detective, haunted by the death of her mother when she was 15, is still subject to "nights [where] I wake up missing her so much that a physical pain sucks at my diaphragm" (85). She is afraid she will lose Lotty as well. Her worries and exhaustion overwhelm her at times; at the end of a particularly trying day, she longs for "some remote mountainside, for snow and a sense of perfect peace" (113). There is considerable strain between V. I. and Carter, who leaves his old firm of Crawford, Mead when it goes aggressively up-market as "Crawford, Mead, Wilton, and Dunwhittie ... in a new building on LaSalle" (103–04). Carter sets up his own practice. There is a major misunderstanding between Carter and V. I. over the Diamond Head pension fund and Dick's involvement in it. Carter, who had some inkling about the illicit activities of his old firm and Dick's probable culpability, but who has also been critical of V. I.'s efforts to trace paper trails and computer records at the firm, eventually apologizes to Vic. He leaves the question of their continuing professional relationship open, suggesting that she take her time "to decide whether you want me to work for you in the future or not" (357).

On another front, the long association between Lotty and Carol Alvarado, "her nurse and right arm at the clinic" (12), becomes strained when Carol wants to quit her clinic job to look after a distant relative with AIDS; Lotty objects to Carol's sense of family duty and quarrels with both Max and V. I. over the matter.

Aspects of society's unexamined racism, sexism, and ageism also pervade the novel. When V. I. is referred to as "babe" and "the girl" by a morgue attendant, she responds by addressing him as "sugar" (108). The 77-year-old Mr. Contreras is addressed as "boy" (108) and "old man" (107); and the white sheriff's deputy mutters "jigaboo" (109) when the black policeman Terry Finchley, "a violent crimes detective from Area One" (108), turns up at the county morgue. The slurs have a shock value because they emerge so casually, and yet deliberately, from a range of characters whose venom is palpable. In a touchy meeting with Milt Chamfers, the plant manager at the factory where Mitch Kruger used to work, Chamfers tries to diminish Vic by addressing her as "Nancy Drew" (121). V. I.'s efforts to resolve the mystery of Mitch's death and to sort out Mrs. Frizell's affairs eventually pay off when she sees that the two cases are connected through several people associated with her ex-husband's law firm. She patiently unpicks the complex web of corporate white-collar crime and faces down those responsible. She "plea bargains" the greedy Picheas into resigning their illegally acquired "guardianship of Mrs. Frizell" (362) who is "making real progress" (360) in the hospital. The fraudulent pension reversion scheme that had been set up for employees at Diamond Head and that Mitch had planned to use to blackmail his former employer is revealed when V. I. discovers that both her ex-husband and his father-in-law have positions on the Diamond Head board. "At the heart of the mystery," reviewer Vincent Patrick writes, are "illicit activities [at] Diamond Head ... pension-fund looting, the evasion of Justice Department decrees and the manipulation of junk bonds" (45). V. I. traces all of this "through paper trails and computer records guarded closely" (ibid.) by the upscale law firm to which Carter belonged and in which V. I.'s ex-husband is a partner. The disgraced Dick confesses his misdeeds and his regrets to V. I. before he departs on a six-month leave of absence. Another piece of V. I.'s past falls into place when Dick asks her, "We had some good times together, didn't we, Vic? It wasn't all fighting and contempt, was it?" (367). Because she remembers, "Dick going with me every weekend to stay with my dad when Tony was dying," she replies, with uncharacteristic gentleness, "We had some important times together" (367). Mr. Contreras persuades V. I. that they should keep one of Peppy's puppies; he chooses "an all-gold male with two black ears [and] insisted on naming it Mitch" (368). V. I. and Conrad become closer, and their affair starts at the end of the novel when V. I. admits "an erotic spark had always jumped between us" (356). Mr. Contreras takes great exception to this development, confessing to his own "prejudice" and his worries about "how ugly people can be in this town" (356). Conrad indicates his own worries about his relationship with V. I. when he points out to her: "you have to keep everyone around you on pins and needles…. So guys like me, or even the old man downstairs, don't get enough of a hold on you to leave you in the lurch" (370). The novel closes with an introspective V. I. in Conrad's embrace, but shivering "in the summer air" (370). Throughout the novel V. I. comments on the ethics and responsibilities of friendship. Trying to mend matters with Lotty, the detective says, "[T]he longer Lotty and I went without speaking, the harder it was going to be to get back together" (291–92). In a discussion with Murray about the case, V. I. keeps an important piece of information to herself on the grounds that "Murray hadn't been supportive enough lately to get a free blue-plate special" (291). When she and Mr. Contreras set out on a nerve-wracking plan to break into a law firm's office, V. I. takes a moment to "reflect on how evil I'd been all those times I'd left my neighbor pacing the floor unhappily at night while I jumped from gantries" (318).

Frances Fyfield's appreciation in a limited edition of this novel comments on the extent to which this series character is, in the hands of her author, "expanding the range of her sympathies and her moods … becom[ing] ever more powerful and brittle" (vi). The book is dedicated to Matt and Eve (younger Paretsky family members) with a quote from W. B. Yeats's poem "The Wind Among the Reeds." A photograph of then-candidate Bill Clinton exiting an airplane with the book cover clearly visible under his arm gave the novel and the author some unexpected publicity. In 1993 the novel won the German Crime Writers Association Marlowe Award.

## Hammett, Dashiell *see* "Long Shadow of the Falcon"; "The Maltese Cat"

### Hard Time (1999)

"'Women can be detectives, and I am one,' I announced" (45).

After a gap of five years, during which Paretsky published the standalone *Ghost Country*, V. I. made her ninth appearance in a suspenseful case involving jail time for the detective. Halfway through the story, V. I. is arrested, foregoes bail, and spends a harrowing month locked up in the fictional Coolis Prison outside of Chicago. While struggling to hold on to her sanity and personal safety behind bars, the detective learns a great deal about conditions in women's prisons, including the sweatshop labor system and human rights violations. The title puns on the slang for doing a term in prison and also suggests an homage to Charles Dickens's crusading Victorian novel *Hard Times*. "Paretsky's rage was ignited by the privatization of America's prisons and the potential this new system creates for abuse and exploitation," suggests S. J. Rozan's review (44).

The novel hits the topical theme of women in prison, tackles the issue of aging in a society and culture that values female youth and beauty, explores the ethics of corporate news conglomerates, and demonstrates the author's emerging preoccupation with a more contemplative side of V. I.'s persona. In addition to enduring the everyday humiliations and the ever-present dangers of sexual and physical assault that characterize the lives of women prisoners, the detective is betrayed by her old buddy, investigative reporter Murray Ryerson, who smears her character in a broadcast news piece.

The story starts late one night in a dark, deserted Chicago neighborhood. V. I. is at the wheel of her beloved Trans Am—now "ten, with the dents and glitches to prove it,

## Meet the author!
# SARA PARETSKY

when she visits to read from
and talk about her latest
mystery

# HARD TIME
## A V.I. WARSHAWSKI NOVEL

• • • • • • • • • • • • • • • • • •

## WEDNESDAY, OCTOBER 13
## 7:30 P.M.

**BORDERS**
BOOKS • MUSIC • CAFE

Baileys Crossroads, Virginia
5871 Crossroads Center Way, on Rt. 7
at Columbia Pike • 703-998-0404

**Original publicity for meet-the-author book-store event while Paretsky is on the road promoting *Hard Time*.**

but it still hugged corners like a python" (12)—taking Mary Louise Neely and her foster daughter, Emily Messenger, home after a media bash at the Golden Glow bar. The party honored Hollywood celebrity Lacey Dowell, who has returned to her native Chicago after "a series of horror flicks about a medieval woman who supposedly died in defense of her chastity" (3). When V. I. swerves to avoid hitting something in the road, she and Mary Louise discover a young woman who is barely breathing. The victim later dies in the hospital, and an aggressive pair of investigating police officers try to pin homicide and drunk driving on V. I. Anxious to clear herself of the hit-and-run charge, V. I. begins to investigate the woman's circumstances and the events leading to her death. It is unusual for the detective to take up a case on her own behalf rather than one at the behest of a relative, friend, or client; and V. I. is wary about this one, reminding herself of a vow she'd made "a few years back to stop diving into other people's wrecks: I only got battered on the spars without getting thanks—or payment" (33). But having acted as a Good Samaritan when she stopped to help the accident victim and then becoming the target of the police investigation, Vic cannot turn her back on the stranger's story. She discovers that Nicola Aguinaldo was an undocumented Filipina immigrant on the run from the newly built women's prison, Coolis, where she was doing time for stealing from her wealthy employers, the Baladine family. Robert Baladine owns Carniface Security, a billion-dollar firm that operates state prisons; he and his family live in one of Chicago's ritziest suburbs. Robbie, Baladine's troubled son who is at odds with his ruthless parents and his competitive siblings, is a familiar Paretsky construct—the youngster whose values and conscience make him or her a misfit in their own family. V. I. is puzzled about the connection among Aguinaldo, the Baladines, and the Coolis prison—and cannot figure out why Aguinaldo would have been wearing a promotional Lacey Dowell T-shirt and why it looked like she had taken a beating when Vic finds her in the street. In the meantime, V. I. is concerned about changes in the media industries and the effect on Murray, who is reinventing himself as a TV reporter. Murray seems to have secured himself a future, but at the expense, V. I. fears, of his scruples and his sharp investigative skills. Skimming the morning edition of the *Herald-Star*, Murray's former employer that has been acquired by the Global conglomerate, V. I. complains to herself: "First the paper spends four days hyping Global's new television network. Then the network makes its debut. Then they write up what they showed on television. It made a neat loop, but was it news?" (27). Themes of aging and its attendant decline in physical agility and stamina permeate the novel, as well as an understanding that one must move with the times. Murray and his newspaper are on the scrap heap; he has to adapt to reality if he is to have a career in the future. Technology is changing V. I.'s work of private investigation. No longer clinging to her mother's Olivetti typewriter and less reliant on her long-suffering answering service, V. I. is now fully accessorized with networked computer systems, a palm pilot, and a mobile phone. In prison, her "wrist camera" (317) enables her to take pictures of the evidence she needs to document sweatshop conditions. When cocaine is planted in her office, and she is targeted with threats from the powerful Baladine, V. I. knows she is getting close to some uncomfortable truths. When Robbie turns up on her doorstep as a runaway, V. I. is arrested on the charge of kidnapping him and ends up in Coolis awaiting bail. Realizing she is in the best possible place to continue the Aguinaldo investigation, V. I. foregoes bail and endures a harrowing month of incarceration. Prison is unfamiliar territory for V. I.—she suffers from isolation, loneliness, and the ever-present threat of violence and sexual assault from vindictive guards, corrupt wardens, and other prisoners. Increasingly unnerved and disoriented, she becomes pensive about her long-deceased mother, a love affair that has ended, and her beloved friend Dr. Lotty Herschel, to whom she later writes a tender letter. As well as witnessing the systemic brutality endured by the prisoners in the Coolis system, V. I. is threatened and beaten herself. When her untreated injuries endanger her life, she is smuggled out of prison by the sadistic corrections officers who beat her and is left to die on a Chicago roadside. Recovering later at an institute for torture victims, V. I. struggles to regain her confidence and trust in people, finding herself "feeling unbearably helpless, as I had in Coolis … and moving away as fast as I could, my legs wobbly, as if I expected to be hit again with fifty thousand volts of electricity" (327). The *Publishers Weekly* review notes how "Paretsky weaves a thread of loss throughout this journey to hell and back" (55). The aftereffects of her time in prison haunt her when she tries to get back to work and finds herself feeling "dull and drained…. [T]here were still too many nights I dreaded going to sleep because of the dreams that lay on the other side" (379). Morrell, the journalist and human-rights activist who becomes V. I.'s new love interest, makes a modest debut in this novel as a man "who's writing a book about people who ran away from jail" (44). He helps with the investigation into the Aguinaldo story and comforts V. I. at the end of the novel when she is worried about loose ends, assuring her, "You can't save everyone or fix every broken part of this planet. But you do more than most" (385). When V. I. takes temporary refuge at Father Lou's Catholic rectory, the priest who is "a local legend" (375), and the detective strike up an unlikely friendship. Father Lou asks V. I. to assist at Mass one morning, and to her surprise, she finds herself "reading the lesson … from the book of Job about how God desires humans to see the light" (347). Father Lou turns up again in a small role in the later *Blacklist*.

There is a noticeably more reflective side to V. I. emerging in this novel; even after she leaves the sanctuary of the rectory and returns home, she tells the reader: "for some reason I found myself getting up nearly every day and driving over to St. Remigio's for the six o'clock mass" (377). She thinks twice about her desire for revenge on Robert Baladine, discussing the matter with Father Lou. These developments seem to signal some inner changes in the detective's ways of thinking and understanding herself in relation to the world around her. In the end, her revenge takes the form of a video/slide presentation she compiles with material from Baladine's own security cameras. Assisted by Morrell, V. I. calls a press conference and screens the evidence she has collected to substantiate her version of events, demonstrating the links among Carniface Securities, Global Entertainment and their spin-off products, Coolis Prison, and Aguinaldo's death.

V. I.'s beloved Trans-Am never recovers from the damage done to it when V. I. stops to help Aguinaldo. Mr. Contreras undertakes the project of finding her an affordable replacement, and by the end of the novel, V. I.'s fantasy of owning a Jaguar gives way to a "late-model green Mustang" (383), a "car for a working detective who has to use her wheels in the grime of Chicago" (384). The money for the car comes from the check for "forty thousand dollars" (HT 384) that Lacey gives V. I. as a thank you for finding out who had killed her friend, Frenada, in the course of the Aguinaldo case. Even though V. I. is uneasy knowing that the money was "made from T-shirts sewn by women in prisons here or abroad," she does not reject it, seeming to accept Morrell's reassurances that "if Lacey's money comes in part from sweatships, you still brought some relief to women in prison here in Illinois" (HT 385). The novel concludes on a characteristically ambivalent note, with V. I. registering that her efforts have brought some measure of justice into play and that she has made a difference in some people's lives even though the bigger picture remains stubbornly the same.

As one reviewer notes, "regular characters are supposed to change, but not that much. The presence in the book of real jeopardy and real betrayal makes *Hard Time* a good series thriller" (Kaveney 21). A *Sunday Times* (London) review by John Dugdale claims the novel "reaffirms Paretsky's Dickensian conception of the genre as investigative journalism plus thrills, in a powerful attack on private jails" (44). Val McDermid, writing in the *Sunday Express* (London), finds the novel "a compulsive read, revealing its author at her most passionate ... the contrast between prison life and the false glamour of the entertainment industry alone is worth the cover

price" (60). A *Daily Mail* (London) review says the author's "most impressive creation is the women's prison of Coolis, where casual exploitation and sexual harassment are the norm ... the crusading seems entirely justified, and adds to rather than detracts from the momentum of the story" (Brett 60). In a 2000 interview, Paretsky told Jane Ammeson the idea for *Hard Time* "was suggested by a sister-in-law of mine who [told] me that 20 years ago, no town wanted a prison built in it. Now towns bid with each other to have prisons ... we incarcerate a greater percentage of our population than any other country in the world" ("Fifth" 51). Stephanie Merritt's *Observer* interview and review describes the novel as "a harrowing read in places, particularly in her exposure of the way women prisoners are treated" (13). Paretsky told Merritt of her concern about "the way government is for sale these days, and the massive amounts of money companies can spend to buy the legislation they want. So if you don't have an independent press that is really diligent there's no way that abuses will be exposed or people called to account" (ibid., 13).

## *Hardball* (2009)

> "I could curb my pit bull personality for three more minutes" (180).

The 13th V. I. novel is an ambitious work that goes deep into the heart of racism as part of the American national identity. It evokes the turbulent events of summer 1966 in Chicago when Dr. Martin Luther King was in town leading a housing desegregation movement. Hostile white, working-class communities took to the streets provoking riots and bloodshed; the Chicago police force was ineffective in keeping the public order. The novel is foreshadowed in Paretsky's short story "A Family Sunday in the Park," published in the 2007 anthology *Sisters on the Case*, in which a young, headstrong V. I. (10-year-old "Tori") rushes into the mayhem of the 1966 protest march to Marquette Park, where the Chicago police were unwillingly protecting the peaceful black marchers. The novel's titular source (and double-entendre) is the 40-year-old baseball autographed by Chicago White Sox second-baseman Nellie

Fox that turns up in the belongings of V. I.'s deceased father, Tony Warshawski. The peculiar holes in the surface of the ball and the fact that Tony was a diehard Cubs fan like his daughter hint at some mysterious circumstances attaching to Tony's possession of the object.

V. I., age 50 in this novel, is still coping with the end of her affair with the journalist Morrell (their breakup is recounted in chapter 3). Two new series characters make their debut in *Hardball*: the lively Petra (the college-age daughter of Peter Warshawski, V. I.'s uncle—the same Peter who was so unhelpful to his sister, Elena, in the earlier *Burn Marks*—) and the musician Jake Thibaut who moves into the apartment next door and is a potential love interest. Petra is the classic millennial, navigating her way in the world via a cellphone and social media sites. She arrives in Chicago to work on the charismatic Brian Krumas's campaign for a Senate seat. Her curiosity about family history both annoys and intrigues Vic, whose patience is often worn thin by Petra's enthusiasm.

The plot involves torture of black suspects in police custody that extends back to the 1960s, with collusion between the police and Chicago politicians keeping the secret safe. Hired by the elderly African American sisters Miss Claudia and Miss Ella to find Lamont Gadsden, the missing son of Miss Ella, V. I. is soon delving into a disappearance that might be linked to the murder of a young black protester marching with Dr. King in summer 1966; she also digs up a secret about her late father, Tony, a city-beat cop idolized by V. I. The search for Lamont, who was last seen in 1967, leads V. I. to her father's colleagues in the Chicago police force. They send her to imprisoned Anaconda gang leader Johnny Merton, who V. I. had once represented in her public defender days. He provides information that leads V. I. to Steve Sawyer; he and Lamont served as bodyguards for Dr. King in 1966. Digging deeper into the civil rights protests in Chicago, V. I. discovers that black activist Harmony Newsome was killed when a peaceful march in support of integrated housing turned into a riot in Marquette Park after the local whites at-

tacked the march. V. I. remembers that her aunt, Marie, was "one of the crowd of furious St. Czeslaw parishioners who vowed to do everything they could to show King and the other agitators he'd brought with him that they should stay in Mississippi or Georgia where they belonged" (124). Looking for Harmony's killer, the police swept up all the young black men providing protection for Dr. King. Steve is set up by the police to take the rap; he eventually confesses and serves 40 years in prison. V. I. learns that Lamont was probably at the march where Harmony was murdered but disappeared before he could present evidence that would exonerate Steve. To V. I.'s horror, she learns that her father arrested Steve. Also there was Tony's brother, Peter, with a few of his buddies from the hostile white neighborhood. When Petra is kidnapped (after gossiping online about V. I.'s investigations), the private eye realizes she must be on the trail of things that no one wants revealed. Things escalate with a final showdown revealing the shameful sequence of events that led to the framing of Steve and the disappearance of Lamont. The truth about Harmony's death is closer to home than even V. I. suspects; both she and Petra suffer from V. I.'s discoveries about their fathers' actions and culpabilities all those years ago. Petra's relationship with her father is fractured when his role in the events of that day is revealed, and he is arrested. Betty Webb's 2010 review for *Mystery Scene* notes that "Petra combines innocence and idealism with a sense of entitlement; Johnny 'The Hammer' Merton is a ruthless gangbanger whose idealism … matched Petra's" (Web).

V. I. uses increasingly sophisticated technology on this case to track down the past, whereas the more techno-savvy, but gullible and unsuspecting, Petra is glued to her cellphone night and day with no thought of the possible consequences of posting on Facebook pages. Their various uses of the Web mirror the way in which the plot shows how people's actions can be tracked by police and other authorities with access to social media networks. V. I. suffers considerable confusion and pain over her past—both what she knows and what she imagines. V. I.'s introspection—some of it triggered by her ambivalence about the young, vibrant Petra and some by her sadness after the breakup with Morrell—lends the story depth. She asks herself some hard questions. Remembering a belligerent childhood argument with her grandmother, V. I. wonders if her own trait of self-righteousness is "what made it hard for me to live with someone else? Was it what Mr. Contreras had just accused me of: that, in my book, I was always the only one who knew anything?" (169). Later, she thinks, with regret, "of the many times I let my temper get the best of me, turning difficult situations into impossible ones" (178). In the hospital recovering from serious burns she has suffered in a vain attempt to save the life of a witness she was interviewing when a fire bomb is lobbed through the window, the detective gives into more doubts about her personality: "Did I bring destruction to everyone around me?" (227). Bobby Mallory also has an introspective time in this novel following a police department investigation into racist torture of suspects that shows "active collusion up and down the chain of command" (433); Eileen Mallory tells V. I. "how betrayed [Bobby] felt by the relentless revelations of abuse" on the force (ibid.). Paretsky's characteristic music motif is prominent in *Hardball*. The opening chapters have V. I. musing over her recent visit to Italy in search of her mother's roots and tracing her early training as a singer. The closing chapter marks the beginning of her affair with Jake; they listen to a remastered tape recording of her mother singing an aria by Mozart.

Paretsky experiments with narrative voice in this novel, departing from the detective's characteristic first-person narration in two short sections titled "In the Detective's Absence I and II." These two interludes are set in Lionsgate Manor, the assisted living facility of Miss Claudia and Miss Ella. The point of view is Miss Ella's, as she sits with and talks to her bedridden sister, suffering from the after effects of a stroke: "sometimes Ella felt herself slipping back in time … to when she was five and Claudia was the darling baby of the block … so cooed over in church that Ella would steal Claudia's dolly…. [P]ure

meanness. She knew it then and she knew it now" (87–88). The passages characterize the still-fractious relationship between the sisters, document some of the indignities and frailties of old age, and report on the progress made by V. I. in finding Lamont.

An early draft of the novel drew an enthusiastic response from one of Paretsky's editors: "The way the story is framed and the way the plot unspools is fantastic; I love the mixture of urban and family history, the deep presence of long-held secrets, the way the mystery … builds to a dramatic crescendo before all is revealed." (Handwritten letter to Paretsky, signed "Chris," 2.15.09, in Sara Paretsky Papers-Addition, Accession 2012–12, Box 20 ("Publicity") of 22, Newberry Library, accessed October 2012). Marilyn Stasio's 2009 review notes that "there's a real sting to both the anger of a black man who took care of a friend beaten to insensibility by racist cops and the grief of an old white woman displaced from her family home. Voices like these can ring in your ears…" (22). A *Spectator* (London) review observes how "the lost idealism of the 1960s provides a haunting backdrop … the recurring characters continue to develop and engage the reader … [and] moral intelligence informs the writing" (A. Taylor 36). The *Kirkus* review describes the novel as "a tormented, many-layered tale that seems to have been dug out of Chicago history with a pickaxe" (15).

## Hard-Boiled Subgenre

Hallmarks of the hard-boiled mode include the first-person narrative voice with its characteristic wise-cracking humor, the tough and cynical detective figure, a gritty urban locale, and violent action. Stereotypes and clichés abound in this area of popular fiction, making it a narrative form easy to imitate yet one with elasticity open to subversion and innovation. Historically male authors and their sharp-talking, trigger-happy detectives such as Race Williams, Philip Marlowe, and the Continental Op dominated the hard-boiled subgenre. As Priscilla Walton points out, the "male-focus and male-oriented structure of early hard-boiled detective fiction … [portrays] a world in which … men were men, and women were dangerous" ("Form" 128). Female characters were largely confined to the roles of vamp, femme fatale, or victim with the attendant expectation of temptation, betrayal, and violence. Women characters often caused trouble, but rarely solved it. The underlying misogyny of the form has been much discussed by contemporary genre scholars such as Sally Munt, Manina Jones and Priscilla Walton, Scott Christianson, Glenwood Irons, and many others. John Cawelti's early study of formula fiction pointed to how "the intense masculinity of the hard-boiled detective is in part a symbolic denial and protective coloration against complex sexual and status anxieties focusing on women" (154). Anne Cranny-Francis's discussion of feminist popular fiction locates the endemic violence of the hard-boiled mode as "largely an expression of misogyny, a fictional recompense to the conservative male reader for the growing autonomy of women in the real world" (168). Although there is a long history of fictional female detectives dating from the nineteenth century in both American and British crime fiction, the role of the private eye was not significantly imagined as a suitable job for a woman in fiction until the late 1970s and early 1980s, when authors such as P. D. James, Marcia Muller, Sara Paretsky, Liza Cody, and Sue Grafton began publishing novels with female private investigators in urban locales at the center of the narrative. One of the earliest of these was P. D. James's 1972 *An Unsuitable Job for a Woman*, featuring the London-based detective Cordelia Gray who inherits a detective agency when her employer dies; however, James abandoned the series after *The Skull Beneath the Skin* in 1982. By the late 1980s, the small early cluster of pioneering writers and their female protagonists had become a critical mass of women novelists creating commercially successful mystery series featuring a wide variety of female detective figures—hard-boiled private eyes, police detectives, investigative journalists, legal investigators, and security agency operatives. When Paretsky first imagined writing a mystery novel with a female private eye, she was working for a large multinational insurance com-

pany in Chicago as a marketing manager in the mid–1970s. Drawn to the Raymond Chandler–type novels that she herself enjoyed reading, she set aside her first attempts to create a convincing character. In a 1990 interview, Paretsky told Jean Ross, "I realized that I was trying to create a character who was aping the Raymond Chandler tradition, only in female form, and what I really wanted was a woman who was doing what I was doing, which was trying to make a success in a field traditionally dominated by men. With that realization, I was able to find V. I.'s voice" (335). V. I.'s distinctive voice emerged in *Indemnity Only* (1982), the debut novel that staked its claim to the hard-boiled tradition even as it marked the start of a transformation in which Paretsky and her protagonist created new spaces within genre conventions. Paretsky also found her location in the city where she has lived and worked since the 1970s—Chicago—placing the street-smart detective in a setting as unexpected in the genre as the idea of a female private eye who specializes in white-collar financial fraud and crime. V. I. has affinities to, and significant differences from, the type of hero outlined in Chandler's famous 1944 essay "The Simple Art of Murder." Chandler describes a "man … who is not himself mean, who is neither tarnished nor afraid … an unusual man … a man of honor … [who] take[s] no man's money dishonestly…. [T]he story is this man's adventure in search of a hidden truth … [and it happens] to a man fit for adventure" (3). Comparisons with Chandler's private-eye Marlowe and Hammett's earlier Continental Op are inevitable. Paretsky gave her protagonist the characteristics of honor and fearlessness, and V. I.'s first-person voice has some of Marlowe's terse and laconic style. She can perform the traditional hard-boiled style with the best of them—using the "direct, evocative colloquial language that represents the hard-boiled hallmark of the genre" (Christianson, "Talkin' Trash" 129). She also can draw attention to the performance, using talking tough to maintain her control over herself and over situations, to express autonomy, or to make a joke. V. I. is physically and mentally fit for adventure. Quick-witted, agile, strong, and courageous (although not averse to confessing the occasional anxiety when faced with thugs intent on beating her up), V. I. values honesty in herself and others. She casts a cold eye on corporate greed, civic neglect, fraud, and entrenched male power and privilege. Her sympathies lie naturally with the underdog—those people on the margins of society who are suffering from the greed and neglect of the corporate and political hegemony. Lehmann-Haupt's review of *Guardian Angel* points out, "despite being anticliche, Warshawski fulfills the traditional fictional role of the private investigator as rebel, existentialist, provocateur and critic of the status quo ... not much different from all the great American detectives, from Dashiell Hammett's Continental Op to Robert B. Parker's Spenser" ("Detection" C22). One factor that distinguishes the Warshawski character from the earlier models, readers and reviewers agree, is that Paretsky allows her character to grow by "expanding the range of her sympathies and her moods" and portraying V. I.'s "aching vulnerabilities in the midst of the volcano" (Fyfield vi). Kate Saunders's review of *Tunnel Vision* observes that what Paretsky "brings to the classic private-eye novel is something entirely original; a dry crackle of wit and a deep emotional sympathy with her characters ... V. I. [is] a detective who matures through the novels like good wine" (14). Another differentiating aspect is V. I.'s reluctance to take violence for granted. She thinks twice about carrying her gun, often torn between a desire to protect herself and the knowledge that a gun can escalate matters. Although comfortable handling a gun due to her policeman father's careful training, V. I. prefers to rely on her quick tongue and physical agility when in tight spots. She is attuned to her own mental and visceral responses when faced with danger and often provides a running commentary on what she is imagining and how she is experiencing fear and anxiety. In *Guardian Angel*, when V. I. becomes nervous about involving Mr. Contreras in a plan to get into Dick Yarborough's office for some crucial files, she says, "...my stomach heaved uncontrollably; I retched up a mouthful of bile.... Marlowe never let his nerves get the better of him" (GA 317). In *Hardball* cousin Petra wants to know if V. I.'s father kept a diary about his work life. V. I. references mystery writers P. D. James and Ian Rankin when she tells Petra: "You're thinking of storybook cops like Adam Dalgliesh or John Rebus, endlessly second-guessing themselves" (HB 170). In *Blood Shot* V. I. confesses, "I've always been a little jealous of Kinsey Milhone's immaculate record-keeping" (BS 159)—a nod to Paretsky's contemporary, author Sue Grafton's popular private investigator character. These self-conscious and self-referential in-text jokes draw attention to genre stereotypes at the same time as the humor works to subvert and renovate the traditional patterns of the detective novel. Paretsky also uses chapter headings to refer to canonical texts in the genre such as the chapter title "Shadow of the Thin Man" in *Critical Mass*. V. I.'s humor functions to identify herself as belonging to the crime and mystery genre while creating a distance from which she can mock certain aspects of the private-eye canon. Biamonte argues that Paretsky "transforms the detective figure" by using humor to create "a dialogue between the traditionally perceived hard-boiled detective and the newly evolving, socially conscious professional" (323). There is a parodical exchange referencing Chandler's famous detective when, in *Blacklist*, Geraldine Graham offers V. I. bourbon because she knows "detectives are used to stronger beverages than tea." V. I. responds with "[t]hat's only Philip Marlowe. We modern detectives can't drink in the middle of the day: it puts us to sleep" (BL 11). The reappropriation of the hard-boiled formula by writers interested in creating female characters who behave like real women has met with both critical and commercial success over the last 30 years. Paretsky's V. I. series played a pioneering role in transforming the landscape of the private-eye novel. Walton and Jones's study of the late–twentieth-century female private-eye figure notes the extent to which the figure is now "solidly entrenched in the genre" (39).

**See also "Mean Streets"**

## "Heartbreak House" (1996)

This short story blends two popular fiction forms—the romance and the mystery—and it explores some of the commercial pressures and personal rivalries of the publishing world. First published in Otto Penzler's *Murder for Love* anthology, it later appeared in the *Mary Higgins Clark Mystery Magazine* and in Jeffrey Deaver's 2003 anthology.

The story opens with a paragraph from a romance novel manuscript that is being read by Amy, editor of the commercially successful novelist Roxanne. Roxanne's publishers, Clay and Amy, are anxious to keep her churning out the books. But Roxanne is absorbed in working with her psychiatrist on personal issues and retreats to Santa Fe to take a break. Her psychiatrist dies in mysterious circumstances, and Roxanne, distraught but apparently cured, produces a new book to the delight of Clay and Amy. Amy uses her knowledge of how the doctor probably died to secure her own future in Clay's publishing house as Roxanne's preferred editor and blackmails Clay into signing the new author Lisa Ferguson who has "written an extraordinary novel about life in western Kansas during the sixties" despite Clay's objection that "rural Kansas is of no interest to anyone these days except you" (Deaver 443). Here, Paretsky is no doubt commenting on publishers' initial reactions to her plans to write *Bleeding Kansas*, a novel set in rural Kansas and eventually published in 2008. In a nod to two contemporary authors of detective fiction, the fictional Amy tells Clay that she has persuaded Roxanne to change the title for her latest book from "An Unsuitable Job for a Woman" to "Life's Work." The reference is to P. D. James's 1972 novel *An Unsuitable Job for a Woman* featuring a female private eye. Val McDermid subsequently adapted the phrase for the title of her book on real-life women private detectives, *A Suitable Job for a Woman*.

## Heilbrun, Carolyn G.

Professor and writer Carolyn G. Heilbrun (1926–2003) was the first female academic to receive tenure at Columbia University (in the English Department). Well known for her feminist literary critical essays and studies of modernist women writers, Heilbrun had another life. Under the pen name Amanda Cross, Heilbrun published 14 mystery novels featuring the outspoken English professor Kate Fansler. The popular series began in the 1960s and was an important precursor to the female private-eye figures that appeared from the late 1970s on in novels by authors such as P. D. James, Liza Cody, Marcia Muller, Sara Paretsky, and Sue Grafton. In common with Paretsky's long-running V. I. series, the Amanda Cross novels explore women's friendships, misogyny, and other social and political issues. The novels are infused with Fansler's wit and quick thinking, much as V. I. is noted for her quips and wry humor. In a 1987 mysteries column for *Ms* Magazine, Heilbrun mentions Paretsky and *Bitter Medicine* amongst a number of new women writers in the mystery genre. Paretsky contributed "Remarks in Honor of Carolyn Heilbrun" (see entry) to a 2005 issue of *Tulsa Studies in Women's Literature*, published as a special issue commemorating Heilbrun.

## Herschel, Dr. Charlotte ("Lotty")

Dr. Charlotte "Lotty" Herschel is V. I.'s cherished friend and mentor from V. I.'s undergraduate days at the University of Chicago; Lotty was "one of the physicians who performed abortions in connection with an underground referral service I'd belonged to at the University of Chicago in the days when abortion was illegal and a dirty word to most doctors" (IO 108). When the series opens, Lotty is a neo-natal surgeon at Beth Israel Hospital, has a residency in family medicine, and runs a neighborhood clinic for poor families on Chicago's north side "about three miles from [V. I.'s] apartment, near the corner of Damen and Irving Park" (Burn 65). Lotty's significant other is Max Loewenthal; she and Max maintain independent households and share a rich professional, cultural, and intellectual life. According to V. I., Lotty has "a streak of European intellectual arrogance in her.... [A]ll the information she had about the world came from the *New York Times* and the *New Statesman* ... swell if you live in New York or Manchester" (Bitter 46). In the first several novels Lotty lives not far from Vic, on N. Sheffield in a second-floor apartment. In *Hard Time*, V. I. is relieved that Lotty, who "turned sixty-five last year ... [has] bought herself a condo in one of the art nouveau buildings overlooking the lake ... a place more secure than the fringes of Uptown" (HT 41–42). In the next novel, V. I. reiterates her pleasure that Lotty has "moved to a high-rise on the lakefront, to one of the beautiful old buildings where you can watch the sun rise with nothing between you and water but Lake Shore Drive and a strip of park.... Max and I had both been relieved to see her in a building with an indoor garage" (TR 107).

Readers first meet Lotty in the debut novel *Indemnity Only* as "Lotty, Austrian war refugee, brilliant London University medical student, maverick doctor, warm friend" (IO 8 in Gollancz ed.). V. I. further describes Lotty's early life in *Bitter Medicine*: "Lotty had grown up in Nazi-dominated Vienna. Somehow her parents had managed to ship her and her brother to English relatives in 1938" (*Bitter* 46–47). The two women have close emotional and intellectual bonds. V. I. says, "I know myself better when I talk to Lotty" (KO 57). "[Lotty] is the one person I never lie to. She's—not my conscience—the person who helps me see who I really am, I guess" (BS 295). In *Total Recall*, V. I. remembers how Lotty had taken her, a young college student, "under her wing, giving me the kind of social skills I'd lost when I lost my mother, keeping me from losing my way in those days of drugs and violent protest" (107). Aged about 20 years older than V. I., Lotty is—like the detective's mother, Gabriella—a refugee from Hitler's Europe in the 1930s; Lotty's Viennese family sent her to London via the Kindertransport system that took Jewish children to safety. "Lotty's grandfather had sent her and her brother from Vienna to London with the Kindertransport in the summer of 1939" (BD 67). Once in London, Lotty finished her schooling and undertook her medical training. Although the two characters are separated by age and background, they have bonded over their experiences together in the Chicago Women's Liberation Movement of the early 1970s; their devotion to feminist principles and each other has deepened over the years. Lotty is energetic, opinionated, and well informed; V. I. is convinced that "sometime in her Viennese youth she had discovered the secret of perpetual motion" (IO 83). Lotty's medical skills often are applied to patching up V. I. after her various run-ins with hired thugs and sabotaged cars, and accidents that put V. I. temporarily out of commission. They share a social life (dinners, opera, concerts); they offer each other counsel on professional and personal matters; and for the most part are respectful of the other's autonomy and privacy, although this often gets tested when V. I. ignores her friend's advice. Lotty, who is as outspoken as V. I., is not shy about expressing an opinion, especially when she thinks V. I. is behaving recklessly: "Am I angry? Maybe so. I sometimes think you're too arrogant with other people's lives.... I worry, Vic, when you decide to intervene in other people's lives. Someone usually suffers'" (TV 13–14). In the novel *Guardian Angel* Lotty is savagely beaten in an unprovoked attack when she is mistaken for V. I. because they have swapped cars. As V. I. reminds herself in the subsequent novel, "Her anger and my remorse had cut a channel between us that we rebridged only after months of hard work" (TV 14). Lotty is a notoriously poor driver; being a passenger with her friend at the wheel is one of the few situations that can frighten V. I.: "Lotty's driving, on a sunny day and with no one else on the road, was still a fine test of anyone's nerve endings. In the snow, with a cell phone in her ear, I wouldn't want my life to depend on her" (BW 64). Offered a lift by Lotty in *Hard Time*, the detective takes up the theme again: "[D]riving with Lotty is almost more adventure than I wanted at the end of a difficult day. She thinks she's Sterling Moss and that urban roads are a competitive course" (42). In *Total Recall*, Lotty's dark-green Infiniti is parked in Max's driveway, "its battered fenders an eloquent testimony to her imperious approach to the streets. She hadn't learned to drive until she arrived in Chicago at the age of thirty, when she apparently took lessons from a NASCAR crash dummy" (122). V. I. regularly seeks safety and solace at Lotty's home—staying in her spare room or turning up late at night in need of Lotty's special Viennese coffee. Lotty also facilitates the medical care needed by V. I. when she is attacked; waking in Lotty's hospital after suffering major burns in a fire-bombing in *Hardball*, Vic tells herself "Lotty was protecting me, I could rest, I could relax and be safe" (208). On several levels, Lotty is not only V. I.'s best friend, but the mother V. I. lost in her teens, and V. I. understands this; she wakes from a dream in *Total Recall*, in which "Lotty and my mother are inter-twined" (TR 72). In *Hard Time* V. I., locked up in Coolis Prison, writes to Lotty explain-ing what her friend means to her: "Some-thing ... restless drives me, a kind of terror that if I don't take care of things myself I will be left with a terrible helplessness.... You've kept that helplessness at bay. Thank you for your years of love" (HT 315).

Lotty's background is most fully revealed in *Total Recall*; she is given her own voice as she experiences a considerable personal cri-sis due to the claims of a Holocaust survivor who may be exploiting Jewish history. In six first-person, italicized passages interspersed throughout the main narrative, Lotty finally tells V. I. the secrets she has kept for decades. It is V. I. who rescues Lotty this time, whose impulse to bury the past and her memories has endangered the doctor's sense of self. V. I. understands something about the danger of detachment from cultural memory, and her patience in waiting for Lotty's story to emerge helps restore Lotty. In *Total Recall*, readers learn that Lotty studied medicine in postwar London and, as a result of a passionate but ultimately doomed love affair with the mu-sician Carl Tisov, bore a child and gave the child up for adoption. She recalls the anguish of this period in a heated exchange—wit-nessed by V. I., Morrell and Max—with Carl, who is in London to give some concerts. Many years later, Carl is still baffled and angry over Lotty's behavior when she disap-peared for six months "with no word.... [N]o response to my letters. No explanation" (TR 147). Lotty tells him, "I loved you, Carl. But

no one could reach me in the alone place I was. Not you, not Max, no one" (TR 147). Their lives take separate directions after the war; Carl develops his career as a musician with "three marriages in forty years and ... many mistresses in between" (TR 147). Lotty arrives in Chicago in the late 1950s to finish her medical residency and begin her career as a doctor. In the 16th novel, *Critical Mass*, Lotty's story again comes to the fore, when V. I. is involved in a case concerning a Vien-nese physicist whose family history inter-sects with Lotty's childhood. Members of Lotty's family who survived the Holocaust appear now and again in the novels and short stories. For instance, her brother, Hugo, "lives in Montreal—he runs a small chain of upscale women's boutiques" (TR 118). Hugo's daughter, Penelope, appears as a character in the V. I. short story "Settled Score." Lotty's Uncle Stefan "came to Chicago in the 1920s and spent most of the war as a guest of the federal government in Fort Leavenworth. Forgery" (TR 118), as V. I. explains to Mor-rell. Uncle Stefan features in *Killing Orders* where his forgery skills help V. I. solve a case involving counterfeit bonds. Lotty has never married, although Max has asked her repeat-edly over the years; later in the series, they reach an understanding that allows them to function as a couple while maintaining sep-arate residences and professional identities. She is portrayed as a woman of integrity, loy-alty, and great moral stature; these personal qualities, like those of Mr. Contreras, mirror V. I.'s characteristics. An intense and ener-getic woman, Lotty is also known for her sharp tongue—more reflections of aspects of the detective figure herself. What V. I. says about her friend—"Lotty's ferocity creates periodic sparks in all her relationships" (GA 13–14)—could equally be applied to Vic. A specific reference is made to her age in the short story "The Case of the Pietro Andro-mache" when she complains to Max about a colleague: "I am fifty-eight years old. I am a Fellow of the Royal College of Surgeons be-sides having enough credentials in this coun-try to support a whole hospital, and to him I am a 'little baby doctor'" (VIFS 77). In *Crit-ical Mass* (2013), Lotty is still running her

Damen Avenue storefront clinic and performing surgery at the hospital; she asks for V. I.'s help when Judy Binder, the daughter of Kitty Saginor who was a childhood acquaintance of Lotty's in Vienna, leaves a message for Lotty stating that someone is trying to kill her. The subsequent investigation takes both V. I. and Lotty deeper into the past and strengthens the bonds between them. At the conclusion of the novel, V. I. restores some long-missing documents to Lotty with her grandfather's handwriting on the title page; Lotty's response is heartfelt: "Oh, Vic, oh, daughter of my heart. For this—oh, thank you" (CM 460).

### "The Hidden War at Home" (1994)

In this op-ed piece on domestic violence for the *New York Times*, Paretsky addresses a "problem as pervasive and intractable as murder, drug dealing or armed robbery" (A13). She explores the shame felt by many women about admitting "they live with an abuser, and many, especially those with young children, are more afraid of ending up on the streets.... [T]hey also fear that if they do leave, their partners will get angry enough to kill them" (A13). Paretsky argues for more training and sensitivity in the Chicago police force's responses to the issue, suggesting that "officers could help abused women with a change in attitud.... [I]f they stopped calling battered women "domestics" they might see the women differently" (ibid.).

### "Imagining Edgar Allan Poe" (2009)

In this short essay for a Poe anthology edited by Michael Connelly, Paretsky considers readers' responses to Poe, noting that "the blood-drenched Poe, the racially charged Poe, the analytic, the poetic—all are aspects of this complicated writer; none explains him fully" (328).

### "In Chicago, We've Fought to Stand Together" (2008)

This short essay for the *Washington Post* explores the history of racial tension and segregation in Chicago. She offers a testimonial to then-presidential candidate Barack Obama "who arrived in Chicago with high hopes and a passion for social justice ... [and who] has come of political age in one of the roughest states in the nation."

### *Indemnity Only* (1982)

"If things get heavy, I'll figure out a way to handle them—or go down trying" (Dial ed. 9).

Paretsky's first V. I. Warshawski mystery and her idiosyncratic character were met with enthusiasm from early reviewers such as Barbara Bannon, who noted the novel "looks like the start of a very winning new mystery series" (43). *Indemnity Only* sold 3500 copies in its first print run, sufficient to convince its publisher, Dial, to offer a contract to Paretsky for a second book with the same character.

The novel's title is a nod to James M. Cain's 1943 hard-boiled novella *Double Indemnity* (a clause used in life insurance policies that doubles the payout in certain cases of accidental death) and to the 1944 noir film of the same title, signaling both the author's identification with the hard-boiled tradition of the crime and mystery genre, as well as her detective figure's specialty in white-collar financial crime. In this first novel, readers learn that V. I. was raised on Chicago's blue-collar South Side by Italian and Polish-American parents (now deceased); that she has a law degree from the University of Chicago; that she worked for the public defender's office before becoming an independent private investigator; and that she was married briefly to a law school colleague. She has a sharp tongue, a direct manner, an engaging sense of humor, and street smarts.

In the closely plotted story, the detective is hired by Chicago banker John Thayer to find his son's girlfriend. When she discovers the dead body of Peter Thayer in the Hyde Park student apartment he shared with the missing girlfriend "Anita Hill," V. I. is caught up in the duplicitous corporate worlds of banking and trade unions, where murder, fraud, and greed rule. Facing those who do not hesitate to use violence in pursuit of their goals, V. I. works fast to track down Anita before hired killers do. The deadly secret discovered by Anita and Peter is that her father, Andrew McGraw (a trade union official for the International Brotherhood of Knifegrinders who masqueraded as John Thayer to V. I.), has betrayed his personal and professional values. He has been using the union as a front for phony claims from the Ajax Insurance Company, where Peter's father leads the firm and Peter worked as a summer intern. When Peter is murdered because he was asking questions, Anita goes into hiding, choosing the name "Jody Hill" as an alias because, as she explains later to V. I., "[Famous labor organizer] Joe Hill has always been a big hero of ours" (241). V. I.'s inquiries lead her to the wealthy Thayers in Winnetka, where the real John Thayer offers her $5000 to drop the case; predictably, this has the opposite effect, as V. I. becomes more determined to find the truth.

Back in Hyde Park, she searches Peter and Anita's apartment and finds the carbon copy of incriminating Ajax paperwork hidden by Peter. The next day, John Thayer is shot dead as he leaves his Winnetka home. The distraught Jill Thayer, Peter's younger sister, asks V. I. to find out what happened to her father and brother and why. When the remaining members of the Thayer family try to buy V. I. off again, she affirms her intention to investigate the murders: "You guys up here on the North Shore live in some kind of dream world. You think you can buy a cover-up for anything that goes wrong in your lives, just like you hire the garbagemen to take away your filth" (133). She refuses to be intimidated by their threats or by the roughing-up of those in the mob-connected Knifegrinders Association. With important financial information gleaned from her reporter friend, Murray Ryerson, and from the Ajax Insurance budget manager Ralph Devereux who knew Peter, V. I. finally puts the pieces of the insurance scam together and connects McGraw to Ajax. She also tracks down the missing Anita (Hill) McGraw and persuades her to return to Chicago and face the truth about her father's activities. After nearly losing his daughter to the murderous thugs who are key to John Thayer's planned cover-up, Anita's father eventually confesses, "[A]ll I saw was the money" (244). Evoking the King Midas myth and the notion of repentance, the novel concludes with father

and daughter on the brink of reconciliation as V. I., with Murray's help, plans to hold McGraw publically accountable for his actions: "Murray was waiting for his story. I didn't say good-bye" (244).

This debut novel puts in place several features that come to characterize the whole series: the vivid setting of Chicago; the fearless detective figure who refuses to be intimidated (when asked by an irate corporate executive what the *V* stands for, she responds, "My first name, Mr. Masters" (19)); the investigation of white-collar financial crime; and V. I.'s community of friends and collaborators who bring contemporary Chicago to life. Close friend Dr. Lotty Herschel, journalist Murray Ryerson, homicide detective Bobby Mallory of the 21st Division, and Golden Glow Bar proprietor Sal Barthele are all introduced in this first novel. The detective's personal and professional relationships with such a diverse collection of friends and colleagues become an important strand in subsequent novels, providing humor, warmth, tension, conflict, and continuity. Paretsky also introduces a number of themes in *Indemnity Only* that can be identified with her oeuvre. The novel explores corruption and betrayal of ethical standards in the top levels of Chicago's powerful institutions, in this case focused on insurance indemnity scams in a leading bank and an important trade union. The question of female autonomy pervades the book, whether V. I. is portrayed confidently on her own at night in the deserted city streets outside her office or guarding herself against a potentially overprotective lover, Ralph Devereux, as she tells him, "I have some close women friends, because I don't feel they're trying to take over my turf. But with men, it always seems, or often seems, as though I'm having to fight to maintain who I am" (160). The importance of education and strong friendships is signaled through the idealistic college students Peter Thayer and Anita McGraw, as well as the University Women United group; V. I. attends one of the group's meetings in her search for the woman she knows as Anita Hill. The gap between rich and poor, to which V. I. is very sensitive, is signaled in her warning to the wealthy Thayer family that they are not invulnerable. Important recurring motifs also appear in this debut novel; the figure of the resilient teenage girl, at risk from family and/or friends, is suggested in both Anita McGraw and in Peter's sister, Jill, who is temporarily taken under V. I.'s wing and given sanctuary until it is safe to return home. V. I.'s ardent support of the Cubs baseball team provides a running motif and symbolizes her characteristic willingness to take the side of the underdog; as she tells Murray, "I am a person with very few illusions about life. I like to have the Cubs as one of them" (149). Music, another repeating motif, is introduced in the novel, as V. I. sings Mozart in her car and whistles a bit of Simon Boccanegra. The eight Venetian wineglasses that link V. I. to her mother, Gabriella, are introduced when V. I. entertains Ralph; the glasses, "a beautiful clear red with twisted stems," were brought by Gabriella to the United States when she "left Italy right before the war" (77). V. I. is devastated when intruders smash "one of Gabriella's glasses" (103); the remaining goblets make subsequent appearances throughout the series. In a clear homage to the mean city streets traditions of the private-eye genre as exemplified by Raymond Chandler, Paretsky gives V. I. a first-person narrative voice, a predilection for wise-cracking, and a rundown office in the Pulteney Building at the corner of Monroe and Wabash in the South Loop. V. I.'s office, however, has personal touches that Chandler never allowed Philip Marlowe, such as the desk from a police department auction (V. I.'s father, Tony, was a Chicago cop) and an Olivetti typewriter that belonged to her mother. Although the genesis of Paretsky's private-eye character owes certain features to the hard-boiled tradition, the author explained in an interview with Alistair McKay: "I wanted someone, like me and my friends, who was doing a job that hadn't existed for women when we were in school, and was facing some of the same kinds of challenges, obstacles, that we did ... because she didn't have to make people like her, she said what was in the balloon over her head" (4). Readers learn about V. I.'s personal circumstances and her day-to-day routines; she lives in a "large, cheap apartment on Halsted," and she often makes the 5-mile run from home "over to the lake and around Belmont Harbor and back" (10) in an effort to keep in top physical shape. She drives a Chevy Monza; she likes Johnnie Walker Black Label whiskey.

Paretsky dedicates this debut novel to mystery author Stuart Kaminsky; she attended his Northwestern University evening course on "Writing Detective Fiction for Publication" in fall 1979. With Kaminsky's encouragement, she finished a manuscript in 1980 and sent it to Kaminsky's agent, Dominick Abel, in New York. After Abel accepted the manuscript, "there were 13 rejections before Dial Press decided it would publish the novel," as Helen Dudar's profile in *Lear's* magazine documents (96). Two years later, *Indemnity Only* was published because Dial Press were, according to Paretsky in the 30th anniversary edition of the novel, "willing to take a chance on a woman private eye in the Midwest" (Dell pb 2011 ed. xi). Paretsky's introduction further notes that "[m]uch has changed in thirty years…. A woman working as a private eye is no longer a bold or unusual creation" (xi). In March 2012, the first chapter of *Indemnity Only* was given a staged reading at the Harold Washington Library Center in Chicago by actors from the Steppenwolf Theatre company to mark the city's "Sara Paretsky Day" in commemoration of the book's 30th anniversary.

**See also Sal Barthele; Chicago; hardboiled genre; Lotty Herschel; Bobby Mallory; music; Murray Ryerson; Gabriella Sestieri Warshawski; Tony Warshawski; V. I. Warshawski; Red Venetian Glasses**

## "Independent Sleuth" (1992)

An entry for the *Oxford Companion to Crime and Mystery Writing* discusses the figure of the independent sleuth as it appeared and developed in the genre. Paretsky links the prototypical private-eye figure to the heroes and codes of honor depicted in the western. She concludes that "late twentieth-century women feminists have proven that the mean streets are not the exclusive preserve of male private eyes, and that the lonely search for the truth can be achieved by a woman" (234).

## "Introduction" (2007)

Paretsky's introduction to her collection of autobiographical essays *Writing in an Age of Silence* tells readers that the "memoir traces the long path I followed from silence to speech ... [and] deals with the dominant question of my own life, the effort to find a voice" (xiii). She describes her 1950s childhood in a Kansas town "obsessed by the threat of Communism" (xvi). She identifies herself as "the descendant of immigrants ... [who] came here to escape religious persecution" (xvi–xvii). Paretsky explains that she "began speaking on the topic of speech and silence to state library associations in 2002, since libraries were on the frontline of some of the [Patriot] Act's most pernicious sections" (xviii). In response to people asking for written copies of her lectures and speeches, she offers them in this volume "expanded, rewritten, updated" (xviii).

## "The Inventory: Sara Paretsky" (2014)

This feature for the *Financial Times* (London) magazine is based on a set of questions posed by the newspaper to which Paretsky responded. Her earliest ambition was "to become a dancer"; in reply to the question of her political commitment, Paretsky writes, "[A]lmost frothing in the mouth, but I try to dial it back in public" (8). Asked about the greatest achievement of her life, she says, "I'm proud of supporting women and girls."

## "Keeping Nancy Drew Alive" (1991)

Paretsky's short introductory essay for a facsimile edition of *The Secret of the Old Clock* points out that the Nancy Drew character "offered girls of 1930 an amazing alternative to the career choice of secretary and milliner that other children's books provided. Her enduring popularity probably has no deeper cause than that: little girls need to see a bigger girl act competently and solve problems they keep being told belong to boys" (n.pag.). The essay explores the phenomenon of Nancy Drew's continuing popularity in relation to a recurring theme in Paretsky's nonfiction—that "girls today still grow up without a strong sense of themselves as people or of their right to play active roles in adult life" (n.pag.).

**See also Drew, Nancy, and Carolyn Keene**

## Kilian, Michael *see* "Mysteries"

## *Killing Orders* (1985)

> "Of course, a hard-boiled detective is never scared. So what I was feeling couldn't be fear" (226).

The third V. I. mystery takes her head to head with the power structures of the Catholic Church in Chicago and beyond in a plot "involving mysterious share movements and the murkier depths of the Catholic mafia" (Berlins 1986). Provisionally titled *V. I. & the Vatican* and then *Iphigenia* before settling on the published title with its characteristic double entendre, *Killing Orders* is dedicated to Courtenay (Courtenay Wright is Paretsky's husband) with an epitaph from John Donne's poem "The Anniversary."

In a pattern that continues throughout the series, it is a member of V. I.'s family that draws her into the investigation. A year after the death of V. I.'s cousin Boom Boom in the previous novel, she finds herself unwillingly responding to a summons from her estranged cousin, Albert, and his elderly mother, Rosa Vignelli, in suburban Melrose Park. Rosa is the aunt of V. I.'s mother, Gabriella, and thus her great-aunt. Making the long drive out of the city on a blustery autumn day, V. I. remembers the bad history between Rosa and Gabriella. Hostilities have carried through to the next generation, as V. I. reminds her great-aunt: "You know the only reason I'm here: Gabriella made me promise that I would help you if you needed it. It stuck in my gut and it still does ... [but] let's leave the past in peace: I won't be sarcastic if you'll stop throwing around insults about my mother" (14). Rosa, in the course of her responsibilities as the volunteer treasurer of St. Albert's Priory, has inadvertently "gotten herself involved with some counterfeit securities" (15). Albert and Rosa want V. I. to help clear Rosa of the Dominican order's suspi-

IPHIGENIA

By Sara X. Paretsky

*Pat — Type as standard ms — put # # on top except when starting new chapter — then they go on bottom. Left margin = 1½ inch, ditto top — right & bottom = 1 inch. Double space*

*For final draft I'll have chapter titles, so please leave space (1 line)*

*When I've inserted pp, such as 14a, just type + number as continuous part of text*

*I decided at the last minute to rewrite part of pp 32-36, so my husband will bring another hundred pages or so over tomorrow*

*Many thanks*

*Sara*

822-2194 (day)
947-9570 (evening)

The draft title page of *Killing Orders* shows original title as "Iphigenia" referencing V.I.'s middle name. The name means "strong-born" and in Greek legend also refers to Artemis the huntress. From Paretsky Papers Newberry archive (Box VII of 9, 1992 gift). Photograph by Linda Erf Swift.

cions that she planted the forged securities in the safe. Embarked on an investigation into "the troubles of an aunt I loathed" (22), V. I. also confronts some unresolved matters from her own past—why, for instance, all those years ago, "Rosa had thrown Gabriella out on the street, an immigrant with minimal English," and why the dying Gabriella had "made me promise to help Rosa if her aunt ever needed me" (18). Newgate Callendar's review for the *New York Times* describes Rosa as "a harridan and religious hypocrite" (1985). With no love lost between the two family members V. I. nevertheless honors the promise made to her mother.

At St. Albert's Priory, V. I. meets the Dominican prior Boniface Carroll; Father Stephen Jablonski, the student master; and Augustine Pelly, the priory's procurator. They are ostensibly helping the Securities Exchange Commission (SEC) and the FBI with their formal inquiries into the matter of the counterfeit securities. An initially cordial meeting becomes somewhat testy when V. I. criticizes the church's political practice of allowing local pastors "to influence their congregations to vote for antichoice candidates regardless of how terrible their qualifications may be otherwise" (31). Paretsky's character is, like the author herself, an outspoken advocate of women's reproductive rights and does not hesitate to express her views. Rosa and Albert try to call off V. I.'s investigation when the stock certificates mysteriously turn up in the priory safe. In spite of this, as well as some warnings from an anonymous caller, V. I. enlists the help of her friend Lotty Herschel's elderly Uncle Stefan, whose expertise as an engraver and former forger is put to good use in resolving the mystery of the fake stock certificates. However, his assistance to Vic puts him in considerable danger, much to Lotty's dismay. V. I. also calls on stockbroker Agnes Pacoriak, an old friend from law school, when Roger Ferrant (the English insurance broker at Ajax who V. I. knows from an earlier case) needs help in understanding the workings of the American stock exchange. Agnes has been looking into the financial dealings of Corpus Christi, a secret Roman Catholic lay organization with which her

wealthy and arch-conservative mother has become involved. When Agnes is shot and killed, and Father Pelly turns up at her funeral, V. I. begins to suspect a link between her friend's death and the priory theft. The Church, trusted by Rosa, turns out to have exploited her loyalty; when V. I. takes on the corrupt church hierarchy that has links to the Mafia, she invokes the wrath and vindictiveness of both entities as they scramble to keep their secrets buried. The intrepid detective survives an acid attack on her eyes and an arson attack on her apartment, from which she and Roger (with whom she has a brief romance) barely escape with their lives. She loses her home and her mother's piano in the fire, and one of Gabriella's precious red wineglasses suffers "a jagged piece broken from it" (170). The relationship between V. I. and Lotty is deepened and made more complex when they quarrel over the detective's single-mindedness that has put Uncle Stefan at risk. When he is stabbed, and Lotty and V. I. are temporarily estranged, V. I. begins to take Lotty's criticisms more seriously: "Lotty wouldn't speak to me. That hurt" (180). Uncle Stefan survives the brutal attack and, based on what he has discovered about the forgeries, he makes an astonishing accusation against the Vatican financial official, Archbishop Xavier O'Faolin. This sets the scene for the final dramatic events in the novel, including a killing that V. I. has a shadowy hand in arranging. She makes risky contact with local mobster Don Pasquale and negotiates with him about the forgeries, the arson attack, and those involved in both. She tells him what she wants invoking the codes of honor so dear to the Italian mafia. The bomb that detonates in O'Faolin's car is never traced. Eventually clearing Rosa's name and identifying the real culprits, V. I. hears Rosa's self-serving explanation of why she always hated Gabriella—years ago, her husband, Carl, planned to leave Rosa for Gabriella. When Rosa blamed Gabriella for her husband's infatuation and threw her niece out of the house, Carl committed suicide. The embittered Rosa is fiercely ashamed of this family history and still locked in her anger and humiliation.

At the end of the novel, Ajax Insurance compensates V. I. handsomely for her part in thwarting the takeover of Ajax shares planned by O'Faolin to cover his financial tracks; she uses the fee to pay for "a Steinway grand to replace Gabriella's old upright" (285). Another sum of money—"twenty-five crisp thousand-dollar bills"—arrives in her office mail with "no note, no return address" (ibid.). "It seemed churlish to try to trace it" (ibid.), she decides. Before Roger returns to England, he helps her "find a co-op on Racine near Lincoln, in a clean, quiet little building with four other units and a well-cared-for lobby" (ibid.). Parts of Lotty's backstory spill out in the final chapter when she and V. I. effect a heartfelt reconciliation that acts as a counterpoint to the conclusion of the more public investigation into the financial crimes of the church and the mafia. Lotty talks about her family, the war, and her protective feelings for Stefan; she tells the detective, "You have been the daughter I never had, V. I. As well as one of the best friends a woman could ever desire" (286–87). V. I. expresses unusual remorse and self-reflection over her "narrow-minded, pigheaded, bullying" (287) behavior that has led to Agnes's death, Uncle Stefan's near-death, and the estrangement from Lotty. Together they pick up the threads of their friendship as V. I. weeps in Lotty's arms, overwhelmed by the grief for her dead mother and her sense of herself as Gabriella's sacrificial victim. V. I. reveals her middle name to Lotty, and the novel ends with Lotty telling her, "They named you well, Victoria Iphigenia. For don't you know that in Greek legend Iphigenia is also Artemis the huntress?" (288). Richard Goodkin's scholarly essay explores the novel's complex and indirect intertextual relationship to Racine's tragedy *Iphigénie* and to Euripides's play *Iphigenia in Aulis*; he suggests that all three texts explore a concern with "a familial order and a heroic order which is meant to protect or insure it…. The heroic order ultimately establishing its hegemony over the familial order" (83). Goodkin's unusual reading of *Killing Orders* makes a persuasive case about detective fiction and tragedy being "about the impossibility of ever killing disorder completely and of doing away with sacrifice" (ibid., 106).

## "Let's Have a Big Smile Now, Please" (1988)

A short story published in an anthology of stories and poems by Chicago women writers titled *Naming the Daytime Moon*, Paretsky's contribution is included in the section themed "For Those Who Thought That Equal Privilege Came With the Vote." The story features three airline attendants who have just come off duty and is written from the point of view of Tracy, one of the attendants. Resting in a hotel room, they nurse their sore feet and swap stories about the passengers and coworkers who expect them to smile no matter what. Tracy tells her colleagues of a recurring dream in which she looks down and sees that "my feet are bound. You know, like they used to do to Chinese girls. My feet are bleeding. I can hardly walk. But I'm grinning." (46). She falls into a reverie about her childhood where she was an isolated middle child who understood that "perky smiles keep Daddy happy." (47). Tracy remembers learning about China in geography class and tells her friends about the time she and two schoolfriends "try binding their feet … thing[ing] they're brave Chinese princesses, enduring pain to be beautiful" (48). The fragmented story ends with Kathy's response to Stacy's "gross" memory: "Anyway, those Chinese had it backwards. I've gone from a size seven to a nine since I started flying." (48). The elliptical tale draws attention to the cultural and social restrictions that historically have curtailed the lives of women and girls.

## "A Letter to My Grandmother on Coming Home from Europe" (2004)

This op-ed piece appeared in the *Illinois Brief* winter issue and was reprinted in the *Guardian* (London) newspaper in January 2005 under the title "Grannie, Look What We're Doing to the Land of Freedom." Paretsky voices her concerns regarding President George W. Bush's Patriot Act legislation and queries whether the resulting "arrests and interrogations of writers, artists, ordinary citizens" is a "necessary price to pay for protection against terrorism" (2).

### "Lily and the Sockeyes" (1990)

This short story about a child abuser first appeared in the Japanese magazine *Suntori Sisters Quarterly*, then in the 1990 *Third Womansleuth* anthology and subsequently in a Penguin anthology edited by Peter Robinson in 2008. Paretsky's longtime interest in baseball comes to the fore in the story, where she creates a female PR manager Clementine Duval for the "Vancouver Sockeye baseball team" (Zahava anthology 187). Duval's appointment has raised eyebrows; she is an athlete and a journalist, but still, "a woman handling the press for a men's pro team?" (187). One antagonist is Jimmy-Bob Reedy, a sportscaster on both TV and radio for the Sockeyes. A number of women have left the station after working with him—they have "quit [with] handsome severance pay to stop possible attempted-rape charges" (187).

Lily, Clementine's grandmother and a notable actress, decides to take action when he starts describing Clementine as a "lesbian-communist" (193) on the airwaves. Lily throws a grand party and treats Jimmy-Bob as a special guest of honor; she then screens a video to the 300 or so partygoers showing "a montage of Jimmy-Bob's greatest blunders, on and off the air" (195). In the ensuing uproar, Jimmy-Bob is found with "one of the carving knives for the salmon [stuck] into him" (196). Lily and Clementine come under suspicion for the murder. However, it turns out that the killer (who is close to home in the Sockeyes) was being blackmailed by Jimmy-Bob, who was using information about the perpetrator's child-molesting history to retain his broadcasting job. The story highlights the issues of sexual harassment, child sexual abuse, and the collusion of men with dubious morals and secrets to hide.

### "Lives: Le Treatment" (2009)

Paretsky's short essay for the *New York Times Magazine* describes the encounters of the author and her husband with a bureaucratic French medical system on a recent trip abroad. She praises the doctors and the treatment given for her husband's pneumonia. The article was also printed in the *Herald Tribune* on 18 August 2009 (17).

### Loewenthal, Max

Max first appears in *Bitter Medicine* as a friend and associate of Lotty's. An "executive director of Beth Israel [hospital]," he is a "short, sturdy man of sixty or so with curly white hair" (*Bitter* 259). Beth Israel Hospital, on the northwest side of Chicago, is "one of the big Jewish charities in town" (TR 268); the widower Max is an effective fund-raiser as a board member, and Lotty practices there. Like Lotty, sent to safety as a child on the Kindertransport from Prague to London, Max has "asked her several times to marry him, but she always replied that she wasn't the marrying type" (TR 259). Their relationship deepens over the course of the novels and, together, they strengthen their bonds with V. I., who often turns to each of them for advice, practical help, moral support, and companionship. An important figure in the Chicago Jewish community, Max is a skilled administrator and philanthropist. His large house in the northern suburbs—"part of a small block that shared a private park and beach at the south end of Evanston" (GA 99)—is often the center of family gatherings, as well as more formal fund-raising receptions and events. The house is "immaculate and beautifully furnished" (GA 99). Max becomes a repeating character, part of V. I.'s extended family of affiliation; his legendary hospitality offers a domestic normality that contrasts with V. I.'s more disorganized home life. In *Guardian Angel* V. I. tells herself, "The serenity of his Evanston home would make a welcome relief from the places and people I'd been seeing lately" (97). In *Fire Sale*, the detective and her current lover Morrell "joined a cast of thousands at Max's for Thanksgiving dinner" (394), and in *Total Recall*, V. I. takes on the role of babysitter for his granddaughter, Calia. It is in this novel that the tangled web of Lotty's past is revealed; it overlaps with the stories of Max and gifted musician Carl Tisov, all of whom were together in postwar London. Michael, Max's son and a cellist, lives in London with his photographer wife, Agnes, and their daughter, Calia. Michael's career often brings him to Chicago for performances. In *Guardian Angel*, Michael is in town for a "solo recital at the Auditorium as a benefit for Chicago Settlement, the refugee assistance group [which] had been a favourite charity of Max's wife Theresz, before she died nine years ago" (GA 10). The whole family is visiting Max during the events of *Total Recall*; the demands of dealing with the lively Calia, when V. I. is pressed into emergency babysitting duties, nearly finish off the detective: "I don't think Race Williams or Philip Marlowe ever did babysitting, but by the end of the morning I decided that was because they were too weak to take on a five-year-old" (TR 8). Usually supportive of V. I.'s efforts to solve her cases, Max spars with her when he feels she is endangering Lotty or putting herself into unnecessary jeopardy. His linguistic skills in Eastern European languages help V. I. untangle a subplot involving the exploitation of Romanian immigrant laborers in *Tunnel Vision*. His medical background is often useful, and his steady presence as Lotty's devoted friend and companion serves as a living reminder of what V. I. valued in the relationship between her deceased parents. He is an art and music lover, a wine connoisseur, and a philanthropist. The stresses and strains of the events in *Total Recall*, which involve Lotty's dramatic disappearance, take their toll on Max, who, according to V. I. "doesn't often look his age, but this afternoon his skin was drawn tight and grey across his cheekbones" (TR 279). Max and Lotty, and their backstories as refugees from Eastern Europe, come to the foreground again in the 16th novel, *Critical Mass*. V. I. is searching for the details of Martina Saginor, an Austrian physicist who disappeared after the war; as her story overlaps with Lotty, the doctor is forced to look into her own past again. Max makes a number of characteristically wise and generous gestures in this novel such as helping to fund a trip to Vienna for the detective's party of six and helping to secure a place at college for Martina's

grandson, a promising computer-designer. Max is both a comfort and an inspiration to V. I.; a father-figure of sorts, he has less of the baggage with V. I. than her other father figures, Bobby Mallory and Mr. Contreras. Fiercely protective of Lotty, he also is appreciative of V. I.'s skills and guts; he rarely judges her harshly. The 1988 short story "The Case of the Pietro Andromache" is narrated in the third-person voice from Max's point of view; the events that unfold involve Lotty being suspected of playing a part in the death of a medical colleague with whom she has quarreled publicly; Max calls on V. I. to help exonerate their beloved friend.

## "The Long Shadow of the Falcon" (2000)

This feature article for the *Guardian* (London) newspaper is an edited extract from her introduction to the 2000 Folio Society edition of *The Maltese Falcon* by Dashiell Hammett (9–19). She describes Hammett's creation Sam Spade as the "father to every gumshoe that ever walked down a mean street" (1). Paretsky explains that in creating her own detective, she "wanted a woman who could, like Sam Spade, be a physical, sexual person without being evil" (3).

## Mallory, Bobby

Bobby Mallory—a "[h]omicide lieutenant from the twenty-first district" (IO 27)—was a close friend and colleague of V. I.'s father, Tony Warshawski, on the Chicago police force, with Tony mentoring the younger Bobby in the beginning. Bobby and his wife, Eileen, have known V. I. since she was born. When the series begins, Tony Warshawski has been dead for some time, but Mallory is still at the precinct where he was stationed with Tony. As V. I.'s investigations frequently bring her into the orbit of the Chicago police force, he often feels conflicted by his protectiveness toward his deceased pal's daughter and his professional judgments about her sometimes illegal and dangerous activities. He and V. I. regularly rub each other the wrong way; although antagonism between police and private eyes is a staple of the genre, Paretsky invests this tradition with the more personal conflict of the relationship that V. I. no longer has with her deceased father. According to V. I., "Mallory hates talking to me about crime. He thinks Tony Warshawski's daughter should be making a better world by producing happy healthy babies, not by catching desperadoes" (KO 93). Bobby's loyalty to V. I.'s parents, his duties as a cop, and his old-fashioned views about women all make for combustion with the fearless detective, who gives as good as she gets whenever Bobby becomes cross. In *Killing Orders*, when Bobby reluctantly returns her confiscated gun, V. I. says, "He didn't want me carrying it, he didn't want me in the detective business, he wanted me in Bridgeport or Melrose Park with six children, and presumably, a husband" (222). Much later in the series, V. I. notes how little has changed concerning Bobby: "Despite the many good women who have worked for him in the last fifteen years, my presence at a crime scene still gives him heartburn" (HB 12). Now and again, the dedicated and loyal policeman Bobby comes up against some hard truths about other members of the force and about his own judgment of their characters. In *Burn Marks*, his young protégé and godson, Michael Furey (who has been romancing V. I. with Bobby's tacit approval), turns out to be a killer; he and Ron Grasso, Michael's childhood friend turned corrupt Chicago businessman, threaten to kill V. I. and her Aunt Elena in a dramatic scene at the top of a construction site. Bobby finds it hard to accept that he was wrong about Michael, unable to comprehend police officers who do not subscribe to the motto "to protect and serve" in the same way that he does. In this novel V. I. and Bobby go head-to-head over V. I.'s suggestion that there are corrupt cops in his department; he reminds her, "I've told you dozens of times that you're in a line of work that's bad for you.... You don't know how to reason, how to follow a chain of evidence to a conclusion ... women your age who don't marry start getting strange ideas" (Burn 297). Enraged as V. I. is about this statement, she realizes that "Bobby wouldn't listen to me spreading stories about his fair-haired boy ... even though I was furious right now with Bobby, I didn't look forward

to bringing him that much pain" (298). In the 13th novel *Hardball* (2009), which exposes long-standing issues of the Chicago Police Department's reputation for brutality with black suspects in their custody, Mallory takes part "in a special housekeeping task force ... [although] it was painful for him to have to recognize the history of corruption and abuse among the men he'd spent his life with" (HB 433). In that same novel, the wise Eileen Mallory comforts V. I., who is distraught at the discovery of her father's failure to address adequately the brutality he witnessed; Eileen reminds her: "Families are terrible hostages for men like your father.... [W]hat other work could he get to support you and Gabriella.... Tony did the best he could under very painful circumstances. He spoke up. Do you know how much courage that took?" (HB 434). V. I. realizes that Bobby's feelings toward her are complicated, "compounded of guilt at flourishing when my father had stayed in beat patrol, at living while Tony had died—and frustration at my being grown up and a professional investigator instead of a little girl he could dandle on his knee" (TS 89). She refers to the same paradoxical feelings in *Burn Marks* when she realizes Bobby might have bad-mouthed her to an official who is giving her a hard time: "Bobby talks about me one way and thinks about me quite another—he might easily have told the fire commander I was a pain in the butt.... [M]issing would be Bobby's affection as an old friend of my parents'" (Burn 80). In the same novel V. I. reveals an unexpected side of Bobby who shares her mother's "love of opera; she used to sing Puccini for him. He would be a happy cop if I'd fulfilled her dream and become a concert singer instead of aping my dad and turning into a detective" (133).

**See also *Guardian Angel, Hardball, Tunnel Vision***

## "The Maltese Cat" (1990)

The short story "The Maltese Cat" in the collection *Windy City Blues* (aka *V. I. for Short*) "provides a glimpse of V. I. in three-dimensional action—playing family social worker" (24), according to Josh Rubins's review of the anthology. The title signals an homage to Dashiell Hammett, author of *The Maltese Falcon,* a defining text in the private-eye subgenre. Further references to the Hammett novel are seen in the horse's name of Flitcraft (from a parable in *Falcon*) and a character named Joel (as in *Falcon's* Joel Cairo). The story involves a gone-to-seed former football star who is found dead. His ex-wife, Brigitte, hires V. I. to find her sister. The unhappy and overweight Corinne has disappeared with the priceless family cat, a rare blue Maltese. Brigitte is eager for the money offered by a cat breeder for the Maltese. Corinne is the troubled teenager figure familiar in the Paretsky oeuvre. Vic achieves a family reconciliation.

## "The Man Who Loved Life" (1990)

The short story "The Man Who Loved Life" takes as its theme the underlying misogyny and violence behind the pro-life agenda as it is taught and enacted within the conservative Christian right; this is a theme Paretsky visits often in fiction and nonfiction. The story was first published in the collection *New Chicago Stories* (ed. Fred L. Gardaphe) and subsequently appeared in the 1993 anthology *The Country of Herself* and in the Penguin 60 *A Taste of Life and Other Stories.* The protagonist of the story is Simon Peter Dresser, whose name signals the biblical Simon Peter, on whose rock the Catholic Church was built. Simon Peter and his wife, Louise, are attending a banquet given by the House of Bishops to honor Simon's work as "a staunch fighter for the unborn.... Untold thousands of lives saved because of him ... wouldn't rest until babies were safe all over America" (Penguin 60 ed. 48–49). As the lights dim for the slide show titled "The Fight to Protect the Unborn," Simon's "glow of satisfaction extended to his well-run family. None of his five daughters ever talked back to him ... except Sandra..., but he'd sure as hell beaten that nonsense out of her" (46). He remembers how his own father "had been tough. [T]ough, but fair.... [H]ad a hand as strong as a board. He wasn't afraid to use it, not even when you got to be as big as him. Bigger" (43–44). The slide show, with footage

of pro-life marchers at rallies and outside abortion clinics, will be used after the banquet "to educate high-school students and church groups on how to fight for Life" (49). When the screen shows a "Pro-Life counsellor ... exhorting a girl in a lime-green parka" as she approaches a DeKalb abortion clinic, Simon realizes he is looking at Sandra. Humiliated and enraged, Simon lashes out at his wife who flees the banquet table in tears. The story closes as the accompanying soundtrack informs the audience that the young woman on the screen was "one of our failures.... [W]e didn't have the resources to give this girl the help she needed to choose Life" (55). The chilling terror tactics and fear experienced by Simon in his own childhood, which he in turn is inflicting on his family, is veiled in the language of Christian morality about the sacredness of life and the imperative to respect those who "know right from wrong and teach it to you" (45).

**See also *Bitter Medicine*; *Killing Orders*; "Our Bodies, Our Fertility"; "Poster Child"; "Terror in the Name of Jesus"**

## McGonnigal, John

Sergeant John McGonnigal is a minor character running throughout the V. I. series; he is a policeman colleague of Bobby Mallory, Conrad Rawlings, and Mary Louise Neely. He first appears in *Indemnity Only* as Lt. Bobby Mallory's sergeant. His professional dealings with V. I. are less combative than those between the detective and Bobby. In *Blood Shot* they almost embark on a romance, but V. I. pulls back from inviting him in late one night when she needs some company. She goes to Lotty's and is glad she decided "to come back here instead of going off with McGonnigal" (296). At the end of that novel, V. I. mentions him as "another loose end that never got tied up.... I knew I was better off not getting too cozy with a cop, however empathic, but we never talked about it" (323–24). When McGonnigal turns up again in *Burn Marks*—"the sergeant Bobby most preferred to work with" (100)—he is in a squad car with Michael Furey, another Chicago policeman with a romantic interest in Vic. In this novel, Vic is embarrassed when Bobby tells her he knows "there's been something between you and John, even though neither of you admits it"; she is stung into replying, "There's never been anything between McGonnigal and me ... we had one kiss and both knew we couldn't cross that line again" (*Burn* 134). McGonnigal is usually portrayed as the reasonable face of Chicago policing; V. I. describes him in the short story "Three-Dot Po" as "a stocky young man, very able, and I had a lot of respect for him" (WCB 231). Their professional relationship functions on a fairly even keel, with McGonnigal more likely than some of his colleagues to listen to V. I. and to follow through on some of her hunches. In the 2001 short story "Photo Finish," McGonnigal—"a Chicago police sergeant I used to do a lot of work with ... [until] the Department transferred him from downtown to one of the far northwest precincts" (*V. I. x 3*, 9)—and V. I. find themselves involved in the same case.

## "Mean Streets" (2007)

This essay for the *Guardian* review section explores how "America idealises the myth of the emotionally self-sufficient hard guy" with reference to the popular fiction genres of the western and the private-eye novel. Paretsky writes that her own fictional creation, V. I., was imagined as a woman with connections to others and so "a community began infiltrating my heroine's life from the start" (22).

## Media Adaptations

Paretsky's work has been adapted for radio and film, and is available for ebook readers and on CD. *Indemnity Only*, the first novel, appeared in an unabridged audio version by the BBC in 1991, read by Kathy Bates. The film *V. I. Warshawski* starring Kathleen Turner came out in 1991. *Deadlock* and *Killing Orders* were adapted by the English feminist playwright and novelist Michelene Wandor for BBC Radio 4 broadcast in 1995. Turner played V. I., and Eleanor Bron took the part of Dr. Lotty Herschel. A BBC Radio 4 adaptation of *Bitter Medicine* followed with Sharon Gless as V. I. *V. I. for Short* is a Redback audiobook, produced in 1995 by Dove Audio, with five unabridged short stories (from the

anthology of the same title) read by Jean Smart. Two short stories read by Turner, "Strung Out" and "Skin Deep," were issued by Durkin Hayes in 1997 as an audio cassette. The short story "Publicity Stunts" has also been adapted for BBC Radio 4 transmission in 2007. In 1999 Dove Audio produced a set of eight audio cassettes composed of an abridged version of the novel *Tunnel Vision* and five unabridged short stories from its 1995 production. *When Danger Follows You Home* is a 1997 USA Network film in association with Universal Television based on original characters created by Sara Paretsky. Two short stories "Dealer's Choice" and "Lily and the Sockeyes" were released in 2014 by Audio Holdings.

**See also *V. I. Warshawski* (the film)**

## "Miss Bianca" (2014)

The short story "Miss Bianca" was published in the Mystery Writers of America anthology *Ice Cold*, a collection of 20 tales of intrigue set during the cold war. Paretsky's story features 10-year-old Abigail, whose mother works as secretary to Dr. Kiel at a research lab. After school, Abigail is allowed to feed the lab mice; she picks up on tensions and rivalries amongst the research staff and PhD students, although she cannot always make sense of the adult dynamics. As Abigail fears for the safety of Miss Bianca, her favorite amongst the lab mice that are used in bacteriological research, she takes the mouse home in her pocket and succumbs to a fever. Afraid to tell her mother how she became ill, Abigail keeps Miss Bianca hidden until researcher Elena Mirova (accused of being a communist spy) seeks help from Abigail's mother. The delirious Abigail, taken hostage by the KGB man in pursuit of Elena, puts Miss Bianca down his shirtfront and frees herself when the mouse bites him. It is revealed that Elena fled Czechoslovakia after the authorities imprisoned and tortured her writer husband. The couple were accused of treason. Elena smuggled her scientific research out of the country and, with the secret help of Dr. Kiel, came to his lab to continue her work. In a brief afterword to the story, Paretsky notes that "Abigail grew up to be a doctor working for Physicians for Social Responsibility.... [A]s for the five lumpy Kiel children, one of them grew up to write about a Chicago private eye named V. I. Warshawski" (Paretsky, "Miss Bianca" 118).

## Morrell

The independent journalist Morrell first appears in *Hard Time*, where he becomes involved in V. I.'s investigation into the death of Nicola Aguinaldo and helps her recover after her month-long incarceration at Coolis Prison. His courtship of her is slow and gentle, with V. I. grateful that "he would respect my distance as long as I felt I needed to maintain it" (HT 379). When she decides to step closer, he becomes her lover and companion in a tender conclusion to the novel: "if my sleep was still disturbed, if the images of terror still sometimes woke me, at least I had the comfort of a friend to share my journey" (HT 385). Morrell, a "journalist who often covers human-rights issues," lives in Evanston (not far from Max Loewenthal's home), and like most of V. I.'s close circle, he has a love of classical music: "I could hear Morrell tinkering with a Schumann piano concerto, too loudly to hear my arrival" (TR 17, 184). Morrell's first name is never revealed, and very little of his own background emerges apart from what he reveals one night on the eve of a trip to Afghanistan. He talks to V. I. "about himself, his parents—whom he almost never mentioned—his childhood in Cuba when they had come as emigrants from Hungary" (TR 185). Morrell uses V. I.'s nickname bestowed by her father—*pepaiola* (pepper mill in Italian)—telling her, "You keep me stirred up, sneezing, with your vigorous remarks" (TR 119). He is a loving presence in V. I.'s life, although often absent on long assignments covering international human rights stories. When Morrell has to leave for Afghanistan, an unusually eloquent V. I. tells him, "it will be very hard for me to live without you these next few months" (TR 119). Morrell offers her wise counsel in *Total Recall*, when V. I. is terrified about Lotty: "Let her bring the story to you when she's strong enough to," he tells her (TR 118). In the subsequent novel *Blacklist*, V. I. is

"anxious, and feeling alone" (BL 1), because of her worries about Morrell; the book is set just after the September 11, 2001, terrorist attack on the World Trade Center. The opening chapter details Morrell's trip to "Kabul in the summer of 2001 ... with a contract for a book about daily life under the Taliban" (BL 2). After September 11, "Morrell disappeared for ten days" (2); in the weeks and months that followed, he "stayed on in Afghanistan to cover the war up close and personal" (2). In his continuing absence, with only intermittent email contact, V. I. takes to "wearing myself out running ... ten miles most days, instead of my usual five or six" (3). When she challenges him with her worries for his safety, his email response is robust; "Victoria ... if I come home tomorrow, will you faithfully promise to withdraw from every investigation where I worry about your safety?" (3). His absence, the reason for it, and V. I.'s fears about the dangers he faces constitute a major subcurrent throughout the novel. *Blacklist* concludes with a Humane Medicine colleague of Morrell phoning V. I. to inform her that Morrell "was shot, out in the Afghan countryside.... [W]e airlifted him to Zurich ... he gave us your telephone number and told us to ring you" (BL 415). Overwhelmed by the news, the detective expresses her relief in the last line of the story: "Once in a blue moon, in the midst of pain and helplessness, life hands us a reprieve" (BL 415). In the subsequent *Fire Sale*, Morrell is back in Evanston recovering from his serious wounds. V. I. is jealous of glamorous British journalist Morcena Love who is staying at Morrell's home while she is on assignment in Chicago; the detective is uncertain about the exact nature of the relationship between the two. *Hardball*, the 13th novel in the V. I. series, opens with the detective just returned from a ten-week trip to Italy "with Morrell, where we'd rented a cottage in Umbria" (HB 18). He is in the final stages of recovery from "the bullets that almost killed him in the Khyber Pass two years earlier," and V. I. is tracing the "remnants of Gabriella's [her mother] family" (HB 18). This trip marks the end of their affair as they leave Italy for different destinations, both having "realized we were ready to say good-bye" (HB 19). Later in the same novel, V. I. takes refuge in Morrell's empty apartment when she needs to stay out of sight for a while. She finds traces of her life with Morrell at his place and remembers that during their two years together, they had helped each other recover from a near-death experience. She wonders if "that was the only time we could really help each other, when we were near death. When we were near life, we couldn't sustain the relationship" (HB 345). A somewhat shadowy figure who makes relatively few demands on V. I., Morrell serves as a reminder of the importance of independent journalism in the Paretsky/Warshawski worldview and as evidence that V. I. is capable of sustaining an intimate relationship over an extended period of time.

## Music

Music is a running motif throughout the V. I. novels and functions on several levels. Often V. I. hums or sings a snatch of opera or popular song to indicate her mood, a frame of mind, or her deepest feelings. In *Blood Shot*, she sits at the piano and picks her way through "*Ch'io scordi di te*," a favorite aria of her mother, Gabriella, that suits her "mood of melancholy self-pity" (312). Suffering from a head cold in *Blacklist*, V. I. "lay down on the couch … [with] an old LP of Leontyne Price singing Mozart and watched the shadows change on the ceiling" (38). Music is a way that V. I. talks to herself as well as the reader. Sometimes it features as a leisure activity, attending a concert or other live music event is relaxing for V. I., and it is something she can do with Lotty Herschel, Max Loewenthal, or Jake Thibaut. It is also a powerful connection to Gabriella, who had trained to be an opera singer but never achieved pursuing it as a career. Although V. I. does not become the professional singer envisioned by her mother, the detective has an abiding knowledge and appreciation of music—a legacy from Gabriella. When Gabriella's upright piano is ruined through arson in *Killing Orders*, she replaces the instrument with a Steinway baby grand. V. I. knows opera well and can sing snatches of

it; Paretsky's choice of this particular cultural form—a form that often explores the darkness of grief and loss—hints at the consolation to be found in the singing voice. The love of music connects V. I. not only to her mother but also anchors her in the here and now as well as the people with whom she shares this passion. In *Total Recall*, V. I. lingers at a party to hear a recording of Rosa Ponselle singing "*L'amero, saro costante*"— "one of my mother's favorite arias" (124). The music motif seems to suggest the absence (of Gabriella) that is always present in V. I.'s life, perhaps a reminder that the dead exist as a counterpoint to the melody of the living. In the 14th novel, *Body Work*, V. I.'s cellphone "chirp[s] out a few bars of Mozart" (54).

Throughout the series, V. I. goes out dancing with various friends and lovers. The journalist Morrell—her lover in *Hard Time*, *Total Recall*, and *Blacklist*—also loves classical music and can play the piano. Her most recent lover, bass player Jake, is often out of town on long concert tours. He remasters a tape of Gabriella's voice for V. I., and as they listen together, V. I. says, "it seemed natural to bring out her red wineglasses and toast her memory, and exchange our life stories … while Mozart and my mother filled the room" (HB 446). Max and Lotty share V. I.'s love of music. In *Total Recall*, Michael, Max's cellist son, is in town "with the Cellini Chamber Ensemble, the London group started back in the forties by Max and Lotty's friend Carl Tisov" (TR 6). Tisov turns out to be the father of the child given up for adoption by Lotty long ago in London, when she was a medical student and he was a struggling musician. V. I. and Morrell attend a concert given by the Cellini Ensemble, and V. I. is moved by the music: "In a Schubert trio, the richness of Michael Loewenthal's playing, and the intimacy he seemed to feel—with his cello, with his fellow musicians- made me ache with longing" (121). In further twists to the motif, there are in-text references to contemporary singers such as Canadian singer-songwriter Sarah McLachlan (BL 43), and American vocalist Eva Cassidy, who died of cancer at age 33 in 1996. Paretsky often uses or adapts musical titles and phrases for chapter titles, as seen in *Total Recall* with "Tales of Hoffman," "Heartbreak House," and "Heard on the Street" and in *Blood Shot* with "Highway 41 Revisited," "The Old Folks at Home," and "Muddy Waters." *Critical Mass* has chapters titled "Eye on the Prize" and "Subterranean Homesick Blues." *Hardball* has a chapter title "The Boys in the Back Room."

## "My Hero Elizabeth Barrett Browning" (2010)

This short piece for the *Guardian* (London) Review section describes Paretsky's admiration for Victorian poet Elizabeth Barrett Browning, who "dedicated her life to her art [and] also had a passion for social justice" (6).

## "Mysteries" (1983)

This early review by Paretsky of *Northern Exposure* by Michael Kilian and *Deadlines* by Desmond Ryan was published in the *Chicago Tribune Book World*. Written only a year after her first novel was published, the review praises these mystery writers for ambitious plotting and careful control of pace but is critical of their treatment of female characters, signaling Paretsky's enduring concern about the stereotypical ways in which women often are portrayed in fiction. She writes, "the story is hampered by Kilian's treatment of women" and "the women in [Ryan's] 'Deadlines' … seem wooden" (5).

## Neely, Mary Louise

This character debuts in the fifth V. I. mystery *Blood Shot* (aka *Toxic Shock*) as a young "[P]atrol Officer … quiet and serious" (BS 217), whose commanding officer is Terry Finchley—aka the Finch. She works with other repeating police characters, including Lt. Bobby Mallory, Sgt. John McGonnigal, and Detective Conrad Rawlings. Mary Louise Neely appears in the subsequent novel *Burn Marks*, a slightly inscrutable figure on the fringes of V. I.'s usual scuffles with Mallory, and one with whom V. I. tries unsuccessfully to express some solidarity: "[S]he was looking rigidly ahead, making it impossible to know if she was embarrassed, disgusted, or just not very responsive" (*Burn* 295). The Finch explains to V. I., "She's the first female

in the unit … maybe she's afraid if she acts friendly around you, the lieutenant will think you've corrupted her" (ibid., 67). A minor character 12 or more years younger than V. I. at her debut, her role enlarges two novels later in *Tunnel Vision*, Mary Louise becomes involved in the life of the young Emily Messenger when V. I. and the police investigate the story behind the murder of Emily's mother, Deirdre. It is in this novel that Mary Louise reveals that her father sexually abused her. By the end of *Tunnel Vision*, Mary Louise has taken on the role of foster parent to Emily, Joshua, and Nathan Messenger and resigns from the police force to join V. I. on a trial basis as a private investigator. She explains to V. I. that she is "not much good in a hierarchical organization when I don't agree with the hierarchy" (TV 429); she and Vic agree to a freelance arrangement for six months "before considering a more formal arrangement" (TV 431). By the opening of *Hard Time*, Mary Louise is "going to law-school part time besides her part-time work for me [V. I.]" (HT 12). In the later *Total Recall* V. I. understands that her assistant's interest in a controversial recovered memory therapist probably stems from her own story: "Mary Louise had run away from an abusive home when she was a teenager. After a tumultuous ride through sex and drugs, she'd pulled herself together and become a police officer" (57). Mary Louise continues her foster parenting for the Messenger children and makes exasperated efforts to influence V. I.'s office habits: "Gosh, Vic, if you can clean out a briefcase, maybe you can learn to put papers into file jackets" (TR 164). In *Hard Time*, Mary Louise abruptly withdraws from her work for V. I. when she is threatened by anonymous callers who seem to know a lot about her foster children. Frightened, she retreats without explaining to V. I., and it takes courage for the two of them to rebuild their professional relationship when Mary Louise asks Vic to give her a second chance. Although Vic tells Mary Louise that "what hurt was the way you were judging me. Claiming I was running hotheaded into danger when I was fighting for my life" (378), they agree to "give it three months and see how we felt about the relationship then" (HT 379). By the 11th novel, *Blacklist*, Mary Louise has moved on to a "full-time job with a big downtown [law] firm" (BL 49) and left V. I. with a gap. The detective has "interviewed a number of people but hadn't found anyone yet who had both the street smarts and the organizational skills to take her place" (49). In the 2001 short story "Photo Finish," Mary Louise is still working as V. I.'s part-time assistant; V. I. notes "she had me fill out an expense report and time sheet—an important reason I keep her on my payroll" (*V. I. x 3*, 8). Mary Louise is one of a number of professional working women whose lives intersect with V. I.'s in her contemporary Chicago. Like Sal Barthele and Tessa Reynolds, these characters reflect many of the social and legal changes in the United States from the 1960s on that affected women's personal and professional circumstances. For instance, female Chicago police officers were first assigned to patrol duties in the mid–1970s, having previously been restricted to specialized assignments.

## "The New Censorship" (2003)

This essay for the *New Statesman* is subtitled "Sara Paretsky on the chilling climate in America, where a visit to a foreign-language website can get you arrested, and the FBI can search library records for dissenting books" (18). The article explores concerns about the changing marketplace in publishing, the cuts in public library budgets, and the effect of the Patriot Act on civil liberties; Paretsky is worried about a public climate in which "we are once again allowing fear to silence our speech" (ibid.). Some of the material in this essay was included, along with material from a public lecture given by Paretsky, in a May 2004 essay titled "Truth, Lies and Duct Tape" published in *Booklist* (a periodical of the American Library Association). An expanded and updated version of the material appears under the chapter title "Truth, Lies and Duct Tape" in Paretsky's 2007 memoir *Writing in an Age of Silence*.

## Newberry Library

A world-renowned independent research and reference library in Chicago since the late 1800s, the Newberry's noncirculating core collections focus on the humanities, with significant holdings in American history and culture, Chicago, the Midwest, music, and religion. It is a free library open to any member of the public conducting research on a topic covered by the collections. The library and its staff support a wide range of exhibitions, speaker events, seminars, and book events. Paretsky's own relationship with the Newberry dates back to the 1970s and 1980s when the library was under the leadership of Bill Towner and when Paretsky attended seminars and short adult education courses. Towner is named on the dedication page of *Breakdown* (2012) as one of the "librarians who've helped me navigate the great sea of learning." In 1992, Paretsky made her first gift to the library's archives: nine boxes of correspondence, manuscripts, photographs, clippings, publicity, and published books. This first set of boxes includes materials related to her education, early marketing career, Sisters in Crime, manuscripts, research notes and page proofs from early novels and anthologies, and folders of fan mail. A second gift in 1999 was composed of one box of six folders containing the outtakes for *Hard Time* published in autumn 1999. The archive was supplemented in 2000 with a further set of seven boxes including materials on short stories, publicity tours, speaking engagements, fan mail, *Ghost Country* galleys and notes, interviews given, and press kits for book launches. A fourth addition was made in 2012, a Works series in six labeled boxes, and a set of printed editions of the works accompanying it. The printed books include editions in Swedish, Spanish, Italian, Japanese, Dutch, Danish, Finnish, Icelandic, and German. The archive is titled the Paretsky Papers.

## "One Trial, Many Angles to Investigate" (1995)

This review of the new ABC series *Murder One* for the *New York Times* praises the tough but compassionate defense lawyer at its center. Paretsky says of the series' writer, "Mr. Bochco tries to make us think about where we are as a society: obsessed with exposing, even eviscerating a public figure, then moving like sharks to the next, without thinking again about the carcass left behind." The review subsequently appeared in the *Cape Cod Times* under the title "It's No Trial to Watch 'Murder One.'"

### "Ode to the Season: When Your Landlord Is a Precinct Captain" (2008)

"Ode to the Season" is a short piece for the *Chicago Tribune* in which Paretsky remembers the bitter winter of 1969 when she lived "in a three-flat on 51st Street, which I shared with three other women" and their struggles to obtain adequate heating for the apartment.

### "Our Bodies, Our Fertility" (2012)

In this article for the *Chicago Tribune* Perspective section, Paretsky describes the continuing assaults on the rights of women to make their own decisions about sexuality and fertility. She highlights "access to contraception" (15) as the next front in the reproductive rights wars being played out in the courts, the churches, and the legislature. Paretsky notes that the recent decision of the Obama administration requiring "most insurers to cover contraception, even in Catholic hospitals" is already under threat as "churches are fighting this and other regulations on the grounds that they infringe on their religious liberty" (15). She poses the following question: "[H]ow can bishops, legislatures or judges … believe that their judgment is superior to that of the women who will have to live with the consequences of an unwanted pregnancy for the rest of their lives?" (ibid.).

### Paretsky's Writing Career

Sara Paretsky has worked with Dominick Abel as her U.S. agent and David Grossman as her UK agent for all of her professional writing life. Her fifth novel *Blood Shot* is dedicated to "Dominick." While *Indemnity Only* was still in galleys in the United States, Gollancz and Hayakawa bought the novel; the UK edition appeared in 1982 and the Japanese edition in 1983. Since its first publication, it has sold upward of 100,000 copies. All of the V. I. novels have subsequently been published continuously in the United Kingdom, Japan, and Denmark; foreign editions have also been published in Germany, Italy, Norway, Sweden, the Netherlands, Finland, Iceland, Spain, Brazil, France, Hungary, Poland, Bulgaria, Korea, Slovakia, Portugal, Russia, Greece, and Indonesia. After the first two novels with the American publisher Dial, she moved to William Morrow for the next two and subsequently to Delacorte, where she remained through the publication of *Total Recall*, the 10th in the V. I. series and including the first standalone *Ghost Country*. Douglas A. Stumpf worked with Paretsky at both Dial where he was an associate editor and then at William Morrow as a senior editor and vice-president in 1989. During the period at Delacorte, then under the executive editorship of Carole Baron, *Burn Marks* and *Tunnel Vision* (sixth and eighth in the series) earned places on the *New York Times* bestseller list. In March 1991 the paperback print run for *Burn Marks* was 419,000 copies. *Hard Time* (ninth in series) was on the *Publishers Weekly* hardcover bestseller list for 16 weeks ("Hardcover" 88). Paretsky paid tribute to her Delacorte editor, Jackie Farber, as "one of a vanishing breed of editors [with] the capacity to look at the book you're trying to write, not the book she would have written" (Rozan 44). *Hardball* (2009) is dedicated posthumously to another inspiring editor, Kate Jones (at Hamish Hamilton), who died in London in 2008; the epigraph reads, "[T]he world, and my words in it, are poorer for your leaving." In 2003, Putnam published *Blacklist* (11th in the series), which reached the *Publishers Weekly* bestseller list ("Paperback" 94), and it remains her U.S. publisher.

After Paretsky had published with Gollancz over several years in the United Kingdom, Nicolette Jones's note in *The Bookseller* broke the news that "Paretsky … has been snatched from Gollancz (who published her last five books), by Carmen Callil at Chatto.… Paretsky goes from strength to strength in America, where the print run of her latest paperback, *Toxic Shock*, was five times the run for her previous book" (4). Chatto & Windus published the sixth novel, *Burn Marks*; the next five novels in the V. I. series and the standalone *Ghost Country* were published in the United Kingdom by Hamish Hamilton. In 2005, the author moved to Hodder & Stoughton with *Fire Sale* published in 2006; the firm remains her UK publishers. *Fire Sale* was listed in the "Top 20 Original Fiction" bestsellers in *The Bookseller* ("Horror Story" 46). *Critical Mass*, published in 2013, was named in a *Sunday Times* (London) list of the 50 best crime/mystery novels in the last five years (*Sunday Times* 2014). Several of the novels have been adapted for radio broadcast and audiobooks. As her career developed, Paretsky gained experience in the world of publishing and began to speak out about matters of interest to her, in particular strategies for furthering "the careers of women in the mystery field and … correcting imbalances in the treatment of women" (Trembley 266) in the review pages of the print media. In 1998, she spoke at the Upper Midwest Booksellers Association Trade Show in St. Paul, Minnesota. Her speech, titled "Damned by Dollars," references Melville writing to Hawthorne in the middle of the nineteenth century with a complaint about the pressure of the dollar on his writing. Paretsky's speech discussed today's climate, pointing out that "the forces of silence can come as readily from the market as from a totalitarian state" (160). As Paretsky was born in Iowa, her books are shelved in the "Iowa Authors" section of the University of Iowa Library's Special Collections in Iowa City. Another Iowan, Mildred Wirt Benson (aka Carolyn Keene), author of many of the famous Nancy Drew mysteries, is shelved in the same section; Benson's papers and manuscripts are held at the nearby Iowa Women's Archives. Throughout the Paretsky oeuvre (including the standalone novels, short stories, and nonfiction), the themes of female voice and agency are worked and reworked; framed and reframed; enlarged and refined. Arguably it is the abiding concern in all her material. Writing a successful series character is a challenging proposition. Paretsky has kept it fresh in a number of ways such as incorporating a range of secondary characters with stories that sometimes come to the fore (such as Lotty's story in *Total Recall* and *Critical Mass*);

taking breaks to write standalone novels; building up V. I.'s backstory through the histories of her biological family and close associates such as Mr. Contreras; introducing younger continuing characters such as Mary Louise Neely, cousin Petra, and Boom-Boom's goddaughter Bernie; allowing V. I. to age in real time; and responding to modern technological developments such as computers and hand-held devices. Paretsky, in common with other modern mystery authors, often references famous detectives, authors, and methods in her texts as in-jokes—such as in *Total Recall*, V. I. puzzles over the scenario behind the dead body she has just discovered: "He tried to blackmail his mystery caller, who told Fepple they needed to talk privately in his office—where he shot Fepple, staging it to look like suicide. Very [British thriller author] Edgar Wallace" (159). References to Nancy Drew, the famous girl detective created in the 1920s, turn up frequently. Paretsky's introduction to the 1991 facsimile edition of *The Mystery of the Old Clock* pays tribute to the influence of the smart girl detective figure. In the 2013 *Critical Mass*, a young librarian addresses V. I. as "Nora" in homage to Dashiell Hammett's witty amateur detectives Nick and Nora Charles from *The Thin Man*; the same novel references Edgar Allan Poe in the phrase "like the purloined letter" (236), and P. D. James and T. S. Eliot in the phrase "the skull beneath her skin" (359). Paretsky's broader erudition is evident in her epigraphs, dedications, in-text allusions to forgotten painters and artists, punning titles, chapter titles, and paraphrases of poets such as W. H. Auden and W. B. Yeats. Paretsky's famous detective is intelligent, independent, and intrepid, unafraid to speak her mind. In a broadcast for the American Library Association Paretsky described V. I. as "tall, thin and stronger than she looks." Speaking at the Library of Congress Center for the Book in 2007, the author tells her audience that V. I. "practices truth and honesty and expects the same of others" and that she created the character as a woman who "can act and solve problems" (www.loc.gov). Interviewer Susan Ferraro described V. I. as a "hard-boiled, hard-hitting female private eye in Chicago whose wise-guy patter and glorious self-confidence turned the mystery genre inside out" (23). Paretsky told mystery writer S. J. Rozan that "V. I. is about voice, not action.... She speaks for people on the margins who have no voice" (44). Like the young Nancy Drew, another principled and fearless detective, V. I. became a role model for generations of women wanting to read about women like themselves and wanting to live meaningful lives that made a difference. The signature character has appeared in 17 full-length novels and a dozen short stories to date. "One of the most critically and commercially successful of contemporary urban crime writers," Paretsky is "arguably the most prominent of a group of women crime writers ... who both used and challenged the conventions of hard-boiled detective fiction by producing politically committed, feminist private investigators" (Dempsey 306). The oeuvre of "laconically two-word-titled novels ... adheres to the conventions of the hard-boiled crime story, but these conventions are largely undercut because the protagonist is a woman" (ibid.). Paretsky's novels explore complicated issues of racial and sexual oppression in contemporary U.S. society—the roots of both oppressions run deep into American economic and political history.

## Peppy and Mitch

Peppy and Mitch are the dogs that V. I. shares with her downstairs neighbor, Mr. Contreras. Peppy, the golden retriever acquired by V. I. at the end of *Bitter Medicine*, becomes a devoted companion to the detective and Mr. Contreras. Mitch, named in memory of Mr. Contreras's friend and comrade Mitch Kruger, is added to the household in *Guardian Angel* when Peppy gives birth to a litter of eight pups fathered by a neighborhood black lab. Peppy and Mitch are a constant presence in the novels and are V. I.'s best excuse for getting regular exercise along the lakefront. The dogs give V. I. daily responsibilities, anchoring her into a domestic routine of sorts. They are a source of comfort and companionship for the loner detective; unlike others in her like, they do not judge her. They provide a joint focus for V. I.

and Mr. Contreras, both of whom love the dogs, although they sometimes quarrel over the best way to look after them. The dogs provide comic relief when their exuberance threatens to get the better of stiff-necked neighbors and nosy cops. They are less successful as guard dogs, as they are more inclined to try to make friends with humans than to scare them off. Peppy and Mr. Contreras save V. I.'s life in a dramatic rescue scene in *Blood Shot* when they find her tied up and close to death in Dead Stick Pond. In *Hard Time* Mitch takes a bullet in his shoulder during a showdown between V. I. and the murderous CEO Robert Baladine, but survives thanks to an able veterinarian and a blood donation from Peppy. Two novels later, in *Blacklist*, V. I. wears out herself and the dogs by running off her anxiety about her lover Morrell's dangerous assignment in Afghanistan: "the two dogs I share with my downstairs neighbor ... started retreating to Mr. Contreras's bedroom when they saw me arrive in my sweats" (BL 3). In *Body Work* the dogs once again prove to be "physically taxing, but emotionally rewarding, what I needed these days (BW 435). They are a much-loved part of the series with personalities of their own; the accuracy with which they are portrayed no doubt owes something to Paretsky's own love of golden retrievers.

## "Photo Finish" (2001)

This V. I. short story explores the human desire for revenge and was first published in *Mary Higgins Clark Mystery Magazine*. It subsequently appeared in a 2005 anthology edited by Tony Hillerman and Rosemary Herbert and in the 2007 collection of V. I. short stories *V. I. x 3*. A young man from Charleston, SC, tells V. I. that he is in Chicago looking for his photographer father, Hunter Davenport, last seen when the young man was 11. The detective tracks down the elusive photographer but is mystified when he denies having any children. Eventually the truth behind the client's story emerges when V. I. realizes he is the son of Lady Helen Banidore, a beautiful, wealthy, and titled celebrity who died years before in a car crash in Kenya on safari. Lady Helen was followed throughout her adult life by the paparazzi who were "supplying the insatiable appetites in America and France for beautiful women with titles" (*V. I. x 3*: 11). Her son, Andrew, had been taken to the crash site, and newspapers "had used a photograph of the white-faced boy kneeling by his dead mother, cradling her head on his knees" (op. cit., 12). Davenport was one of the pack following Lady Helen, and Andrew holds Davenport responsible for his mother's death. When Andrew tries and fails to kill Davenport, V. I. demonstrates her capacity to see justice done and her conviction that mercy is also important. She obtains Andrew's agreement to underwrite Davenport's lifetime medical expenses in exchange for not finding "evidence that links you to that Toyota" (ibid., 4). The story has echoes of the real-life story of Diana, Princess of Wales, who was hounded by paparazzi and whose untimely death fleeing from the press became the topic of considerable public interest.

### "The Pietro Andromache" (1988)

This short story involves V. I.'s friend Dr. Lotty Herschel and has V. I. as a character, but it is told from the third-person point of view of Lotty's lover/colleague Max Loewenthal. First published as "The Case of the Pietro Andromache" in *Alfred Hitchcock's Mystery Magazine* in 1988, it has been republished a number of times including the 1995 volume of V. I. short stories *Windy City Blues* (aka *V. I. for Short* in UK). When Lotty and Max attend a reception at the home of the new chief of staff at the Beth Israel Hospital, Lotty encounters an alabaster sculpture in Dr. Lewis Caudwell's fabled private art collection. She recognizes the statue of Andromache mourning Hector as one that belonged to her family in Vienna before the war. She points out the chip on Hector's foot that she remembers. Drs. Herschel and Caudwell have tangled in the past at hospital board meetings over "their radically differing approaches to medicine" (WCB 62), and now Lotty argues violently in public with Caudwell over the provenance of Pietro's sculpture. When the statue goes missing and Caudwell is found strangled, the police arrest Lotty on suspicion of

murder and theft. The distraught Max, who is not entirely convinced of Lotty's innocence, hires V. I. to investigate on behalf of Lotty, although Lotty refuses to speak to anyone. V. I.'s inquiries about Caudwell's party lead her to focus on "three people with an ax to grind" (WCB 85). She travels to Arkansas and North Carolina in search of crucial background information about Caudwell's family—his ex-wife, his two grown children, and his brother. Matters are resolved when V. I. gives the police the story of what really happened and identifies the perpetrator. The statue mysteriously ends up back in Lotty's possession; she explains to Max that it was "Victoria…. I told her the problem and she got it for me. On the condition that I not ask how she did it" (WCB 90). The story concludes with Max accepting that natural justice of a sort has been done.

### Poe, Edgar Allan *see* "Imagining Edgar Allan Poe"

### "Poster Child" (2011)

The short story "Poster Child" was published in the anthology *Send My Love and a Molotov Cocktail* that offers a hint of the hard-hitting content. Paretsky's tale opens with a woman walking her dog and discovering the body of a man hidden under a bench near the Monroe Street harbor in Chicago. His mouth is stuffed with anti-abortion leaflets. Police officer Pacheco is on the scene in minutes, pulled away from his nearby assignment to monitor a demonstration with right-to-life supporters and pro-choice campaigners. Pacheco's job was to "make sure protestors and baby killers didn't get physical with each other" (50). The policeman recognizes the victim as Mr. Culver, a high-profile, right-to-life demonstrator known for involving his children in his guerrilla tactics outside abortion clinics. The victim is described as "a bully and a thug" (52) by Dr. Adair, who works in a clinic targeted by Culver. Dr. Adair subsequently comes under suspicion for his murder. Lawyer Leydon Ashford, a recurring character in the V. I. series, represents Dr. Adair and protests her innocence. Pacheco and his partner, Liz Marchek, eventually uncover the truth of the murder as a result of a visit to the family home, where they discover the teenage son's rage and despair over his father's physical violence and coercion to participate in the pro-life campaign. The son admits to killing his father on the park bench and hiding the body underneath. The story concludes with Leydon's hope that the youth will be treated with some sympathy and understanding by the judicial system.

The motif of the bullying parent and the suffering child is a familiar one in the Paretsky oeuvre, as is the subject of women's reproductive rights and the issue of the serious money that backs the right-to-life campaigners. There are references in the story to sexism and racism in the police force—also familiar territory. Lieutenant Terry Finchley, another repeating character in the V. I. series, makes a brief appearance. There is reference made by the police to the Chicago private-eye V. I. Warshawski who is, according to them, "able to operate outside standard systems with impunity" (60).

## "Preface" (2004)

Paretsky was invited to write the foreword to a coffee-table book of photographs of famous *Chicago Apartments* by Neil Harris. Paretsky's introduction discusses the Chicago buildings in which she imagines her rich criminals live. She points out that one convention of American crime fiction, particularly the private-eye genre as embodied in Raymond Chandler's novels, is that "the rich are definitely corrupt"; and so Paretsky, like Chandler, is prone to using luxury apartments and dwellings as "the setting for lies, secrets, and villainy" (11).

## "Private Eyes, Public Spheres" (1988)

Paretsky's article for the *Women's Review of Books* traces how "the reaction of men to the changing social role of women is writ large in genre fiction" (12). She expresses her concerns that two films in circulation at the time of writing her article (*Presumed Innocent* and *Fatal Attraction*) feature central female characters who destroy the lives of others; Paretsky argues that this reflects a social

and cultural "underlying unease, this fear that men have become superfluous" (13). The essay concludes that if "women have become so threatening that men can only tolerate them if they are crippled[, it] is a sobering thought for feminists" (13).

## "Protocols of the Elders of Feminism" (1994)

This essay for the Australian journal *Law/Text/Culture* explores the obstacles confronting women writers who seek a public voice and the contested relationship between women's voices and the public sphere. Paretsky characteristically defines the problem as "the rage our culture feels against women" (26).

## "Publicity Stunts" (1996)

This V. I. short story was first published in the 1996 anthology *Women on the Case* edited by Paretsky. It has subsequently appeared in several other collections, most recently in the 2007 *Chicago Blues* edited by Libby Fischer Hellman. V. I. is approached by the successful crime novel writer Lisa Macauley who wants to hire a bodyguard. The celebrity author has been receiving hate mail in response to her fictional detective "who goes against all the popular positions that feminists have persuaded the media to support" (*V. I. x 3*, 16). When V. I. turns her down, Macauley persuades media darling and local radio evangelist Claud Barnett to broadcast diatribes against the detective; he willingly uses his program to urge the public to boycott V. I. because she "investigate(s) the politics of all [her] potential clients and won't take anyone who's given money to a Christian or a Republican cause" (17). The vindictive Barnett continues to smear V. I. on air while giving Lisa and her new book considerable free publicity. Murray Ryerson, the investigative reporter for the *Herald-Star* and V. I.'s "one time lover, sometime rival, occasional pain-in-the-butt, and even, now and then, a good friend" (17), comes to V. I.'s defense with a "nice story on me in the Star's ChicagoBeat section, recounting some of my great past successes" (19). Matters do not improve when V. I. and Macauley engage in a public verbal altercation when they accidentally meet at a jazz club—a glass of champagne is thrown, and photos are taken. When Macauley's body is found by her personal trainer the next morning, V. I. ends up in jail. Her lawyer Freeman Carter intercedes to have her released on bail, and V. I. sets out to discover who and what is behind Macauley's murder. She finds some dark secrets lurking from the time of Macauley's Christian fundamentalist upbringing in Wisconsin and an unexpected connection between Macauley and the right-wing talk show host. When Macauley's killer is exposed as a child molester and found guilty of second-degree murder, V. I. "got a lot of public vindication," but the celebration champagne cannot wipe out the "bitter taste" in her mouth over the public opinion poll results that suggest many still believe the killer to be "innocent of all charges" (28). The story explores the dangers inherent in the increasingly corporate, celebrity-driven world of broadcast media: as independent investigative journalism disappears and as funds for the global media companies increasingly come from "high-end sponsors" (18) eager to promote their own agendas, V. I. and her author fear for the future of a free press.

## Rawlings, Conrad

Chicago police detective Conrad Rawlings first appears in *Bitter Medicine* as, according to V. I., "a solidly built black man about my age ... [with] a soft voice, rather husky" (*Bitter* 51). They work together to flush out the guilty parties at the hospital where the interests of commercial medicine have led to some tragic and unnecessary deaths. At the close of this novel, Conrad asks V. I., "You want to get a drink someplace? Something to eat?" (311). The surprised V. I. admits that this sounds appealing but takes a rain check and reflects, "Rawlings was amusing, but it's not good for a PI to get too sociable with the police" (320). Three novels later he becomes V. I.'s lover in *Guardian Angel* and breaks up with her at the end of *Tunnel Vision*. Their romantic relationship has both tender and tough moments. Their professional relationship continues beyond the break-up of the

affair, and to some extent it changes her prickly confrontations with the police force, though tensions remain between V. I. and Bobby Mallory. Conrad is a Vietnam vet with a gold tooth, and he lives in Hyde Park. His best friend is Terry Finchley, aka the Finch—another African American Chicago policeman. Conrad's family consists of his possessive widowed mother and four sisters; his sister Camilla is a year younger than Conrad and "the closest to him" (TV 23). More of her backstory emerges in *Tunnel Vision*; she "eschewed the pink-collar jobs she'd trained for in high school and become an apprentice welder" (TV 23). Later she starts a "woman-only company" in construction, working on "low-cost housing for single mothers" (23); in this novel she and Vic encounter each other via V. I.'s current case and develop a friendship of sorts. However, the family is not altogether approving of V. I. or her relationship with Conrad, as she discovers when he tells her, "My sister heard about you from some busybody on the grapevine and won't let me sully her living room now" (GA 369). Mr. Contreras, V. I.'s downstairs neighbor, also has trouble with the relationship between V. I. and Conrad. His old-fashioned views about women and his prejudices about black people lead to some offensive opinions that he does not hesitate to express to Vic, telling her, "I grew up in a different time.... I don't like seeing you with him, it makes me uncomfortable" (GA 356). At the close of *Guardian Angel* V. I. and Conrad are embarked on a love affair, although she wonders "how long we could stay close before our careers collided" (369). He comforts her when she wakes from "nightmares of my mother's death, dreams in which Lotty and Gabriella are inextricably entangled" (369); in spite of his reassurances that he will not leave her "in the lurch" and his embrace as they stand at the window looking out, the novel ends on a melancholy note as V. I. "shivered in the summer air" (370). By the start of the next novel, *Tunnel Vision*, the relationship is already strained, with arguments about V. I.'s habit of breaking the law when she is investigating a case. Conrad is badly wounded in this story when his attempt to rescue V. I.

from a life-threatening situation goes wrong; his own life is endangered, and he ends up in hospital with both his pride and shoulder in need of rebuilding. His withdrawal from V. I. is hard for her; not mincing his words, he tells her: "I think you and I need to cool things off for a while. The last month has taken a real toll on my love for you. You don't have enough room in your breast for compromise" (414). Sad at his intransigence, she accepts his decision. He appears again in *Fire Sale*, by which time he has been promoted to "watch commander ... down at 103rd and Oglesby" (5), but things are still frosty between them. He makes a brief appearance in *Hard Ball*.

## Red Venetian Wine Glasses

The eight red Venetian wine glasses, brought to Chicago in the suitcase of V.I.'s mother, Gabriella, when she left fascist Italy for an uncertain future with relatives in the United States, are amongst V. I.'s most treasured possessions. They are first described in *Indemnity Only* when she offers a drink to her guest Ralph Devereux. The glasses, "a beautiful clear red are an heirloom and" (77), appear throughout the series, oblique reminders of Gabriella's story as a refugee and her early death from cancer. They are vulnerable objects. Throughout the series the glasses are usually V. I.'s first concern when her apartment suffers from a number of break-ins and a horrific arson attack in *Killing Orders*. One goblet lies "shattered on the wood floor" (IO 101) after intruders ransack her apartment, and another "had a jagged piece broken from it" (KO 170) after a fire that guts her home. However, V. I. guards the remaining glasses carefully and is still using them in the 15th novel, *Breakdown*, when she and her current lover, Jake, fortify themselves with some Black Label. The red wine glasses function on several levels: they suggest Gabriella's past and her connection to the crafts of her native country; they signal a graciousness in life that Gabriella appreciated but that is not predominant with Vic; they symbolize conviviality in V. I.'s life when she retrieves them to share with friends and lovers. The glasses suggest another side to

the unsentimental detective. Further than that, the breakable glasses serve as a reminder at the fragility of memory and the importance of memory. When the glasses shatter here and there, they also hint at the broken dreams of Gabriella, who has exchanged her longing to become an opera singer for the protection of her husband, Tony. In an argument with the overprotective Roger Ferrant, V. I. remembers "Protection. The middle-class dream. My father protecting Gabriella in a Milwaukee Avenue bar. My mother giving him loyalty and channeling her fierce creative passions into a South Chicago tenement in gratitude" (KO 188). The fragile glasses also suggest the sadness of a life cut short (Gabriella's death when V. I. is a teenager). The mother's story is remembered and reinscribed each time V. I. uses them and takes a moment to tell her guests something about the background to the glasses. The wine glasses seem to help V. I. gain a sense of belonging to her mother's past. The detective's love of Italy, and especially her appreciation of Italian food and wine, come from Gabriella and are symbolized in the glasses. V. I.'s identification of herself as a resisting person, as well as her capacity for surviving fragmentation and bruising, also come from Gabriella, who has herself resisted and survived. Gabriella is the child of a Catholic mother and a Jewish father in Benito Mussolini's prewar Italy. This means trouble, not only between the warring families but also in the wider context of the persecution of the Jewish population in the 1930s. In this sense, the glasses perhaps signal something about the shattered dreams and lost lives of Holocaust victims. The glasses also connect V. I. to her mother's musical ambitions: playing some scales on her mother's piano, V. I. reminds herself to practice because, "along with the red glasses, my voice was my legacy from Gabriella" (KO 154). In *Hardball* (2009) she and Jake (also a musician) listen to Gabriella's voice on a remastered tape: "it seemed natural to bring out her red wineglasses and toast her memory, and exchange our life stories ... while Mozart and my mother filled the room" (446).

## "Refusing to Allow Pressure to Silence a Critical Voice" (2007)

This short biographical op-ed piece for the *Chicago Tribune* Perspective section looks back to the 2003 U.S. invasion of Iraq and the author's speech at the Toledo Public Library that addressed issues of censorship and silence and the powers of the Patriot Act. Although she had been "advised" to tone down her remarks, she gave the speech she intended to deliver and received a standing ovation. Material in that speech made its way into one of the essays in Paretsky's memoir *Writing in an Age of Silence*. In the op-ed piece, Paretsky introduces the newly published memoir as a text that deals with "the questions of who gets to speak, and who listens…. These are the issues I explore in my new collection of essays…. Silence is more dangerous and more crippling than dissenting from power" (1–2).

See also **"Sara Paretsky Replies"** 2007

## "Remarks in Honor of Carolyn Heilbrun" (2005)

Paretsky's testimonial, given at a memorial service for Carolyn Heilbrun, was printed in a special issue of the academic journal *Tulsa Studies in Women's Literature*. Heilbrun had a career as an English literature professor at Columbia University in New York and, under the pseudonym Amanda Cross, also published a series of classic detective stories featuring the academic Kate Fansler throughout the 1960s, 1970s, and 1980s. Heilbrun's novels and her outspoken, witty protagonist found a ready audience. Although the character Kate Fansler was slow to identify herself as a feminist academic (several novels into the series), the debut novel marked out new territory in the crime and mystery landscape of the 1960s; Heilbrun continued the series through the 1980s. Paretsky pays tribute to the way in which Heilbrun, writing as Cross, "opened a window and let fresh air blow in on the crime novel and on the world's way of thinking about women and our stories" (243) when she created Kate Fansler in 1963.

## Reynolds, Tessa

Tessa Reynolds makes her first appearance in *Bitter Medicine*—a "tall, flamboyant" artist (*Bitter* 541)—focused on her work as a sculptor. The lover of Dr. Malcolm Tregiere, Lotty's medical associate, Tessa refuses to accept that Tregiere's death was at the hands of a local gang (as the police believe); together, she and Lotty urge V. I. to investigate the murder further. Tessa turns up later in the series in *Tunnel Vision* as V. I.'s co-tenant in an industrial office building in gentrifying Wicker Park/Bucktown, when V. I. is forced to leave the Pulteney Building in the Loop. Tessa's half of the building is a studio, where she "welds big metal chunks into space-age sculptures" (HB 5), whereas V. I.'s half comprises an office and a room where she keeps a camp bed. There is a shared kitchen and bathroom. Tessa comes from "African-American aristocracy, her mother a famous lawyer, her father a highly successful engineer" (HB 10). Tessa's mother lives in a "palace on the Gold Coast" (HT 205). The co-tenancy functions well for the most part, although Tessa (and her worried parents) suffer occasionally when V. I.'s cases result in office break-ins (in *Hardball* for instance). They are still sharing a lease on the building on Leavitt Street, near the junction of North Avenue with Milwaukee, in the 16th novel *Critical Mass* (2013).

## "The Rough Landing We Give Refugees" (1999)

This op-ed piece for the *New York Times* is on the subject of the reform of U.S. welfare laws. Paretsky argues that the "new temporary-assistance program is out of sync with the needs of refugees" and that the "Federal Government should provide specialized cash and medical assistance to refugees during their first year in this country" so that "the states could concentrate on the needy families that already live here."

## Ryan, Desmond *see* "Mysteries"

## Ryerson, Murray

Murray Ryerson is a city desk reporter for the *Herald-Star* newspaper and one of V. I.'s most significant partners in crime. Red-haired, bearded, and scruffily dressed, he is always after a good story and knows Vic is likely to give him a scoop. He first appears in *Indemnity Only* when V. I. calls him for some background information on prominent Chicago figures and promises that "if a story breaks, you can have it" (IO 145). In the early novels Ryerson's reputation as an independent investigative reporter who breaks stories about the misdeeds of the rich and powerful is important; a justice of sorts is provided as he and V. I. work in tandem to expose in print people who are often beyond the reach of the law. This partnership, however, changes across the oeuvre, as independent print media and investigative reporting in the real world give way to corporate market forces. Murray's own career and agency, as outlined in the novels, reflects twenty-first-century changes in the news world. In *Burn Marks*, the sixth novel, V. I. describes him as "Chicago's leading crime reporter ... a leading authority on the frequent intersection of crime and politics in town" (144). By the ninth mystery, *Hard Time*, V. I. is expressing some sympathy for Murray who has had to reinvent himself as a TV reporter assigned to celebrity stories when his newspaper is acquired by the GEN conglomerate (Global Entertainment Network), which prioritizes entertainment over hard news. Paretsky's use of the name Ryerson for her character signals a possible echo of the prominent Chicago family of the same name, who settled in Chicago before the Civil War and who have been active in business, cultural, and civic organizations ever since. The Ryerson Library at the Art Institute of Chicago was established with a legacy from the family. The Ryerson family origins can be traced back to Norway; in *Tunnel Vision*, V. I. describes her friend as "an outsize Viking in a red beard" (TV 171). Suspicious of the Democratic party-machine control of Chicago and the county, Murray is good at sniffing out dubious connections among elected officials, big-business executives, and state agencies. As dogged an investigator as V. I., Murray tends to follow the money and follow the vote. He has all the qualities of a good investigative journalist that V. I. has as a detective: persistence, determination, and a moral compass. He shares V. I.'s passion for the Cubs. In *Burn Marks*, V. I. explains some of the complications in their relationship:

"[A]t times we've been friendly enough to be lovers, but both of us covering the same scene and having strong personalities make it hard to avoid conflict" (*Burn* 144). She refers again in the later *Tunnel Vision* to the brief romantic past between them: "Murray and I go back to my days in the PD's Office when he'd been a rookie reporter trying to find who was leaking defense files to the state's attorney.... For a brief time we'd compounded the mess by becoming lovers" (TV 172). In the subsequent *Hard Time*, V. I. refers to their past as "history so ancient there weren't even any archaeological remains to look through ... going to bed with someone that competitive had been a colossal mistake" (HT 28). She reports they have long since settled for irascible friendship and loyalty as they "collaborated and competed on financial scandal in Chicago" (HT 5). As the series develops, he and V. I. are portrayed in a mutually exasperating and mutually beneficial relationship, with many opportunities to exchange personal and professional insults. On a fishing trip made by V. I. to Murray's office, he refuses to cooperate, reminding her, "I never got anything from you except with a crowbar, and then only if you needed a favor back" (TV 172). The bottom line, however, is that they usually have each other's back. Murray's career has suffered over the years; the *Herald-Star*, "which used to be a great newspaper until, like papers all over America, they began cutting staff and pages to keep Wall Street happy" (BW 117), has been acquired by the GEN corporation, whose cable news channel has eclipsed the print media. Murray makes the uneasy transition to TV news at Global in *Hard Time*, the ninth novel in the series, accepting a role as host of a "Behind Scenes in Chicago" segment in the hopes of placing his investigative stories. At a Global reception held at the Golden Glow on the eve of his TV debut, V. I.'s sympathy is invoked: "Somehow it made my heart ache—foolish Murray, anxiously decking himself for the media gods" (HT 5). She knows Murray "had been having a tough time since Global bought the paper. They hadn't stopped any of his digging, but they wouldn't print any stories they considered politically sensitive" (HT 11). Later in this same novel, however, Murray prints a discrediting story about her based, unknowingly, on information planted to manipulate him; V. I. finds it hard to forgive him for this betrayal, although he apologizes to her in a letter. In the 2010 *Body Work*, V. I. worries that although he is "still a good reporter ... he's depressed a lot of the time and turns to me way too much for news" (BW 117). Together, they stage a spectacular news-scoop on Murray's live TV show that results in GEN firing Murray. He finds a job on a political campaign.

### "Sara Paretsky: My First Car" (2014)

This brief column for the *Chicago Tribune* is accompanied by a video clip of Paretsky next to the red Jaguar convertible she owns. She used to fantasize about such a car as a younger woman who drove more ordinary cars.

### "Sara Paretsky on Liza Cody" (2011)

In a column for the *Guardian* (London), five crime writers were invited to nominate their favorite living author in their field. Paretsky selected the British crime writer Liza Cody, as she admires Cody for her "gift for language and storytelling, and [being] willing to do the hard work of digging into real emotional life" (23).

### "Sara Paretsky Replies" (2007)

Paretsky's letter to the editor of the *Library Journal* was written in response to an article published by the journal that revisited the author's 2003 speech in Toledo "on censorship and the silencing of dissent" (10). Paretsky recalls that "many people, after my lecture, told me they had thought they were alone in their opposition to our government's policies, so skillfully had the government silenced dissent. The library made it possible for them to feel less isolated" (10). Paretsky's commitment to public libraries and her conviction that they play an important role in the development of a well-informed public is made clear in this piece

and in her promotional work for the American Library Association.

### "Settled Score" (1991)

The short story "Settled Score" was first published in the anthology *A Woman's Eye* edited by Paretsky. The story later appears in the 1995 collection *Windy City Blues* (aka *V. I. for Short*). The title signals the story's connection to the world of professional musicians. Penelope, niece of Dr. Lotty Herschel and daughter of Lotty's only brother Hugo, is in a wintry Chicago to scout locations and designers for her father's chain of dress shops and to see her lover Paul Servino, who is an analyst friend of Lotty's. Over the dinner table at V. I.'s apartment Lotty and Paul argue about the question of "legal versus moral responsibility" (WCB 187); the issue of claiming personal responsibility for one's actions provides the theme of the story. The dinner guests include Lotty, Max Loewenthal, Penelope, Paul, and Chaim Lemke—"a clarinetist ... [and] a slight melancholy man" (WCB 188). Chaim knows Lotty and Max from their time together in London as refugees during the war; he is leaving the next day for a two-week concert tour. At the end of the dinner, V. I. suggests "some appeasement.... Chaim brought his clarinet and Max his violin. Paul, if you'll play the piano, Penelope and I will sing" (op. cit., 190). The detective spends the "next two days forcing my little Chevy through unplowed side streets" (op. cit., 191) with her attention on a fraud case and a missing witness. A distraught Penelope visits V. I. and tells her that a janitor in Paul's office building had "found the doctor dead on the floor of his consulting room" (WCB 193); Penelope comes under suspicion because someone resembling her was seen near his office that morning, and the previous evening several people had witnessed a quarrel between Penelope and Paul in a restaurant. Lotty prevails on V. I. to look for Paul's murderer, reminding Vic how she has always "come out in any wind or weather to patch you up" (WCB 198). When the police charge Penelope, V. I. finally agrees to "undertake an independent investigation" (WCB 200). Freeman Carter, V. I.'s attorney, handles Penelope's defense. A "not guilty" verdict is returned, and Penelope returns to Montreal. Not long after, when V. I. accidentally stumbles on the murder weapon, she confronts the killer who confirms her suspicions. Knowing the murderer is suffering in mind and body, and does not have long to live, the detective chooses not to reveal the truth until after the perpetrator's death. Natasha Cooper's review of this story states that the author "has fallen into the trap of excessive earnestness" ("Going" 24).

## "Sexy, Moral, and Packing a Pistol" (1997)

Paretsky's article for the *Independent* (London) newspaper discusses the new figure of the female sleuth who is allowed autonomy and agency in the hands of a growing number of crime authors. Looking back, Paretsky writes: "For women to find a voice, a voice telling them that they may have adventures, that action is a woman's appropriate sphere, has been the difficult task of the last several centuries" (22). She describes her own protagonist, V. I., as "a woman of action [whose] primary role is to speak…. [H]er

success depends … on her willingness to put into words things that most people would rather remained unspoken" (ibid.).

## Sisters in Crime (SinC)

At the autumn 1986 Bouchercon convention in Baltimore, Sara Paretsky convened a meeting of 26 women. Earlier that year Paretsky had spoken at a Hunter College conference, organized by B. J. Rahn, on Women in the Mystery; Paretsky's remarks on the increasing use of graphic sadism against women in crime and mystery fiction set off a huge response in the crime fiction world. The women who met in a hotel room in Baltimore discussed shared concerns in their careers as crime writers, including the lack of award nominations for female authors and the small percentage of review space given to women reviewers and authors in the print media. A year later, the advocacy organization Sisters in Crime was born, with a steering committee of writers (Sara Paretsky, Dorothy Salisbury Davis, Charlotte MacLeod, Susan Dunlap, and Nancy Pickard), bookseller Kate Mattes, and corporate executive

Leslie Budewitz (2015–16 President of Sisters in Crime) and Sara Paretsky (founding member) at the 70th annual Edgars Awards Banquet in New York City, April 2016. Budewitz is holding the 2016 Raven Award from the Mystery Writers of America in honor of Sisters in Crime. Photography by Steven Speliotis.

and reader Betty Francis. Paretsky steered the organization until 1988, when Pickard became the first elected president. Sisters in Crime played an important role in "growing the market for mystery readers" (*Sisters on the Case* xii) and in highlighting the unequal treatment of women writers in such review pages as the *New York Times Book Review*, *Washington Post*, and *Chicago Tribune* as well as in trade publications such as *Publishers Weekly* and *Kirkus*. Membership today is just over 3,000, including some "misters" in crime and local chapters in the United States, Canada, Europe, and Australia. The national organization has been successful in expanding markets for and awareness of women mystery writers. A standing committee monitors print reviews of female authors, reporting on parity in the space given to books by women compared to male-authored books. Its first tabulation in the late 1980s revealed that "although women wrote more than a third of mystery fiction, they received less than 20% of the genre's reviews" (Ferraro 42). Sisters in Crime circulates a national newsletter; offers training and workshops to women working in the field of mystery and crime writing; and holds annual meetings at Malice Domestic and Bouchercon, the two big mystery conferences in the United States. In 2004, president Kate Grilley told Natalie Danford that "Sisters in Crime is unique in that it does not give awards or sponsor contests, nor does it place one author's work over another" (Danford 31). The organization and Paretsky's part in it were pivotal in enhancing the profile of women mystery writers in general and in providing valuable networking and training opportunities for women entering the field. The name Sisters in Crime was used for a series of short story anthologies published throughout the 1990s that promoted and published women mystery authors.

Another concern of the founding members of Sisters in Crime was their sense that "graphic descriptions of rape and violence are very much on the rise," Paretsky told Mary Schmich in a 1987 interview. The organization hoped to educate the public about this trend in recent crime and mystery fiction. In a letter dated 8 November 1995 written in response to interview questions posed by Julie Simmich, Paretsky registers disappointment that her "hope that it [SinC] would also address some social issues about the depiction of women in crime fiction has not, however, been realized" (letter in author's private papers, accessed March 1998, Chicago). In 1998 the Sisters in Crime archive (a collection that includes "everything from correspondence to videos of television programs based on books by member authors" according to Diane Nottle's 1998 article in the *New York Times*) was donated to the Mabel Smith Douglass Library at Douglass College, Rutgers University.

### Sisters on the Case (2007)

An anthology edited by Sara Paretsky in celebration of 20 years of the Sisters in Crime organization, the anniversary collection has stories by a number of popular contemporary women mystery writers, including Margaret Maron, Dorothy Salisbury Davis, Linda Grant, Carolyn Hart, and Barbara D'Amato. The collection features 20 mostly original short stories by the founders and leaders of the organization. Paretsky's "A Family Sunday in the Park" (aka "Marquette Park") tells the story of V. I.'s first case when, as an 11-year-old, she is caught up in a race riot in Chicago and accidently solves a mob murder.

### "Skin Deep" (1987)

A V. I. story originally written for the *New Black Mask*, "Skin Deep" was later published in *Windy City Blues* (aka *V. I. for Short*) in 1995 and re-released in *Chicago Noir: The Classics* in 2015. Sal Barthele, V. I.'s long-standing friend and owner of the Golden Glow bar, wakes the detective in the middle of the night when Sal's sister is arrested for murder. Evangeline Barthele gives facials at "a high-prestige beauty salon on North Michigan" (WCB 210–11). She had left her lunchtime client, Mr. Darnell, to relax in the cubicle after applying the usual creams and potions; when she returned to clean his face, she found him throwing up repeatedly. He is taken to the hospital where he dies a few hours later from the effects of poison rubbed into his skin. The police arrest Evangeline on suspicion of murder. When

V. I. accompanies Evangeline the next morning to bond court, she discovers the police have evidence linking her client to the victim. Evangeline reluctantly tells V. I. the truth about her personal relationship with Mr. Darnell. When V. I. looks into his past history, she discovers an arrest for drug smuggling, a short prison sentence, and a missing partner in crime. Vic successfully unmasks Mr. Darnell's former drug-smuggling partner as the killer who infiltrated the beauty salon and turns him over to the police. Evangeline's name is cleared, and a grateful Sal tells her friend "We owe you a lot, Vic. The police would never have dug down to find that" (op. cit., 224).

## "Soft Spot for Serial Murder" (1991)

This short op-ed piece for the *New York Times* expresses Paretsky's concerns about the trend toward increased violence in mysteries and movies, in particular violence and sadism against female characters. She argues that such depictions reflect the problem that many women see themselves as "inevitable, acceptable targets for violation" (E17). Paretsky has raised this issue in more than one arena; it was something she hoped that would be taken up by Sisters in Crime and was disappointed when the organization decided not to do so.

## "Strung Out" (1992)

This V. I. short story was first published in a joint Private Eye Writers of America/Sisters in Crime anthology. It subsequently appeared in the V. I. collected stories *Windy City Blues* (aka *V. I. for Short* in UK). "Strung Out" takes V. I. back into old acquaintances and rivalries from high-school days in South Chicago; the tale invokes the world of pro tennis players, rising young stars, pushy parents, and tetchy coaches. The cast of characters includes V. I.'s old high-school basketball coach Mary Ann McFarlane (who also appears in the V. I. novels *Blood Shot* and *Fire Sale*) and Nicole Rubova, one of "the dazzling Czech players who'd come to the States in Martina [Navratilova]'s wake" (WCB 98). Nicole seems to be a sexual predator in relation to her younger tennis rival, Lily Oberst;

Lily's mother, Monica, played basketball with V. I. in high school under Mary Ann's coaching. When the young tennis star's overbearing father is found garrotted by a racket string in the locker room at the all-important Virginia Slims tournament in Chicago, V. I. is called on to clear Nicole, whose racket seems to be missing a section of string. V. I. succeeds in establishing Nicole's innocence by flushing out the real killer, but not before she and Mary Ann go head to head over their differing loyalties to the people involved. V. I. is stung when Mary Ann tells her, "Maybe Monica is right about you, Victoria: too high-and-mighty" (WCB 122). Their estrangement ends a year later when Mary Ann invites V. I. to watch Lily make "her first public appearance at the Slims" (WCB 123). The theme of V. I. and her complicated relationship to the part of Chicago where she grew up is one often explored by Paretsky in the longer novels and in many of the short stories. In this short story, V. I. once again comments, "[I]t's a clannish place, South Chicago, and people don't leave it easily" (WCB 92).

## "Sweet Home Chicago" (2000)

This brief article on "how Chicago won and kept [Paretsky's] heart" appeared in *Publishers Weekly*. She remembers summer 1966 when she came to the city to do community service work, and she provides tips on where to go for food, theater, music, and ball games.

## "The Takamoku Joseki" (1983)

This early V. I. short story was first published in *Alfred Hitchcock's Mystery Magazine* before appearing in the collected V. I. stories *Windy City Blues* (aka *V. I. for Short*) in 1995. In the story, V. I.'s neighbors Mr. and Mrs. Takamoku approach the detective for advice about American etiquette regarding house guests. Puzzled, V. I. visits their apartment where they show her the scratch that now mars the bottom of a table; its top is "criss-crossed with black lines which formed dozens of little squares" (WCB 248)—the go-ban on which the traditional Japanese/Korean board game Go is played. The following week V. I. is again summoned to the Takamoku apartment where one of the assembled Go players is found "sprawled on the floor … [smelling of] hydrocyanic acid" (WCB 250–51). With the help of Charles Welland, another Go player and "a physicist at the University of Chicago" (251), V. I. persuades the couple to call the police and agrees to represent them in any inquiries about the death of Folger. Welland explains to her that the dead man "was trying one of the Takamoku *josekis*" (252)—a complicated opening move not often used in play. The move, Welland tells her, "wasn't named for our host. That's just coincidence" (253). The killer turns out to be one of the Go players in the apartment that afternoon; he and Folger worked for rival electronics firms and were involved in "passing Series J secrets to…. Kawamoto over the go boards" (256). The FBI was closing in on both of them, and Folger had been offered "immunity if he would finger the guy from Kawamoto" (256). As the police begin to handcuff the guilty party, "he popped a gelatin capsule into his mouth [and] was dead almost before they realized what he had done" (257). In the aftermath of clearing the dead bodies from the Takamoku apartment, V. I. and the physicist exit together. He invites her for a drink to "salute a lady clever enough to solve the Takamoku joseki unaided" (258). The epigraph to this story (printed in the *V. I. for Short* edition) reads: "Written for S. Courtenay Wright Christmas Day, 1982." The story and the initials of Welland's name commemorate Paretsky's physicist husband, Courtenay Wright, and his own love of the board game Go.

## "A Taste of Life" (1989)

This cautionary tale was published first in a Women's Press anthology of original crime stories, and subsequently in a Penguin 60 collection by Paretsky and in another collection edited by Lawrence Block. The title hints at the subject matter—greed, appetites, matricide, and cannibalism. The mother/daughter relationship at the heart of the story is an unhappy one with food symbolizing the power struggle between the slender Sylvia and her overweight daughter.

Sylvia is a successful model whose infant daughter Daphne showed "an angelic beauty"

(*Taste of Life* 3). For a while, all was well until Sylvia realizes that if the child is growing up, "the mother must be ageing" (ibid.). Sylvia takes to force-feeding her daughter "until Daphne weighed close to 300 pounds" (op. cit., 4). As an adult, Daphne still eats constantly and also "longed for love" (ibid.). She starts a tentative romance with a young man in her accounting department and discovers she can lose weight; they move in together. When the overbearing Sylvia turns up unexpectedly, things go downhill. Daphne wishes Sylvia would "drop dead"; Sylvia, for her part, "could not rest. Daphne happy and in love? Impossible. Daphne thin? Never!" (7). Sylvia's subsequent "courtship of Jerry was long and difficult," although eventually she succeeds in separating the couple. When she turns up to collect his clothes and tells her daughter, "Jerry won't be coming back" (9), Daphne snaps. In a rage, but "scarcely knowing what she was doing," she beats Sylvia with a lamp. Later, next to her mother's body, she "wanted to die herself, to eat and eat until she was engulfed by food. Mechanically, methodically, still weeping, she lifted Sylvia's left arm to her mouth" (10). The exploration of powerlessness and voicelessness are characteristic Paretsky themes, as well as the problematic family relationships.

## "Terror in the Name of Jesus" (2009)

This op-ed piece for the *Guardian* (London) mourns the murder of Dr. George Tiller whose abortion clinic in Kansas was frequently targeted by fundamentalist Christian groups. Paretsky hopes the shock of his death "begins a real search for common ground" (26) on the issue of women's reproductive rights and privacy. This is a subject often visited by the author in her fiction and nonfiction.

**See also "Bush's Pick a Reminder of What's Not Right";** *Bleeding Kansas*; *Killing Orders*; *Bitter Medicine*; **"Poster Child"; "The Man Who Loved Life"**

## Thibaut, Jake

Jake Thibaut is introduced in the 13th V. I. novel *Hardball*, when he moves into the unit next to the detective's apartment on the third floor of the co-op on Racine. The first time V. I. sees him, he is "dressed in the quintes-sential artist's costume: faded black T-shirt and jeans ... older than I'd first thought, per-haps in his forties" (HB 46–47). A bass player with a chamber music group and a music teacher, his schedule is as erratic as V. I.'s, and they see little of each other over the summer; however, by the end of the novel, he and the detective have embarked on a ten-tative romance. His musical background makes a powerful connection with V. I.'s love of music, inspired by her mother's training as an opera singer. When V. I. discovers some old reel-to-reel tapes with Gabriella's voice on them, Jake offers to have them profes-sionally mastered for her; late one night they listen together to Gabriella singing Mozart while Jake "played the aria through, first in company, then in counterpoint, with my mother's voice" (HB 446). In the next novel, *Body Work*, set in the winter seven months after the events of *Hardball*, Jake and V. I. have "been dating for a few months now" (BW8), although the demands of their pro-fessional lives mean that they see one an-other infrequently. After a Christmas day to-gether, "he left to visit his mother and sister in Seattle" (BW 23), and "at the end of Jan-uary, he was leaving for a European tour" (21). Jake, in common with some of V. I.'s previous lovers and with her close friends, worries about her predilection for engaging in verbal and physical fights and her knack for placing herself and others in danger. On a night out, Jake, seeing that V. I. is about to chase some nearby suspects, warns her: "Vic, not that I'm trying to tell you what to do, but you know I'm not going to risk my fingers if you go after them," (17). This novel con-cludes on a romantic note when Jake, still on tour with his group High Plainsong, salutes V. I. on a live BBC Radio 3 broadcast from London, which she hears while having break-fast with Max and Lotty. In *Breakdown*, the 15th V. I. adventure, Jake and V. I. have been "spending a fair amount of our free time with each other" ever since he "moved in across the landing from me two years ago" (35). In most of this novel, Jake is again offstage spend-ing the summer in Vermont where he is

"artist-in-residence at the Marlboro Festival" (65). V. I. has plans to join Jake for the last week of the festival for "a real vacation ... we would drive up to Canada, where we would hike the Laurentian Mountains" (65). How-ever, V. I.'s present case disrupts these plans, and at the end of the novel Jake and V. I. re-turn to Chicago to attend the funeral of V. I.'s law-school friend Leydon Ashford, who has died alone and estranged from her family. Jake's group provides the music, and V. I. takes part "in singing the Stravinsky setting of Psalm 39, which Leydon had liked all those years ago" (430). In the next novel, *Critical Mass*, Jake is touring the West Coast with one of his chamber groups; V. I. notes "his absence made my schedule easier in some ways, but it also meant I was lonely at the end of a long day" (CM 76). At the end of the story, Jake accompanies V. I. on a trip to Vienna where she, Lotty, and Max tie up loose ends in her current case; she and Jake "wandered through the city's parks, where we met his musician friends for drinks that lasted until dinner and then became informal recitals at one apartment or another" (CM 454).

## "This Is for You, Jeannie" (1972)

Paretsky published this early short story in the feminist magazine *Women: A Journal of Liberation*. It is a little-known part of her oeuvre. The main characters, a scientist and his wife, may be modeled, in part, on Paret-sky's parents, David and Mary Paretsky. The story about a woman whose life as a middle-class wife and mother slowly sends her into a state of helpless madness is also obviously influenced by the women's liberation move-ment and consciousness-raising in which Paretsky was participating. The protagonist is unable to put a name to "her clever, terri-ble enemy [which] followed her all the way to the edge of her mind" (51).

Jeannie and Roger appear, on the surface, to be the ideal couple; they enjoy a comfort-able lifestyle, have two children, and soon will welcome a third. Roger keeps long hours as a scientist. Jeannie, who looks after the house and children, is increasingly frustrated. After the birth of the third child, her apparently inexplicable rages intensify to the point where she chases two of the children with an ax. Nothing seems to assuage the anger; she drinks too much, and tries pills and therapy. Roger attempts to pay more attention. Jeannie seems unable to escape the terrible knowledge of her powerlessness in a marriage that has given her "a man, three children, a lot of furniture, and a house. All of which belong to the man, who is gone all day doing something else" (46). After several years of miserable family life and Roger embarking on an affair, he moves his wife into a separate apartment accompanied by a psychiatric nurse. The story concludes with Jeannie in the "apartment designed for calm…. [T]here was only one place further she could go … there would be rest. And so she went" (51).

K. Edgington's discussion of this short story draws attention to the ways in which it echoes Charlotte Perkins Gilman's 1892 short story "The Yellow Wall-Paper" and Jean Rhys's 1966 novel *Wide Sargasso Sea*—both with female protagonists who are trapped in rigid gender roles and who escape into madness. Edgington further links "Jeannie's black thing" to "Betty Friedan's 'problem that has no name,' the generalized malaise of middle-class housewives examined in *The Feminine Mystique* (1964)" (57); and recognizes "autobiographical connections between the author [Paretsky] and the outspoken V. I., whose backgrounds as feminist activists in the sixties are notably similar" (58).

## "This Was My Destiny: Housework, Babysitting, Marriage" (2000)

This long article for the *Guardian* (London) newspaper explains that as a reader and a writer, Paretsky is "pulled by stories … of people … who can't speak for themselves, who feel powerless and voiceless in the larger world" (11). The theme of voicelessness is an important one to Paretsky and one to which she frequently returns in both her fiction and nonfiction. In this piece, she writes about how she always felt a "need to start writing down the lives of people without voices" (11).

## "Three-Dot Po" (1984)

Another early short story featuring V. I., "Three-Dot Po" was published first in 1984

in a Private Eye Writers of America anthology. It next appeared in a *Ms Murder* anthology edited by Marie Smith and in 1995 in *Windy City Blues* (aka *V. I. for Short*). In the middle of a bitter Chicago winter, V. I. goes out jogging to Belmont Harbor, expecting to meet her friend Cinda, with Cinda's golden retriever, Three-Dot Po. When V. I. finds Po "on a flat slab of rock … [near] the mist-covered water, barking furiously," she is not surprised to discover "Cinda's body … just visible beneath the surface" (WCB 229). Cinda's musician boyfriend, Jonathan Michaels, is arrested, accused of strangling her and pushing her into Lake Michigan. V. I. agrees to look after Po and to find a lawyer for Jonathan who can handle the musician's upcoming bail hearing.

Po is the heroine of this short story; a police sergeant tells Jonathan, "Looks like your dog saved your hide, Mr. Michaels" (WCB 244). Po helps V. I. chase down the cocaine-dealer culprit at Belmont Harbor, and she recovers vital evidence that the killer throws into the lake. The dog's loyalty, good nature, and exemplary behavior is praised throughout; she is not dissimilar from the golden retriever Peppy acquired by V. I. at the end of the 1987 novel *Bitter Medicine*. Po's unusual name is explained at the close of the story when Jonathan and V. I. celebrate his release from jail. He tells the dog, "you get the steak and I'll eat Butcher's Blend tonight, Miss Three-Dot Po of Blackstone, People's Heroine, and winner of the Croix de Chien for valor" (WCB 245).

A wintry Chicago provides a frozen and desolate background in the story, which V. I. likens to "a wasteland … no people, freezing cold, snow blowing across in fine pelting particles like a desert sandstorm" (WCB 228). Members of the Alvarado family—repeating minor characters in the series—make a brief appearance in this short story when Lotty leaves V. I. recovering at home on Christmas day to "eat dinner with her nurse Carol Alvarado, and her family" (WCB 230).

## "The Tornado" (1959)

This brief account of a tornado in Kansas was written by Paretsky at age 11 and is her first published work. Submitted to *American Girl* magazine, the piece won a nonfiction award and was published in the August 1959 issue. The report of the eighth graders huddled in the school tunnel used for a tornado shelter foreshadows some familiar characteristics of the later detective novels. The description of the schoolchildren enduring a lengthy and cramped period in the shelter parallels the uncomfortable physical conditions often suffered by V. I. in the course of her sleuthing, and the slight preoccupation of the children missing their lunchtime may point to V. I.'s constant interest in food.

## Total Recall (2001)

> "I could have kept my temper—my besetting sin" (63).

The 10th V. I. mystery, published in 2001, uses a title that refers to photographic memory and also references Arnold Schwarzenegger's 1990 action film, loosely based on a Philip K. Dick short story, and Schwarzenegger's 2012 autobiography. Paretsky's novel, in common with the film, Dick's short story, and Schwarzenegger's memoir, is concerned with the nature of memory and illusion. Dedicated to Paretsky's great-grandmothers— "Sara Krupnik and Hannah Paretsky, whose names I bear"—the novel deals with the Holocaust, the validity of recovered memory, and legal and moral issues such as slavery reparations and the ethics of contemporary multinational corporations. In a departure from the traditional hard-boiled use of the first-person voice for the detective story, Paretsky structures the novel differently. The novel opens and closes with the voice of Dr. Lotty Herschel, "chief perinatologist at Beth Israel" (6) and V. I.'s beloved friend. In a flashback where the detective is "sitting on a hillside ... listening to Lotty until she could talk no more" (4), the doctor recollects the bitter cold in England "the second winter after the war" (1) at the beginning of her medical training. Lotty's voice, filtered through V. I.'s, continues to punctuate the narrative in five additional flashbacks that detail how she left her Austrian home and family before World War II as part of the Kindertransport program; her subsequent studies in London;

her wartime lover and secret pregnancy; and her anguish and loss in that period. Alternating with V. I.'s voice in the present, as the private eye gives an account of her part in Lotty's memories, the two first-person narratives allow both women to speak for themselves and give Lotty's story an unusual prominence in a novel targeted, as Cooper's TLS review notes, at "the peddlers of Recovered Memory Syndrome and the financial institutions that are determined to deny restitution to victims of the Holocaust" (Cooper 2001). Then-President Bill Clinton, who had worked on the Holocaust assets issue, wrote to Paretsky after reading the novel, "Thanks for writing about a little known chapter of that sad time" (handwritten letter, 7.1.2001, in author's private papers accessed November 2013).

The present-day setting and circumstances of *Total Recall* is September in Chicago; Lotty calls on V. I. to provide some emergency baby-sitting for Max Loewenthal's 5-year-old granddaughter, Calia, so that he can participate in a panel on "his postwar experiences in trying to track down his relatives and their assets" at the Birnbaum Foundation's conference on "Christians and Jews: a New Millennium, a New Dialogue" (7). Max and Lotty have argued about this issue; she claims such exposures of past difficulties "only reinforced a stereotype of Jews as victims" (7), whereas Max, who serves on "the national committee dealing with missing assets for Holocaust survivors" (19), does not want to wallow in the past but believes "it can be healthy for people to understand it" (7). Their conflict is at the heart of the novel, and their quarrels unsettle V. I. Nonetheless, she agrees to look after Calia for a few harrowing hours, commenting, "The private eye as baby-sitter: it wasn't the first image you got from pulp fiction" (7). When she drops Calia off at Max's conference hotel, she encounters demonstrators "carrying signs demanding passage of the Illinois Holocaust Asset Recovery Act" (9–10) and led by the ultra-Orthodox Joseph Posner, "son of a Holocaust survivor" (10). A second group, "mostly black, was carrying signs with a large red slash through *Pass the IHARA*. NO DEALS WITH SLAVE OWN-

ERS ... their signs proclaimed" (10, emphasis in original). This crowd is led by Alderman Louis "Bull" Durham, who "wants the state to make it illegal for a company to do business here ... unless they pay restitution to the descendants of slaves" (12). The head-to-head picketers and the conference proceedings make the evening news and further upset Lotty. In the meantime, V. I. has much on her mind. Her lover Morrell, who she has "been seeing for the past year, was leaving on Tuesday for Afghanistan" (17). The hard-working South Side Sommers family hires V. I. to investigate how and why their late Uncle Aaron's life-insurance policy, taken out 30 years ago and worth $10,000, had apparently been cashed in before his death and without his or his family's knowledge. She also is "trying to run my business, and juggle the nonprofit work I do, and pay my bills" (4). Unpicking layers of local and international swindle concerning the Sommers insurance policy, V. I. also is concerned about Lotty. Lotty has become distraught by conference-attendee Paul Radbuka claiming to have recovered repressed memories of surviving the Nazi concentration camps; he now seems to be claiming kinship with Lotty's friends, Max Loewenthal and Carl Tisov, who lost loved ones in the Holocaust. Lotty clearly has secrets of her own, which V. I. tries patiently to learn; tension builds between the two friends, until V. I. realizes that Lotty's continued refusals are expressing "a ragged fury born of grief" (65). Lotty is convinced that parading one's private sorrows about the war years is offensive; in a bitter moment, she tells V. I. her belief that "publishers and movie studios make fortunes from titillating the comfortable well-fed middle class of Europe and America with tales of torture" (65). She is furious that "to many people [the Holocaust] is a game. Something to romanticize or kitschify or use for titillation" (64). When Lotty disappears, V. I. starts to investigate Radbuka's past in the hopes of discovering something that will help Lotty. The Sommers case brings her to the offices of the Ajax Insurance Company, now owned by the Swiss firm Edelweiss Re, and her old acquaintance Ralph Devereux,

now "head of claims" (33). The two plots—the Sommers insurance claim and its connection to cheating international insurance companies, and the mysteries around Lotty and her friends—along with themes of reparation, guilt, complicity, and pain that can endure—are brought together in a moving resolution narrated by Lotty as she and V. I. start on "the long road back" (405) to Chicago.

The novel refers frequently to V. I.'s expanding familiarity with the modern world of technology. She looks online for background on the Radbuka name and family, forgets to charge her cellphone, and copies an address into her palm pilot. "The Web," V. I. ruminates, "has transformed investigative work, making it for the most part both easier and duller" (167). In a characteristic Paretsky nod to the accomplishments of little-known women, V. I. mentions looking at "the Isabel Bishop painting on the wall by my desk ... the angular face staring at a sewing machine" (168). Bishop was a twentieth-century American artist who often painted studies of working women in urban settings. V. I. also is concerned about the gentrification of her office locale—a "fifteen-minute drive from the financial district where most of my business lies" (37). When she and sculptor Tessa Reynolds moved into the "converted warehouse on Leavitt ... [it was] still a grimy no-man's-land between the Latino neighbourhood farther west and a slick Yuppie area nearer the lake" (37). In addition, she reflects on the legacy of her parents when she takes her mother's diamond-drop earrings—a 20th anniversary present from her father—from her wall safe, commenting, "Diamonds from my mother, handguns from my father" (256).

Stephanie Zvirin's *Booklist* review notes that "Paretsky is in good form in this new V. I. Warshawski mystery" (2001). Paretsky has, according to Maureen Corrigan's review, "created a memorable character in Lotty, whose moving tale of survivor guilt shames every other voice into silence" (T13). Dick Adler's review concurs, writing that the novel gives "new insights into one of the genre's most interesting character actors, Lotty Herschel" (3). The managing director of Penguin in the United Kingdom wrote to Paretsky about this novel: "I do think it is an absolutely triumphant achievement…. We are so delighted to have the book…. [I]t is a very long time since I have had a weekend of such undilutedly pleasurable reading" (letter to SP from Helen Fraser, dated 13 March 2001, in Newberry Library Paretsky Papers-Additions, Accession 2012–12, Box 20 of 22, Manila folder titled "Total Recall Editorial").

## Tregiere, Malcolm

Malcolm Tregiere is a young Haitian medical associate of V. I.'s friend Dr. Lotty Herschel and lover of sculptor Tessa Reynolds, who becomes V. I.'s co-tenant in an office building in the gentrifying Wicker Park neighborhood of Chicago in *Tunnel Vision*, the eighth V. I. novel. Dr. Tregiere appears in the 1987 *Bitter Medicine* as the attending obstetrician to Consuelo Alvarez: "[A] slight, quiet black man, Tregiere had the enormous confidence needed by successful surgeons without the usual arrogance that accompanies it" (*Bitter* 25). His brutal murder sparks an investigation that leads V. I. deep into the world of for-profit health-care organizations and medical malpractice.

**See also *Bitter Medicine*, Lotty Herschel, Tessa Reynolds**

## Tunnel Vision (1994)

"They could have listened to me…. It's what they get for not believing women's stories" (362)

The eighth V. I. novel signals many changes in V. I.'s life. Aware she is pushing 40, she knows she must face some challenging difficulties in her personal and professional life: "Nothing about my life these days looked remotely successful, let alone professional" (171). The punning title points to the detective's own preoccupations, the tunnels under the Chicago Loop, and society's blind spots in relation to vulnerable people. V. I. acknowledges her weariness borrowing an image from *Hamlet*: "I was tired of taking arms against a sea of opposition. All it got me was knocks on the head, my home trashed, and accusations" (358).

After 10 years, V. I. is forced to vacate her

The cover for the Japanese edition of *Tunnel Vision* features graphic of V.I. character in action. From author's private papers. Photograph by Linda Erf Swift.

office in the Pulteney Building when the decaying building falls victim to property developers; she states, "I should have realized long since that the Culpepper boys were … waiting for the day when the building would be worth more dead than alive" (1). She has unpaid bills. Her relationship with policeman Conrad Rawlings is under stress; they argue repeatedly about his constant lectures to her on matters such as "illegal search and seizure" (255), as well as her tendency to leave himself, caution, and police procedure behind when she is working on a case. Laura Shapiro's review in *Newsweek* finds that "one of V. I.'s most winning features is the way she is aging: not a bit gracefully" ("Does It" 67).

The plot characteristically weaves two seemingly unconnected story lines into a tightly constructed tale of political and financial shenanigans that encompasses money laundering, murder, child abuse, exploitation of illegal immigrants, and an agricultural conglomerate's business dealings with Iraq in direct contravention of the Boland Amendment. The first story line involves issues of homelessness and emergency housing/shelter responses in the public and private sectors. As V. I. prepares to move out of her office, she finds a homeless family in the basement, on the run and distrustful of official intervention. V. I. and Lotty struggle with the best approach to helping Tamar Hawkings and her children, as they need medical attention as well as housing. As board members of Arcadia House (a nonprofit battered women's shelter), Lotty and V. I. are aware of the shortcomings in appropriate and safe housing options for families in emergency situations. Despite their efforts to meet the Hawkings' needs without splitting up the family, the mother and her undernourished children disappear. Not long after, V. I. attends a retirement party at the home of another Arcadia board member, Deirdre Messenger, whose husband, Fabian, is an ambitious University of Chicago law school professor and an acquaintance of V. I.'s from law school days. V. I. notices that Deirdre—a volunteer at Home Free, an organization that advocates on housing issues at state level and contracts housing for the

homeless—seems unusually stressed and anxious. The second plotline emerges in Fabian's reputation for giving "highfalutin advice to Republican bigwigs" (13) such as Senator Alec Gantner, founder of successful agricultural conglomerate Gant-Ag. When the murdered Deirdre is found in V. I.'s office, her troubled daughter, Emily, becomes a suspect in the subsequent police investigation. V. I.'s sympathies for the teenager draw the detective into investigations on Emily's behalf. She also is doing some pro bono background work for Capital Concerns, a small venture-capital firm run by Phoebe Quirk, an acquaintance of V. I.'s from the days when they had "worked for the abortion underground where [V. I. had] met Lotty" (21). Capital Concerns works on funding social programs such as Lamia Housing, a project run by Conrad Rawlings's sister, Camilla. Phoebe and Camilla ask V. I. to find out why there is trouble obtaining zoning permits required from City Hall and why their funder, Century Bank, has backed out. In the meantime, V. I.'s long-standing client Darraugh Graham is leaning on her to find an internship for his computer-hacking son who must do some court-mandated community service for readmittance to college. She reluctantly takes on MacKenzie "Ken" Graham as a community service volunteer, and he promptly develops a crush on her. Irritated by Ken's attentions, she finally snaps at him, "I don't need perpetual youth to keep me from feeling my age" (224). Phoebe subsequently attempts, with some poor excuses, to take V. I. off the background investigation into the Lamia investors; by this time, V. I. is discovering some interesting connections among Century Bank, City Hall, Home Free's construction projects, and Gateway Bank. The deeper she digs, the more she uncovers evidence of political ambition meeting big-time financial fraud in the nonprofit housing sector. She and Ken break into the Home Free premises in search of computer and paper evidence; after a narrow escape from the office, V. I. and Conrad have a robust discussion about her habit of breaking and entering in search of vital information. Conrad's patience wears thin as he reminds her, "You can't go around breaking the law like you're above it ... we have laws ... so everyone doesn't go buzzing through the streets defining justice however it suits them that morning" (233). More layers to V. I.'s melancholy in this novel are added in her dreams about babies and young children. Her helplessness in the face of Emily's situation—the characteristic figure of the valiant girl who is up against great pressures from within the family—surfaces in a dream where Vic is "following Emily down endless flights of stairs while Phoebe, Lotty, and my mother stood in doorways along the way mocking my blindness" (196). The detective finally discovers that Century Bank is running a line of credit for a Home Free housing construction project, which is linked to the Lamia building collective and seems to be using illegal Romanian immigrants on their building projects. Both Home Free and Century Bank are money laundering for Gant-Ag. Max's linguistic abilities assist in interviewing some of the Romanian crew living in abject conditions in a large metal container on a Home Free building site. Convinced that Century Bank is violating the Community Lending Act and is involved in money laundering, trying to help Emily by looking for Deirdre's murderer, and still on the lookout for the Hawkings family, V. I. is tired of people who do not listen to her. V. I. uncovers some compromising information about Fabian's involvement with Gant-Ag's violation of the Boland Amendment, a federal law forbidding financial deals with terrorist organizations—Fabian's advice to Gant-Ag on circumventing this embargo has resulted in the company trading with Iraq. In providing the corrupt Gantner with valuable legal advice, Fabian is hoping for a spot on the federal bench. Fabian is also a child molester and a wife-beater, secrets well kept within the family. Emily and her brothers disappear. In a dramatic set piece, based on a real event in 1992, water breaks through a wall between the Chicago River and the tunnels under the Loop, flooding the maze of underground tunnels—the Loop goes dark when the authorities cut off the electricity as a safety measure. Lehmann-Haupt's review notices

that "[t]he image of flooding tunnels ... is an effective touch, suggesting as it does both the corruption of the city's power and the deluge of irrational passion that are the novel's main themes" (C18). V. I. and Mr. Contreras set out to rescue the Hawkings, who have taken refuge in the tunnels. Battling against the rising water in the dark, rat-infested tunnels, they find Emily and her brothers as well as the Hawkings family and manage to take them to safety. There is another dramatic scene when V. I. attempts a showdown with the corrupt Gantner in the Gant-Ag cornfields outside Chicago. Conrad comes to her rescue but is wounded in the subsequent shootout. Although Vic saves his life, their relationship does not survive. From his hospital bed, he says: "I can't go through another episode like this, Vic ... watching you plunge ahead without regard for anything or anyone except your own private version of justice" (414). The devastated V. I. retreats to nurse her wounds in private.

The novel opens and closes on the note of friendship. The dedication "For Dorothy" refers to mystery writer Dorothy Salisbury Davis, who is described in the epigraph taken from E. B. White's *Charlotte's Web* as a "true friend and a good writer." In the final chapter of the book V. I. attends her surprise 40th birthday party. Sad from the break-up with Conrad, she is comforted by the gathering where "champagne flowed like water, and we danced until the pale moon sank" (432). The theme of the battered woman unites the homeless mother—Tamar Hawkings—hiding in the tunnels and the wealthy Deirdre Messenger with her privileged lifestyle. The theme of incest and child molestation unites the 14-year-old Emily (another one of Paretsky's teenage girls in danger from their family) with police officer Mary Louise Neely, who suffered the same as a young girl. At the end of the novel Mary Louise tells V. I. that she is resigning from the police force, is becoming a foster parent to the three Messenger children, and wishes to work for V. I. The detective takes her on to do "freelance work ... for six months before considering a more formal arrangement" (431). According to Kate Saunders, the novel provides "exactly the right quantities of tension, human insight and cliffhanging drama" (14). Donna Bickford's 2007 scholarly discussion of the novel examines "how Paretsky confronts and resists the inaccurate stereotypes of those who experience homelessness" (47). The theme of homelessness—as manifested in the plight of the Hawkings—allows Paretsky to question the assumptions often made by society about homeless people (such as that they are street people by choice, traumatized vets, mentally ill people, or drunks), to elaborate some of the causes of homelessness (such as domestic violence), and to demonstrate the need for more emergency and long-term shelter. V. I.'s resistance to contact with the authorities regarding the Hawkings demonstrates the limitations of the criminal justice system and social services: "And what would they have done? Arrested her for neglect and put the children into foster care" (9), the detective points out to Lotty. Bickford's essay concludes that Paretsky's handling of the homelessness theme challenges her readers to ask, "Why do we, as members of a relatively affluent society, permit anyone to be without safe, decent, and affordable housing?" (51). Stasio's review highlights "the war of ethics that V. I. wages against a conspiracy of bankers, elected officials and corporate brigands who have their snouts in the city's social services funding trough" ("Crime" 42).

## V. I. Warshawski (Film)

V. I. Warshawski, starring Kathleen Turner in the title role, was released in 1991 to a mixed reception. Directed by Jeff Kanew for Buena Vista Pictures, the film involves 13-year-old Kat Grafalk (Angela Goethels) hiring V. I. to investigate the murder of her father (Stephen Meadows), a former player for the Blackhawks hockey team.

The film was generally agreed to have been "a commercial and critical disappointment" (Graham 443). Cindy Pearlman's article on V. I.'s transition from page to screen traces the history of Hollywood's attempt to film the character: "Paretsky sold the rights to her first four

V. I. books and the Warshawski character to Chestnut Hill Productions, which option[ed] it to Tri-Star [which] volleyed the project over to Disney's Hollywood Pictures" (35). Pearlman quotes producer Jeffrey Lurie on the problems he encountered: "We embraced the idea of a female hero, a woman as a thinker. But Hollywood … freighted the movie plot with lots of standard action-flick motifs—things blowing up, bathtub suds, chases, guns, blood" (35). Janet Maslin's review points out that the film "does a lot to take the edge off Vic's feminism," but she enjoyed "the rapport that develops between Vic and Kat as they join forces" (C17). Caryn James's review also picks up on the young Kat character as "a V. I. in training" (H7). In an early scene the precocious Kat asks V. I., "What does it cost to hire you?"; V. I. replies, "A just cause." An apologetic 1991 letter to Paretsky from John P. March, vice president of production at Chestnut Hill Productions, states, "this did not turn out to be the kind of movie I envisioned when I first read the books … [because] the homogenizing tentacles of Disney do indeed run deep" (The Paretsky Papers, Newberry Library Box 5 of 9 in 1992 gift accessed November 2012).

DVD cover for the 1991 movie *V.I. Warshawski* starring Kathleen Turner.

Paretsky sent a mailgram to Kathleen Turner on 19 July 1991 that stated, "I saw Warshawski last night. You were terrific. Thanks. Love Sara Paretsky" (ibid.). Dave Kehr's review for the *Chicago Tribune* also praises Turner's presence as "responsible for whatever interest and conviction the film retains" and suggests the screenwriters seemed to be "looking for ways to diminish Warshawski's strength and independence" (B7). Paretsky told interviewer Susan Ferraro, "I wish it had been a better movie, that it hadn't had that adolescent humor. But I felt the movie was so *different* from what I do … that *my* V. I. is intact" (23, emphasis in original).

The film grossed $11.1 million domestically, although this did not make it a box-office success. Kathleen Gregory Klein's 1994 discussion of the movie looks at the commercial imperatives of Hollywood and concludes, "[N]either Sara Paretsky's independent character nor Kathleen Turner's star status nor V. I. Warshawski's lead role can rescue *V. I. Warshawski* from its commercial parameters and its consequent failure" (56). The original plan for a series of V. I. movies has not been realized. At the time of this writing the screen rights to the V. I. character remain with Disney.

The 2011 Hammer award from Private Eye Writers of America honors V.I. Warshawski as Best P.I. Series Character." From author's private papers. Photograph by Linda Erf Swift.

## Violence

British mystery writer P. D. James published a novel in 1972 featuring Cordelia Gray, a professional female investigator who inherits a detective agency from her London employer. The ironic title *An Unsuitable Job for a Woman* draws attention to the challenge of putting a female protagonist at the center of a type of fiction noted for the glorification of a male world of fast, often violent action. The hard-boiled genre is marked by expressions of violence, as John Scaggs's definition of the mode explains: "[T]he hard-boiled style is terse, tough, and cynical … and the typical hard-boiled story is one of violence, sex, and betrayal" (145). The association with violence extends to the city settings typical of the private-eye novel, urban landscapes where danger and corruption lurk in dark seedy streets, and underpinning the genre's claim to realism. The hard-drinking male detective figure of the early *Black Mask* stories is known for strength, a gun in his hand, and a willingness to use it. In this 1920s era of the genre women's roles were restricted to those of femme fatale, vamp, victim, or the occasional secretary to the private eye. John Cawelti's discussion of the hard-boiled detective story notes that "the hard-boiled detective faces assault, capture, drugging, blackjacking, and attempted assassination as a regular feature" (143) of the investigation. Women writers stepping into the arena of the hard-boiled from the 1970s on were to discover it was a contested area. "Switching the gender of the detective requires a reconsideration of the meaning of violence and of the value of fighting back," Maureen Reddy observed ("Female Detective" 1058). If female detectives are portrayed as suffering from violence, does this in some way condone the image of the woman as victim, or does this confront the problem by naming it and claiming the right to express it in terms of female subjectivity? If female detectives are initiating and enacting violence, does this suggest they are imitating the characteristics of the male detective in a bid to be just as tough? Contemporary women writers of crime and mystery have examined and responded to such questions in a variety of ways. The project of appropriating or transforming the narrative conventions, particularly those associated with the tough, action-prone hero, is full of contradictions and of pleasures, as Reddy's discussion points out: "one of the pleasures women readers find in the female hard-boiled novels is a vicarious feeling of power, as the detective successfully fights her way out of dangerous situations" ("Female Detective" 1058). Although the breed of new fictional private eyes such as Kinsey Millhone and V. I. Warshawski might carry guns and know how to use them when necessary, there is an ambivalence about relying on them; their authors found other ways of demonstrating the strength and agility of their heroines and to hint at the problematic aspects of engaging with the motif of violence. Marilyn Stasio's 1985 feature on up-and-coming fictional female detectives comments on the complexities of their characterization: "Less brutal than their male counterparts, these new private eyes are more willing to admit physical weakness and emotional vulnerability and much more inclined to use their wits rather than their fists to solve a case" (39). For many of the new private eyes, using their wits includes a reliance on self-defense tactics acquired through, for instance, the disciplines of the martial arts such as karate and kung fu. They also rely, when they can, on taking the upper hand verbally when faced with danger—using voice and verbal skills to try to control the situation. Another characteristic of some of the newer female detective figures is a refusal to eroticize physical violence, instead expressing an ambivalence about their responses to it. This is a particular concern of Paretsky's, who told interviewer Jane Sullivan she notices a current tendency in mystery novels to emphasize descriptions of violence done to bodies; the

trend "seems to have no purpose other than to be pornographic or sexually titillating…. I'm not interested in a graphic description of what a dead body will look like" (7). Paretsky is more interested, writes Sullivan, "in the violating power of emotional or psychological violence" (ibid.). The traditional first-person voice used in hard-boiled narratives is helpful to Paretsky in several respects. V. I.'s subjectivity filters her experiences, so the reader is both acquainted with and slightly distanced from what happens to her body when she is beaten up, threatened with physical violence, or pushed around. V. I. is capable of giving as good as she gets when she is in danger; but her agency and authority in such circumstances is as often signaled by her verbal skills and mental strength as it is by her fists. Her gun is rarely used, although carrying it sometimes gives her the illusion of protection, as she confesses in the first novel *Indemnity Only* when she reluctantly acquires a Smith & Wesson because she feels threatened by "a lot of hired muscle…. [A] gun wouldn't completely protect me, but I thought it might narrow the odds" (IO 93). In *Blood Shot*, she prepares for a possible encounter with housebreakers by "going to the little wall safe I'd built into the bedroom closet" (151) to take out the Smith & Wesson, even as she expresses her doubts about the habit of carrying a gun because "if you do, you get dependent on them and your wits slow down" (152). V. I.'s actions and her habit of reflecting on her actions seem to open up textual spaces that explore the female fear of violence and the vulnerabilities felt by many women in a culture and society in which they are often held responsible for both provoking and preventing attacks on their person. V. I. refuses the category of victim that is implied by the chorus of concern from Lotty and others who voice many a reprimand to the detective over her "reckless" behavior. In time-honored genre tradition, V. I. often stirs things up by taking action that she knows is provocative. In *Killing Orders,* for example, she turns to other weapons, throwing up twice on a thug who has kidnapped her on the instructions of his mob boss; his humiliation does not go unnoticed. There is an emphasis on V. I.'s various fitness routines—running, going to the gym, exercising the dogs—which conveys her physical strength and agility as well as her commitment to staying strong so that she can take care of herself and others in a tight situation. More than once, her "good physical condition and [being] used to defending [her]self" (HT 323) has saved V. I.'s life after run-ins with people intent on killing her. The cost of violence to the body is established repeatedly throughout the series whenever V. I. has to recover from attacks. Sometimes she is hospitalized; other times she recovers at Lotty's apartment where her doctor friend can keep an eye on her. After a particularly vicious prison beating and being left for dead "on the Belmont exit ramp to Kennedy" (ibid.), V. I. is visited by Lotty at the Grete Berman Institute for torture victims. Lotty acknowledges that although luck played its part in V. I.'s survival, Vic herself deserves credit because she also does not "have the habit of victims" (ibid.). A fistfight between V. I. and two attackers on the landing outside her apartment is recounted move by move in a long, detailed paragraph early in *Indemnity Only*; this echoes Chandler's technique of offering choreographed accounts of fights, as he does, for example, in the brawl involving Moose Malloy at Florian's Bar in *Farewell, My Lovely*. V. I.'s account of her own actions and responses, and her refusal to play the victim, serve some important functions. Paradoxically the detailed description of the movement and action helps to distance the reader from the brutality; at the same time, the text reminds the reader of V. I.'s considerable physical and mental capabilities: "He was stronger, but I was in better shape.... I was on my feet way in advance of him" (IO 59). V. I.'s narrative voice—telling the reader what is happening to her as it happens—resists the voyeuristic gaze. Another of Paretsky's strategies is to characterize V. I. as imagining, rather than initiating, violent acts: "I wondered hopefully if he could be tortured into talking"; "I wished I'd smashed in Howard's face" (ibid., 2). In a later novel, during a tense confrontation between V. I. and the trigger-happy Lt. Montgomery, V. I. knows she has to keep her temper, although she wants "to jump up from behind the table and seize his long stork neck and pound his head against the wall" (*Burn* 294). V. I.'s self-mocking manner and vivid fantasies about how she might behave but chooses not to underscore the different spaces being claimed in relation to the motif of violence. In *Deadlock*, for example, V. I. makes an ironic reference to the traditional role of the femme fatale: "I gave my most ingratiating smile—Lauren Bacall trying to get Sam Spade to do her dirty work for her" (DL 173). Textual jokes about genre conventions serve to draw attention to the traditions while distancing this detective and her strategies from the earlier models of the private eye. Neither the author nor her character is above using, and drawing self-conscious attention to, traditional female roles and strategies to further a cause. The use of humorous asides helps to undercut the imperatives of both gender and genre expectations particularly in relation to the motif of tough behavior. Frequent references to V. I.'s visceral responses signal the fear with which she is often contending. In a showdown with a mobster who is threatening her with a beating V. I. hopes she "wasn't shaking; my stomach was knotted with nervousness" (IO 63). Her body betrays her in other ways. Facing down a couple of gangsters in her apartment building, although she realizes they are not going to shoot her, "my hands didn't believe me. They started sweating and I was afraid they might be trembling so I stuck them into my pockets" (KO 270). It is in this same novel, *Killing Orders*, that V. I. participates, but at a distance, in a supremely violent act—she plays a part in setting up the murder of the person instrumental in her friend Agnes's death and in the acid attack on herself. In the early novels, V. I. often finds herself at the mercy of her own rage and prone to launching physical attacks on people guilty of criminal actions. In *Blood Shot*, she is goaded by anger at Dr. Chigwell's complicity with the cover-up of medical statistics that showed the effect of a poisonous chemical on factory employees, to the point where she finds herself "pounding him over and over, screaming at him that he was a traitor to his oath, a miserable worm of a man"

(BS 284). Dr. Chigwell's sister intervenes, pulling V. I. away from her victim. Disgusted by her "own destructive rage" (ibid.) and loss of control, V. I. feels "the gorge rise within" and retreats "behind a vat to throw up" (ibid.). In the earlier *Killing Orders*, V. I.'s rage drives her into a nearly murderous encounter with the corrupt killer Archbishop O'Faolin; she pushes her crooked fingers into his eyes, telling him, "I might blind you. I might kill you. If you fight, you up the pressure" (265). Someone else in the room pulls her off him. Such graphic physical descriptions and close-up fights diminish as the series progresses.

V. I.'s relationship with guns is a complex one. In the first novel, she explains her confidence in handling firearms comes from her policeman father: "I used to go down to the police range with my dad on Saturday afternoons and practice target shooting" (IO 92). After her father died, V. I. gave his gun to his colleague and friend, Bobby Mallory, as a memento. However, in her current profession she has come to terms with owning one and keeping in practice, although it is not her first weapon of choice. The reader is made party to the dilemma she faces frequently in trying to decide whether or not to get the gun out of the safe, knowing that carrying a gun is in itself a provocative act. The text often talks the reader through V. I.'s thought process as she decides whether the situation merits carrying the gun, what to wear so as to conceal it, and considers other options for protecting herself. Her more characteristic response in a tight situation is to talk—to insult, jeer, taunt, demand answers, and shout accusations. Her tough talk is a potent weapon because so many of her antagonists and assailants are not expecting it from a woman. The verbal skills often buy her time when she is cornered. She survives in the combative milieu of her profession and her city by using her wits and physical skills whenever possible; guns are a last resort. In *Burn Marks* she uses her gun to save her own life and that of her elderly Aunt Elena when they are threatened by the corrupt building contractor Ron Grasso and when she has exhausted any other means of fending him off. In a dramatic night-time scene at the top of a skyscraper under construction, V. I. aims to kill Grasso and succeeds. Although she continues to push herself physically and mentally, V. I. ages in semi-real time and is aware that her physical powers at 50 are not what they were at 30. Another of Paretsky's strategies vis-à-vis the motif of violence is to treat it as a theme. In *Tunnel Vision* episodes of wife-beating and child sexual abuse link a middle-class family, a homeless family, and a young policewoman at the start of her career—domestic violence has touched them all. Each of these individuals—the battered wives and the molested children—are impotent, at the mercy of general indifference to their stories, and helpless to change things. When a long-buried story of sexual abuse of a niece by an uncle threatens to surface in *Blood Shot*, the abuser is provoked to murder and V. I. herself is driven by fury to use her gun in a showdown with the guilty uncle and two more criminals involved in the cover-up. In *Bitter Medicine* Paretsky describes the violence that is instigated by a group of pro-life campaigners outside Dr. Lotty Herschel's streetfront clinic that offers safe abortions to women. In a city famous for the heavy-handed tactics of the Mob, political party machines, and police force, V. I.'s experiences of violence emanate from encounters with the good guys as well as with out-and-out crooks and thugs. In *Hardball*, Paretsky focuses on the provocative strategies used by the Chicago police during the civil rights movement of the 1960s: intimidating witnesses, taking short cuts in protecting the right of peaceful assembly, and planting evidence. In *Burn Marks*, the murderous Michael Furey hits the handcuffed V. I. across the mouth telling her she needs to learn a lesson; she replies, "I have to wonder if beating me while I'm defenceless would make you feel powerful or ashamed?" (320). When he tries to hit her again, she kicks him in the kneecap "hard enough to break it" (ibid.). Paretsky addresses the issue of violence against women in some of her nonfiction pieces such as a 1991 op-ed piece for the *New York Times* on the subject of domestic violence and in the long essay "Protocols of the Elders of Feminism" for an Australian law journal.

## Voice and Agency

In an article for the *Independent* (London) newspaper in 1997, Paretsky wrote, regarding her heroine V. I. "her primary role is to speak.... [S]he says those things which I—which many women—are not strong enough to say for ourselves" (22). V. I.—a female private investigator created in the wake of the hard-boiled tradition—is given the wisecracking mouth associated with the likes of Philip Marlowe and the Continental Op. She offers a running internal commentary, laced with wit and cynicism, on her own thoughts and actions, and can spar in conversation with hoodlums, police officers, petty officials, white-collar corporate executives, and anyone else who crosses her path or her code of ethics. Beyond that convention, however, V. I.'s voice is constructed as particularly and consistently attentive to the relationships between gender systems and institutional relations of power in society. What V. I. says is more often than not inherently unsettling to the way things are, in genre terms and in social and cultural terms. To the enduring delight of her reading public, V. I. is a woman who behaves badly—a disorderly, rebellious, lippy female "out of place" in a genre that historically serves to trivialize and demonize women, and in a society that functions according to rules and regulations that tend to subordinate women. The corrupt police officer Michael Furey accuses V. I. of just this "crime" when he tells her, "[Y]ou're not interested in the things a normal girl is" (*Burn* 316). In the same novel, Bobby Mallory also reminds V. I. that "you just didn't seem like a real girl to me, the things you wanted and wanted to do" (*Burn* 339).

Paretsky's work has, from the beginning, occupied a key position in the foregrounding of gender in relation to genre. Commercially and critically successful, she is a self-identified feminist whose interventions in the patterns of crime and mystery fiction have proven at once pioneering and enduring. The figure of V. I. is a subversive image of what women are supposed to be like, whether in fiction or in reality. By the standards of many readers, as well as by those of some of V. I.'s friends, V. I. is a woman behaving outside of conventional parameters. She is unmarried, rude, outspoken, and a reluctant housekeeper. Conducting on-again, off-again sexual relationships with a series of partners, she shows little interest in settling down and having children, and refuses to countenance any injunction that there might be places where she cannot or "should not" go. She lives on her own, is skilled in the ailing electric and plumbing systems in her office building, and has been known to eat out alone in restaurants. She engages in work involving the world of ideas and action; she is positioned to take action, influence events, and demonstrate competence. These are all underpinned by some narrative patterns that Paretsky puts in place in the debut novel and that continue to characterize the female detective whose methods and presence subvert even as they entertain. What V. I. says, those she says it to, and what they say back to her is not so much an obvious demonstration that "women can do it too" but rather the more subtle exploration of what is in the way of women doing it. When V. I. encounters an obstruction and names it to another character (plus the reader), she forces both the textual and the reading audience to participate, if only for a moment, in a slightly different order of things. For example, in *Indemnity Only*, V. I. parries a gendered pattern of interaction in an exchange with a corporate executive who is unable, or more likely, unwilling, to use her last name. He asks, "What does the V. stand for?," and she replies, "My first name, Mr. Masters" (IO 19). In refusing Masters the information he assumes it is his right to have, V. I. momentarily disrupts the privilege and power taken for granted in the Ajax Insurance world where secretaries are female and addressed by their first name, and CEOs are male and called Mr. Masters. Speech exchanges in the V. I. novels are often accompanied by V. I.'s accounts of her extremely reactive physiology. She tells the reader about her visceral responses—the throbbing pulse, the husky voice, the tight throat, the deep breathing to calm herself, the sweating, the occasional bout of vomiting. The narrative space occupied by the female private eye's body attests to the nonstop physical and mental effort involved in claiming one's place as a competent woman with a legitimate voice. The police force—another bastion of male privilege and a staple of the private-eye novel with the historically troubled relationship between the cops and the private investigator—gives Paretsky another opportunity to generate V. I. as an image that opens up gendered structures. For Lt. Bobby Mallory, the old friend and colleague of V. I.'s father on the Chicago police force, V. I. is, in social and cultural terms, completely out of place. He has difficulty accepting her as a detective or as a competent person. Appalled at her housekeeping, her attire, and her life choices, and suspicious of her chaotic professional methods, he complains that she does not behave as a "nice" or "decent" young woman ought to (IO 32). This debate continues throughout the series with some robust arguments between the two of them. The conflict between Bobby and V. I. allows Paretsky to locate V. I. generically, capable not only of solving the crime but also of tackling the nonstop, wider task of reframing the female self in the face of institutional doubt. V. I.'s voice is strengthened further by Paretsky's decision to represent some of V. I.'s fantasies about how she would like to behave. In *Indemnity Only,* the detective imagines pumping bullets into the evil and brutal Smiessen who has victimized her and others in the story; this strategy is a means of legitimizing what is often denied to women— the right to express the rage and anger that attends the helplessness of being the victim. Finally, V. I.'s voice is located not as a singular (although very distinctive) one, but as part of a chorus of other (predominantly female) voices throughout the novels claiming their spaces from the edges of social and cultural boundaries. Where the historical experience of women (as well as black people, the elderly, and the gay community) is fragmentation and obliteration from the record, the collective presence of other nonconformist characters and voices in the novels (such as Mr. Contreras, Sal Barthele, and Lotty Herschel) adds up to a collective project. Speaking her mind—whether out loud, in her imagination, or in concert with her friends and neighbors—has served V. I. well in maintaining the complexity of her position as a "deviant" detective figure in the landscape of the mystery novel.

## Warshawski, Anton "Tony"

V. I.'s father, a Polish cop in the mainly Irish Chicago police force, has died "from emphysema" (*Burn* 73) at the start of the series with *Indemnity Only*. In the debut novel, V. I. tells the young grieving Anita about her own dad, who has "been dead ten years now … a bit of a dreamer, an idealist, a man who had never shot another human being in all his years on the force" (IO 240). Much later in the series, V. I. fills in some Warshawski family background for Petra (the daughter of Tony's brother, Peter; Peter left Chicago for Kansas City and a successful career as a company executive). Petra, who first appears in *Hardball*, is curious about the uncles she never knew. Tony and his brother, Bernie, were the two oldest in the Warshawski family that started out near the stockyards in a "row house in Back of the Yards" (HB 42), with no indoor plumbing. Later, "Grandma Warshawski … bought a bungalow in Gage Park [and t]hen she moved to Norwood, up on the Northwest Side" (HB 42), which is where V. I. remembers visiting her grandmother. Going through a photo album in *Hardball*, V. I. comes across Tony and Gabriella's wedding picture: "City Hall, 1945. My mother, in a severely tailored suit, looking like Anna Magnani in *Open City*. My father, in his dress uniform, bursting with astonished pride" (HB 126). In *Burn Marks*, more is revealed about Tony's adolescence and young adulthood in the Norwood Park neighborhood. He and Bobby Mallory (a Chicago police officer still on the force) know each other from this period; their friendship is forged through strong family ties and years together as Chicago cops, when Tony mentored Bobby. In addition to Peter and Bernie, Tony has a sister, Elena (who becomes the family problem because of her fondness for the bottle). Elena and Peter both feature in *Burn Marks*, although relations between Peter and V. I. are strained when he refuses to help his destitute sister.

Tony met Gabriella as a beat cop; "he rescued her in a Milwaukee Avenue bar where she'd thought she could use her grand opera training to get a job as a singer" (TR 16). Tony died 10 years after Gabriella, at a time when V. I. was finishing law school and entering the public defender's office, and 10 years before the series starts, which suggests V. I. is in her mid-thirties when she debuts in *Indemnity Only*. According to V. I. in *Hardball*, her "dad died, in 1982" (43). An earlier reference to Tony's death in *Blood Shot* is made when V. I. visits her childhood neighborhood: "I'd last been on the block in 1976 when my father died and I came back down to sell the house" (9). Here V. I. remembers that Gabriella had been "dead ten years at the time" (ibid.). This suggests a slippage in the fictional family timeline. In *Total Recall*, V. I. remembers arguing with her father forty years ago about "my joining anti-war protesters in Grant Park when he was assigned to riot control duty…. I'd run wild with the Yippies for a night" (11). The events in Grant Park to which V. I. refers took place in 1968, making the time frame for *Total Recall* 2008 and suggesting that, by the late 1960s, V. I. is in college. At the close of *Burn Marks* she gives Tony's police shield to Bobby as a token of reconciliation. Tony is commemorated in the wooden desk bought by V. I. "at a police auction" (IO 3) for her office in the Pulteney building. Tony's reputation is that of a "gentle, good humoured father" (BS 9) and an honest, hard-working beat cop who never was promoted because, as Gabriella once said to V. I.'s Aunt Marie, "Tony, he must do many hard jobs at the police, they are Irish, they not liking Polish peoples" (HB 125). In *Hardball*, V. I. is startled to wake up from a dream about Tony that leaves her "sweating and weeping … there are still nights when I need my father so badly that the pain of losing him cuts through and takes my breath away" (HB 123). In the short story "A Family Sunday in the Park," the 11-year-old "Tori" (V. I.'s childhood nickname) ends up in the riot-filled Marquette Park, searching for her father who is guarding the civil rights demonstrators.

## Warshawski, Gabriella Sestieri

Long before readers meet V. I. at age 30 or so in *Indemnity Only*, both of her parents have died. She refers frequently to both parents throughout the series; however, it is the death of her mother, Gabriella Sestieri Warshawski, from cancer when Vic is 15 years old that continues to haunt her memory and dreams. The loss of her mother at an early age is something from which Vic has never quite recovered. Gabriella frequently appears in V. I.'s dreams and thoughts, and she is further remembered through the recurring motif of music as well as some personal belongings that V. I. has inherited. For instance, in the ninth V. I. novel, the detective comes across her mother's concert gown stored in a trunk: "The fabric brought her to me as intensely as if she were in the next room … holding her gown I longed to have her with me, guarding me against the great and little blows the world inflicts" (HT 28). Thus, throughout the mystery series, Gabriella suggests both a palpable absence and the presence of a somewhat idealized mother figure. Her musical gifts, femininity, and ability to appreciate the beauty of the world she is in, rather than living in a world of regret, are all character traits that V. I. respects but does not display herself. Gabriella connects V. I. to the arts, crafts, and culture of her native Italy, a heritage that V. I. appreciates as representing a graciousness that is missing in her own life in Chicago.

The highlights of Gabriella's back story are revealed through the use of various narrative strategies across the series and the 1995 short story "Grace Notes." Gabriella was born in the Umbrian town of Pitigliano, "a Jewish cultural center before the war" (VIFS 206), to Laura Verazi, who converted from Catholicism to Judaism to marry Matthias Sestieri. V. I.'s Grandpa Matthias was "considered a real catch" (VIFS 206); his family "were harness makers who switched to automobile interiors in the Twenties," and Matthias was "rich until the Fascists confiscated his property" (VIFS 206). As a teenager, the half–Jewish Gabriella leaves fascist Italy to live with her Catholic aunt, Rosa Verazi, in Chicago and takes with her "the eight Venetian glasses that were her sole legacy of home. Fleeing in haste in the night, she had chosen to transport a fragile load, as if that gained her control of her own fragile destiny" (VIFS 215). The red Venetian wine glasses were "a wedding present to Nonna Laura" (VIFS 209), V. I.'s grandmother who perished in Auschwitz. The glasses, which pass into V. I.'s possession after the death of her mother and which gain meaning throughout the series, come to symbolize all that V. I. remembers and treasures about Gabriella and her family of origin.

In Chicago, Gabriella struggles to fit in with Aunt Rosa's judgmental branch of the family and longs to develop a singing career. After Aunt Rosa kicks her niece out, for reasons not revealed until *Killing Orders*, Gabriella marries the Polish policeman Tony Warshawski. According to V. I., Gabriella "struggled to create domestic harmony. She had married my father out of gratitude, and out of fear, an immigrant alone on the streets of the city, not knowing English" (TR 16). Gabriella's final illness and death continues to trouble V. I., who often dreams of her mother's last few months, remembering how she would "approach Gabriella's bed through the maze of tubes and oxygen that shrouded her" (GA 24). The strong connection between V. I. and her mother is symbolized by concrete objects that V. I. treasures—such as the red wine goblets, a pair of diamond drop earrings, and a necklace—as well as by more abstract motifs such as their shared love of music and the values by which they conduct themselves. The Olivetti typewriter in V. I.'s office in the Pulteney Building is, V. I. says "one of my few tangible legacies from her; its presence comforted me through my six years at the University of Chicago"(GA 90); she is reluctant to part with it when she begins to acquire computer and desktop copier equipment in *Guardian Angel* and *Tunnel Vision*. Other treasured items include Gabriella's framed engraving of the Uffizi gallery in Florence hanging in V. I.'s office and Gabriella's upright piano that is burned beyond repair in *Killing Orders*.

V. I. often "hears" Gabriella's voice giving her instructions, advice, and loving support, urging her to do the right thing and offering her comfort and protection. In *Killing Orders*, Vic wakes up one morning remember-ing a dream in which "Gabriella had come to me, not wasted as in the final days of her illness, but full of life. She knew I was in danger and wanted to wrap me in a white sheet to save me" (213). Making a getaway from an illicit raid on some crucial files in an office building, V. I. bluffs her way past two policemen by wearing a cleaning staff smock and "donning Gabriella's thick accent.... I started shouting in Italian, trusting none of them knew the words to 'Madamina' from *Don Giovanni*" (KO 135–36). In *Bitter Medicine*, the detective reminds herself, "[D]on't trouble trouble, and trouble won't trouble you, Gabriella used to tell me—advice I occasionally followed" (*Bitter* 37). More of Gabriella's early family background in Italy is revealed in the opening chapters of *Hardball* when V. I. returns from a trip to Italy. On vacation in Umbria with Morrell, they have visited "the remnants of Gabriella's family, elderly Catholic cousins … who wouldn't talk about the years she'd had to live in hiding with her father, an Italian Jew" (HB 18). The cousins also claim "not to remember my grandfather, who had been denounced and sent to Auschwitz the day after someone smuggled Gabriella to the coast and a Cuba-bound freighter [and n]o-one knew what had become of Gabriella's younger brother, Moselio … [after] he joined the partisans in 1943" (HB 18). V. I. and Morrell tour "the Siena Opera House, where Gabriella had performed her only professional singing role, Iphigenia, in Jomelli's opera," and V. I. meets an elderly opera singer "who remembered Gabriella from their student days together in the conservatory" (HB 18). In the short story "Grace Notes," a distant Verazi cousin shows V. I. "a stage photo from 1940" (VIFS 208) when Gabriella starred as Iphigenia. V. I. is Tony and Gabriella's only child, although V. I. remembers that Gabriella "had a miscarriage the summer of sixty-five.... Tony and I thought she was dying then" (VIFS 205). Gabriella teaches her daughter to sing and play the piano, and earns money giving music lessons in their South Chicago neighborhood. Although V. I. does not become the professional singer envisioned by her mother, the detective has an abiding appreciation of music and will often break into song as a way of expressing her mood or in response to an obstacle in her current case. V. I. inherits a sturdy set of values from her mother—loyalty, courage, stubbornness, frugality, determination—and V. I. spends a good deal of her adult life trying to live up to Gabriella's high expectations of her daughter. This did not always make for an easy relationship, as V. I. remembers in comparison to her friend Nancy Cleghorn's relaxed mother/daughter "camaraderie, which I'd envied. Even though I loved my mother, she was too intense for an easy relationship" (TS 101). However, in the later *Body Work*, V. I. encounters an angry and alienated young woman who grew up rudderless and remembers she was "the lucky one, getting to live under Gabriella's fierce protective wing until I was old enough to fly on my own" (435). V. I. also gets her habit of defending the underdog from Gabriella's history of speaking up for vulnerable people. In *Blood Shot*, V. I. remembers how Gabriella took the part of a young unwed mother who lived near them; "I felt fiercely proud of my mother for standing up to her righteous neighbors" (BS 31).

## Warshawski, Petra

Petra, the oldest daughter of Peter Warshawski and cousin of V. I., debuts in *Hardball*, the 13th V. I. adventure. A member of the millennium generation, she becomes a regular character in the series, with subsequent appearances in *Body Work* and *Breakdown*. V. I. and the impetuous, privileged Petra experience a stormy start, when the latter unexpectedly turns up in Chicago, "fresh out of college to work as an intern on [a] Senate campaign" (HB 6) for the son of an old Chicago buddy of her father's. "Tall and blond" (HB 40), Petra is full of energy and enthusiasm, and inseparable from her cellphone. Her beauty and confidence work their magic on Mr. Contreras, who tells the unimpressed V. I., "You know what they say, doll: you catch more flies with honey" (HB 71). When V. I.'s patience snaps over a small dispute with her unrepentant cousin, she tells Petra, "you are a wonderful young woman with a lot of energy and goodwill, but you've lived your whole life in a privileged bubble" (HB 176). By the end of *Hardball*, V. I. and Petra have achieved an uneasy truce, although the detective decides that "neither of us was ready" (HB 438) for the young woman's suggestion that she work for V. I. for a while.

Petra's father, Peter, is the much younger brother of Tony, V. I.'s father; the family lived on Ashland Avenue near the famous Chicago stockyards, and Peter worked in the slaughterhouses as a teenager. "When the stockyards left Chicago in the sixties, Peter had followed Ashland Meats to Kansas City" (HB 43); he became a successful businessman, married Rachel, and had five daughters. At the end of *Hardball*, Petra has learned some hard truths about her father's role in the death of a young female civil rights activist in the 1960s. Petra is unable to forgive him, and there is a rift in the family. In *Body Work*, Petra's indiscretions about V. I.'s current case on social media networks endangers her own life; when Petra is kidnapped, V. I. successfully tracks her down. Mr. Contreras is fond of Petra, and the young woman dubs him her Uncle Sal. By the 16th novel, *Critical Mass*, Petra has "left Chicago for the Peace Corps … [in] a remote El Salvoradoran village [which] doesn't often get an Internet connection" (CM 60).

## Warshawski, V(ictoria) I(phigenia)

Victoria Iphigenia Warshawski is the signature private-eye character created by Paretsky. After some early experiments with a fictional detective called Minerva, who was more of a Philip Marlowe figure in drag, Paretsky realized that she wanted a female character who was like women in the real world of the United States in the late 1970s—and so V. I. came into being in *Indemnity Only* in 1982. In common with other famous fictional detectives, it is V. I. herself, rather than the plots and cases, who figures most prominently in the series and whose rebellious personality and lifestyle distinguish her. She is a strong, single-minded woman, confident in her profession and capabilities; as the series progresses, she suffers from the occasional self-doubt about "her stubborn devotion to work, which often wreaks havoc with those she cares about most" (Zvirin, "Hardball" 7). Her fictional friends and real readers, reviewers, and critics draw on a similar lexicon to describe her distinctive personality traits: courageous, smart, stubborn, loyal, intelligent, hot-tempered, independent, tough, resourceful, gutsy, feminist, compelling, witty, impertinent, fearless, outspoken, suspicious, self-reliant, principled, capable, sharp-tongued, ethical, compassionate, and emotionally vulnerable.

V. I. has appeared in 17 novels and several short stories to date. The desire to make women feel powerful lies at the center of the Paretsky oeuvre; V. I.'s spirited, resourceful voice and stubbornness (her greatest asset as well as her greatest handicap) express female agency and power. In a 1999 fax to a publicist preparing a press kit for *Hard Time*, Paretsky wrote about V. I.: "I wanted her to be a substantial figure so that her taking on criminals in a physical way would be credible. I made her about 5'8" and she's muscular with it. Her appearance also combines her Italian mother's olive skin and dark hair with her Polish father's grey eyes and strong Slavic cheekbones…. I suppose that V. I. is the acting part of our partnership and I'm the reflecting one" (Paretsky Papers, Newberry Library, Box 20 of 22, 2012 addition).

In the 1988 short story "The Case of the Pietro Andromache," Max Loewenthal describes V. I as "five foot eight, athletic, light on her feet" (WCB 73). Earlier, the detective herself tells the reader that she looks her best "in the summer. I inherited my Italian mother's olive coloring, and tan beautifully" (IO 11). This moment of self-approval is immediately undercut by Vic's recollection of her mother telling her, "Yes, Vic, you are pretty … but to take care of yourself you must have brains. And you must have a job, a profession. You must work" (ibid.). According to an "interview" of V. I. by Murray Ryerson, the fictional investigative reporter for the *Chicago Herald-Star*, which was published on Paretsky's early Web site, the detective was named by her soprano-trained Italian mother for Victor Emanuel ("the second, who helped unify Italy, not the third") and for Iphigenia because her mother once sang the role in

Jommelli's opera by that name. It is the brilliant and erratic Leydon Ashford, a friend of V. I.'s from law school days, who calls V. I. "her little huntress" (BD 75), because Leydon knows that the detective's "middle name, Iphigenia, was an avatar of the Greek goddess Artemis, the huntress" (ibid.). The private eye is known primarily as V. I., although friends such as Lotty call her Vic or Victoria. Her childhood nickname, Tori, is referenced in *Hardball* and in the short story "A Family Sunday in the Park." In *Deadlock*, the detective notes that policeman Bobby Mallory, her father's friend and colleague, is the "only person allowed to call me Vicki" (3). The author's Web site includes a profile of the fictional character that explains "V. I. Warshawski was born on July 27th, [circa 1950] with the sun in Leo and Gemini rising. Her chart reads: 'Extremely active by nature, you like to get around and meet people. Very restless, you can't seem to stay put. Because of the high nervous tension you always have, athletic ability would be a good way for you to burn off energy'" (http://www.saraparetsky.com/about-v-i/). She works to keep in shape by running and exercising at home.

Famous for her intelligence, quick wit, energy, and "a temper that could bend cutlery" (Stasio "Firebrand" 22), the character attracted praise from the beginning. Kathi Maio's 1982 review of *Indemnity Only* suggests that "Vic shows great potential as a strong but sensitive woman sleuth" (17). A 1984 review by Emily O'Leary of Paretsky's second novel, *Deadlock*, credits "her inspired creation, female private-eye V. I. Warshawski" as a reason why the author "manages skilfully to elude the second-novel jinx that sinks so many promising authors" (18G). Mouthy from the start, V. I. is renowned for speaking her mind. In *Indemnity Only*, she famously faces down a doubting client who calls her a "girl" and questions her capabilities in case "things get heavy" by telling him, "I'm a woman, Mr. Thayer, and I can look out for myself. If I couldn't, I wouldn't be in this kind of business…. I'll figure out a way to handle [things]—or go down trying" (5). Paretsky portrays V. I. in relation to a wide circle of friends and associates; several of the repeating characters such as Dr. Lotty Herschel, Sal Barthele, Mary Louise Neely, and Tessa Reynolds are women like V. I., with careers, energy, agency, and principles. In the memoir *Writing in an Age of Silence* (2007), Paretsky comments on the significance of V. I.'s affiliated "family" and her community ties, so different from the isolated prototype of a private eye such as Philip Marlowe: "My detective couldn't survive with so much loneliness.... She needs friends, dogs, lovers—she needs continuity and connectivity" (121). As the series develops, the detective becomes known for her doggedness, trustworthiness, courage, and refusal to compromise. She claims the privilege of thinking and acting for herself, even when this leads her into disagreements with friends and lovers, and often into real danger. Lehmann-Haupt's review of the seventh V. I. adventure *Guardian Angel* explains the character's appeal as "her willingness to defy decorum and raise absolute hell in defense of her outrage. She has the courage of her low boiling point" ("Warshawski" C22). Another reviewer notes that "in spite of her doubts and fears, she still tries to act ... with integrity. She keeps on trying to make sense of the chaos that surrounds her" (Metcalf 7). V. I. is motivated, in case after case, by "an extreme sensitivity to injustice, which she is always inclined to test for hidden neurotic motives" (Lehmann-Haupt op. cit., C22). She is chronically short of sleep and characteristically eats on the run. Her lax relationship to housework and the domestic sphere is a running gag throughout the series, exemplified in repeating motifs of the heap of clothes on the floor, the empty fridge, the piles of dirty dishes in the sink, and any number of throwaway remarks to the reader. In *Burn Marks*, after a night of champagne, V. I. staggers "into the kitchen looking for orange juice. The maid or wife or whoever looked after these things hadn't been to the store yet" (*Burn* 257). One of her biggest fears is finding herself helpless, as she explains in *Burn Marks* when she reluctantly takes pity on her elderly and indigent Aunt Elena: "The thought of being sixty-six, alone, living in a little room with three plastic drawers to hold my clothes—a shudder swept

through me" (*Burn* 32). Her instinct is to take action, and although vulnerable to occasional attacks of doubt, she never hesitates for long. Temporarily unnerved after discovering yet another break-in at home, V. I. briefly collapses on her mattress "for a quarter of an hour before forcing myself to abandon self-pity and start thinking" (KO 234).

In a radical departure from genre tradition, Paretsky fills in a great deal of the detective's background over the course of the novels. Chicago born and bred, V. I. is the only daughter of policeman Tony Warshawski, whose immigrant Polish family settled originally near the stockyards in Chicago, and the Jewish-Italian Gabriella Sestieri, who fled fascist Italy when she was a young opera student. Gabriella came to live in South Chicago with maternal relatives; struggling to support herself and her fledgling singing career, she marries Tony, and they settle in a blue-collar neighborhood on the southeast side of Chicago. In *Hardball*, V. I. takes her cousin Petra, who has become interested in the family background, "on a tour of our family's South Side history" (HB 183), including V. I.'s "childhood home on South Houston" (ibid.). V. I. grew up in a five-room bungalow in South Chicago; she lived in a working-class industrial neighborhood near steel mills and factories during a time when "men poured from those tidy little homes every day into the South Works, Wisconsin Steel, the Ford assembly plant, or the Xerxes solvent factory" (BS 1). Athletic and smart, V. I. did well in high school, in spite of the devastation of her mother's death from cancer when "I was sixteen" (HB 175). (It should be noted that V. I.'s age when her mother died varies in the series.) The private eye is proud of her South Chicago roots: "I was a street fighter, a product of the mills and ethnic wars of Chicago's Steel City" (BD 52). In spite of the frequent references to her family's Polish Catholic and Italian Catholic and Jewish backgrounds, and the Catholicism of her South Chicago neighborhood, V. I. was not brought up in a religious framework. Her familiarity with Catholic rituals stems from the more observant branches of her family (Italian American Aunt Marie and her son, Boom Boom), and early exposure to death: "In my child-hood, although I wasn't a Catholic, I attended a lot of funeral masses for classmates—one of the by-products of growing up in a rough neighbourhood" (BW 74). Much later in life, V. I. seems to get in touch with an unexpected spiritual side, most notably in her encounters with Lou, a helpful neighborhood priest who appears in *Hard Time* and *Blacklist*.

With the help of a basketball scholarship, V. I. attends the University of Chicago, study-ing hard and singing "in the chapel choir in my student days" (BD 101). By the time she is in law school, her father, Tony, is dying from emphysema. In *Hard Time*, she remembers, "His illness affected everything about me then, from my decision to marry [fellow law student Richard "Dick" Yarborough] in the hopes I'd produce a grandchild … before he died … [to taking] the public defender's job so I could stay in Chicago and be with him" (HT 29). Two years later, Tony has died, and V. I.'s marriage ends not long afterward. Meanwhile, her career in the public de-fender's office is something she pursues with diminishing enthusiasm.

Although V. I.'s parents have died before the series begins with *Indemnity Only*, they remain a strong presence in her life. Through-out the novels, V. I. remembers their advice and encouragement, their deep love of her, and their values of frugality, honesty, loyalty, fairness, and helping others. Gabriella and Tony appear in V. I.'s dreams, often to com-fort her, and sometimes to exhort her. De-tails of her parents' back stories and of V. I.'s childhood, emerge particularly in the early novels *Deadlock* (Tony's family); *Killing Or-ders* (Gabriella's family); *Blood Shot* (V. I.'s childhood and Gabriella's family); and *Burn Marks* (Tony's family). More of Gabriella's story is revealed in the short story "Grace Notes" in *Windy City Blues* (aka *V. I. for Short*). Another short story, "A Family Sunday in the Park," depicts a very young V. I., her cousin Boom-Boom, and other family members in summer 1966. Further memories of V. I.'s up-bringing surface throughout the oeuvre, often stirred up as the sleuth cruises areas of Chicago associated with her family, and also in dreams—a favorite Paretsky motif.

In the debut *Indemnity Only*, set in sum-mer 1979, V. I. is in her thirties, working as a private investigator and specializing in cor-porate financial crime. She earns a modest living by performing background financial checks on individuals and businesses and tracking people who have stolen assets. Ex-plaining why she became an investigator to an inquisitive suitor in *Burn Marks*, she tells him it is because she can be her own boss: "I should have given that as my first reason—it continues to be the most important with me" (*Burn* 95). She lives alone in a "large, cheap apartment on Halsted" (IO 10), not far from Belmont Harbor where she likes to run for exercise. On the housekeeping front, she admits to being "messy, but not a slob" (IO 11). V. I. drives a dark blue Chevy Monza and rents an office in the gently decaying Pul-teney Building at the corner of Monroe and Wabash in the South Loop, next to the El. The office is sparsely furnished, with objects that link V. I. both to her mother (the print of the Uffizi gallery and the Olivetti portable typewriter), and to her father (the wooden desk she acquired at a police benefit auc-tion). She charges $125 per diem plus ex-penses and runs her business singlehanded with backup from an answering service. Al-though she operates alone as an investigator, the artifacts that symbolize her parents con-nect V. I. to a collective remembered past and underscore V. I.'s sense of self as cultur-ally attached to identities that are Polish, Ital-ian, Catholic, and Jewish. Her father, Tony, was a policeman in the city's 21st district, where his friend, Lt. Bobby Mallory, still works in the homicide division. Gabriella is further symbolized in the debut novel by ref-erence to one of V. I.'s most treasured pos-sessions, a set of red Venetian wine goblets brought to the United States by her mother—"wrapped carefully in her underwear to take in the one suitcase she carried" (IO 77) when she left Italy just before the war broke out. These red glasses appear throughout the se-ries.

V. I.'s. family timeline in the novels includes some slippages. From *Blacklist*, the reader learns that V. I.'s father Tony is age 9 in 1931. In the same novel, it appears that V. I.'s parents marry in 1946, although in the later *Hardball*, the marriage date is given as 1945 (126). According to the author's Web site, V. I. is born to Gabriella and Tony on 27 July, ca. 1950 (http://www.saraparetsky.com/about-v-i/). In the later *Hardball*, V. I. remembers "the big storm of 'sixty seven. I'd been ten then" (30), which would make her birth year 1957. However, in *Total Recall* V. I. also remembers arguing with her father about hanging out with the Yippies during the famous events in Grant Park during the 1968 Democratic Convention in Chicago; this would suggest she was older than 11 by then. Gabriella dies of cancer when V. I. is 15, according to *Killing Orders* (18); and when she is 16, according to *Hardball* (175)—the latter age makes the date of Gabriella's death 1973, although another novel, *Blood Shot*, suggests she died in 1966—10 years earlier than Tony's death in 1976 (BS 9). However, the date of Tony's death also changes; *Hardball* gives 1982 as the year in which Tony died (43). Whatever the inconsistencies in dates, it is clear that V. I.'s mother dies when V. I. is still in high school in the mid to late 1960s; 10 years later, her father dies after a long illness.

V. I.'s brief marriage is first mentioned in *Indemnity Only*; she relates how she met Dick at a bar association meeting. He is an attorney with Crawford, Mead, and she is working in the public defender's office (IO 160). However, in the later *Guardian Angel*, the story of their meeting is referred to slightly differently, as V. I. remembers "six months of sweetly tormented eroticism as we finished law school and studied for the bar, and eighteen of simple torment after we married" (GA 14). In the first novel, motifs are set in place that continue throughout the series: V. I.'s dedication to an exercise routine; her love of music, particularly opera; her fondness for classy clothes and shoes; her ardent support of the Cubs baseball team; her wide knowledge of places to eat and drink across Chicago; her small circle of friends and colleagues who function as a "family" of sorts; and her prickly relationship with the Chicago Police Department. She is a self-identified feminist whose principles are informed not only by her parents' values but also by an un-

derstanding of gender, race, and class politics. She has a strong sense of solidarity with the cultural and political traditions of her forebears—her social conscience has been nurtured by examples of loyalty to her own, doing service to others, hard work, and frugal habits. She is impatient, quick to take the side of the underdog, fearless in battle, and determined to do the right thing. As Marilyn Stasio's review of *Tunnel Vision* notes, "This principled private eye intimidates people because she doesn't know the meaning of compromise and won't tolerate moral slackers" ("Crime" 42). She prefers to solve her own problems, and she places great value on taking responsibility for her own actions, even when those actions endanger her. In line with the traditionally cynical private eye, V. I. is under no illusions about the flawed society in which she operates and the hypocrisies of the American Dream, which seems to promote personal gain at the expense of social responsibility. As Australian journalist Jane Sullivan notes, what V. I. "burns to do is to make sense of crime … she fights for truth, justice and the American underdog against the corruption that overwhelms the highest institutions in the land" (7). In a twist to the Chandler tough-guy tradition, where the detective hero gives little away about his inner feelings, V. I. often filters emotions such as anger, frustration, and fear through visceral expression: "My neck muscles had turned so stiff from rage that when I got to my own front door I was trembling violently" (GA 71). In *Tunnel Vision*, in retreat after a tense encounter with a homeless family in the basement of the Pulteney Building, the detective notices, "I couldn't stop the unreasoning part of my body from sweating clammily as I went" (6). She is also prone to throwing up when distressed. One such incident occurs in the first novel, *Indemnity Only*, when she vomits on the jacket of a would-be kidnapper who is manhandling her in the back of a car. On another occasion she confesses, "I'd thrown up after leaving Mrs. Frizzell, a sudden, spontaneous retching to purge myself from the lie I'd had to tell" (GA 81). Throughout the series, V. I. has affairs, some of which end badly. V. I.'s romances include some short affairs in the early novels with a succession of Ajax Insurance agents: Robin Bessinger (*Burn*), Ralph Devereux (IO, TR), and Roger Ferrant (DL, KO). In *Deadlock*, V.I. has a brief encounter with shipowner Martin Bledsoe during her investigation into the shipping industry. Similarly, in *Bitter Medicine*, she and the corrupt Dr. Peter Burgoyne have a short affair, which Burgoyne has pursued to extract information from her. The legacy of this relationship is the golden retriever Peppy that becomes part of V. I.'s household when her owner dies. Peppy and her offspring, Mitch (a dog that is half labrador), play lasting roles in all the subsequent V. I. novels. In *Blood Shot*, she toys with the idea of a romantic interlude with Sergeant John McGonnigal, but thinks better of it with apparently few regrets on either side as she notes, "[H]e acted pretty cold until he realized I wasn't going to blow the whistle on his late-night lapse from policeman decorum" (BS 324).

V. I. and *Chicago Herald-Star* reporter Murray Ryerson had a short fling in the past but have settled for a slightly edgy and competitive relationship as friends and collaborators. She has a longer, although ultimately troubled, relationship with Chicago policeman Conrad Rawlings, who becomes her lover in *Guardian Angel* and separates from her at the end of *Tunnel Vision,* although they remain friends of sorts. As well, she has an intense relationship with the independent investigative journalist Morrell. Morrell's work often takes him to the Middle East on long assignments; their affair starts in *Hard Time* during a period when he is based in Chicago. She parts from him by the beginning of *Hardball.* The breakup of these long-term affairs leaves her melancholy and reflective about her capacity for commitment; at the end of the Morrell affair, she wonders if "[m]aybe I was too prickly, as some of my friends suggested, for anyone to get close to me" (HB 19). By the end of this novel, she is embarked on a tentative romance with her new neighbor, musician Jake Thibaut. That relationship continues as of the 17th novel, *Brush Back* (2015).

The lovers and affairs function in several ways: to allow V. I. emotional depth; to portray her as an adult female character with sexual autonomy; to underline her struggle for independence and autonomy within the parameters of intimate relationships and social expectations. Her friendships with Dr. Lotty Herschel and Mr. Salvatore Contreras, her elderly neighbor from downstairs, further locate her in a community of people whose values and personal histories she shares. With both Lotty and Mr. Contreras come extended family members of their own, work associates, and friends who become part of V. I.'s wider network, taking her into cross-generational relationships and sometimes into personal disagreements and showdowns. Despite the lone-ranger persona she likes to think she is projecting, V. I. is anything but rootless or friendless. On the contrary, she is, in some ways, weighted down by family history and friends. While they anchor her, their demands and expectations can be invasive and draining for someone who prefers to operate solo. At various points V. I. experiments with part-time assistants who help her manage her workload and administrative tasks, and sometimes take on background research on a case. The most notable of these is Mary Louise Neely who leaves the police force, becomes a foster parent to the Messenger children, and starts working for V. I. at the end of *Tunnel Vision.* Eventually Mary Louise earns her law degree and obtains a position at a downtown law firm. Another assistant is history student Amy Blount, who does research for V. I. in *Blacklist.* Much later in the series, V. I.'s eager millennial cousin Petra has a brief stint as V. I.'s assistant, although they come to the conclusion that it is not an advisable situation.

Throughout the oeuvre, V. I. lives alone, although in close proximity to dogs, neighbors, and friends. Often in the company of Lotty or Murray, she frequents a range of restaurants. V. I. runs a tab at Sal Barthele's Golden Glow bar in the Loop where her favorite tipple is Johnny Walker Black; V. I. and Murray often meet there to compare notes on their investigations. V. I. frequently pauses for snacks and meals on the road; she is also portrayed cooking for herself and others at home. The food motif functions not only to indicate her knowledge of her own city but also to establish V. I. in the reality of needing to eat and as a way of breaking up the action and giving the reader a pause from the heightened tension and temperature of the investigation.

The events of the second novel *Deadlock* take place in spring 1982; V. I. is still living in her "tired 3-flat" (11), but the blue Monza she drove in *Indemnity Only* has been replaced by a green Mercury Lynx. In 1990, the time frame for *Burn Marks*, V. I. buys an '89 Pontiac Trans Am that she is still driving in *Guardian Angel* (1992). At the end of *Killing Orders*, third in the series, V. I. is burned out of her apartment and relocates to a third-floor flat in a six-flat building on Racine, in a "quiet blue-collar neighborhood" (GA 6). In the next novel, *Bitter Medicine*, Mr. Contreras, her new downstairs neighbor and a retired machinist, becomes a devoted friend and supporter of V. I. and a regular character in the series. Mr. Contreras and V. I. take on the joint care of Peppy, the golden retriever who was left homeless when her owner died at the end of *Bitter Medicine*. Later in the series, Peppy's offspring Mitch joins the household. Their low-key neighborhood near Belmont Harbor eventually gives way to the forces of gentrification. By the time of *Guardian Angel*, V. I.'s "upwardly mobile neighbors" have formed a local development committee that she declines to join. Her apartment is "four rooms arranged boxcar style. From the kitchen you went into the dining room and then into a little hall that fed the bedroom, bath, and living room" (GA 5). Although she lives quite frugally, she often has trouble making ends meet. In *Guardian Angel* for example, she worries about her cash flow: "Besides Peppy's [vet] bills and new running shoes, I had payments on the Trans Am and my apartment to keep up" (GA 32). V. I.'s early physical fitness routine of jogging is amplified in *Deadlock* with a reference to the Irving Park YWCA, which she joins for an annual fee of $90 so she can use its pool and Nautilus room. As the series progresses, V. I.'s main fitness routine consists of running, exercising the dogs at Belmont Harbor, and doing sets of stretches at home. Allowed to age in a "slow" real time, she reports more physical aches and pains as she hits her fifties; although she claims she is slowing down, this is not reflected by the pace of her activities in the recent novels. Usually attired in jeans, running shoes, and a jacket, V. I. is also famous for a certain amount of self-conscious power-dressing: in *Tunnel Vision*, for example, she dresses "carefully for my meeting with Darraugh Graham, in black wool with a white silk shirt and my red Magli pumps…. [T]hey bring me luck, my red Magli pumps" (15). In the fourth V. I. novel, she prepares for a meeting with the police by dressing "professionally … in a wheat-colored suit with a silk shirt about the same color" (*Bitter* 50). This tendency to dwell on her outfits diminishes in the later novels.

By *Tunnel Vision*, she has installed an alarm system, seeking to avert the frequent break-ins by those looking for evidence accumulated in her cases. V. I.'s detecting m.o. references classic detective fiction. She is as good as Sherlock Holmes at disguise and disappearance; in *Breakdown*, for example, she drops off the radar screen when a killer leaves her for dead, only to stage a dramatic reappearance some days later on Murray's live TV program where they expose the criminal Wade Lawlor. Like Miss Marple, she can bluff her way past gatekeepers and persuade people to talk to her. She is not above breaking and entering with her picklocks; she burgles offices as well as copies or steals files. As adept with insulting putdowns as she is with picklocks, V. I. uses her wits and verbal skills to face down antagonists, but she can resort to physical violence when necessary. Her sardonic putdowns and challenges often buy her time in tight situations.

V. I.'s somewhat contentious relationship with the Chicago police force is true to genre tradition that historically portrays conflict between the amateur or professional detective and the official law enforcement agencies. However, in the hands of Paretsky the somewhat formulaic expectation of an uneasy antagonism between the solo detective and the official police is given a number of twists and complications. First, V. I.'s father, Tony, was a "beat cop on the south side" (*V. I. x 3* 2007 29) for all of his working life. Tony's career never advanced beyond neighborhood cop, no doubt hindered by his Polish background in a historically Irish police force and his gentle personality. V. I. grew up with an understanding of precinct politics, the demands and dangers of the job, the sense of duty and honesty of her father, and the constant fear of her mother that harm would come to him. As the daughter of a policeman and as a former lawyer for the public defender's office, V. I. has an insider's understanding and knowledge of the workings of the system—from the rules and regulations that govern the police service and the courts to the loyalties and pressures that also influence police behavior. Vic's professional relationship with Bobby, her father's best friend on the force, is underpinned by the personal history between her family and that of Bobby and his wife, Eileen, who regard V. I. as a daughter. Spats between Bobby and V. I. are as likely to be over their differing personal opinions on appropriate roles for a woman in today's society as over the details of a case in which they are both involved. In addition to Bobby, V. I. encounters several other police officers with whom her personal and professional boundaries sometimes blur. Officers John McGonnigal and Michael Furey, who are favorites of Bobby's, express a romantic interest in V. I. Bobby encourages the personal relationship between V. I. and Furey, but it does not last long in *Burn Marks* when Furey's corrupt dealings with an old friend in the construction business are revealed. Other repeating police detective characters are Terry Finchley ("The Finch"), and Conrad Rawlings, V. I.'s lover for two novels. Paretsky spotlights a police force with its own friendships, loyalties, betrayals, history, and internal conflicts over professional standards and behavior, thus widening the traditional focus on conflicts between the private eye and police.

Another aspect of the traditional genre trope is the detective's stubborn refusal to cooperate with the police. In genre convention, the private eye is usually one step ahead of the police; the police refuse to listen until too late; then, when the police finally engage, the private eye refuses to cooperate. Paretsky's variations on this theme include the faintly comic with V. I. keeping the police waiting in her kitchen while she makes coffee or breakfast, leaving an officer on the phone while she showers, and napping in the squad car when she is being hustled down to headquarters. In *Breakdown*, V. I. responds to an unwelcome police presence in her apartment by "asserting my right to remain silent"; she then "turn[s] on the radio and went down on my hands and knees to do some core strengthening moves" (42). In the ensuing showdown, she continues to exercise with a "sequence of abdominal presses" and refuses to say anything because of her view that "the Supreme Court's recent ruling on the right to silence had alarming implications for anyone who said anything during an interrogation" (43). So the antagonism can be provoked by the personal face of the cop in front of her but behind that there is V. I.'s constant suspicion of the misuse of power and the rules as well as her difficulties with the way in which the rules keep changing and making inroads into individual rights. Underneath all the bluster and the trouble between V. I. and the police, however, is a fundamental sense that she can rely on them now and again when all else fails and she needs help. This is because her father's reputation still counts for something amongst present-day personnel and also because the Chicago police force tolerates V. I. When she asks a doubting rural police officer to call a few people in the Chicago force who can vouch for her, she overhears one of the assessors saying, "[H]onest but a pain in the ass" (CM 13). The detective is also alert to the iniquities imposed by gender and fearless about drawing attention to them. On a visit to the police station with Lotty, who becomes impatient at being kept waiting, V. I. reminds her, "This is what it's like at the average gynecologist's office.... [B]ecause they treat only women and women's time has inherently no value, it doesn't matter that the average patient wait is over an hour" (*Burn* 50). In the same novel, she spars with Furey when

Furey tells a security deputy not to look at V. I.'s invitation while they are on a date because "she's with me" (36). The furious V. I. tells a bewildered Furey that she does not like being treated as his "appendage" (37). Some of the novels and story lines (such as in *Hardball* and with Mary Louise) directly confront the issues of historical racism and sexism both inside and outside the force. Humor is part of V. I.'s toolbox. Knowing she has a short fuse, she jokes about her celebrated temper: "I could have kept my temper—my besetting sin" (TR 63). Her famous aversion to domestic labor is a frequent source of jokes: "No one who knows me has ever accused me of being germ-phobic, but ticks and fleas turn even a sloppy housekeeper into a compulsive Lady Macbeth" (15), she observes in *Critical Mass* after acquiring a rescue dog. V. I.'s legendary wit and self-deprecating humor "functions on multiple levels," as Biamonte's discussion observes, "from the distancing of comic relief to the rejuvenation of parodied genre conventions to the highly politicized nature of [the detective's] penetrating social commentary to the provocative self-examination of [V. I.'s] biting sarcasm" (234). Biamonte argues these are "emancipatory strategies" that allow V. I. "to enter into conversation with society and with herself" (ibid.). In more serious moods, she often reflects on her propensity for driving close friends and family away because of her need for autonomy and independence; and she reflects on the vicissitudes of aging. Turning 40 at the end of *Tunnel Vision*, V. I. tells the reader, "The dreams I'd had at twenty—the twin yearnings for glory and altruism—seemed ... ghostly and futile" (69).

Yet, in a nod to modern times, the detective can hold her own in making use of technology and social media for investigative purposes as well as for releasing confidential and embarrassing material when it serves her purposes in uncovering secrets and lies. V.I .uses an Apple computer in *Hardball*, the 13th novel. By the 15th novel, *Breakdown*, V. I. has acquired an iPad and discusses the implications of text messaging and posting on Facebook with the teenagers she is trying to help. By the time of *Total Recall* (2001),

V. I.'s fee is "a hundred dollars an hour, with a minimum of five hours' work ... [and] all non-overhead expenses, as well" (14). In the 2009 *Hardball,* her fee has gone up to "a hundred fifty an hour" (23). In the early short story "The Maltese Cat" (1990), V. I.'s billing method is per diem: "I got Ms. Leblanc ... to sign on the dotted line for $400 a day plus expenses" (VIFS 109).

A 1991 profile of the author by Helen Dudar summed up the appeal of V. I.: "a friend to legions of readers who ... know her as a committed feminist, a nifty dresser..., a karate artist skilled enough to break a thug's arm, a flinty spirit whose heart can turn to mush" (72). Frances Fyfield describes V. I. as "a lost soul of conspicuous intelligence and hectic kindness" who is "led by the kind of energy which can destroy as well as reform" (v). William Storrar's review of Paretsky's memoir *Writing in an Age of Silence* notes that "a constant theme in the novels" is the detective's "deep sense of outrage at the violation and silencing of ordinary people, especially women, by powerful institutions with no public accountability" (35). Laura Shapiro's 1987 *Newsweek* column on Paretsky's novels to date summarized the appeal of V. I.: "the detective many mystery fans have been waiting for. A great cook, terrible housekeeper, onetime '60s activist and amateur opera singer, she has a powerful sense of justice and a healthy disrespect for authority figures" (64). A 1994 *Publishers Weekly* review of *Tunnel Vision* describes Paretsky's V. I. as "a rare literary entity, a woman quick to anger and action, yet sympathetic and credible" (57), a summary as accurate in 2015 as it was in 1994.

**See also Sal Barthele; Chicago; dreams; Lotty Herschel; Bobby Mallory; Morrell; Conrad Rawlings; Murray Ryerson; Tony Warshawski; Gabriella Warshawski; Dick Yarborough; Jake Thibaut**

### "Why I Write ..." (2011)

In this piece for *Publishers Weekly* Paretsky explains she writes because stories come to her: "I love language, I love playing with words, and rewriting and reworking, trying to polish" (27).

## "Wild Women out of Control" (1989)

This early autobiographical essay, published in the Carolyn Anthony-edited volume *Family Portraits*, explores the author's recollections of childhood struggles for self-realization as a writer and describes the importance of the adult figure Agnes who listened to her stories. A revised version of the essay appears in *Writing in an Age of Silence* (2007) where "Agnes" is revealed to be a fictional muse based on four women who influenced Paretsky's longings to write and be published.

## *Windy City Blues* (*V. I. for Short* in UK, 1995)

This book collects nine short stories featuring V. I. that were written between 1982 and 1995. Eight of the tales are narrated by the detective in her familiar, if slightly less combative than usual, first-person voice. The exception is "The Pietro Andromache," a story that puts Lotty Herschel center-stage and is told from Max Loewenthal's third-person point of view. In a change from the usual focus of the V. I. novels on Chicago's mean city streets and its reputation for corporate crime, this collection displays a more introspective approach, with several of the stories looking inward and back in time. With settings that range from domestic interiors and a hairdressing salon to the locker rooms at tennis courts and swimming pools, the stories focus on V. I.'s family background, on current friends such as Lotty and Sal Barthele, on long-forgotten friends from school days, on old family rivalries, and on household pets. A lengthy introduction by the author, "A Walk on the Wild Side: Touring Chicago with V. I. Warshawski," which appears in the U.S. Delacorte edition, takes the reader on a tour of the rundown industrial Southeast Chicago neighborhood where V. I. grew up and where herons used to nest before the steel mills were built. Paretsky explains what made her choose this location for V. I.'s childhood: "[I]t is the gallantry of this old neighbourhood that made me take it for the home of my detective…. V. I. came of age under the shadow of the mills, with weekend treks to Dead Stick Pond to watch the herons

feed" (WCB, Delacorte ed. 7). The dedication, "For Isabel—always Agnes's star pupil," references the author's "mentor and friend Isabel Thompson, who took me under her wing" (WIAAOS 23–24) during Paretsky's time as a graduate student at the University of Chicago in the late 1960s. Isabel is further commemorated in a character in the opening story (WCB Delacorte ed.) "Grace Notes"; the title signals a musical theme and the character "Isabel Thompson, an authority on rare music from the Newberry Library" (58), plays a part in the proceedings. The *Publishers Weekly* review notes that the collection has to "get by largely on plotting" as there is no space for the "extended Chicago set pieces" characteristic of the novels (106). Emily Melton's review finds that V. I. "presents a somewhat softer side in this series of stories" (6).

## *A Woman's Eye* (1991)

This anthology of 21 original short stories by an international collection of mystery writers is edited by Paretsky; her long introduction, "Eye of a Woman," traces the predicament of the female author through history with reference to Virginia Woolf's essay "Professions for Women" and outlines the particular history of women writers in mystery writing. Paretsky's essay discusses the ways in which women writers still wrestle with the Victorian ideal of womanhood—the "Angel in the House" domestic phantom described by Woolf. Paretsky writes, "[I]t is a difficult phantom to overpower because it speaks in so many voices and with so much authority behind it" ("Eye of a Woman" vii–viii). The collection includes stories by Liza Cody, Maria Antonia Oliver, Dorothy B. Hughes, Antonia Fraser, Margaret Maron, Gillian Slovo, Mary Wings, and others, who write about homelessness, revenge, and hard-won sobriety from many different points of view. Their protagonists include private eyes, amateur detectives, grandmothers, social workers, police detectives, perpetrators of crime, and intended victims who outsmart the perpetrators. What the stories have in common "is the message that there is no one way to view women" (ibid. xiv). Craig's review for the *Times Literary Supplement* appreciates "the handful of stories in which a 'feminist' outlook isn't at odds with astringency, or plausibility," singling out the story by Amanda Cross ("Women" 21). The *Publishers Weekly* review states that "the female sleuth proves once and for all in this fabulous anthology that testosterone is no prerequisite for success in criminology" (65). Paretsky received the Anthony Award for best anthology of the year in 1992 for this collection. A second volume in the occasional series *Women on the Case* appeared in 1996; a third volume *Sisters on the Case* was published in 2007.

**See also *Women on the Case*; *Sisters on the Case***

## Women and Children First

This independent bookstore opened in 1979 in Chicago with a manifesto "to promote the work of women writers and to create a place in which all women would find books reflecting their lives and interests" (http://womenandchildrenfirst.com); it has become one of the largest feminist bookstores in the county. It was important early on in championing Paretsky's novels and supporting her work. Paretsky gave her first reading at Women and Children First, for the debut V. I. novel *Indemnity Only* (1982). To date, Paretsky still gives a reading for her new books at Women and Children First. The V. I. novels often feature as a staff choice on the bookstore's Web site, and some of Paretsky's book covers appear in the local authors section. *Critical Mass* was launched at the bookstore in autumn 2013 with a joint event with the Girls into Science project, a local Chicago initiative supported by Paretsky that encourages high school girls to explore science topics.

## Women of Mystery: Three Writers Who Forever Changed Detective Fiction (2000)

*Women of Mystery* is a 53-minute color documentary film on mystery writers Sara Paretsky, Marcia Muller and Sue Grafton, their famous detective figures, and the home locations of the authors. The movie was made in 2000 by Pamela Beere Briggs and William McDonald and distributed by New Day Films.

The film visits each author in her home city where "the writers are seen researching their projects, talking about their craft, and offering insight into the "alter egos" of their respective characters," according to the *Booklist* review (Holzberg 492). The film switches between the first-person voices of each author and her protagonist, drawing attention to parallels and differences between writer and fictional character. Kinsman's review notes that "the writers comment on how they engage with questions of violence, how they research their novels, and the nature of both theirs and their characters' relationships with the reader" (651). In the film, JoBeth Williams reads book excerpts and provides the voiceover. The script includes a short history of the mystery novel with reference to nineteenth-century writers of the gothic and sensation novel. Maureen Reddy, a scholar of detective fiction, contributed to the script; her wide knowledge of the genre lends the program an instructive context and points the viewer to "significant continuities between the active heroines of the sensation novels and the contemporary female private eye figure" (ibid., 52). Beere Briggs explained the genesis of the film in her own reader's appreciation of authors such as Paretsky, Linda Barnes, and Marcia Muller who "were raising compelling questions about such social issues as spousal abuse, the environment, homelessness, and the death penalty; about crime and justice; and about the importance of women's voices to literature, and the intimate connection between readers and the female hero" (44). In collaboration with the Center for the Book at the Library of Congress, the documentary became part of a book and film discussion series designed for use in public library systems in Kansas and California. According to librarian Natalie Cole, "*Women of Mystery* is one of the California Center for the Book's most successful and popular programs ... it inspires its participants to appreciate the writing process and to become more active readers" (Beere Briggs & Cole 44).

## Women on the Case (1996)

*Women on the Case* is an anthology of 26 original stories by women writers edited by

Sara Paretsky, whose introductory essay draws attention to the "wide range of voices" represented in the collection that offers "an alternative vision to the anorectic, sex-crazed [female] victim of much contemporary popular culture" (ix). This is "the second in an occasional series of original short stories by women crime writers" and returns to the theme of "what it means to speak in a woman's voice" (vii). Paretsky's introduction tackles the problem of "what if anything I am doing to acknowledge my duty to other women writers, and to the suffering of women in my own age" (ix), and points to the inclusion of new and international women's voices. Authors include Linda Barnes, Liza Cody, Amanda Cross, Dorothy Salisbury Davis, Frances Fyfield, Marcia Muller, Ruth Rendell, Barbara Wilson, and others. The *Publishers Weekly* review praises "a collection that endorses good politics at least as much as good storytelling" (54). Emily Melton's review for *Booklist* notes that Paretsky "has included a well-rounded assortment of crime fiction from both well-known American authors and from foreign writers whose works have never before appeared in English" (1681).

**See also** *A Woman's Eye*; *Sisters on the Case*; **Sisters in Crime**

### "Writers on Writing: A Storyteller Stands Where Justice Confronts Basic Human Needs" (2000)

In this short essay for a *New York Times* series, Paretsky explains "the stories that speak most to me are those of people … who can't speak for themselves, who feel powerless and voiceless in the larger world" (B1). The theme of voicelessness is one that appears often in Paretsky's fiction and nonfiction.

**See also** *Writing in an Age of Silence*

### Writing in an Age of Silence (2007)

This collection of autobiographical essays traces Paretsky's difficult journey as a writer from "silence to speech" (Paretsky, WIAAOS xiii).

The essays are based, in some instances, on material used in earlier speeches and public talks. The memoir is dedicated to Tom Phillips, the Chicago pastor whose summer day-care project in 1966 brought the college-age Paretsky to Chicago as a volunteer. She writes that she came away from that summer "filled with the sense that change for good was possible" (ibid., 6), a sentiment echoed in the book's epigraph taken from Tennyson's *Ulysses* that salutes those who remain "strong in will." The individual pieces include personal details of her oppressive childhood in rural Kansas and her experiences as a PhD student in Chicago, describing how she "became angry at my powerlessness—my personal powerlessness in my patriarchal family and my patriarchal history department—and the powerlessness that society bestowed on all women" (ibid., 7–58). The essays raise a number of linked questions about the obstacles confronting women who seek a public voice. Rooted in her experiences growing up in the decades after World War II and developing a writing career in the 1980s and 1990s, Paretsky broadens the personal into the political. The essays show her pondering, for instance, about the role of misogyny as part of the price paid by women for their voice(s) to be heard; how the words of women can be trivialized and overlooked from the classroom to the boardroom; the challenge of hearing authority in a woman's voice. As one reviewer

**Publicity photograph of Sara Paretsky. Photograph by Alex Garcia, courtesy Tuesday Agency.**

noted, the memoir "stands as an example of the difficulties feminist writers face as they write against the backdrop of a political culture that is often openly hostile to their message" (Gott 9). Tones of anger and frustration infuse the chapters. The British mystery writer P. D. James's review in the *Spectator* described the book as a "poignant and compelling personal testimony" about how Paretsky "grew up to be a passionate advocate for her own sex and a doughty fighter for liberty and social justice" (41). Closer to home, Samuel Freedman's *Chicago Tribune* review finds the first half of the book, which outlines the writer's "journey from love-starved childhood to adult celebrity, and the essential role of literature in the metamorphosis" more powerful and compelling than the material later in the book, which he finds lacking in "thematic unity" (4). These are the sections where Paretsky explores the traditions of political and literary dissent that inform her work and where she shifts her attention from the personal (her childhood and the idealism of the 1960s), to the political (aspects of the prevailing post–9/11 U.S. culture of selfishness and individualism that concern her). As in many of her V. I. novels, Paretsky's epigraph, taken from Tennyson's *Ulysses*, suggests her purpose in the memoir: to honor and recognize those private and public individuals who are "strong in will/Born to strive, to seek, to find, and not to yield." The memoir's title also points to the author's abiding concerns about meaningful free speech, civil liberties, and the importance of dissenting voices in a current climate of censorship. As reviewer Brian A. Klems notes, "at the heart of this book is a fear of silence, no matter its source" (18). The ACLU of Illinois gave Paretsky the 2007 Harry Kalven Freedom of Expression Award in honor of "outspoken defence of the first amendment through your published opinion pieces, particularly your inspiring new book, *Writing in an Age of Silence*" (from letter in author's private papers, accessed November 2012, Chicago). It was subsequently shortlisted for the 2007 National Book Critics Circle awards and was selected as a Kansas Notable book by the State Library of Kansas. In 2010, Paretsky

was invited to speak on the book at the 76th PEN International Congress in Tokyo. Particularly exercised by the effect of the Patriot Act in allowing law enforcement to search libraries, bookstores, and people's homes without probable cause, she took up this issue not only in *Writing in an Age of Silence* but also on many public platforms across the United States. She also made it a theme in the V. I. novel *Blacklist*, which won the British Crime Writers Association Gold Dagger award for best crime novel of the year in 2004.

**See also *Blacklist***

## "The Written Word" (2012)

This short essay on storytelling and the written word was published in *Booklist* and adapted from a speech "given in Chicago on March 1, 2012, at the annual conference of the Association of Writers and Writing Programs" (14). Paretsky points out that "writers have a selfish as well as a public duty to work for a literate nation" (14).

## Yarborough, Richard (Dick)

Successful corporate attorney Richard "Dick" Yarborough, V. I.'s ex-husband, is first mentioned in *Indemnity Only* when V. I. explains her marital background to the curious Ralph Devereux: "Dick was a terrible husband for someone like me.... I was an eager young lawyer on the Public Defender's roster … he saw my independence as a challenge" (IO 160). Nine months after V. I. and Dick divorce, he marries Terri, the "suburban-chic second wife" (*Bitter* 65); they and their children live in Hinsdale and later in Oak Brook, two wealthy suburbs in the Chicago area. Dick's career at Crawford, Mead, one of the "outsize law firms in Chicago that work for the state's heaviest hitters in politics and business" (BD 36), is rewarding—he becomes a managing partner. Dick and/or his firm crop up often in V. I.'s cases; V. I.'s attorney Freeman Carter is an associate at the firm, so the paths of all three cross frequently. In *Guardian Angel* V. I. is attending a concert with Max and Lotty when she bumps into Dick and Terri; she recalls how Dick was never comfortable with "the taint of immigrant squalor that clung to me" (GA 15). In *Breakdown* (2012), she muses that he "wasn't a bad guy, just one who wanted power and money badly enough to sacrifice anything that got between him and his goal—such as my career, my feelings, little kittens. Not that I was still bitter or anything, twenty years later" (36). In the earlier *Hardball*, V. I. encounters Dick at a dressy VIP fundraiser event and admits that "I enjoyed it when my once-upon-a-time husband ... gave me a silent whistle in greeting and kept an arm around my bare shoulder a moment too long for his current wife's peace of mind" (114). On the other hand, she just as often cannot resist a scathing comment on his values and ethics. When she and Mr. Contreras break into the Crawford, Mead building in search of evidence about a pension fraud, she finds herself "tiptoeing into Dick's office, as if my steps on his Kerman could raise his hackles out in Oak Brook.... [H]e had ... a slab of burled blong wood that apparently was a desk and an elaborate sideboard housing German ceramics and a wet bar" (*Burn* 323–24). Yarborough's continuing background presence in the series acts as a reminder of the many lifestyle choices rejected by V. I.: matrimony, children, suburban life, a corporate career, and fancy material possessions.

# Annotated Bibliography

Abbe, Elfrieda. "Risky Business: Sara Paretsky Pushes the Boundaries of Her Detective Series." *The Writer* Oct. 2003: 22+. Print. Author interview.

Adler, Dick. "Fraud and Murder in Chicago and the Suburbs." *Chicago Tribune* 9 Sept. 2001, sec. 14: 3. Print. Review of *Total Recall* enjoys being "allowed to see another side of Dr. Lotty Herschel, Warshawski's raspy, much-loved friend."

_____. Rev. of *Guardian Angel. Chicago Tribune Books* 2 Feb. 1992: 3. Print. Favorable review.

_____. "In Sara Paretsky's Latest Tale of Intrigue, There's No Resting Easy." *Chicago Tribune* 5 Oct. 2003. Review of *Blacklist* notes that V.I.'s "sleep deprivation" plays a major role in the thriller.

_____. "Sara Paretsky's Non-Mystery Novel About Faith and Family." *Chicago Tribune* 24 May 1998. Web. http://articles.chicagotribune.com/1998–05–24/entertainment/9805240034_1_warshawski-homeless-woman-sara-paretsky Enthusiastic review of *Ghost Country* says author has created "scene after scene of power and poignancy," although he finds that the failed opera singer Louisa Montcrief character to be mostly "an annoying distraction."

Ahern, Mi-Ai. "V.I. the P.I. Is Back." *Chicago Sun-Times* 12 Sept. 1999: 17E. Print. Review of *Hard Time* welcomes detective back after 5-year absence "just as vivid, flawed and impassioned as when we last saw her." Describes novel as "vintage V.I., with detailed, interlocking talks of hidden corruption ... [and a] carefully drawn portrait of Chicago neighborhoods."

Akbar, Arifa. "Crimes of a Century." *The Independent* 26 Feb. 2010: 26–27. Print. Author interview on publication of *Hardball* describes Paretsky as "an ardent, self-proclaimed second-wave feminist."

Algren, Nelson. *Chicago: City on the Make.* Garden City, NY: Doubleday, 1951. New York: McGraw-Hill, 1983. Print. Algren's elegiac prose-poem salute to Chicago based on article first published in *Holiday* magazine. Portrays Chicago as a city in mid-century decline as its industrial past and neighborhood order give way to postwar pressures.

Allen, Susan. "Revels to Perform 'The Ballad of Scavenger Gulch' on January 28–9." *States News Service* 25 Jan. 2011. Web. Press Release from U of Chicago. Academic OneFile Gale Doc GALE/A247644165. Brief article on notable Hyde Park residents, including Sara Paretsky, appearing in annual U of Chicago Revels at the Quadrangle Club.

Ames, Katrine. "Blood Shot." *Newsweek* 26 Sept. 1988: 73, 75. Print. Review of *Blood Shot* finds it "her best book yet."

Ames, Katrine, with Ray Sawhill. "Murder Most Foul and Fair." *Newsweek* 14 May 1990: 66–67. Print. Feature article on "new breed of mystery heroines" with reference to Sara Paretsky, Sue Grafton, Marcia Muller, Linda Barnes, and Sharyn McCrumb as authors creating heroines who are "intuitive and brainy, ... more apt to shoot from the lip than the hip."

Ammeson, Jane. "An Interview with Sara Paretsky." *Chicago Life* July/Aug. 1996: 14–15. Print. Feature interview with writer who "by her own admission ... is also a slightly neurotic writer, who incessantly worries about how her next book will be received."

_____. "Sara Paretsky's Fifth 'V.'" *Northwest Airlines World Traveler* Jan. 2000: 51–52. Print. Author interview and brief review of *Hard Time* describes plot wherein "our intrepid detective is falsely accused of a crime and uses her time in prison to discover the connection between a murder, a correctional facility and a multimedia conglomerate."

Anderson, David R. Afterword. *The Cunning Craft: Original Essays on Detective Fiction and Contemporary Literary Theory.* Ed. Ronald G. Walker and June M. Frazer. Macomb: Western Illinois U, 1990. 188–90. Print. Short summative essay points to innovation in the genre, asserting that "current theory is being expertly employed to challenge received ideas about the genre, [though] traditional assumptions about the rigidity of the formula persist."

Anderson, Michael. "Out of the Attic." *Times Literary Supplement* 26 Oct. 2007: 22. Review of *Writing in an Age of Silence* criticizes the book as "all long shots without close-ups" and continues "[t]he best chapter in the book is a scathing denunciation of the Patriot Act.... [E]lsewhere, the righteousness of her passion drives her to a disregard for accuracy that is hard to credit in someone who holds a doctorate in history."

Babener, Liahna. "Sara Paretsky." *The Authors.* Ed. Philip A. Greasley. Bloomington: Indiana UP, 2001. 399–401. Print. Vol. 1 of the *Dictionary of Midwestern Literature.* Short biographical/critical overview of author and work to date. Describes V.I. as "a female revision of the prototypical hard-boiled sleuth, but her character was endowed from the beginning with a nuanced personal history and a complex nature that transcends her formulaic roots" (400). Misidentifies Paretsky's three stepsons as the children of Paretsky and her husband, Courtenay Wright; they are Wright's children and Paretsky's stepsons.

Bakerman, Jane S. "The Criminal Element." *Belles Lettres* Summer 1990: 36–37. Print. Review of *Burn Marks* notes the novel "transports women's perennial quandary—what do they owe to others? What dare they grant themselves?—from the hearth onto the mean streets with stunning effect."

_____. "The Criminal Element." *Belles Lettres* Spring 1989: 15. Print. Review of *Blood Shot* praises Paretsky's sophisticated use of "her traditional urban setting, Chicago ... coupling it with the social criticism that figures importantly."

_____. "Living 'Openly and with Dignity'—Sara Paretsky's New-Boiled Feminist Fiction." *Midamerica XII.* Ed. David D. Anderson. East Lansing, MI: Midwestern P, 1985. 120–135. Print. An early academic essay explores Paretsky's use of hard-boiled tradition "as a means of making useful statements about contemporary women's lives."

Bannon, Barbara. Rev. of *Indemnity Only.* *Publishers Weekly* 4 Dec. 1981: 43. Print. Praises debut novel as "[E]xciting, intelligent and truly involving in terms of making you want to find out everything there is to know about the characters you are meeting."

Barnes, Geraldine. "Medieval Murder—Modern Crime Fiction." *Medieval Cultural Studies: Essays in Honour of Stephen Knight.* Ed. Ruth Evans, Helen Fulton, and David Matthews. Cardiff, UK: UP of Eales, 2006. 241–54. Print.

Article discusses medieval accounts of murder in, e.g., Chaucer noting a focus on "the centrality of the messenger's role [including] the details of his trips to and from Westminster" with comparison to how "V.I. Warshawski keeps a similarly close professional measure of Chicago times and distance" (246).

Barr, Allyson. "Turning the Tables on Sam Spade." *Inside Chicago* Mar./Apr. 1988: 52–53. Print. Feature profile of Paretsky as Chicago writer concludes, "[G]iven her already substantial recognition as a pioneer in modern mystery writing, and her concomitant devoted following, Paretsky is remarkably modest."

Basbanes, Nicholas A. "Successful Author Tries a New Tack." *Eugene* [OR] *Register-Guard* 7 Jun 1998: 3B. Print. Interview with author on publication of *Ghost Country.* Paretsky tells interviewer, "[W]hen you've written about a series character ... you run the risk of repeating the same story. I really needed some time away from her [V.I.]."

Beard, Mary. "Corrupt in Chicago." *Times Literary Supplement* 5 June 1992: 21. Print. Review of *Guardian Angel* finds the detective's "obsessive interest in her clothes and in her jogging shoes" irritating.

Beere Briggs, Pamela, and Natalie Cole. "Women of Mystery: A Filmmaker and a Librarian Team Up." *American Libraries* Nov. 2003: 44. Print. Filmmaker Beere Briggs and librarian Cole discuss the film "Women of Mystery: Three Writers Who Forever Changed Detective Fiction," outlining the genesis of the movie and "how it developed into an innovative program for libraries."

Benedict, Helen. Rev. of *Ghost Country. Women's Review of Books* July 1998: 27–28. Print. Review states that Paretsky's attempt to move out of the mystery genre is disappointing because "stock characters" are not believable and the fable-like story does not work.

_____. "Helen Benedict Responds." *Women's Review of Books* Nov. 1988: 5–6. Print. Author responds to Kinsman's letter to the editor regarding her July 1998 review of *Ghost Country,* saying there is a "difference between an academic's reading of fiction and a reading by a fiction writer" (5).

Benenson, Laurie Halpern. "FILM; Kathleen Turner: Going Public as a Private Eye." *New York Times* 14 Apr. 1991: H20. Print. On-set interview with Kathleen Turner who says, "We have a little slogan in this film—'no bimbos.'"

Berch, Bettina. "Tunnel Vision." *Belles Lettres: A Review of Books by Women* Fall 1994: 68. Print. Brief review notes, "[A] nice twist this time is the way Warshawski's tiresome cop-boyfriend, unable to deal with her Lone Ranger style, decides to 'cool the relationship.'"

Bergland, Lisa. "Sara Paretsky: The Detective and the Didactic Urge." *The Drood Review of Mystery* May 1987: 1, 8. Print. Feature article on *Bitter Medicine* and its theme of medical malpractice based on a conversation with the author.

Berlins, Marcel. "Books: Female Cop at the Top of the Lot." *The Times* (London) 23 Jan. 1986: 15. Print. Review of *Killing Orders* praises "intelligent plot."

_____. "Crime." *The Times* (London) 7 July 2012: 47. Print. Review of *Breakdown* suggests "Paretsky and V.I. have tried to move with the times, and yet I had a definite feeling that the formula had dated."

_____. "Femcop of Windy City; Crime." *The Times* (London) 31 May 1990: 15. Print. Review of *Burn Marks* notes that the detective "grows more interesting, quirky, and admirable" and that Paretsky's setting of Chicago "is proving to have layers of decadence and corruption that not even Los Angeles can match."

_____. "From Seaside Noir to Gruesome Victorian Gothic: Crime." *The Times* (London) 19 Mar. 2011: 12. Print. Review of *Body Work* finds it "relatively light on the social, political and feminist issues that were usually an important aspect of her books." Wonders if author, "like her heroine, was a little tired."

_____. "Stalin's Bloody Treasure Hunt." *The Times* (London) 20 Feb. 2010: 12. Print. Review of *Hardball* praises Paretsky for "continuing to mix the detection in her novels with a lot of angry and intelligent comment on Chicago's social, political and racial ills."

_____. "Still with the Fire in Her Belly; Crime." *The Times* (London) 11 Mar. 2006: 16. Print. Rev. of *Fire Sale* notes "there's nothing feel-good about *Fire Sale*, which doesn't stop it being among her best."

Beuttler, Bill. "A Sense of Crime." *Southwest Airlines Spirit* magazine July 1994: 43–45, 106–08. Print. Lengthy author interview on publication of *Tunnel Vision* quotes author on V.I. being "grounded in that history, that civil-rights/Vietnam war/feminist kind of revolutionary history."

Beyer, Charlotte. "Life of Crime: Feminist Crime/Life Writing in Sara Paretsky. *Writing in an Age of Silence*, P.D. James, *Time to Be in Earnest: A Fragment of Autobiography* and Val McDermid, *A Suitable Job for a Woman: Inside the World of Women Private Eyes.*" *Constructing Crime.* Ed. Christiana Gregoriou. London: Palgrave, 2012. 209–23. Print. Essay explores connections "between female crime writers' life writing and their crime fictions," arguing that the life

writing "is central to a fuller understanding of their crime fictions" particularly in relation to the authors' "feminist engagements with the politics of language and writing" (209).

Biamonte, Gloria A. "'Funny, Isn't It?' Testing the Boundaries of Gender and Genre in Women's Detective Fiction." *Look Who's Laughing: Gender and Comedy.* Ed. Gail Finney. Langhorne, PA: Gordon and Breach Science Publ, 1994. 231–51. Print. Essay explores the use of humor and comedy by several contemporary women writers of detective fiction, singling out "V.I.'s unflagging and penetrating wit."

Bickford, Donna M. "Homeless Women and Social Justice in Sara Paretsky's *Tunnel Vision.*" *Clues: A Journal of Detection* 25.2 (2007): 45–52. Print. Scholarly essay considers Paretsky's nonstereotyped characterization of the homeless Tamar Hawkings and her children as informed by a "more accurate understanding of the life experiences of homeless populations, particularly of women" (47).

Binyon, T. J. "Criminal Proceedings." *Times Literary Supplement* 30 Nov. 1984: 1391. Print. Review of *Deadlock* finds it "well told, with good background, good characters, and good business detail; but Warshawski herself is just a little bit too good to be true."

_____. "Criminal Proceedings." *Times Literary Supplement* 13 Nov. 1987: 1262. Print. Review praises *Bitter Medicine* as "more thoughtful, more credible and better organized than the earlier Warshawski stories."

Rev. of *Bitter Medicine*, by Sara Paretsky. *Publishers Weekly* 3 Apr. 3 1987: 66. Print. "This fourth story narrated by the spiky detective is the series' most suspenseful so far."

Rev. of *Bitter Medicine*, by Sara Paretsky. *Kirkus Reviews* 15 May 1987. Web. https://www.kirkus reviews.com/book-reviews/sara-paretsky/bit ter-medicine-2/ Review notes "a dense, convincing, fast-moving plot, a dauntless but vulnerable heroine, a fine-tuned ear for real-life dialogue and a sharp eye for the Chicago scene."

Blachman, Ed. "The Detective and the Didactic Urge." *The Drood Review of Mystery* May 1987: 1, 8. Print. Review of *Bitter Medicine* praises it as "a fine story of detection, [which also says] some important things about the state of health care in this country."

_____. "An Industrial Strength Solution." *The Drood Review of Mystery* Aug. 1988: 1, 3. Print. Review of *Blood Shot* says Paretsky's latest work "accurately reflects her stature as one of the finest PI novelists active today."

Black, Claire. "The Politics of Paretsky." *The Scotsman* 19 Mar. 2011: 8. Print. Interview with Paretsky on occasion of British publication of *Body*

*Work* and author's UK tour. Describes content of novel as "political."

Rev. of *Blacklist*, by Sara Paretsky. *Kirkus Reviews* 15 July 2003: 941. Print. Short review notes that novel "emphasizes the political but doesn't neglect the personal here: a compelling tale of secrets that can't stay buried."

Rev. of *Blacklist*, by Sara Paretsky. *Publishers Weekly* 15 Sept. 2003: 48–49. Print. Short review describes novel as a "riveting exploration of guilt and fear."

Blain, Virginia Clements, et al. "Paretsky, Sara." *The Feminist Companion to Literature in English: Women Writers from the Middle Ages to the Present*. London: Batsford, 1990.830. Print. Short biographical entry on Sara Paretsky describes her as creator of "V.I. Warshawski, a tough, fit, gun-packing political feminist" (830). Inaccurately identifies Paretsky's place of birth as Eudora, Kansas.

Rev. of *Bleeding Kansas*, by Sara Paretsky. *Kirkus Reviews* 15 Nov. 2007. Web. https://www.kirkus reviews.com/book-reviews/sara-paretsky/blee ding-kansas/ Describes novel as "[b]ig, ambitious and heartfelt."

Rev. of *Bleeding Kansas*, by Sara Paretsky. *Publishers Weekly* 15 Oct. 2007: 38. Print. Review finds the novel "a timely tale of fear and conflict in heartland America."

Block, Lawrence, ed. *Opening Shots*. Nashville: Cumberland, 2000. Print. Anthology includes Paretsky's short story "A Taste of Life."

Rev. of *Blood Shot*, by Sara Paretsky. *Kirkus Reviews* 15 Aug. 1988. Web. https://www.kirkusre views.com/book-reviews/sara-paretsky/blood-shot/ Brief review notes that V.I.'s case is a "strong indictment of gentlemen with sorry morals and old-time ward politics."

Blumenstock, Kathy. "V.I. Warshawski, seeking murder clues in the detritus of war." *Washington Post* 13 Sept 2010: CO2. Print. Short review of *Body Work* notes the author "shows how the war in Iraq has affected those who've seen it up close, as well as those who've endured its losses back home."

Rev. of *Body Work*, by Sara Paretsky. "Crime." *Bookmarks* Nov/Dec 2010: 42. Print. Round-up column of critical reviews states, "For readers interested in a complex, multistrand story, *Body Work* is another thoughtful, timely entry in the series."

Rev. of *Body Work,* by Sara Paretsky. *Publishers Weekly* 19 July 2010: 110. Print. Describes "superb" novel with "her aging neighbor and a new love interest giv[ing] a much needed balance to the serious plot."

Rev. of *Body Work*, by Sara Paretsky. *Kirkus Reviews* 1 July 2010. Web. https://www.kirkusre views.com/book-reviews/sara-paretsky/body-work-2/ Review describes novel as "compelling story of lives shattered by pride, greed and fear of the unknown."

Rev. of *Body Work*, by Sara Paretsky. "*Body Work.*" *Healthcare Traveler* 18.5 (Nov. 2010): 45. Print. Brief review praises novel that "hurtles like a runaway L-train to its conclusion."

Rev. of *Body Work*, by Sara Paretsky. "Something Rotten." *Sunday Times* (London) 17 Apr. 2011: 52. Print. Enthusiastic review describes novel as "memorable ... in this fine series."

Brandt, Kate, and Paula Lichtenberg. "On the Case with V.I. and Kinsey." *Hot Wire: The Journal of Women's Music and Culture* 10.1 (1994): 48–50. Print. Article on Sue Grafton and Sara Paretsky compares the characterization of their two detectives and speculates about what a friendship between the two might be like.

Brashler, William. "Two Private Eyes Stalk Chicago's Mean Streets." *Chicago Tribune* 31 Jan. 1982, sec. 7: 1, 5. Print. Review of *Indemnity Only* notes that with the creation of V. I. Warshawski, "Paretsky ... has the makings of an engaging sleuth."

\_\_\_\_\_. "Sisters in Crime." *Chicago Tribune Magazine* 8 Dec. 1991: 18–26. Lengthy feature article tracing history and success of Sisters in Crime organization.

Braun, Susan Clifford. "Bleeding Kansas." *Library Journal* 1 Nov. 2007: 60. Print. Review notes "a powerful tale with overtones of the Wild West that illustrates the ease with which communities become zealous, ignited by fear and ignorance."

Rev. of *Breakdown*, by Sara Paretsky. *Publishers Weekly* 28 Nov. 2011: 39. Print. Review identifies a "mudslinging political race" and a group of teenage girls' obsession with their favorite "vampire" supernatural novels at the heart of the novel and notes the detective "once again proves a dogged champion for the truth at any cost."

Rev. of *Breakdown*, by Sara Paretsky. *Kirkus Reviews* 1 Dec. 2011: 2173. Print. States that the novel is "[p]lotted with all Paretsky's customary generosity ... [and] harnesses her heroine's righteous anger to some richly deserving targets."

Breen, Jon L., and Ed Gorman, eds. *Sleuths of the Century*. New York: Carroll, 2000. Print. Anthology includes Paretsky's short story "Grace Notes."

Bremer, Sidney. "Willa Cather's Lost Chicago Sisters." *Women Writers and the City*. Ed. Susan Merrill Squier. Knoxville: U of Tennessee Press, 1984: 210–28. Print. Bremer identifies several Chicago women writers during the late 1800s and early 1900s whose novels, poetry, and drama expressed a communal vision that was eclipsed by the dominant male literary constructions of the period.

Brett, Simon. "Tough Cookie Shows Her Soft Centre." *Daily Mail* 17 Sept. 1999: 60. Print. Review of *Hard Time* by British mystery writer endorses "an excellent novel by any standards…. V.I. Warshawski is getting richer and more complex with every book."

Briggs, Pamela Beere, prod. and dir., and William McDonald, prod. and cinematographer. *Women of Mystery: Three Writers Who Forever Changed Detective Fiction.* Harriman, NY: New Day Films, 2008. (ca. 2000). Film. Fifty-three minute film (videodisc/videorecording/DVD) in which Sara Paretsky, Sue Grafton, and Marcia Muller discuss their characters and locales, and how they research their novels. Voice-over provides well-informed background on history of women crime writers from nineteenth century onward.

Brunsdale, Mitzi M. "V.I. Warshawski." *Gumshoes, A Dictionary of Fictional Detectives.* Westport, CT: Greenwood, 2006. 404–06. Print. Short profile of detective and her cases through *Fire Sale* (2005) describes V.I. character as "tough as nails" (404).

Rev. of *Brush Back*, by Sara Paretsky. *Kirkus Reviews* 1 June 2015. Web. https://www.kirkusreviews.com/book-reviews/sara-paretsky/brush-back/ Review notes that Paretsky "plots more conscientiously than anyone else in the field" in a novel that digs deep into the past.

Rev. of *Brush Back*, by Sara Paretsky. *Publishers Weekly* 25 May 2015. Web. http://www.publishersweekly.com/9780399160578. Review notes "Paretsky never shies away from tackling social issues … she targets political corruption without ever losing sight of her dogged sleuth's very personal stake in the story."

Budd, Elaine. "Burn Marks." *New York Times Book Review* 17 June 1990: BR17. Print. Review praises author for embedding her books in "the fabric of problems that confront us all—the poisoned environment, for example, or urban blight … add[ing] an immediacy to 'Burn Marks' that is not found in many private-eye novels."

Rev. of *Burn Marks*, by Sara Paretsky. *Kirkus Reviews* 15 Feb. 1990. Web. https://www.kirkusreviews.com/book-reviews/sara-paretsky/burn-marks/ Short review finds novel "suffers from bloat … [with] too much domestic detail."

Byron, Jennifer. "Challenging the Male Paradigm: A Comparative Analysis of the protagonists V.I. Warshawski and Nurit Iscar as Models of Postfeminism in Crime Literature." *Out of Deadlock.* Ed. Enrico Minardi and Jennifer Byron. Newcastle upon Tyne, UK: Cambridge Scholars Publishing, 2015. 135–53. Print. Essay argues the work of Argentinian writer Claudia Pineiro demonstrates, in common with that of Paretsky, a postfeminist model of detective.

Callendar, Newgate [Harold C. Schonberg]. "Crime." *New York Times Book Review* 18 Mar. 1984: 27. Print. Brief review of *Deadlock* says character "seems more confident, less strident, less eager to impress. And the author handles a rather complicated plot smoothly."

_____. "Crime." *New York Times Book Review* 15 Sept. 1985: 33. Print. Review of *Killing Orders* is impressed with the subject matter of corruption in the Catholic church and the author's apparent willingness "to take on any institution, no matter how sacred."

_____. "Crime." *New York Times Book Review* 2 Aug. 1987: 29. Print. Review of *Bitter Medicine* notes "the characters are well drawn" and says the author "writes with sympathy and understanding for the downtrodden."

Callil, Carmen. *Subversive Sybils: Women's Popular Fiction This Century.* London: British Library, 1996. Print. A talk given by Callil for the British Library Centre for the Book's lecture series on "People and Popular Literature" in which she focuses on work of writers such as Georgette Heyer, Jackie Collins, and Judith Krantz, and examines the ways in which they tell "subversive moral tales" (11).

Campbell, Bryce Robert. "Detecting Resistance/Resisting Detection: The (Re)Codification of Sexuality and Gender in 19th and 20th Century Anglo-American Detective Fiction." PhD diss. Washington State U, 1999. Web. ProQuest document ID: 304539523. Contains some discussion of Grafton's and Paretsky's detectives as figures capable of "disrupting a static conception of gender and sexuality within the genre" (143), although concludes these are not radical interventions compared to contemporary lesbian-identified mystery novels.

Campbell, Peter Joseph, Jr. "Watching the detectives: The evolution of the hard-boiled detective." PhD diss. U of Notre Dame, 1997. Web. ProQuest document ID: 304360949. Explores five hard-boiled authors' detective figures as exemplars of changing social values in USA. Discusses V.I.'s beliefs in independence and "the right to self-determination" (201) as a reflection of later twentieth century mores.

Cannon, Margaret. "Hard-Boiled Women Step Out." *Globe and Mail* (Toronto) 20 June 1987. *Lexis-Nexis Academic.* Web. Brief review of *Bitter Medicine* finds it a "finely crafted and immensely readable book."

Capp, Fiona. "Writing in an Age of Silence." *The Age* (Melbourne) 11 Aug. 2007: 26. Print. Short review describes memoir as "rambling essays, held loosely together by strands of autobiography, [which] chart the personal and political forces that have shaped her as a writer, such as the civil rights movement, the women's movement, and the heroic loner of hard-boiled American crime fiction."

Cappetti, Carla. *Writing Chicago: Modernism, Ethnography and the Novel*. New York: Columbia UP, 1993. Print. Cappetti identifies a "larger tradition of urban writing" (2) associated with Chicago writers such as Nelson Algren and Richard Wright and shaped by their "appropriations from Chicago urban sociology" (ibid.). No mention is made of crime and mystery fiction, another literary tradition with a strong relationship to city streets.

Cawelti, John G. *Adventure, Mystery, and Romance, Formula Stories as Art and Popular Culture*. Chicago: U of Chicago P, 1976. Print. Groundbreaking theoretical discussion of the dynamics of "formula" fiction draws attention to the cultural function of popular formula stories. Lengthy descriptions and analysis of the hard-boiled mode, the western, and romance.

Chandler, Raymond. "The Simple Art of Murder." *Atlantic Monthly* Dec. 1944. Chandler, *The Simple Art of Murder*. New York: Vintage, 1988. 1–19. Print. Seminal critical essay outlines Chandler's template for the heroic private-eye detective figure and the hard-boiled style. He critiques the classic British Golden Age detective story as "contrived" and praises the work of American writer Dashiell Hammett, who "gave murder back to the kind of people that commit it for reasons, not just to provide a corpse."

Rev. of *Chicago Blues*, ed. Libby Fischer Hellmann. *Publishers Weekly* 13 Aug. 2007: 47. Print. Brief review notes "a classy anthology of mostly original short stories from 21 renowned Windy City authors blends the blues, crime and Chicago…. This impressive volume has soul, grit and plenty of high notes." Includes Paretsky's short story "Publicity Stunts."

Christianson, Scott. "A Heap of Broken Images: Hardboiled Detective Fiction and the Discourse(s) of Modernity." *The Cunning Craft: Original Essays on Detective Fiction and Contemporary Literary Theory*. Ed. Ronald G. Walker and June M. Frazer. Macomb: Western Illinois UP, 1990. 135–48. Print. Discusses interventions of recent women writers working in hard-boiled mode, noting that "in the matter of its misogyny, hardboiled detective fiction undergirds the whole system of Western patriarchy" (146).

_____. "Talkin' Trash and Kickin' Butt: Sue Grafton's Hard-boiled Feminism." *Feminism in Women's Detective Fiction*. Ed. Glenwood Irons. Toronto: U of Toronto P, 1995. 127–47. Print. Essay discusses Grafton's detective Kinsey Millhone as successful example of appropriating "hard-boiled language … [which] in the process transforms the classic private eye genre into a place from which a woman can exercise language as power" (128–29). Refers briefly in footnote to Paretsky's V.I. as "more consciously feminist" (145) in comparison to Millhone.

Christopher, Joe R. "The Christian Parody in Sara Paretsky's *Ghost Country*." *Mythlore* 26.3–4 (2008): 165–85. Print. Scholarly article exploring the novel's thematic and character-identified parallels to Christianity, Judaism, and Babylonian and Assyrian myth. Concludes that the novel is "a curious, deliberately provocative, feminist reshaping of the life of Christ."

Clifford, Susan. *Library Journal* 1 Nov. 2007: 60. Print. Review of *Bleeding Kansas* recommends book as "different in style from her crime fiction, this will nonetheless prove popular among her readers."

Coale, Sam. "Tenacious as Ever, Warshawski Takes on the Holocaust." *Providence Journal* 14 Oct. 2001: F12. Print. Review of *Total Recall* focuses on novel's thematic concern with "the duty the present has to deal with the past as honestly and as forthrightly as possible" and praises Paretsky for "wrestl[ing] with some extremely complex and tortuously contemporary issues, which adds to the book's brooding and serious perspective."

Cody, Liza, and Michael Z. Lewin, eds. *1st Culprit, A Crime Writers' Association Annual*. London: Chatto, 1992. Print. Anthology includes Paretsky's short story "Freud at Thirty Paces."

Cody, Liza, Michael Z. Lewin, and Peter Lovesey, eds. *3rd Culprit, a Crime Writers' Association Annual*. London: Chatto, 1995. Print. Anthology includes Paretsky's short story "The Great Tetsuji."

Cogdill, Oline H. "Strong Characters Save 'Bleeding' from Gimmicks." *South Florida Sun-Sentinel* 30 Dec. 2007: 7G. Print. Review of *Bleeding Kansas* finds the novel "captures the hardships of family farms, the money woes and each family's dependence on the other. Kansas is vividly presented, giving not just a view of its beauty but also its political and social landscape."

Collins, Max Allan, and Mickey Spillane, eds. *A Century of Noir: Thirty-Two Classic Crime Stories*. New York: New American Library, 2002. Print. Anthology includes Paretsky's short story "Grace Notes," 417–48.

Collins, M. E. "Latest Warshawski Work Not Out of Character." *Chicago Sun-Times* 8 Jan. 2012:

6. Print. Brief review of *Breakdown* notes that the "popularity and charm of V.I. Warshawski continue" but wonders if the author "may be on cruise control when it comes to the care-taking of a groundbreaking character."

Connelly, Michael, ed. *MWA Presents In the Shadow of the Master: Classic Tales.* New York: Morrow, 2009. Print. Anthology includes short essay by Paretsky on "Imagining Edgar Allan Poe" (325–29).

Connolly, John, and Declan Burke, eds. *Books to Die for: The World's Greatest Mystery Writers on the World's Greatest Mystery Novels.* Atria/Emily Bestler Books, 2012. Print. Paretsky pays tribute to Charles Dickens's *Bleak House*; mystery writers Natasha Cooper and Dreda Say Mitchell honor Paretsky's work.

Connolly-Lane, Karen. "Politics and the Private Eye: Ideology and Aesthetics in the Hardboiled Tradition." PhD diss., U of Minnesota, 2006. Web. ProQuest document ID: 305308160. Dissertation explores the genre's flexibility in reflecting contemporary issues, focusing on Paretsky's novel *Blacklist* as an example of using the popular form to confront social and political developments post–9/11.

"Conversation with Sara Paretsky Author of *Body Work*." 1 Sept. 2010 c/o Elizabeth Hohenadel, publicist at penguingroup.com. Print. Five-page, Putnam-sponsored conversation with author in which she answers questions regarding themes and characters in *Body Work* and the challenges of continuing to write about V.I. Comments on the development of Petra, V.I.'s irrepressible niece, as an "energetic foil to V.I.'s overly responsible, problem-solving persona" (5).

Cooper, Natasha. "Going for the Heart." *Times Literary Supplement* 20 Oct. 1995: 24. Print. Brief review of *V.I. For Short* notes it is a collection of stories in which "most of the familiar characters appear … and [which] provide a nice reminder of the best of the full-length novels."

———. "Lotty's Story." *Times Literary Supplement* 23 Nov. 2001: 24. Print. Review of *Total Recall* notes that the "plot also develops the story of V.I.'s best friend and surrogate mother, Doctor Charlotte Herschel."

———. "Sara Paretsky." *Times Literary Supplement* 26 June 1998: 26. Print. Review of *Ghost Country* describes it as "a fable to rival the myths in which strong men are threatened with destruction by gorgons, sirens, mermaids, enchantresses—or Eve … written with all the pace and hot rage of the best of the Warshawski novels."

Cornwell, Bob. "'Anger's a very bad place to start,' says Sara Paretsky." Web. https:/www.twbooks. co.uk/crimescene/Sara-Paretsky-An-Interview-by-Bob-Cornwell.htm Lengthy 2008 interview during author's UK tour for *Fire Sale* describes how a *Wall Street Journal*'s story on "the business activities of the 'big-box' retailer Home Depot" inspired part of novel's storyline.

Corrigan, Maureen. "The Comforts of Home Meet the Criminal Element." *Washington Post Book World* 23 Sept. 2001: T13. Print. Review of *Total Recall* praises it as "a spectacular mystery—complex, fast-paced yet ruminative, and imbued with the grim awareness, shared by all intelligent hard-boiled novels, that the past always catches up with us, sooner or later."

———. "The Past Puts Up a Fight." *Washington Post Book World* 28 Sept. 2009: CO3. Print. Review of *Hardball* praises novel as "a standout, nuanced mystery about civil rights struggles past and present."

———. "Scoundrel Time; A Private Eye Uncovers Powerful Betrayals and Political Secrets." *Washington Post Book World* 30 Nov. 2003: T6. Print. Review of *Blacklist* applauds it as "a thoughtful, high-tension mystery" that "makes pointed connections between McCarthyism and present-day threats to civil liberties in post–Sept. 11 America." Likens the opening chapter, in which V.I. stumbles on a body during a night-time stakeout in the grounds of an abandoned mansion, to a Nancy Drew mystery.

———. "*The Washington Post Book Club*; TOTAL RECALL by Sara Paretsky. A Reader's Guide." *Washington Post Book World* 5 May 2002: T12. Print. Outlines plot lines and themes in novel with invitation to join online discussion of book on 30 May.

Corrigan, Susan. "Undercover Girl." *Times* (London) 19 Aug. 2000: 12. Print. Lengthy interview with author in London on publicity tour for *Hard Time* highlights how "Paretsky's characterisation has influenced younger offbeat female writers."

Craig, Patricia. "Criminal Proceedings." *Times Literary Supplement* 21 Dec. 1990: 1382. Print. Positive review of *Burn Marks* finds it "stylishly written, solidly constructed and immensely entertaining."

———. "Female Virtues." *Times Literary Supplement* 21 Oct. 1994: 20. Print. Brief review of *Tunnel Vision* notes V.I. is given "the freedom … to be as obstinate and authoritative as the case requires, and to stand up to repeated rough handling."

———. "Women on the Streets." *Times Literary Supplement* 1 Nov. 1991: 21. Print. Short review of *A Woman's Eye* edited by Paretsky whose "title has an ironic ring: women's matters, she implies, are no longer confined to a particular sphere: 'It's because we see women doing so much that the horizons of our fiction have expanded.'"

Cranny-Francis, Anne. *Feminist Fiction: Feminist Uses of Generic Fiction.* Cambridge, UK: Polity P, 1990. Print. Discusses the uses made by feminists of a number of fictional forms, including detective fiction, romance, science fiction, and fantasy. Makes brief reference to Paretsky and her work. Acknowledges successful feminist appropriations of forms such as the private-eye tradition are subject to contradictions and is cautious regarding Paretsky's feminist credentials, arguing novels tend to reinscribe the patriarchal order of the world of authors such as Raymond Chandler.

Crawford, Alan Pell. "Lady of Mystery." *Insurance Review* July 1989: 16–20. Print. Lengthy interview quotes Paretsky crediting her background in the insurance world: "[M]y first books grew right out of those discussions the claims guys would have about insurance fraud."

Rev. of *Critical Mass,* by Sara Paretsky. *Kirkus Reviews* 11 Aug. 2013. Web. https://www.kirkusreviews.com/book-reviews/sara-paretsky/critical-mass-paretsky/ Notes "V.I. has a charismatic and blistering way of bringing old secrets to light."

Rev. of *Critical Mass,* by Sara Paretsky. *Publishers Weekly* 2 Sept. 2013: 32. Print. States that Paretsky "builds the suspense by deftly weaving the contemporary narrative with flashbacks to Lotty's Austrian childhood."

Dale, Alzina Stone. *Mystery Reader's Walking Guide: Chicago.* Lincolnwood, IL: Passport Books, 1995. Print. Set of detailed walking tours of Chicago neighborhoods with maps that reference places and restaurants from Chicago mysteries. The guide won Malice Domestic's Agatha Award for best nonfiction work of 1995. Author's acknowledgments thanks "Sara Paretsky, who as MWA Mid-West president, asked Barbara Sloane Hendershott and me to prepare a Chicago 'scene of the crime' bus tour for our first meeting" (vii).

Danford, Natalie. "Such Devoted Sisters." *Publishers Weekly* 19 Apr. 2004: 31. Print. Brief note on Sisters in Crime 17 years after founding meeting reports membership of 3,600 and concludes "sisterhood is powerful."

Dayton, Tim. "New Maps of Chicago: Sara Paretsky's *Blood Shot.*" *Clues: A Journal of Detection* 25.2 (2007): 65–77. Print. Essay places Paretsky within the context of political economy and Marxist literary theory through a close examination of novel *Blood Shot.*

Rev. of *Deadlock,* by Sara Paretsky. *Publishers Weekly* 23 Dec. 1983: 54. Print. Notes that "Paretsky,

an insurance executive, puts her insider's knowledge of the industry to good use in this absorbing, well-written tale, a topnotch mystery."

DeAndrea, William L. "Paretsky, Sara." *Encyclopedia Mysteriosa.* New York: Prentice Hall, 1994. 269. Print. Short biographical entry on author as well as novels and short story collections to date.

Deaver, Jeffery, ed. *A Century of Great Suspense Stories.* New York: Berkley, 2001. Print. Anthology includes Paretsky's "Heartbreak House," pp. 432–44.

Decure, Nicole. "V.I. Warshawski, a 'Lady with Guts': Feminist Crime Fiction by Sara Paretsky." *Women's Studies International Forum* 12.2 (1989): 227–38. Print. Critical article explores the importance of the V.I. character as a female role model in a genre marked by its tendency to subordinate, ignore, or exploit women.

Dempsey, Peter. "Sara Paretsky." *American Mystery and Detective Writers.* Ed. George Parker Anderson. Detroit: Thomson Gale, 2005. 306–20. Print. Vol. 306 of *Dictionary of Literary Biography.* Comprehensive profile of Paretsky and her work through *Blacklist* (2003) claims her as "one of the most critically and commercially successful of contemporary urban crime novelists … the most prominent of a group of women crime writers who began publishing in the early 1980s" (306).

Diehl, Digby. "Books." *Playboy* 41.7 (July 1994): 34. Print. Brief review of *Tunnel Vision* notes "Warshawski goes up against the bankers, bureaucrats and politicos of Chicago to help the homeless."

Dilley, Kimberly JoAnn. "Not Just Sam Spade in a Skirt: Women Redefine the Heroic and Ordinary. Women's Detective Novels in Late 20th Century America." PhD diss., U of Calif., San Diego, 1995. Web. Proquest document ID: 9541989. Dissertation explores how heroism is being redefined and the concept of "family" starts to occupy a place in the genre through the women mystery writers of the 1980s and 1990s with focus on Paretsky and others in chapter 3.

Dobyns, Stephen, et al. "Crime/Mystery—Hooker Malone Is Missing: A Serial Mystery." *New York Times Book Review* 20 Oct. 1991: 1+42–5. Print. A spoof short story about a Yankees pitcher and a female sports reporter. Story coauthored by Dobyns, Loren D. Estleman, Walter Mosley, Sara Paretsky, and David Stout. Sends up genre clichés.

Dudar, Helen. "Queen of the Gumshoes." *Lear's* 4.6 (1991): 70–74, 96–98. Print. In-depth discussion of character and author, tracing story of how V.I. arrived on the publishing scene in

1982, and noting similarities between author and detective. Signals Paretsky's determination to take a break after the eighth Warshawski mystery to write other kinds of fiction.

Duerr, Teri. "Sara Paretsky Announced as 2011 MWA Grand Master." *Mystery Scene.* Web. http://mysteryscenemag.com/blog-newsfeed/55-awards/1686-sara-paretsky-announced-as-2011-MWA-grand-master Notice of Paretsky's being named as recipient of "the highest honor given by the [MWA] in recognition of extraordinary career achievement and contribution to the mystery genre."

Dugdale, John. "Masked by the Mafia." *Sunday Times* (London) 10 Oct. 1999: 44. Print. Short, positive review of *Hard Time* notes author "takes sideswipes at racism, sexual exploitation and local media monopolies."

Dyer, Carolyn Stewart, and Nancy Tillman Romalov, eds. *Rediscovering Nancy Drew.* Iowa City: U of Iowa P, 1995. Print. A record of the proceedings and papers given at the Nancy Drew Conference at the U of Iowa, 16–18 Apr. 1993.

Edgington, K. "Defining the Enemy: Housewives and Detectives." *Clues: A Journal of Detection* 25.2 (2007): 55–63. Print. Essay examines Paretsky's little-known 1972 story "This Is for You, Jeannie"; suggests story demonstrates the 1970s second-wave feminist culture from which the author and the subsequent V.I. series emerged.

Edwards, Harriet. "Women of Mystery: Three Writers Who Forever Changed Detective Fiction." *Library Journal* 15 May 2001: 179. Print. Short review of film about Sara Paretsky, Sue Grafton, and Marcia Muller discussing why they started writing, what the process is, and "what [each] hopes her heroine will bring to the reader." Judges the film as "instructive" and "useful in creative writing and women's studies classes and where there are fans of these writers."

Edwards, Martin, ed. *Mysterious Pleasures.* London: Little, 2003. Print. Anthology includes Paretsky's short story "At the 'Century of Progress.'"

Effron, Malcah. "Sara Paretsky (1947–)." Rzepka and Horsley 523–30. Short biographical/ critical entry on author and 12 V.I. novels to date. Assesses series in terms of its social commentary and interrogation of power structures. Minor mistakes made in names of two secondary characters in the series.

Ellison, Michael. "Wild Card of Windy City." *Guardian* (London) 24 Sept. 1999: 25, 27. Print. Interview with author as *Hard Time* is published in United Kingdom after a five-year gap in the V.I. series. Paretsky tells Ellison about the effect of the temporary separation from the V.I. character: "I think I did a better job on her for having been away. It brought her back to me with more freshness, it was like starting over" (25).

Emck, Katy. "Feminist Detectives and the Challenges of Hardboiledness." *Canadian Review of Comparative Literature* 21.3 (1994): 383–98. Print. Scholarly essay argues that Paretsky's protagonist "combines a highly self-conscious hardboiled machismo with an equally pointed feminism" (383). Author draws on Foucault and Lacan, concluding that Paretsky "effectuates a postmodern re-narration of the hardboiled detective as historical precedent for a feminine mode" (395).

England, Katharine. "Cracking the Concrete." *The Age* (Melbourne) 26 Feb. 1994: 8. Print. Review of *Tunnel Vision* points out that the title "puns on the maze of old tunnels that underlie Chicago's business district and the blinkered responses of most of society when it comes to the probity of the rich and famous."

Ensor, Sarah. "Exposing the Real Criminals." *Socialist Review* Apr. 2008: 18–20. Print. Wide-ranging author interview during Paretsky's UK tour on publication of *Bleeding Kansas.* Paretsky tells Ensor, "I wanted to tell stories that rescued the voices that no one was listening to" (18); and "[f]or me the big issue has always been women's reproductive rights, because that goes to the core of whether we are defining women as human beings or chattels" (20).

Evans, Donald G. "V. I. Warshawski's Cross to Carry." *Cubbie Blues, 100 Years of Waiting till Next Year.* Ed. Donald G. Evans. Elgin, IL: State Street Publ./Can't Miss P, 2008. 78–85. Print. A tribute to Paretsky's love of the Cubs baseball team and an appreciation of how "V.I. and the Cubs are a natural fit; she loves the underdog."

Everson, David H. "My, My. A New Chicago Private Eye." *Illinois Times* 17–23 Dec. 1987: 45–46. Print. Favorable review of *Bitter Medicine* notes how Paretsky "evokes a strong sense of place, especially sweltering Chicago in Aug.."

"Favorite Memories from 30 Years of Printers Row Lit Fest." *Chicago Tribune* 23 May 2014. Web. http://www.chicagotribune.com/lifestyles/books/chi-printers-row-lit-fest-30th-anniversary-memorie-20140523-story.html Feature on Printers Row Literary Festival includes vox pop inserts from writers. Chicago author Luis Alberto Urrea tells readers that Paretsky's work "inspires me. She's a goddess amongst Chicago writers."

Feit, Theodore. "Theodore's Bookshelf." *Reviewer's Bookwatch.* June 2012. Web. http://www.midwestbookreview.com/rbw/jun_12.htm#theodore Lukewarm review of *Breakdown* states, "book never seems to make up its mind whether it is a political tract, murder mystery or something else."

Ferraro, Susan. "A Woman of Mystery." *Los Angeles Times Magazine* 22 Dec. 1991: 22–24, 42–43. Print. Lengthy, wide-ranging feature interview with author prior to book tour for *Guardian Angel*. Author tells Ferraro, "V.I. says and does things that perhaps I'm strong enough to think, but I might not be strong enough to do" (23). Ferraro notes, "[T]he ineffable but stubborn tension that exists between the writer's real self and her fictional alter ego—and the energy that springs to the page when she lets V.I. loose—is central to Paretsky's success" (23).

Rev. of *Fire Sale*, by Sara Paretsky. *Kirkus Reviews* 15 May 2005: 566. Print. Brief review notes, "Corruption and deception are never far behind as V.I. Warshawski … goes back to her South Chicago roots." Incorrectly identifies novel as eleventh in series rather than twelfth.

Rev. of *Fire Sale*, by Sara Paretsky. *Publishers Weekly* 16 May 2005: 36. Print. The review notes, "Packed with social themes and moral energy, held together by humor, compassion and sheer feistiness, this novel shows why Paretsky and her heroine are such enduring figures in American detective fiction."

Fleischer, Leonore. "Talk of the Trade: Step Aside, Miss Marple." *Publishers Weekly* 28 Oct. 1988: 57. Print. Brief history of Sisters in Crime organization to date and its efforts to document members' feelings that women mystery writers "weren't receiving the same review attention as those of men writing in the genre."

Fletcher, Connie. Rev. of *Killing Orders*. *Booklist* 15 May 1985:1296. Print. Notes that Paretsky's "gutsy V.I. Warshawski established a new, intelligently hard-boiled breed of female private eye."

_____. Rev. of *Sisters on the Case: Celebrating Twenty Years of Sisters in Crime*. *Booklist* 15 Sept. 2007: 40. Print. Review notes there is "no thematic glue holding this collection together—other than the involvement of the contributors in Sisters in Crime."

_____. "V.I. Comes a Cropper." *Chicago Sun-Times* 5 Oct. 2003:14. Print. Brief review of *Blacklist* describes novel as "a clunker."

Foley, Dylan. "Mystery Writer Shares a Lifetime of Anguish in Memoir—Behind the Voice." *Denver Post* 10 June 2007: F12. Print. Review of *Writing in an Age of Silence* notes that memoir "addresses her soul-killing childhood in Kansas … [and her efforts] to get a foothold in the misogynistic academic world."

_____. "On My Nightstand." *Star-Ledger* (Newark, N.J.) 27 May 2007: 6. Print. Brief Q&A regarding the author's current reading mentions nonfiction such as Taylor Branch's trilogy on the civil rights movement and Jonathan Weiss's biography on Irene Nemirovsky.

Ford, Susan Allen. "Ruined Landscapes, Flooding Tunnels, Dark Paths: Sara Paretsky's Gothic Vision." *Clues: A Journal of Detection* 25.2 (2007): 7–18. Print. Essay discusses Paretsky's use of Gothic conventions to explore the mysteries of self and identity.

Forshaw, Barry. "Heartache in the Heartland." *The Independent* (London) 28 Mar. 2008: 20–21. Print. Author interview on occasion of UK tour for *Bleeding Kansas* notes that novel's "principal theme is religious intolerance."

_____. *The Rough Guide to Crime Fiction*. London: Rough Guides Ltd., 2007. Print. A reference book that surveys "a selection of the best in crime writing … organized by subject (or sub-genre)" (viii). Short entry on Paretsky, with Forshaw's selected top five V.I. novels (70–71). Description of *Blacklist* misidentifies murder victim as female.

Foster, Jordan. "PW Talks with Sara Paretsky: Bombs Away." *Publishers Weekly* 9 Sept. 2013: 38. Print. Q&A interview with author.

Fowler, Christopher. "Crime Fiction." *Financial Times* 20 Feb. 2010: 16. Print. Review of *Hardball* praises Paretsky for taking "the thinking woman's detective to a new level of excellence."

Frase, Brigitte. "Warshawski in the Hornet's Nest Again." *Chicago Tribune* 3 Mar. 2010: S08. Print. (reprinted as "Warshawski's back on the case and this time, it's war" in *Los Angeles Times* 1 Sept. 2010: D5.) Print. Lengthy review of *Body Work* praises "the subplots and main story [which] come together in a seamless, satisfying way." Notes "Vic's character has unfolded and deepened over the years."

Freedman, Samuel G. "It's No Mystery." *Chicago Tribune* 26 May 2007, sec. 5: 1, 4. Print. Detailed review of *Writing in an Age of Silence* finds the first half of the memoir a powerful exploration of the "essential role of literature in … one writer's artistic education." He judges the second half disappointing "diatribes against Bush administration policy." Praises Paretsky as "not only one of Chicago's civic literary treasures but a transformative figure in detective fiction."

Freeman, John. "Paretsky's Toughest Assignment." *Times* (London) 19 May 2007: Books 8. Print. Interview with author on publication of *Writing in an Age of Silence*, an account of how "she began to associate writing with resistance and breaking silence."

Fyfield, Frances. "An Appreciation of Sara Paretsky." *Guardian Angel*, by Sara Paretsky. Bristol:

Scorpion P, 1992. v–vi. Print. A limited edition of *Guardian Angel* includes Fyfield's appreciation of the author and her character that displays "aching vulnerabilities in the midst of the volcano" (vi).

Galef, David. "Books in Brief: Fiction." *New York Times Book Review* 14 June 1998: 21. Print. Unenthusiastic review of *Ghost Country* warns that "the reader feels the twitch of puppet strings."

Gardaphe, Fred L., ed. *New Chicago Stories.* Chicago: The City Stoop Press, 1990. Print. Anthology includes Paretsky's short story "The Man Who Loved Life."

Garofolo, Denise A. "Hard Time." *Library Journal* 1 Mar. 2000: 141. Print. Review of *Hard Time* audiobook praises story as "an ambitious but satisfying tale, with Jean Smart's clear reading contributing to its success."

Garrison, Jessica. "V.I. Warshawski on the Case Again." *Los Angeles Times* 18 Jan. 2012: 14. (reprinted in *Chicago Tribune* 28 Jan. 2012: C14.) Print. Short review of *Breakdown* notes that story moves quickly because "the dialogue is sharp, the satire of politics and media institutions downright biting, and the descriptions hilarious."

Gavin, Adrienne E. "Feminist Crime Fiction and Female Sleuths." Rzepka and Horsley 258–69. Short essay outlines explosion of female sleuths in crime and mystery fiction beginning with critical cluster of authors Marcia Muller, Sue Grafton, and Sara Paretsky in the early 1980s.

Gavin, Bianca. Rev. of *Total Recall. Times* (London). 30 Nov. 2002: 15. Print. Brief review states that novel is "a fast and furious read that touches while it entertains."

Geherin, David. *Scene of the Crime: The Importance of Place in Crime and Mystery Fiction.* Jefferson, NC: McFarland, 2008. Print. Chapter on Sara Paretsky and Chicago setting, pp. 81–92.

Gentile, Petrina. "Woman of Mystery Loves her Cat; 'It's such a beautiful car. I feel like the coolest person on the planet when I drive it." *The Globe and Mail* (Canada) 3 Feb. 2012: D10. Print. Interview quizzes author re her red 1995 Jaguar XJS convertible.

George, Elizabeth, ed. *A Moment on the Edge.* New York: Harper, 2004. Print. Anthology includes Paretsky short story "The Case of the Pietro Andromache."

Gerrard, Nicci. "Gunning for the girls." *Observer* (London) 23 Apr. 1995: C6. Print. Article on writers such as Paretsky, Cody, Dunant argues that in the 1990s "the female sleuths seem to have lost their way."

_____. "Just the Woman to clean up Chicago." *Ob-*

*server* (London) 18 Aug. 1991: 45. Print. Interview with author on UK book tour promoting *Burn Marks* describes Paretsky as "intense, and gauntly striking."

Rev. of *Ghost Country*, by Sara Paretsky. *Publishers Weekly* 30 Mar. 1998: 67. Print. Describes novel as "modern-day fairy tale" with "characters and plot lines [that] occasionally beggar even the conventions of fictional enchantment."

Rev. of *Ghost Country*, by Sara Paretsky. *Kirkus Reviews* 1 Apr. 1998. Web. https://www.kirkusreviews.com/book-reviews/sara-paretsky/ghost-country/ Notes "Paretsky's ambitious, ambiguously religious novel earns an honorable place in the gallery of straight fiction by mystery writers."

Gibb, Lorna. "The Right to Silence." *Times Literary Supplement* 10 Oct. 2003: 24. Print. Rev. of *Blacklist* describes it as "intelligent and complex ... a comparison between the enforcement of the Patriot Act in America today and the havoc wreaked by the House Un-American Activities Committee (HUAC) during the McCarthy years."

Gibson, Edie. "Guest of Honor: Sara Paretsky." *Bouchercon Program Book.* 1997 World Mystery Convention Monterey, Calif. 30 Oct.–2 Nov. 21–22. Print. Gibson's profile takes form of interview with "renowned Chicago private investigator V.I. Warshawski ... [who] was glad that she had brought her good friend, author Sara Paretsky, along" (21). Gibson asks V.I. about aging and going on working; V.I. replies, "I'll have to use my wits more and strong right arm less. But I won't become Miss Marple" (22).

Gilbreth, Edward S. "Feisty V.I. Warshawski Finds a New Maturity in Sara Paretsky's Latest." *Chicago Sun-Times* 1 June 1994: 59. Print. Enthusiastic review of *Tunnel Vision* notes the novel is set in spring 1992, "when the Chicago River came gushing through a hole into a forgotten network of underground tunnels ... drowning out electrical power and turning the central city into a ghost town ... [the] disaster provided Paretsky with a setting for her intrepid sleuth that had the double advantage of great novelty while retaining the familiar grit of the city she writes about so sensitively."

Givens, Ron. *People* 15 Dec 2003: 52. Print. Brief review of *Blacklist* judges "comparisons between McCarthyism and what [Paretsky] sees as threats to civil liberties after 9/11 ... add to the deeper currents of the story."

Gladsky, Thomas. S. "Consent, Descent, and Transethnicity in Sarah (sic) Paretsky's Fiction." *Clues: A Journal of Detection* 16.2 (1995): 1–15. Print. Discussion of importance of cultural ancestry to the V.I. Warshawski series argues that Paretsky "regards her heroine as a descendant of immigrants and, more important, as a victim of their cultural dispossession" (8). "Ethnic identification for her [V.I.] means being part of a transethnic community defined socio-economically, politically, and crossculturally" (9). Mis-identifies V.I.'s neighbor, the Italian Salvatore Contreras as "a Hispanic male" (2); mis-spells Paretsky's first name.

Glazebrook, Olivia. "Predictable Plots, Familiar Faces." *Spectator* 22 Nov. 2003: 58. Print. Review of *Blacklist* focuses on character of V.I., who "stands up to rich, domineering old ladies and defends the suspected terrorist. She asks the questions other people are scared to ask."

Goheen, Diane. "Tunnel Vision." *School Library Journal* Jan. 1995: 146. Print. Brief review notes, "the world seems to be caving in on V.I. Warshawski" with her dilapidated office building, mounting bills, and pressure from a client to find a community service placement for his computer hacker son.

Goldenberg, Suzanne. "Interview." *Guardian* (London) 22 Mar. 2008, family sec.: 3. Print. Lengthy author interview and review of *Bleeding Kansas* notes author is "revisiting the geography of her troubled childhood" in this standalone novel.

Goldstein, Philip. "The Politics of Sara Paretsky's Detective Fiction." *Reader: Essays in Reader-Oriented Theory, Criticism, and Pedagogy* 55 (Fall 2006): 71–84. Print. Long essay argues that Paretsky's novels "have achieved popularity because the readers, especially the female readers, have acquired a new sophistication" (82) in responding to how "her novels undermine those [genre] conventions and produce forceful and insightful ideological critiques" (81).

Goodkin, Richard E. "Killing Order(s): Iphigenia and the Detection of Tragic Intertextuality." *Yale French Studies* 76 (1989): 81–107. Print. Critical essay discusses the role of the Iphigenia myth in *Killing Orders*.

Gorden, S.A. "Blacklist: A V.I. Warshawski Novel." *Reviewer's Bookwatch* Feb. 2005. Web. http://www.midwestbookreview.com/rbw/feb_05.htm#gorden Brief note describes "gritty detective suspense novel."

Gott, Patricia A. "Sara Paretsky: Writing in Perilous, Paranoid Times." *Feminist Collections: A Quarterly of Women's Studies Resources* 29.2 (2008): 9–11. Print. Appreciative review of *Writing in an Age of Silence* says book is both "a memoir and a manifesto" that "provides readers with an open and inviting doorway into the writing process."

Graff, Keir. Rev. of *Writing in an Age of Silence*. *Booklist* 1 Apr. 2007: 15. Print. Brief review notes that memoir is "written with graceful economy … an urgent cry for dissent and a powerful reminder that liberties taken for granted may someday not be granted at all."

Graham, Judith. "Paretsky, Sara." *Current Biography Yearbook*. Ed. Judith Graham. New York: Wilson, 1992. 441–44. Print. Biographical/critical entry on author discusses "seven enormously popular mystery novels" and profiles author.

Green, Jen, ed. *Reader, I Murdered Him: An Anthology of Original Crime Stories*. London: The Women's P, 1989. Print. Anthology includes Paretsky short story "A Taste of Life."

Green, Michelle, and Barbara Kleban Mills. "Sara Paretsky's Cult Heroine Is a Woman's Woman—V.I. Warshawski, the Funky Feminist Private Eye." *People Weekly* 14 May 1990: 132–34. Print. Interview with author as sixth novel *Burn Marks* is published. Paretsky tells interviewers, "My process of writing involves a lot of screaming and yelling and fear that I will never write another line" (133–34). Green and Mills write, "Paretsky is pleased that V.I. has attracted a loyal audience" (134).

Greenberg, Martin H., ed. *Women on the Edge*. New York: Pinnacle, 1992. Print. Anthology includes Paretsky's short story "The Case of the Pietro Andromache."

Gressette, Felicia. "Mystery Women." *Miami Herald* 24 Apr. 1994: 1J, 41. Print. Author interview re the process of creating V.I. quotes Paretsky as follows: "I didn't want Philip Marlowe in drag. What I really wanted was a woman who was like me and my friends."

Rev. of *Guardian Angel*, by Sara Paretsky. *Publishers Weekly* 6 Dec. 1991: 59. Print. Review praises V.I. who "shakes off stereotypes to become more believable and more complex." Detective "uncovers an intricate bond-parking scheme that reaches deep into her former husband's prestigious law firm."

Rev. of *Guardian Angel*, by Sara Paretsky. *Kirkus Reviews* 15 Nov. 1991. Web. https://www.kirkusreviews.com/book-reviews/sara-paretsky/guardian-angel/ Short review finds V.I. "more short-fused and meanmouthed than ever" in a "densely textured, adroitly plotted" story.

Gutman, Amy. "Review: 'Hardball' by Sara Paretsky." *Chicago Tribune* 3 Sept. 2010. Web. http://www.chicagotribune.com/lifestyles/books/chi-books-review-hardball-paretsky-story.html Detailed review highlights focus on "V.I.'s inner landscape" as one of the strengths of the novel; reviewer finds V.I. emerges as "more nuanced and more sympathetic than the V.I. we've come to know and, for that reason, all the more compelling."

_____. "Troubled Homecoming; V.I. Warshawski Returns to South Chicago as Sara Paretsky Gets to the Heart of the Human Condition." *Chicago Tribune* 26 June 2005: 14. Print. Review of *Fire Sale* describes it as "an engaging read that gives social issues a human face."

_____. "Troubles in the Heartland." *Chicago Tribune* 12 Jan. 2008, books sec.: 3. Print. Lengthy review of *Bleeding Kansas* praises author for showing "a remarkable flair for teasing out the foibles as well as the strengths of her rural protagonists."

Hagestadt, Emma, and Boyd Tonkin. "*Total Recall.*" *The Independent* (London) 7 Dec. 2002: 29. Print. Brief review of novel notes that "V.I.'s South Side savvy is operating at full throttle."

Halligan, Kathleen, ed. *Women of Mystery III*. New York: Carroll, 1998. Print. Anthology includes Paretsky short story "Skin Deep."

Hamilton, Cynthia S. *Sara Paretsky: Detective Fiction as Trauma Literature*. Manchester, UK: Manchester UP, 2015. Print. Monograph moves from the gender politics of the hard-boiled genre to frameworks of trauma literature and historiographic discourse, discussing Paretsky's oeuvre as "a sophisticated analysis of the dynamics and impact of coercive power."

_____. "Strange Birds: Rewriting *The Maltese Falcon.*" *Journal of American Studies* 47.3 (2013): 699–718. Print. Essay explores the debut detective novels of Chester Himes and Sara Paretsky "both of whom borrowed from Hammett's novel, using it as a starting point for their own ambitious projects, which in turn opened new narrative spaces for exploration" (699).

_____. "U.S. Detective Fiction." *A Companion to Twentieth-Century United States Fiction*. Ed. David Seed. Chichester, UK: Wiley-Blackwell, 2010. 122–34. Print. Essay traces roots of hard-boiled detective formula in U.S. fiction with a focus on later twentieth-century innovations regarding race, gender, and ethnicity. Discusses Paretsky's work in some detail.

_____. *Western and Hard-boiled Detective Fiction in America: From High Noon to Midnight*. Basingstoke, UK: Palgrave and Iowa City: U of Iowa P, 1987. Print. Analysis of the American adventure formula from 1890 to 1941 focuses on the western and the hard-boiled genres. Challenges notion that "formula is essentially static" and argues for "the remarkable versatility of ... formula."

Rev. of *Hardball*, by Sara Paretsky. *Publishers Weekly* 13 July 2009: 35. Print. Praises novel that "tracks the poisonous residue of racial hatred that still seeps into Chicago life and politics."

Rev. of *Hardball*, by Sara Paretsky. *Kirkus Reviews* 1 Aug. 2009: 15. Web. https://www.kirkusre views.com/book-reviews/sara-paretsky/hard ball-2/ Review notes "tremendous momentum of the second half" but is critical of slow start to novel.

"Hardcover Bestsellers." *Publishers Weekly* 11 Oct. 1999: 88. Print. Notes Paretsky's *Hard Time*, ninth in V.I. series, listed at nos. 5 and 8 over three-week run in hardcover bestsellers column.

Rev. of *Hard Time*, by Sara Paretsky. *Publishers Weekly* 30 Aug. 1999: 55. Print. Enthusiastic review welcomes series back after five-year break. Praises mix of "illegal aliens, labor problems, political corruption and prison abuse ... Vic ponders the death of her own mother and the end of a relationship, as well as the pain of those caught in the far-reaching tentacles of corrupt power."

Rev. of *Hard Time*, by Sara Paretsky. *Kirkus Reviews* 1 July 1999. Web. https://www.kirkusre views.com/book-reviews/sara-paretsky/hard-time/ Notes "a triumphant return to form for V.I." in "one of [Paretsky's] most satisfyingly ambitious novels yet."

Heilbrun, Carolyn. "The Case of the Missing Woman." *Ms Magazine* Oct. 1987: 76, 78. Print. Brief review of *Bitter Medicine* in mysteries column by feminist and mystery author Heilbrun highlights a range of new women writers in the mystery genre.

Heilbrun, Margaret. "Q&A: Sara Paretsky." *Library Journal* 15 Apr. 2007: 88. Print. Transcribed interview with Paretsky on occasion of publication of *Writing in an Age of Silence*. Discusses role and responsibilities of libraries in the aftermath of the Patriot Act. Paretsky praises "extraordinary courage" of consortium of Connecticut libraries that won "a federal ruling that National Security Letter gag orders are unconstitutional."

Heinzmann, David. "Community of Chicago Mystery Writers Discover the City's Politics, History." *Chicago Tribune* 14 Aug. 2010: C12. Print. Article discusses presence of Chicago in the genre, claiming, "Chicago has become one of the hottest, and biggest, communities of genre authors" and citing Sara Paretsky and Scott Turow as writers whose work helped put Chicago on the map for mystery writers and readers.

Heising, Willetta L. *Detecting Women 2: A Reader's Guide and Checklist for Mystery Series Written by Women*. Dearborn, MI: Purple Moon P, 1996. Print. Entries on author and character.

Heller, Amanda. "Short Takes." *Boston Globe* 3 June 2007: C5. Print. Review of *Writing in an Age of Silence* notes, "Paretsky's descriptions of Chicago seen through the eyes of a young woman newly arrived from small-town Kansas."

Hellman, Libby Fischer, ed. *Chicago Blues*. Madison, WI: Bleak House, 2007. Print. Anthology of 21 (mostly original) stories by Chicago mystery writers writing about the Blues, the Cubs, the Chicago underworld. Collection includes Paretsky's short story "Publicity Stunts."

Henderson, Jane. "Best Books: Here's What We Liked in 2015." *St. Louis Post-Dispatch* 6 Dec. 2015. Web. http://www.stltoday.com/entertainment/books-and-literature/best-books-here-s-what-we-liked-in/article_24176b03-bcb9-537c-aa81-5dc3c5b6facf.html Paretsky's *Brush Back* is selected as one of the best novels of 2015.

Hendry, Kim. "Guns and Roses." *Marxism Today* July 1990: 45. Print. Author interview.

Herbert, Rosemary. "Aiming Higher: Some of Today's Top Crime Writers Are Breaking New Ground in Terms of Setting, Sleuths and Motivations." *Publishers Weekly* 13 Apr. 1990: 30–32. Print. Article comments on how crime writers such as Paretsky are developing extended backstories and communities of friends for their fictional detectives, moving the stories beyond elements of plotting.

Herbert, Rosemary, Catherine Aird, and John M. Reilly, eds. *The Oxford Companion to Crime and Mystery Writing*. New York: Oxford UP, 1999. Print. Informative compendium contains biographies of great mystery writers, articles on famous sleuths and criminals, entries on genre history and development, subgenres, and schools of writing. Authoritative and comprehensive volume includes entries about Paretsky and V.I., and by Paretsky on the sleuth.

Heron, Liz, ed. *Streets of Desire*. London: Virago, 1993. Print. Anthology includes fiction from celebrated twentieth-century women writers such as Djuna Barnes and Margaret Drabble exploring London, Paris, New York, Shanghai, and Cairo. Stories show the cities as places where freedoms can be explored, transgressive encounters can take place, and independence can be negotiated. Heron's introduction points to the ways in which the city offers female characters a place to cast off old roles and models and explore new possibilities.

Higgins, Ellen Freda. "Reconfiguring Detective Fiction: Toward a new paradigm of development." PhD diss. New York U, 2000. Web. ProQuest document ID: 304616339. Dissertation argues for a revision of "the standard histories, canons, and criticism of detective fiction ... to incorporate women and other noncanonical writers into its critical and theoretical paradigms" (viii). Draws on Paretsky's *Bitter Medicine* and *Killing Orders* to demonstrate how inclusion of feminist crime fiction changes perceptions of the canon.

Hileman, Monica, and Sara Paretsky. "Women, Mystery, and Sleuthing in the '80s." *Sojourner: The Women's Forum* 14.7 (1989): 16–17. Print. Transcribed interview with Paretsky discusses author's use of the detective genre, her creation of the detective character, and the question of a "Macha, Feminist PI."

Hillerman, Tony, and Rosemary Herbert, eds. *A New Omnibus of Crime*. New York: Oxford UP, 2005. Print. Anthology includes Paretsky's short story "Photo Finish."

Hoffman, Jan. "Nancy Drew's Granddaughters." *New York Times* 19 July 2009, lifestyle sec.: 1. Print. Article outlines influence of Nancy Drew on range of contemporary American women, including Paretsky "whose own female gumshoe is the cranky smart mouth, V.I. Warshawski."

Holgate, Andrew. "50 Best Thrillers and Crime Novels of the Past 5 Years." *The Sunday Times* (London) 29 June 2014: 36–37. Print. Includes Joan Smith's review of *Critical Mass*.

Holzberg, Carol. "Women of Mystery." *Booklist* 1 Nov. 2001: 492. Print. Brief review of Beere Briggs's film documentary that "travels to the authors' home cities" to hear the writers talk about their craft and their characters. States that "the compelling program also presents a brief history of the mystery novel."

Hopkins, Andy, and Jocelyn Potter, eds. *Crime Story Collection*. Harlow, UK: Longman, 1998. Print. Anthology includes Paretsky short story "At the Old Swimming Hole."

"Horror Story: King and Reichs Lock Out Original and Mass Market Fiction Top Slots." *The Bookseller* 7 Apr. 2006: 46. Brief note regarding Top 20 Original Fiction list with Paretsky's 12th V. I. mystery *Fire Sale* at no. 20.

Horsley, Lee. "From Sherlock Holmes to the Present." Rzepka and Horsley 28–42. Short essay gives overview of main developments in British and American crime fiction since early-twentieth century. References to Paretsky's influences since 1980s.

_____. *Twentieth-Century Crime Fiction*. Oxford: Oxford UP, 2005. Print. A historical overview of Anglo-American crime fiction taking Conan Doyle as the starting point for "the long twentieth century." Horsley takes account "of the fluidity of the genre ... [and] the many different ways in which generic revisions have been accomplished by rereadings and rewritings of what has gone before" (1). Discusses Paretsky with particular reference to *Bitter Medicine*.

Horwell, Veronica. "Best Sellers: Sister Gumshoe—Veronica Horwell Launches a New Series On the Writers We All Like to Read but Who Tend to Be Ignored by the Book Pages/ Sara Paretsky." *Guardian* (London) 25 Apr. 1992: 15. Print.

Brief announcement includes reference to Paretsky.

Hueston, Penny. "Female Crime-Scribes Tackle Woes of Our Age." *The Age* (Melbourne) 3 Jan. 2004: 12. Print. Review of *Blacklist* praises the character and the plot as "complex and convincing."

Humm, Maggie. "Feminist Detective Fiction." *Twentieth-Century Suspense: The Thriller Comes of Age*. Ed. Clive Bloom. Basingstoke, UK: Macmillan, 1990. 237–54. Print. Essay discusses "new group of novels by women … challenging the gender norms of detective writing" (237). Focuses on selected American and British authors, including Sara Paretsky, Gillian Slovo, Barbara Wilson, and Mary Wings who share an "oppositional stance to the constraints of traditional detective fiction" (253).

_____. "Legal Aliens: Feminist Detective Fiction." *Border Traffic: Strategies of Contemporary Women Writers*. Ed. Maggie Humm. Manchester, UK: U of Manchester P, 1991. 185–211. Print. Humm explores the narrative strategies of women mystery writers such as Paretsky who are trying "to situate a female literary subject when the literary canon devalues an articulate female subjectivity" (189). Humm identifies the use of female friendship, an ambivalence about the uses of violence and aggression, and a valorization of female ways of knowing as part of the project of crossing genre boundaries for feminist writers.

Hynynen, Andrea. "Following in the Footsteps of Sara Paretsky: Feminism and the Female Detective in Maud Tabachnik's Crime Novels." Minardi and Byron 19–36. Essay outlines shared features in work of Paretsky and French crime writer Tabachnik such as "a feminist agenda, a remarkable female detective, a special interest in Jewishness and memories of the Holocaust" (23).

Rev. of *Indemnity Only*, by Sara Paretsky. *Kirkus Reviews* 1 Jan. 1981: 1431. Print. Review notes novel is "predictably plotted but written with agreeable plainness."

Irons, Glenwood, ed. *Feminism in Women's Detective Fiction*. Toronto: U of Toronto P, 1995. Print. Collected essays by a range of scholars explore the ways in which a number of contemporary female detective figures are "diffuse[ing] the male-oriented hard-boiled detective formula." Essays draw on examples from the United States and the United Kingdom.

_____. "Gender and Genre: The Woman Detective and the Diffusion of Generic Voices." Irons, *Feminism* viii–xxii. Introduction to collected essays by range of feminist scholars draws attention to Paretsky's construction of V. I. Warshawski.

_____. "New Women Detectives: G Is for Gender-Bending." *Gender, Language and Myth: Essays on Popular Narrative*. Ed. Glenwood Irons. Toronto: U of Toronto P, 1992. 127–40. Print. Essay discusses ways in which detectives created by Amanda Cross (pseudonym of Carolyn Heilbrun), Sue Grafton, P. D. James, and Sara Paretsky are bending "phallocentric elements of the genre in order to impose a feminist perspective" (127).

Jackson, Christine A. *Myth and Ritual in Women's Detective Fiction*. Jefferson, NC: McFarland, 2002. Print. Identifies and discusses ways in which selected contemporary women crime writers' work "conform to quest narratives outlined in classical myths and traditional fairytales." Chapter on Paretsky examines *Tunnel Vision* and *Hard Time*.

Jacobsen, Teresa L. *Xpress Reviews* [*Library Journal*] 13–20 Aug. 2010. Web. http://www.buff alolib.org/vufind/Record/1799978/Reviews. Online review of *Body Work* describes it as "topically relevant and elaborately plotted."

Jacques, Adam. "Sara Paretsky, Credo: The Crime Writer on Her Alcoholic Mother, VI Warshawski, and Longing to Be Free." *The Independent* (London) 20 July 2014: 9. Short Q&A quotes author: "I write stories that I want to tell—then find a way to add the thriller and crime element."

Jakubowski, Maxim. "Big in Crime." *Guardian* (London) 1 Dec. 2001: B10. Review of *Total Recall* says it is "a return to form … [with] a subject that justifies her anger and packs a mighty punch."

_____, ed. *Great TV and Film Detectives*. New York: Reader's Digest Assn., 2005. Print. Anthology includes Paretsky short story "The Case of the Pietro Andromache."

James, Caryn. "These Heels Aren't Made for Stompin." *New York Times* 4 Aug. 1991: H7. Print. Fairly positive review of film *V.I.* says it "blithely uses female stereotypes to unsettle stereotypes of women."

James, Dean. "Interview with Sara Paretsky." *Mystery Scene* 48 (July/Aug. 1995): 18–19, 68. Print. In-depth interview probes writer's thoughts on her career, the Chicago setting, and her famous character. Author tells James that mystery form suits her because it is "where law, justice and society naturally intersect" (19). She also tells interviewer that "Chicago dominates the way in which I think about life, power, and justice … V. I. values integrity and loyalty above all other traits."

James, P. D. "Fearless Freedom Fighter." *Spectator* 24 May 2007: 41. Web. http://archive.spectator. co.uk/article/26th-may-2007/41/fearless-freedom-fighter

Laudatory review of *Writing in an Age of Silence*; "this poignant and compelling personal testimony explains both the influences which made her a writer and the kind of writer she became."

Johnson, George. "New and Noteworthy." *New York Times* 3 Mar. 1991. Web. http://www.nytimes.com/1991/03/03/books/new-noteworthy.html Brief review of *Burn Marks* describes V.I. embroiled in "a case involving real estate developers and the Cook County political machine."

Johnson, M. L. Rev. of *Bleeding Kansas*. *Record* 15 Jan. 2008: 10. Print.

Johnson, Patricia E. "Sex and Betrayal in the Detective Fiction of Sue Grafton and Sara Paretsky." *Journal of Popular Culture* 27.4 (1994): 97–106. Print. Essay analyzes the scenario of the detective's romantic/sexual relationship with a suspect as portrayed by Sue Grafton in *A Is for Alibi* and Paretsky in *Bitter Medicine*.

Johnson, Paul. Rev. of *Blood Shot*. *Chicago Tribune* 29 Sept. 1988: sec. 5, 3+5. Print. Enthusiastic review praises author's "unpretentious prose style" and detective's "essential sweetness of character behind her shrewdness."

Johnston, Darcie Conner. "The Criminal Element." *Belles Lettres* Spr. 1992: 22. Print. Short review of *Guardian Angel* notes "a complex plot involving union fraud, banking shenanigans, and murder—and Vic' ex-husband."

Jones, Kathleen. "Paretsky's Vision." *Ms. Magazine* July–Aug. 1994: 78. Print. Brief review of *Tunnel Vision* notes strong storyline of violence against women who are suffering "physical, sexual and emotional abuse" from "the men who mistreat them."

Jones, Louise Conley. "Feminism and the P.I. Code: or 'Is a Hard-Boiled Warshawski Unsuitable to be Called a Feminist?'" *Clues: A Journal of Detection* 16.1 (1995): 77–87. Print. Scholarly essay discusses the detectives created by Sara Paretsky, Linda Barnes, and Sue Grafton as compatible with the template outlined by Raymond Chandler in the 1940s; argues these fictional female detectives create strong role models, inhabit realistic city settings, and keep physically fit for professional reasons.

Jones, Nicolette. *The Bookseller* 16 June 1989: 4. Print. Brief note regarding Paretsky's move from the Gollancz publishing house to Chatto & Windus.

Kane, Julie. Rev. of *Critical Mass*. *Library Journal* 1 Oct. 2013: 65. Print. Kane's brief review describes book as "an intellectual mystery that will please the author's many fans."

_____. Rev. of *Hardball*. *Library Journal* 1 Aug. 2009: 71. Print. Positive review notes, "race riots, police brutality, political bribery, Chicago's dirty history—this one has it all."

_____. "Paretsky, Sara. Breakdown." *Library Journal* 1 Jan. 2012: 96. Print. Review of *Breakdown* gives a verdict of "nothing less than riveting … topical moments and references to the current socio-political atmosphere keep this book charged and moving."

Kaplan, Alice Yaeger. "On the New Hard-Boiled Woman." *Artforum* 28.5 (1990): 26–28. Print. Article explores dimensions of autonomous V.I. character located in ties of friendship and family in gritty city environment.

Kaufman, Gerald. "Strewth, the Sleuths Are in Peril." *Daily Telegraph* (London) 25 Sept. 1999. Print. Review of *Hard Time* summarizes plot as "Warshawski is framed by a pair of cops odious even by Chicago's standards [and] incarcerated in … jail."

Kaufman, James. "The Further Adventures of Two Delightful Detectives." *Chicago Tribune Books* 7 June 1987: 6. Print. Review of *Bitter Medicine* praises detective as "literate, headstrong, tough enough and steadfastly loyal to her friends, she is also acutely sensitive to all forms of injustice."

Kaufman, Natalie Hevener, and Carrollee Kaufman Hevener. "Mythical Musical Connections: The Mother-Daughter Bond in the Work of Sara Paretsky." *Clues: A Journal of Detection* 25.2 (2007): 19–28. Print. Essay explores the literary mother/daughter relationship in the V.I. series.

Kaveney, Roz. "A Private Eye Takes on the Rich." *Times Literary Supplement* 1 Oct. 1999: 21. Print. Review of *Hard Time* notes that novel "turns on the fact that the very rich are able to buy the destruction of anyone who inconveniences them."

Kaye, Lorien. "Crime Fiction." *The Age* (Melbourne) 11 Feb. 2012: 31. Print. Review of *Breakdown* notes strong "portraits of shock jocks and politicians stirring hate while claiming patriotism." Describes up-to-date V.I. "making full use of search engines, swiping her iPad and up with the teens on Facebook."

Kehr, Dave. "Movie Review." *Chicago Tribune* 26 July 1991, sec. B: 7. Print. Review of the film *V.I.* is critical of director, movie's plot line, and watering down of detective's character.

Keller, Julia. "Welcome Back, Warshawski." *Chicago Tribune* 2 Apr. 2009: S20. Print. Brief review of *Hardball* welcomes V. I. back "in the thick of things, bringing her sarcasm and her intuition" as usual.

Kelly, Katy. "Old Friend Helps Paretsky through a Hard Time." *USA Today* 16 Sept. 1999: D7. Print. Author interview in which Paretsky tells reporter, "[T]he chapters where V.I. is in prison, those were really difficult to write. It was painful to have her be so vulnerable."

Kennedy, Elizabeth. "Sara Paretsky. *Writing in an Age of Silence*." *Library Journal* 1 Apr. 2007: 90. Print. Brief review notes, "this work develops as a conscientious objection to the new American McCarthyism."

Kerridge, Jake. "Sara Paretsky: Interview." *Telegraph* (London) 12 Mar. 2010: R20. Print. Author interview and review of *Hardball* notes that "Paretsky's novels have become steadily more politically engaged since Warshawski's debut."

Rev. of *Killing Orders*, by Sara Paretsky. *New Yorker* 2 Sept. 1985: 87. Print. Review acclaims novel for the V.I. characterization, noting, "there are few private eyes ... about whom we are told so much."

Rev. of *Killing Orders*, by Sara Paretsky. *Kirkus Reviews* 15 Apr. 1985. Web. https://www.kirkusreviews.com/book-reviews/sara-paretsky/killing-orders/ Positive review notes that author weaves in "real-life scandals (Sindona and the Franklin National Bank, Roberto Calvi and the Banco Ambrosiano) to validate her plot."

Kinsman, Margaret. "A Band of Sisters." *The Art of Detective Fiction*. Ed. Warren Chernaik, Martin Swales, and Robert Vilain. Basingstoke, UK: Macmillan. New York: St. Martin's, 2000. 153–69. Print. Essay discusses motif of female friendship with specific reference to Sara Paretsky and Linda Barnes.

_____. "'Different and Yet the Same': Women's Worlds/Women's Lives and the Classroom." Klein, *Diversity* 5–21. Essay discusses authors Linda Barnes, Sara Paretsky, and Barbara Wilson as examples of "what feminist crime and mystery fiction has to offer" (6) to the higher education classroom and to students of literature, cultural studies, and sociology.

_____. "Editor, *The Women's Review of Books*." *Women's Review of Books* Nov. 1998: 5. Print. Letter to the editor regarding Helen Benedict's review of *Ghost Country* in July issue expresses hope "that readers will not be put off by Benedict's cursory reading of the novel—there is more here than meets her eye."

_____. "Feminist Crime Fiction." *The Cambridge Companion to American Crime Fiction*. Ed. Catherine Ross Nickerson. New York: Cambridge UP, 2010. 148–61. Print. Essay outlines history of "feminist counter-tradition in the crime and mystery fiction genre" with particular reference to the hard-boiled tradition and the work of both American and British writers. Draws extensively on Paretsky's work to illustrate impact of the counter-tradition.

_____. "Gabriella's Voice Returned." Minardi and Byron 37–50. Essay explores signifiers of Gabriella's absence and presence across the series, chiefly symbolized in the red Venetian wine glasses treasured by V. I.

_____. "Mid-Life Crisis." *Women's Review of Books* Dec. 1999: 23–24. Print. Positive review of *Hard Time* welcomes V.I. back on the scene like "some galloping Amazon" after an absence of four years during which Paretsky published the standalone *Ghost Country*.

_____. "A Question of Visibility: Paretsky and Chicago." Klein, *Women Times Three* 15–27. Essay explores how a contemporary reader's positioning works to create meaning in the Paretsky texts.

_____. "Sara Paretsky." *Mystery and Suspense Writers: The Literature of Crime, Detection, and Espionage*. Vol. 2. Ed. Robin W. Winks and Maureen Corrigan. New York: Scribner's, 1998. 699–713. Print. Biographical/critical essay on the V.I. series of novels to date.

_____. "Theme Issue: Sara Paretsky Introduction." *Clues: A Journal of Detection* 25.2 (2007): 3–5. Print. Introduces essays in special edition of *Clues* honoring 25th anniversary of V.I. Warshawski's debut in *Indemnity Only*. Essays explore Paretsky's work to date from a variety of theoretical and critical perspectives.

_____. "Women of Mystery: Three Writers Who Forever Changed Detective Fiction." *Journal of Popular Culture* 36.3 (2003): 651–52. Print. Review of Briggs and McDonald's "intelligent and lucid 53-minute documentary" profiling Sara Paretsky, Marcia Muller, and Sue Grafton and their famous detectives.

Kirch, Claire. "Paretsky Defends Arts Funding in Awards Speech." *Publishers Weekly* 9 Mar. 2011. Print. Article summarizes Paretsky's speech given in Topeka after accepting a Distinguished Arts Award from the Kansas Arts Commission whose funds have recently been eliminated by the newly elected Kansas governor. Paretsky's message to him, writes Kirch, is "the arts have always been, and continue to be, vital to people's lives."

Kisor, Henry. "Sara Paretsky's 'Bloodshot' Her Best Whodunit Yet." *Chicago Sun-Times* 28 Aug. 1988:16. Print. Detailed review notes "there are no immovable objects for the irresistible V.I. Warshawski."

Klein, Kathleen Gregory, ed. *Diversity and Detective Fiction*. Bowling Green, OH: Popular P, 1999. Print. A collection of essays focused on "teaching cultural diversity in the classroom and illustrating diversity through [detective] novels." The collection "articulate[s] the pedagogical strategies of using detective fiction texts to investigate the politics of difference" (2).

_____, ed. *Great Women Mystery Writers: Classic to Contemporary* Westport, CT: Greenwood,

1994. Print. Reference volume includes short biographical/critical entry on Paretsky by Elizabeth A. Trembley.

_____. "Sara Paretsky." _St. James Guide to Crime and Mystery Writers._ Ed. Jay Pederson. Detroit: St. James P, 1996. 817–18. Print. Short biographical/critical entry on author.

_____. "Warshawski, V(ictoria) I(phigenia)." Herbert et al. 490–91. Profile of character highlights how Paretsky's creation is "carving out new territory for both women and detectives" (491).

_____. "Watching Warshawski." _It's a Print! Detective Fiction from Page to Screen._ Ed. William Reynolds and Elizabeth Trembley. Bowling Green, OH: Popular P, 1994. 145–56. Print. Discusses commercialization of the character V. I. Warshawski in film of same name, drawing on feminist film and literary theory to argue that the detective figure becomes "a body whose representation valorizes male desire and negates authentic female experience" (55).

_____. _The Woman Detective: Gender & Genre._ 1988. 2nd ed. Urbana: U of Illinois P, 1995. Print. Historical overview of the woman detective figure in print explores ideological problems the genre poses for feminist writers; concludes the inherent conservatism of genre results in compromises between the construction of the detective figure and a feminist sensibility. Identifies five feminist writers (Sue Grafton, Marcia Muller, Sara Paretsky, Susan Steiner, and M. F. Beal) as partially successful in negotiating the contradictions.

_____, ed. _Women Times Three: Writers, Detectives, Readers._ Bowling Green, OH: Popular P, 1995. Print. Collection of essays that explores "the range of relationships among women writers, the women detectives and women-centered novels they create, and women readers ... [and which] employ feminist literary theory and criticism" (1).

Klems, Brian A. "Writing in an Age of Silence." _Writer's Digest_ Feb. 2008: 18. Print. Short review of "part memoir/part political outcry" praises it for Paretsky's "exploration of art and political responsibility."

Koch, John. "Mystery Woman." _Boston Globe_ 5 Feb. 1992: 35, 40. Print. Lengthy feature article linked to author tour to promote _Guardian Angel_, a book that "revolves around old people and hinges on a plot about their exposure to exploitation."

Koch, P. G. "A Crack in the Gray; Sara Paretsky's Latest Offers More Interest and Color." _Houston Chronicle_ 2 Sept. 2001: 17. Print. Rev. of _Total Recall._

Koelsch, Patrice Clark. "Women of Mystery Solving Crimes, Dissolving Stereotypes: The Series Character in Detective Fiction." _Belles Lettres_ July–Aug. 1986: 2–3. Print. Short essay explores what happens when "girl sleuths [aka Nancy Drew] are grown-up women" [whose] "writers often incorporate feminist concerns and perspectives as integral to character and plot." Reference made to Paretsky's first three V. I. novels.

Krotz, Joanna L. "The Power of the Purse: More Women Are Directing Money to Causes They Care About, Setting the Stage for a New Women's Movement: Philanthropy." _Town & Country_ Dec. 2004: 238. Print. Feature article on women's philanthropy cites Paretsky's creation of a private foundation in 2001 so she could "address girls and women in the arts, sciences and sports, mostly in Chicago but not limited to that area."

Landrigan, Linda, ed. _Alfred Hitchcock's Mystery Magazine Presents Fifty Years of Crime and Suspense._ New York: Pegasus, 2006. Print. Anthology includes the Paretsky short story "The Takamoku Joseki."

Langley, William. "Prisoner of Conscience." _Saga_ Mar. 2008: 37, 39. Print. Author interview and review of _Bleeding Kansas_ describes novel as "an ambitious, intricate saga of warring families in the American heartland, shot through with contemporary politics, bigotry, money, redemption, lesbianism and power."

Lanham, Fritz. "Sara Paretsky; 'Hard Time.'" _Houston Chronicle_ 31 Oct. 1999: 4. Print. Review of _Hard Time_ notes that "the latter part of the novel turns into a harrowing portrait of brutality behind bars."

Lavin, Cheryl. "Fast Track." _Chicago Tribune Magazine_ 12 Dec. 1999: 12. Print. Short interview column in which author responds to set questions such as favorite performer ("Dame Margot Fonteyn") and person she would give anything to meet: "Abraham Lincoln. I admire his willingness to do the right thing."

Lawrence, Edward. "Around the Nation (Sara Paretsky Is the Speaker at 2008 Conversation in the Humanities)." _Humanities_ 29.5 (2008): 30–37. Print. Brief note in round-up column re National Endowment for the Humanities funding for speakers for 2008.

Leadbeater, Charles. "Paretsky Fires a Blank." _Financial Times_ 15 Aug. 1994: 9. Print. Review of _Tunnel Vision_ complains that detective "now seems to be shaped by what appear to be Paretsky's political preferences rather than her reflections upon Chicago life."

Leber, Michele. "Crime in Short: Eight Collections of Abbreviated Murder and Mayhem." _Library Journal_ 1 Nov. 2007: 50. Print. Brief round-up review of recent anthologies notes that collection in *Chicago Blues* displays "the work of some of Chicago's finest mystery writers ... [and] should be of interest beyond the Second City area." Includes Paretsky's short story "Publicity Stunts." Notes *Sisters on the Case* anthology, edited by Paretsky and including her short story "A Family Sunday in the Park" (aka "Marquette Park"), which is termed an "accomplished work."

Lehmann-Haupt, Christopher. "Books of the Times; V.I. Warshawski; in Detection and Reflection." *New York Times* 27 Jan. 1992: C22. Print. Review of *Guardian Angel* praises it as "the most engaging yet of Ms. Paretsky's thrillers."

_____. "Books of the Times; The Wet Underbelly of Chicago." *New York Times* 20 June 1994: C18. Print. Review of *Tunnel Vision* praises "clever plotting" but wishes that "for variety the story contained at least one happily married parent, or a generous rich man, or a moral individual of power."

Lehrer, Jim. "Blood Feud." *Washington Post* 13 Jan. 2008: BW06. Print. Appreciative review of *Bleeding Kansas* describes a "serious, multi-layered saga ... as complicated as it is mean."

Leigh, Danny. "Detective Sidelights." *Times Literary Supplement* 28 Apr. 2006: 25. Print. Review of *Fire Sale* observes, "while it is easy to mock Paretsky's didactic tendencies, there are luminous moments in passages as simple as a description of a cavernous By-Smart warehouse, or the corporation's oppressively bland headquarters, the surrounding prairie stripped and concreted with 'a tiny bit of grass Scotch-taped in as an afterthought.'"

Leon, Donna. "Nothing Is as It Seems, Nobody Is to Be Trusted. Betrayal Is Part of the Scenery." *Sunday Times* (London) 16 Dec. 2001: 41. Print. Review of *Total Recall* finds novel disappointing but praises detective for pursuing the case "with her usual tenacity, skill and wit."

Leonard, John. Rev. of *Writing in an Age of Silence*. *Harper's Magazine* May 2007: 87. Print. Brief review of memoir notes that with its passionate focus on the dangers of the Patriot Act, the author "honors a family tree that includes grandparents who met on a picket line at an International Ladies' Garment Workers' Union strike and a great-uncle Wobbly so dangerous to the Republic that he was deported during the red-baiting Palmer raids after World War I."

Leopold, Wendy. "Female Private Eye Packs a Punch, Widens Genre." *Los Angeles Times* 14 Dec. 1988: 11. Print. Short interview with author describes genesis of character and difficulties with getting first novel published because of "a strong bias against the Chicago setting. The sphere of the hard-boiled detective was viewed as Los Angeles or New York."

Lewell, John. "Chicago Private Eye V.I. Warshawski." Femaledetective.com. 17 Mar. 2000. Web. http://www.femaledetective.com/reviews/ Review of *Tunnel Vision* praises detective figure as "an eloquent and convincing narrator ... so free from cynicism that her dismay is almost palpable whenever she finds out new truths about America's infinite ability to organize its crime."

Linnane, Ruth. "*Tunnel Vision*." *Law Institute Journal* June 1995: 595. Print. Brief review of novel notes the "struggling private eye ... with brains and ability ... is involved in a number of good causes, all of which are empowering to women in some shape or form."

Littler, Alison. "Marele Day's 'Cold Hard Bitch': The Masculinist Imperatives of the Private-Eye Genre." *Journal of Narrative Technique* 21.1 (1991): 121–35. Print. Article explores how a range of contemporary women mystery writers are responding to the genre's traditional engagement with violence as "the site around which the narrative action takes place and ... is also a test of the hero's physical and, by extension, moral superiority and fitness to be an heroic figure" and concludes that "the private-eye genre is still a highly problematic site for feminist writers" (124, 133).

Long, Karen. "V.I. Warshawski Creator Paretsky Coming to Dogwood Festival." *Kalamazoo* (MI) *Gazette* 8 May 2005: D1–2. Print. Interview with author on occasion of Paretsky's lecture for the Dogwood Fine Arts Festival; article reminds readers how "V. I. broke the mold, the rules and more than a few noses."

Longhurst, Derek, ed. *Gender, Genre & Narrative Pleasure*. London: Unwin, 1989. Print. Collection of essays on pleasures of reading popular fiction considers thrillers, mysteries, science fiction, and horror. Essay by David Glover discusses codes of masculinity and femininity in the thriller.

Lowry, Mary A. "Crime Time." *Women's Review of Books* July 1989: 41. Print. Brief review of *Blood Shot* notes that novel "has it all—good writing, good characters (even the villains are compellingly real), plus a believable mystery with a satisfying ending."

Mackenzie, Suzie. "Women: Tracking Down Chicago's Crime Queen—Suzie Mackenzie Goes on the Trail of Sara Paretsky, Creator of Fiction's Hardest-Hitting Female Private Eye." *Guardian* (London) 23 May 1990: 17. Print. Interview following publication of *Burn Marks* notes how "Paretsky's success has put V. I. up there in the mainstream of American detective writing ... she gave them a woman who could solve her own problems."

Madden, Leslie. Rev. of *Blacklist. Library Journal* 1 Sept. 2003: 210. Print. Brief review of novel rates it as "Paretsky's most complex novel to date ... a story of betrayal and secrets that spans several generations."

_____. Rev. of *Fire Sale. Library Journal* 15 June 2005: 64. Print. Brief review of novel describes it as "fast-paced and as entertaining as any entry in the series."

_____. Rev. of *Total Recall. Library Journal* Aug. 2001: 164. Print. Review finds that "V. I. is as strong-willed as ever, risking herself at every turn to find the truth." Suggests readers new to series "may find the complex plot and large cast of characters confusing."

Maguire, Susie. "Heroes and Hard Cell." *Scotland on Sunday* 19 Sept. 1999: 7. Print. Review of *Hard Time* finds it "a long tough novel about seeking justice and fighting City Hall."

Maio, Kathleen. "Hard Boiled and Fast Paced." *Sojourner* May 1982: 17–18. Print. Review of *Indemnity Only* notes the detective "has a will to protect women and children, a moral code which has nothing to do with the law, a tendency towards philosophical pomposities, and most disquieting of all, a tolerance for (at times, almost a celebration of) violence."

_____. "Murder in Print." *Wilson Library Bulletin* Apr. 1984: 582. Print. Brief review of *Deadlock* focuses on the sleuth who "relies on intelligence and grit determination. In accordance with hard-boiled precepts, she takes a good deal of abuse and injury before book's end, and she refuses to let it slow her down."

Major, Leslie. "The City Did It." *Eleven Magazine* Jan. 1990: 10–14. Print. Feature article on Chicago's most popular genre writers claims "among the new generation of fictional detectives, Sara Paretsky's V.I. Warshawski packs the most personality."

Makinen, Merja. *Feminist Popular Fiction.* Basingstoke, UK: Palgrave, 2001. Print. Chapter on crime and mystery fiction teases out distinctions between canonical texts and resisting, or counter-canonical, texts, pointing to Paretsky's work as counter-canonical in the private-eye subgenre.

Manning, Anita. "Sara Paretsky Gives Her All to Her Writings and Society." *USA Today* 3 Aug. 1994: 2D. Print. Brief review of *Tunnel Vision* notes that author's own "sense of powerlessness puts the edge in Paretsky's personality and her writing."

_____. "Woman of Mystery V.I. Warshawski Creator Sara Paretsky/Detective Is the Author's Alter-Ego." *USA Today* 25 July 1991: D1+. Print.

Author tells interviewer, "I think what V.I. does for me is give me a voice out of a feeling of helplessness."

Mansfield-Kelley, Deane, and Lois Marchino, eds. *The Longman Anthology of Detective Fiction.* New York: Longman, 2004. Print. Anthology for use in high school and college classrooms: contains short stories, author biographies, outline history and development of genre, and sample literary criticism. Paretsky is referred to in a brief author entry (308–09) as a "major influence in contemporary women's detective fiction" (308); short story "Skin Deep" included (309–19).

Mapstone, E. R. "The V.I. Warshawski Series by Sara Paretsky." *Feminism & Psychology* 6.2 (1996): 324–28. Print. Brief article outlines Mapstone's admiration for the series and speculates about the appeal of the character for feminist psychologists: "Champion of the underdog and the disenfranchised, generous, warm, honest, reliable, courageous, she may be fictional, but offers a not unworthy ideal at which to aim."

Maslin, Janet. "Kathleen Turner as Private Eye." *New York Times* 26 July 1991: C17. Print. Review of film "V.I. Warshawski" praises "Ms. Turner's winning nonchalance and expert timing."

Matthews, Christine, ed. *Deadly Housewives.* New York: Harper, 2006. Print. Anthology includes Paretsky's short story "Acid Test."

Matthews, Christine, and Robert J. Randisi, eds. *Lethal Ladies II.* New York: Berkley, 1998. Print. Anthology includes Paretsky's short story "Publicity Stunts."

McCracken, Scott. *Pulp: Reading Popular Fiction.* Manchester, UK: Manchester UP, 1998. Print. Explores the pleasures of reading and studying detective fiction, popular romance, science fiction, and gothic horror. References Sarah (sic) Paretsky and V. I. Warshawski as examples of successful entry into "the previously masculine world of the thriller and hard-boiled detective fiction" (167).

McDermid, Val. "Book of a Lifetime." *The Independent* 18 Sept. 2009: 33. Print. McDermid credits Paretsky's *Indemnity Only* as the book that inspired her own "career in writing that I could never have imagined."

_____. "Counting the Cost of a Sinister Superstore." *The Independent* 31 Mar. 2006: 28. Print. Review of *Fire Sale* notes Paretsky's "evenhanded" approach to "the commercial conglomerate.... Walmart ... thinly disguised as By-Smart."

_____. "Sleuth's Nightmare When Hunter Becomes Hunted in the Windy City." *Sunday Express* (London) 26 Sept. 1999: 60. Print. Detailed review of *Hard Time* gives it four stars and says author "did more than anyone to change the face of contemporary women's crime fiction." Version of review [title wrongly printed as *Hard Times*] appeared in *Manchester Evening News* 8 Oct. 1999: 11.

McGlone, Jackie. "Prairie Home Companion." *The Scotsman* 22 Mar. 2008: 15–16. Print. Author interview and review of *Bleeding Kansas* quotes author as saying, "I've written about the ultimate insiders in my childhood—farmers who have worked the land for a century and a half.... It's the insider's world that I wanted to explore—to see how it looked, how it felt and why someone like me had no place in it."

McKay, Alistair. "Hall of Femmes." *The Scotsman* Aug. 2000, S2: 4–6. Print. Author interview preceding Paretsky's appearance at the Edinburgh International Book Festival in Aug. 2000. Traces Paretsky's family background and genesis of V.I. character.

McNamara, Chris. "Chicago Mystery Writer Sara Paretsky on Cubs, Sox and Tragedy." *Chicago Tribune* 3 June 2009. Print. Article explores V. I.'s and author's devotion to the Cubs.

Melton, Emily. Rev. of *Ghost Country. Booklist* 1 Mar. 1998: 1045. Print. Brief review notes standalone novel from author whose "gritty adventures of V. I. Warshawski have made the Chicago PI a marquee name among today's sleuths."

_____. Rev. of *Hard Time. Booklist* July 1999: 1894. Print. Fulsome review of *Hard Time* describes it as "brilliantly plotted, full of heart-wrenching emotion, packed with fast-paced action." States that novel "packs a powerful, unforgettable punch."

_____. Rev. of *Tunnel Vision. Booklist* 1 Apr. 1994: 1404. Print. Enthusiastic review praises novel as "her best adventure yet, a complex, authentic, and gripping story that shows our heroine at both her bravest and most vulnerable."

_____. Rev. of *Windy City Blues. Booklist* 1 Sept. 1995: 6. Print. Lukewarm review praises author for "trying a new format for her popular heroine" but judges after the first story "the plots get shorter, shallower, and less engaging."

_____. Rev. of *Women on the Case. Booklist* 1 June 1996: 1681. Print. Detailed review of anthology praises the "star-studded list of contributing authors" for the 26 stories that "range from gritty and realistic to bizarre and laugh-aloud funny." Notes stories are from "both well-known American authors and from foreign writers whose works have never before appeared in English."

Memmott, Carol. "Sara Paretsky by the Numbers." *USA Today* 28 Dec. 2011: 4D. Print. Brief note on publication of *Breakdown* 30 years after *Indemnity Only*.

_____. "Social Issues, Paretsky's Heart Ooze Out of 'Bleeding Kansas.'" *USA Today* 3 Jan. 2008: 4D. Print. Interview/review quotes author saying, "it's about ordinary people whose lives get terribly out of kilter because of events in the big world that they don't have any control over."

Merritt, Stephanie. "If I Hadn't Been a Crime Reader, I Might Never Have Tried to Write." *Observer Review* 13 Aug. 2000: 13. Print. Author interview and review of *Hard Time*, a novel that "has Warshawski confronting high-level corruption: abuses in the prison system, globalisation of the media, the exploitation of immigrant workers."

Messent, Peter, ed. *Criminal Proceedings, The Contemporary American Crime Novel.* Chicago: Pluto P, 1997. Print. Collection of essays provides useful survey of current trends in U.S. crime fiction. Examines work of Paretsky as well as James Ellroy, Walter Mosley, Barbara Wilson, and others.

Metcalf, Mary Ann. "Reviews." *Sisters in Crime Newsletter* (Australia), no. 6 (Winter 1994): 7. Print. Review of *Tunnel Vision* praises the eighth novel "in an intelligent and exciting detective series which offers a particular insight into American society in the eighties and nineties that is often ignored by male writers of the genre."

Miller, K. "Mystery Writer Tackles the A-Bomb." 22 Oct. 2013. Web. http:// www.mprnews.org/ story/2013/10/22/daily-circuit-critical-mass? from=dc# Minnesota public radio interview with Paretsky discusses subject matter of *Critical Mass* and deepening relationship between V.I. and Lotty Herschel.

Miller, Lynn I. "Sara Paretsky: Collaring White Collar Crime." *Crescent Blues* 2.6 (13 Oct. 1999) Web. http://www.crescentblues.com/2_6issue/ paretsky.shtml Q&A as *Hard Time* is published quotes author on the white-collar crimes investigated by V. I.: "[T]he crimes are always the actions taken to further the good of the company or the individual profit of a major officer of a company."

Miller, Sarah Bryan. "Gumshoe Warshawski Embraces Technology Author Q&A." *St. Louis Post-Dispatch* 27 Sept. 2009: D9. Print. Short Q&A with author on publicity tour for *Hardball*.

_____. "Iraq War Plays Role in V.I. Warshawski's Latest Fiction." *St. Louis Post-Dispatch* 29 Aug. 2010: E4. Print. Review of *Body Work* describes it as a "smart, fast-paced thrill ride ... [with] characters who have been wounded, in one way or another, by the war in Iraq and by highly contemporary issues of sexuality and privacy."

_____. "Paretsky Produces Another Gritty, Memorable Tale." *St. Louis Post-Dispatch* 16 Sept. 2001: F8. Print. Review of *Total Recall* notes, "Warshawski inhabits a world that is gritty, real and credible."

_____. "Paretsky's 'Critical Mass' Is Packed with Action." *St. Louis Post-Dispatch* 27 Oct. 2013: C10. Print. Review praises novel which "moves between wartime Vienna and present-day Chicago, the misery of the Jewish ghetto and the luxuries of North Shore privilege."

_____. "V. I. Warshawski Is Back in Top Detecting Form." *St. Louis Post-Dispatch* 8 Jan. 2012: D8. Print. Review of *Breakdown* finds that "as always, Paretsky has a perfectly tuned ear for Chicago and its people [and for combining] social justice issues with acute observation of contemporary life."

Minardi, Enrico, and Jennifer Byron, eds. *Out of Deadlock, Female Emancipation in Sara Paretsky's V.I. Warshawski Novels, and Her Influence on Contemporary Crime Fiction*. Newcastle upon Tyne, UK: Cambridge Scholars Publ., 2015. A collection of essays from a range of international perspectives exploring "Paretsky's fundamental feminist commitment" (5) as the author engages with issues of female friendship, violence against women, gender roles.

Mitchell, Charles. "Favourites Old and New." *Spectator* 8 Dec. 2001: 54. Print. Review of *Total Recall* judges it a "well paced private-eye conspiracy caper, intercut with the fictional reminiscences of a *Kindertransport* survivor."

Mizejewski, Linda. *Hardboiled and High Heeled: The Woman Detective in Popular Culture*. New York: Routledge, 2004. Print. Gives an overview of the woman detective figure in three modes: the novel, television, and film. Discusses the female detectives created by Sara Paretsky, Sue Grafton, and Patricia Cornwell, linking their wide appeal to readers to the "refusal of wife/mother roles" (23) in the novels.

"Monstrous Moms and Tormented Souls." *Washington Post* 22 Nov. 2015: E-8. The newspaper selects Paretsky's *Brush Back* as one of the best mystery novels of 2015; capsule review by Maureen Corrigan calls it "superb" and cites its "uncompromising feminist message."

Moore, Lewis D. *Cracking the Hard-Boiled Detective, A Critical History from the 1920s to the Present*. Jefferson, NC: McFarland. 2006. Print. Critical study analyzes hard-boiled detective character from 1920s origins to twenty-first-century developments. Discusses Paretsky's construction of V.I.'s extended "family" of friends and colleagues as innovative. Concludes that "females play an increasingly significant role" in the genre's current vitality.

_____. "Lies and Deceit: The Family in the Hard-Boiled Detective Novel." *Clues: A Journal of Detection* 21.2 (2000): 67–76. Print. Article discusses the idea of the family as a source of conflict in hard-boiled fiction and explores Paretsky's use of the extended family in the construction of V. I.'s life in Chicago.

Morse, Ruth. "Cold Cases." *Times Literary Supplement* 12 Feb. 2010: 21. Print. Review of *Hardball* notes that "Warshawski herself remains the familiar hot-tempered maverick."

Muir, Kate. "Best Sellers that Pack a Strong Female Punch; Life and Times." *The Times* (London), 16 Aug. 1991: 10A. Print. In-depth interview with Paretsky as author delivers lecture at Edinburgh Festival. Paretsky tells Muir about modeling V. I. on a South Chicago woman who was a friend of her stepsons: "Growing up in that community, girls either had to have basic street-fighting skills, or have a man protect them, or else they were victimised … this pretty, small redhead … used to go to bars, let men buy her drinks, and if they made a move on her, she'd beat them up. It was her hobby."

Muller, Adrian. "Sara Paretsky Interview." *Crime Time* 6.24 (1996): 24–25. Print. Interview quotes Paretsky at length on creation of the V.I. character, the film, Sisters in Crime, and her first non V. I. novel.

Mundow, Anna. "In This Chase, Warshawski Won't Be Caught Flat-Footed." *The Washington Post* 25 Nov. 2013: CO2. Print. Review of *Critical Mass* notes the author's "dense, gratifyingly brief scientific explanations link together the betrayal, theft and murder at the novel's core."

Munk, Erika. "Deadly Delights." *Women's Review of Books* Feb. 1992: 8–9. Print. Detailed review of anthology *A Woman's Eye* praises the contents as "surprisingly various"; observes, in concert with Paretsky's introduction, that "women writers make it easier for women to enjoy mysteries" with the "smart, brave, independent, humane female investigators."

Munt, Sally. *Murder by the Book? Feminism and the Crime Novel*. New York: Routledge, 1994. Print. Critical overview of British and American feminist crime novels of the 1980s; poses questions about the genre's potential for expressing oppositional politics; identifies the lesbian detective figure as the new transgressive superhero. Argues that Paretsky's work (up to 1994)—with its focus on the individual, the family, and the state—sits within a liberal feminist tradition and expresses "a radical charge constrained within an overall conformity" (31).

Murphy, Bruce. *The Encyclopedia of Murder and Mystery*. New York: St. Martin's Minotaur, 1999: 381, 514–15. Print. Entries on author and character; author entry states, "Paretsky's Chicago is teeming with life, but she suppresses none of its drabness" (515).

Nair, Yasmin. "Book Review *Bleeding Kansas* by Sara Paretsky." *Windy City Times* 20 Feb. 2008: 16. Print. Unenthusiastic review of novel says it "strains hard to make a meaningful statement about war and the battle between conservatives and liberals."

Nason, Richard. "A Mystery that Flaunts Healthy Prejudices." *Medical Tribune* 12 Aug. 1987: 21. Print. Thoughtful review of *Bitter Medicine* praises Paretsky's prejudices against "for-profit medicine," against "medical neglect of the impoverished," and against "the right to life movement."

Nelson, Catherine M. "Trouble Is Her Business." *The Armchair Detective* 24.8 (1991): 260–70. Print. Lengthy Q&A interview with Paretsky as *Burn Marks* comes out in paperback.

Newton, P. M. "Crime Fiction and the Politics of Place: The Post–9/11 Sense of Place in Sara Paretsky and Ian Rankin." *The Millennial Detective: Essays on Trends in Crime Fiction, Film and Television, 1990–2010.* Ed. Malcah Effron. Jefferson, NC: McFarland, 2011. 21–35. Print. Theoretical essay examines the politics of place in Paretsky's *Blacklist* and Rankin's *The Naming of the Dead,* comparing and contrasting the novelists' representations of "the same global issue: the impact of terrorism on western liberal democracies."

Ng, Laura. "Feminist Hard-Boiled Detective Fiction as Political Protest in the Tradition of Women Proletarian Writers of the 1930s." PhD diss., Louisiana State U, 2005. Web. Proquest document ID: 304989082. Dissertation seeks to align the work of Sara Paretsky, Sue Grafton, and Marcia Muller as a genre of political protest in common with 1930s women writers such as Josephine Herbst and Catherine Brody.

Nichols, Victoria, and Susan Thompson. *Silk Stalkings: When Women Write of Murder.* Berkeley, CA: Black Lizard Books, 1988. Print. The first comprehensive chronological survey of series characters created by women authors of crime and mystery fiction. An important early reference book. Entry on first four V. I. Warshawski books praises V. I. as bringing "intelligence and competence to her job" but offers personal opinion that detective's "sense of justice … seems self-serving at best" (216).

Nickson, Elizabeth. "Change of Genre Suits Paretsky Fine." *The Globe and Mail* (Canada) 18 July 1998: D14. Print. Review of *Ghost Country* praises author for mixing an "unholy brew into an absorbing story."

Nicol, Charles. "The Hard-Boiled Go to Brunch."

*Harper's Magazine* Oct. 1987: 61–65. Print. Critical essay discussing the figure of the American private eye with reference to Dashiell Hammett, Raymond Chandler, Ross Macdonald, Sara Paretsky, and Robert B. Parker. Examples of "the best of the current, vastly changed hard-boiled dicks" include "Sara Paretsky's V.I. Warshawski, because she gets laid, jailed, knocked out, and shot at, takes the law into her own hands and occasionally has an excessive urge to maim or kill, and generally proves that a feminist can fit hand in glove with the hard-boiled" (62).

Niebuhr, Gary Warren. "Sara Paretsky." *Mystery News* Dec./Jan. 2004. Web. http://www.blackravenpress.com Interview with author shortly after publication of *Blacklist* in which she tells Niebuhr, "I think it's more important to focus on the stories you want to tell than to imagine yourself writing for posterity."

Nolan, Tom. "Bookshelf." *Wall Street Journal* 17 Apr. 1992: A9. Print. Review of *Guardian Angel.*

_____. "Bookshelf: Where Bad Guys Get Caught, Punished Too." *Wall Street Journal* 27 Sept. 2001, sec. A: 16. Print. Review of *Total Recall* finds that "V.I.'s social consciousness is as bracing as ever, as is the realistic depiction of the fatigue and pain suffered in the course of her work. The most affecting aspect of the book, though, is Lotty's recollection of her youth in London."

Norridge, Julian. "A Childhood; Sara Paretsky." *The Times* (London) 4 Sept. 1993: 40. Print. Feature article on Paretsky in which she reveals a painful family background to Norridge who concludes, "her childhood clearly informs her writing. It has done much to shape the feminism, the anger and the intense energy of V. I. Warshawski … who is at the centre of her best-selling crime books."

Nottle, Diane. "Books; Speaking of Crime: In Praise of Shedunits." *New York Times* 25 Oct. 1998: NJ12. Print. Article reports on a symposium celebrating the donation of the Sisters in Crime papers and archive to the Mabel Smith Douglass Library at Douglass College, Rutgers U.

Ogle, Connie. "The Chicago Way: Paretsky Broke New Ground." *Miami Herald* 28 Jan. 2012: WR5. Print. Author interview/review of *Breakdown,* quotes Paretsky as saying "the biggest threat to our democracy [is] the loss of really good, reliable, independent journalism." (a version of this interview appeared in *Miami Herald* 30 Dec. 2011)

O'Grady, Carrie. "Burning Issues: VI Warshawski Is Back. Carrie O'Grady Celebrates Her Return." *Guardian* (London) 25 Mar. 2006: 17.

Print. Review of *Fire Sale* states that after three-year gap, the detective's "prickly feminism, idealism and fury at social injustice are stronger than ever."

O'Leary, Emily. "Books in Brief." *Kansas City Star* 6 May 1984: 18G. Print. Brief review of *Deadlock* notes that Paretsky's "prose is lucid and taut and her inventiveness seemingly unlimited."

Orr, Vanessa. Rev. of *Critical Mass. Mystery Scene.* 2013. Web. http://www.mysteryscenemag.com/blog-article/3433-critical-mass Positive review notes that Paretsky "forces the reader to face what can happen when governments and their leaderships are allowed to run unchecked."

Osborne, Karen Lee, ed. *The Country of Herself.* Chicago: Third Side P, 1993. Print. Anthology includes Paretsky's short story "The Man Who Loved Life."

Ott, Bill. "An Anniversary, a Discovery, and a Resurrection." *Booklist* 1 May 2012: 15. Short article on 30th anniversary of Paretsky's series debut in 1982 describes festivities in Chicago including "Mayor Rahm Emanuel issuing a special proclamation."

_____. "*Bitter Medicine* by Sara Paretsky." *Booklist* 15 Mar. 1987:1075. Print. Review states "Warshawski is an enormously likable, first-class detective who deserves to be released from the liberal straitjacket in which her creator has clamped her."

_____. "Hard-Boiled Gazeteer to the Best Mystery Settings in the World." *Booklist* 1 May 2013: 8+. Print. Guide includes review of *Fire Sale* with correction to 12th in series.

_____. "Paretsky, Sara. *Fire Sale.*" *Booklist* 1 June 2005: 1712. Print. Brief review of *Fire Sale* points out novel effectively utilizes "both the city's broad-shouldered past and its radically globalized present." Incorrectly identifies novel as 13th in series, rather than 12th.

Ousby, Ian. *The Crime and Mystery Book.* London: Thames, 1997. Print. Comprehensive reader's companion tells the story of crime and mystery fiction from its origins to contemporary film and TV adaptations. Emphasis is on British and U.S. chronologies, refers to other Euro traditions. Paretsky's work discussed in Private Eye section with other mentions.

Page, Benedicte. "Anger in America: Sara Paretsky Tells Benedicte Page About the "Shattering" Experience of Living under the Bush regime." *The Bookseller* 30 Sept. 2005: 30. Print. Brief feature on writer who finds "the current political climate in America makes it harder for her to devise successful plotlines for her ballsy, action-loving heroine."

_____. "Fiction Highlights." *The Bookseller* Spr. 2008: 24. Print. Rev. of *Bleeding Kansas.*

"Paperback Bestsellers." *Publishers Weekly* 4 Oct. 2004: 94. Print. Paretsky's *Blacklist* included in paperback bestsellers column.

Paradis, Kenneth. "Warshawski's Situation: Beauvoirean Feminism and the Hard-Boiled Detective." *South Central Review* 18.3/4 (2001): 86–101. Print. Theoretical essay discusses Paretsky's gendered configuration of the classic hard-boiled detective; argues that the novels "express a "feminism" in which the female body and its situational experience become the locus for the articulation of moral agency," with particular reference to *Hard Time* and to de Beauvoir on the female existentialist subject.

"Sara Paretsky." *Contemporary Literary Criticism.* Vol. 135. Detroit: Gale, 2001. 307–70. Print. Lengthy entry includes biographical info, major works, critical reception, and critical essays about the author's works to date.

"Sara Paretsky." *Proquest Information.* Cambridge, UK: Chadwyck-Healey, 2005. Web. Short biographical essay outlines author's career and publications to date, including some reviewers' comments.

Paretsky, Sara. "Acid Test." *Deadly Housewives.* Ed. Christine Matthews. New York: Harper, 2006. 122–55. Print.

_____. "Afterword to *The Brothers Karamazov.*" *The Brothers Karamazov,* by Fyodor Dostoyevsky [sic]. New York: Signet, 2007. 899–906. Print.

_____. "Another Turn of the Screw." 16th Annual McCusker Lecture. Dominican University/Freedom to Read Foundation, Amer. Lib. Assn. 24 Oct. 2012. Repr. *World Libraries* 20.2 (2010 [sic]). Web. http://ojsserv.dom.edu/ojs/index.php/worldlib/article/view/543/465

_____. "Art History." *Kansas State Collegian* 11 Mar. 2011: 4. Print.

_____. "At the 'Century of Progress.'" *Mysterious Pleasures.* Ed. Martin Edwards. London: Little, 2003. 253–77. Print.

_____. "At the Old Swimming Hole." Hopkins and Potter 32–43. *Lady on the Case.* Ed. Marcia Muller, Bill Pronzini, and Martin H. Greenberg. New York: Bonanza, 1988. 277–94. Print. *Murder and Mystery in Chicago.* Ed. Carol-Lynn Rössel Waugh, Frank D. McSherry Jr., and Martin H. Greenberg. New York: Dembner, 1987. 1–20. Print. Paretsky, *Windy City Blues* 124–49. Paretsky, *V.I. For Short* 133–58. Randisi, *Mean Streets* 171–95.

_____. "Baptism in the Bungalow Belt." *Chicago Tribune* 29 Aug. 1996: 1A9. Print.

_____, ed. *Beastly Tales: The Mystery Writers of America Anthology.* New York: Wynwood P, 1989. Print.

_____. *Bitter Medicine.* New York: Morrow, 1987.

London: Gollancz, 1987. New York: Ballantine, 1987. Print.

_____. *Blacklist*. New York: Putnam, 2003. London: Hamilton, 2003. Print.

_____. *Bleeding Kansas*. New York: Putnam, 2008. London: Hodder, 2008. Print.

_____. *Blood Shot*. New York: Delacorte, 1988. Published as *Toxic Shock* in UK. London: Gollancz, 1988. Print.

_____. *Body Work*. New York: Putnam, 2010. London: Hodder, 2010. Print.

_____. "Books-Five Best: A Personal Choice: Sara Paretsky—on bearing witness to the unspeakable." *The Wall Street Journal* 16 Nov. 2013: C10. Print.

_____. *Breakdown*. New York: Putnam, 2012. London: Hodder, 2012. Print.

_____. "The Breakdown of Moral Philosophy in New England before the Civil War." PhD diss., U of Chicago, 1977. Print.

_____. *Brush Back*. New York: Putnam, 2015. London: Hodder, 2015. Print.

_____. *Burn Marks*. New York: Delacorte, 1990. London: Chatto, 1990. Print.

_____. "Bush's Pick a Reminder of What's Not Right." *Chicago Tribune* 7 Jan. 2007. Web. http://articles.chicagotribune.com/2007-01-07/news/0701070087_1_contraception-eric-keroack-pregnancy

_____. "By the Book." *New York Times Book Review* 14 Sept. 2014: 8. Print.

_____. "The Case of the Pietro Andromache." *Alfred Hitchcock's Mystery Magazine* Dec. 1988. *The Year's Best Mystery and Suspense Stories*. Ed. Edward D. Hoch. New York: Walker, 1989. *New Crimes* [1]. Ed. Maxim Jakubowski. New York: Carroll, 1990. Wallace, *Sisters in Crime* 113–35. Greenberg 15–49. Paretsky, *Windy City Blues* 61–91. *V. I. For Short* 76–105. George, *Moment on the Edge* 279–307. *Great TV and Film Detectives*. Ed. Maxim Jakubowski. New York: Reader's Digest Assn., 2005. 474–91. Print.

_____. "Chicago." *Savvy* Sept. 1988: 48–51. Print.

_____. "Chills and Charm." *Entertainment Weekly* June/July 1991: 54 + 56. Print.

_____. *Critical Mass*. New York: Putnam, 2013. London: Hodder, 2013. Print.

_____. "Damned by Dollars." *American Scholar* 68.1 (1999): 160. Print.

_____. *Deadlock*. New York: Dial; London: Gollancz, 1984. New York: Ballantine, 1984. Print.

_____. "Dealer's Choice." *Raymond Chandler's Philip Marlowe: A Centennial Celebration*. Ed. Byron Preiss. New York: Knopf, 1988. 119–33. Print. New York: Simon ibooks, 1999. *The New Mystery*. Ed. Jerome Charyn. New York: Dutton, 1993. 80–95. Print. Paretsky, *A Taste of Life and Other Stories* 11–40. Print.

_____. "The Detective as Speech." Minardi and Byron 11–18.

_____. "Diversions." *Chicago Tribune Magazine* 11 Nov. 2001: 13. Print.

_____. "The Dollus Syndrome: Diversity in Crime Fiction." *Booklist* 1 May 2015: 10–11. Print.

_____. "Evil Yankees, Awful Mets." *Newsweek* 30 Oct. 2000: 68. Print.

_____. "Eye of a Woman—An Introduction by Sara Paretsky." Paretsky, *A Woman's Eye* vii–xiv.

_____. "A Family Sunday in the Park" [orig. publ. as "Marquette Park"]. Paretsky, *V. I. × 3* 29–41. Paretsky, *Sisters on the Case* 248–70.

_____. *Fire Sale*. New York: Putnam, 2005. London: Hodder, 2005. Print.

_____. "Flying Da Coach." TimeOutChicagowww 1–14 Nov. 2012. Print.

_____. "Freud at Thirty Paces." Cody and Lewin 150–67. *The Armchair Detective* 26.3 (1993): 26–33. *The Year's Best Fantasy and Horror: Seventh Annual Collection*. Ed. Ellen Datlow and Terri Windling. New York: St. Martin's, 1994. Print.

_____. "George Eliot's *The Mill on the Floss*: Book of a Lifetime by Sara Paretsky." *The Independent* (London) 23 Aug. 2014: 26–27. Print.

_____. *Ghost Country*. New York: Delacorte, 1998. London: Hamilton, 1998. Print.

_____. "Grace Notes." Paretsky, *Windy City Blues* 11–60. Paretsky, *V. I. For Short* 197–246. *The Year's 25 Finest Crime and Mystery Stories*. Ed. Jon L. Breen. New York: Carroll, 1996. Breen and Gorman 543–79. Collins and Spillane 417–48. Print.

_____. "The Great Tetsuji." Cody et al. 109–15.

_____. "Go Home, Yankee Imperialists!" *Chicago Tribune* 17 Aug. 2006. http://articles.chicagotribune.com/2006-08-17/news/0608170102_1_marshall-field-macy-chicago

_____. *Guardian Angel*. New York: Delacorte, 1992. London: Hamilton, 1992. Print.

_____. "A Gun of One's Own." *Publishers Weekly* 25 Oct. 1999: 44–45. Print.

_____. *Hard Time*. New York: Delacorte, 1999. London: Hamilton, 1999. Print.

_____. *Hardball*. New York: Putnam, 2009. London: Hodder, 2009. Print.

_____. "Heartbreak House." Penzler, *Murder* 279–95. *Mary Higgins Clark Mystery Magazine* Summer/Fall 1997: 15–21. *A Century of Great Suspense Stories*. Ed. Jeffery Deaver. New York: Berkley, 2001. 432–44. Print.

_____. "The Hidden War at Home." *New York Times* 7 July 1994: A13. Print.

_____. "Hooker Malone Is Missing: A Serial Mystery." Short story coauthored by Paretsky, Stephen Dobyns, Loren D. Estelman, Walter Mosley, and David Stout. *New York Times Book Review* 20 Oct. 1991: 44. Print.

_____. "Imagining Edgar Allan Poe." Connelly 325–29.

_____. "In Chicago, We've Fought to Stand Together." *Washington Post* 24 Aug. 2008: BO1. Print.

_____. *Indemnity Only.* New York: Dial; London: Gollancz, 1982. New York: Dell, 1991. 30th anniversary edition with new author introduction dated Nov. 2011 in reissue of Dell 1991 pb.

_____. "Independent Sleuth." Herbert et al. 233–34.

_____. Introduction. Paretsky, *Beastly Tales* 9–13.

_____. Introduction. *The Maltese Falcon,* by Dashiell Hammett. 1930. London: The Folio Society, 2000. 9–19. Print.

_____. Introduction. *Women on the Case.* Ed. Sara Paretsky. New York: Delacorte, 1996. vii–xiii. London: Virago, 1996. vii–xiii. Dell pb ed. 1997. vii–xiv.

_____. "Introduction: A Walk on the Wild Side: Touring Chicago with V.I. Warshawski." Paretsky, *Windy City Blues* 1–10. Plus "Author's Note," n.pag. Paretsky, *V. I. For Short.* "Author's Note" n.pag.

_____. "Introduction to the 30th Anniversary Edition of *Indemnity Only.*" (2011 reissue). *Indemnity Only.* New York: Dell, 1991. vii–xii. reissue of 1991 pb with author intro dated Nov. 2011.

_____. Introduction. Paretsky, *Writing in an Age of Silence* xi–xx.

_____. "The Inventory: Sara Paretsky." *Financial Times* Magazine (London) 9–10 Aug. 2014: 8. Print.

_____. "It's No Trial to Watch 'Murder One.'" *Cape Cod Times* 16 Sept. 1995: C7. Print.

_____. "Keeping Nancy Drew Alive." *The Secret of the Old Clock,* by Carolyn Keene. Facsimile ed. Bedford, MA: Applewood, 1991. n.pag. Print. Foreword for facsimile edition of an early Nancy Drew mystery explores the girl detective's "enduring popularity" as a female character with agency and ingenuity.

_____. *Killing Orders.* New York: Morrow, 1985. London: Gollancz, 1986. London: Penguin, 1987. Print.

_____. "Let's Have a Big Smile, Now." *Naming the Daytime Moon.* Ed. Julie Parson et al. Chicago: Another Chicago P, 1988. 46–48. Print.

_____. "A Letter to My Grandmother on Coming Home from Europe." *The Illinois Brief.* Winter 2004: 2. Repr. as "Grannie, Look What We're Doing to the Land of Freedom." *Guardian* (London) 3 Jan. 2005: 14. Print.

_____. "Lily and the Sockeyes." *The Third Womansleuth Anthology.* Ed. Irene Zahava. Freedom, CA: Crossing P, 1990. 187–99. Print. Robinson, *Penguin Book* 152–72.

_____. "Lives: Le Treatment." *New York Times Magazine* 16 Aug. 2009: 50. Print.

_____. "The Long Shadow of the Falcon." *Guardian* (London) 6 May 2000, rev. sec.: 1–3. Print.

_____. "Making Sense of the Senseless." *Sisters in Crime Newsletter,* no. 7 (Summer 1994). 1+ 7. Print. Interview with Paretsky in which she discusses how her fiction responds to topical issues and addresses social injustice concerns.

_____. "The Maltese Cat." Wallace, *Sisters in Crime #3.* 169–97. *The Year's 25 Finest Crime and Mystery Stories: First Annual Edition.* Ed. Jon L. Breen. New York: Carroll, 1992. 231–54. *Bad Behavior.* Ed. Mary Higgins Clark. San Diego: Harcourt, 1995. 197–225. Paretsky, *Windy City Blues* 150–85. Paretsky, *V.I. For Short* 106–41. Wallace, *Best of Sisters in Crime* 197–227.

_____. "The Man Who Loved Life." Gardaphe 163–74. Osborne 159–69. Paretsky, *A Taste of Life and Other Stories* 41–55. Windrath 85–93.

_____. "Margery Allingham: An Appreciation." *Margery Allingham: 100 Years of a Great Mystery Writer.* Ed. Marianne Van Hoeven. Aylsham, UK: Lucas Books, 2004. xi–xiii. Print.

_____. "Mean Streets." *Guardian* (London) 23 June 2007: 22. Print.

_____. "Miss Bianca." *Ice Cold.* Ed. Jeffery Deaver and Raymond Benson. New York: Grand Central, 2014. 93–118. Print.

_____. "MJ Must Remain Larger than Life." *Chicago Sun-Times* 4 May 1998: 12. Print.

_____. "My Book of a Lifetime: *The Mill on the Floss* by George Eliot." *The Independent* (London) 23 Aug. 2014: 26, 27. Print.

_____. "My Hero: Elizabeth Barrett Browning." *Guardian* (London) 10 Apr. 2010, rev. sec.: 6. Print.

_____. "Mysteries." *Chicago Tribune Book World* 8 May 1983, sec. 7: 5. Print.

_____. "The Naked City." *Great Chicago Stories.* Ed. Tom Maday and Sam Landers. Chicago: TwoPress Publ., 1994. Chapter 45, n.pag. Print.

_____. "The New Censorship." *New Statesman* (London) 2 June 2003: 18+. Print.

_____. "A Note from the Author." *Indemnity Only.* New York: Delacorte, 1990. vii–ix.

_____. "Ode to the Season: When Your Landlord Is a Precinct Captain." *Chicago Tribune* 18 Dec. 2008. Web. http://articles.chicagotribune.com/2007-12-18/features/0712140450_1_precinct-captain-building-department-coal

_____. "One Trial, Many Angles to Investigate." *New York Times* 10 Sept. 1995: 49. Print.

_____. "Our Bodies, Our Fertility." *Chicago Tribune* 22 Jan. 2012: 15. Print.

_____. "Photo Finish." *Mary Higgins Clark Mystery Magazine* June 2001: 37–52. Print. Hillerman and Herbert 282–99. Paretsky, *V. I. x 3* 1–14.

_____. "A Poignant Tribute to Cicero." *Chicago Sun-Times* 20 Dec. 1987: 19. Print.

_____. "Portrait of a City: Chicago." *British Airways Highlife* June 2011. Web. http://www.ba highlife.com/News-And-Blogs/Culture-Blog/portrait-of-a-city-chicago.html

_____. "Poster Child." *Send My Love and a Molotov Cocktail.* Ed. Gary Phillips and Andrea Gibbons. Oakland: PM P, 2011. 49–67. Print.

_____. Preface. *Chicago Apartments,* by Neil Harris. New York: Acanthus P, 2004. 11–12. Print.

_____. "Private Eyes, Public Spheres." *Women's Review of Books* Nov. 1988: 12–13. Print.

_____. "Property Rites: Women, Poverty, and Public Policy." *Illinois Issues* (Springfield, IL). June 1996: 30–34.Print. Commissioned essay on women's legal estate and current attitudes and institutions, funded by the Illinois Humanities Council.

_____. "Protocols of the Elders of Feminism." *Law/Text/Culture* 1 (1994): 14–27. Print.

_____. "Publicity Stunts." *Women on the Case.* Ed. Sara Paretsky. New York: Delacorte, 1996. 392–414. London: Virago, 1996. 374–95. New York: Dell, 1997. 392–414. Matthews and Randisi 17–43. Paretsky, *V. I. x 3* 15–28. Hellman 111–40.

_____. "Refusing to Allow Pressure to Silence a Critical Voice." *Chicago Tribune* 1 Apr. 2007: 1–2. Print.

_____. "Remarks in Honor of Carolyn Heilbrun." *Tulsa Studies in Women's Literature* 24.2 (2005): 241–45. Print.

_____. "The Rough Landing We Give Refugees." *New York Times* 26 June 1999: A13. Print.

_____. "Sara Paretsky: My First Car." *Chicago Tribune* 7 Feb. 2014. Video. http://www.chicagotrib une.com/chi-sara-paretsky-on-her-first-car-20140207-story.html

_____. "Sara Paretsky on Liza Cody." *Guardian* (London) 15 Sept. 2011: 23. Print.

, "Sara Paretsky Replies." *Library Journal* 1 June 2007: 10. Print.

_____. "Sara Paretsky: What I'm Reading." *Entertainment Weekly* 27 Aug. 1993: 105. Print.

_____. "Scouting Out the Best That Baseball Has to Offer." *USA Today* 6 July 1990: 4D. Print.

_____. "Settled Score." Paretsky, *A Woman's Eye* 400–22. *The Year's 25 Finest Crime and Mystery Stories: Second Annual Edition.* Ed. Jon L. Breen. New York: Carroll, 1993. Paretsky, *Windy City Blues* 186–208. Paretsky, *V. I. For Short* 142–64.

_____. "Sexy, Moral and Packing a Pistol." *The Independent* (London) 18 June 1997: 22. Print.

_____, ed. *Sisters on the Case.* New York: Obsidian Mysteries, 2007. 248–70. Print.

_____. "Sisters on the Case: Introduction." Paretsky, *Sisters on the Case* ix–xiii. Paretsky's introduction describes how the Sisters in Crime or-

ganization began twenty years ago when a group of women writers expressed concerns about the amount of review attention given to their work compared to the work of male authors.

_____. "Skin Deep." *The New Black Mask,* no. 8 (1987): 102–20. *Homicidal Acts.* Ed. Bill Pronzini and Martin H. Greenberg. New York: Ballantine, 1988. 151–64. *City Sleuths and Tough Guys.* Ed. D. W. McCullough. Boston: Houghton, 1989. 461–73. *P.I. Files.* Ed. Loren Estleman and Martin Greenberg. New York: Ballantine, 1990. 57–69. *A Modern Treasury of Great Detective and Murder Mysteries.* Ed. Ed Gorman. New York: Carroll, 1994. 197–208. Paretsky, *Windy City Blues* 209–25. Paretsky, *V. I. For Short* 59–75. Halligan 99–112. Mansfield-Kelley and Marchino 308–19.

_____. "Soft Spot for Serial Murder." *New York Times* 28 Apr. 1991: E17. Print.

_____. "Strung Out." Randisi and Wallace 216–38. Paretsky, *Windy City Blues* 92–123. Paretsky, *V. I. For Short* 165–96.

_____. "Sweet Home Chicago." *Publishers Weekly* 8 May 2000: 57. Print.

_____. "The Takamoku Joseki." *Alfred Hitchcock's Mystery Magazine* Nov. 1983. 33–42. *Women of Mystery.* Ed. Cynthia Manson. New York: Berkley, 1993. 227–39. Paretsky, *Windy City Blues* 246–58. Paretsky, *V.I. For Short* 1–12. *First Cases: First Appearances of Classic Private Eyes.* Ed. Robert J. Randisi. New York: Dutton, 1996. 159–70. *Win, Lose or Die.* Ed. Cynthia Manson and Constance Scarborough. New York: Carroll, 1996. 38–46. Landrigan 213–22.

_____. "A Taste of Life." *Reader, I Murdered Him: An Anthology of Original Crime Stories.* Ed. Jen Green. London: The Women's P, 1989. 172–76. Paretsky, *A Taste of Life and Other Stories* 1–10. Block 237–45.

_____. *A Taste of Life and Other Stories.* London: Penguin Sixty, 1995. Print.

_____. "Terror in the Name of Jesus." *Guardian* (London) 2 June 2009: 26. Print.

_____. "This Is for You, Jeannie." *Women: A Journal of Liberation* 3.3 (1972): 46–51.

_____. "This Was My Destiny: Housework, Babysitting, Marriage." *Guardian* (London) 21 Dec. 2000: 10–11.

_____. *Three Complete Novels* [contains *Indemnity Only, Blood Shot* and *Burn Marks*]. New York: Wings, 1995. Print.

_____. "Three-Dot Po." Randisi, *The Eyes Have It* 227–44. *Ms. Murder.* Ed. Marie Smith. London: Xanadu Publ., 1989. 32–43. Paretsky, *Windy City Blues* 226–45. Paretsky, *V. I. for Short* 13–32. *The Big Book of Christmas Mysteries.* Ed. Otto Penzler. New York: Vintage Crime/Black Lizard, 2013. 452–61.

_____. "The Tornado." *American Girl* magazine Aug. 1959: 77–78. Print.

_____. *Total Recall*. New York: Delacorte, 2001. London: Hamilton, 2001. Print.

_____. *Tunnel Vision*. New York: Delacorte, 1994. London: Hamilton, 1994. Print.

_____. *V.I.x 3* [short stories]. Chicago: Sara and Two C-Dogs Press, 2007. Print.

_____. "What Book? ... Are you Reading Now?" *Daily Mail* (London) 17 Apr. 2009: 61. Print.

_____. "Wheezie and Juts Are Still Going at It." *Chicago Sun-Times* 11 Dec. 1988: 18. Print.

_____. "Why I Support Barack Obama." *Huffington Post* 18 Oct. 2008. Web. www.huffingtonpost.com/sara-paretsky/why-I-support-barack-obam_b_126953.html

_____. "Why I Write." *Publishers Weekly* 21 Nov. 2011: 27. Print.

_____. "Wild Women Out of Control." *Family Portraits*. Ed. Carolyn Anthony. New York: Doubleday, 1989. 165–79. Print.

_____. *Windy City Blues* [short story collection]. New York: Delacorte, 1995. Published in the UK as *V.I. For Short*. London: Hamilton, 1995. Print.

_____, ed. *A Woman's Eye*. New York: Delacorte, 1991. London, Virago, 1991. Print.

_____, ed. *Women on the Case*: Twenty-Six Original Stories by the Best Women Crime Writers of Our Time. New York: Delacorte, 1996. London: Virago, 1996. Print.

_____. "Writers on Writing: A Storyteller Stands Where Justice Confronts Basic Human Needs." *New York Times* 25 Sept. 2000: B1–2. Print.

_____. *Writing in an Age of Silence* [essays]. New York: Verso, 2007. Print.

_____. "The Written Word." *Booklist* 1 May 2012: 14. Print.

"Paretsky Wins." *Publishers Weekly* 19 Sept. 2005: 8. Item on Paretsky's Lifetime Achievement Award from the Private Eye Writers of America. Print.

Patrick, Vincent. "In Search of an Old Drunk." *New York Times Book Review* 31 May 1992: 45. Print. Detailed review of *Guardian Angel* praises seventh V. I. novel for a story that "accelerates smoothly" and that allows the reader to "get into the detective's skin much more than is usual in a private-eye novel."

Peach, Linden. *Masquerade, Crime and Fiction, Criminal Deceptions*. Basingstoke, UK: Palgrave, 2006. Print. Chapter on Agatha Christie, Dorothy L. Sayers, and Sara Paretsky argues Paretsky's work "looks back to British, feminist writers of the 1920s and 1930s, especially Virginia Woolf" (104).

Pearl, Nancy. "Hard Time." *Library Journal* July 1999: 42. Print. Review of *Hard Time* notes that V.I. never imagines her current case will result in "a long stint behind bars at a private women's prison overrun with sadistic guards and almost equally distressing inmates."

Pearlman, Cindy. "The Hollywood Shuffle." *Inside Chicago* Mar./Apr. 1991: 35. Print. Article discusses compromises made when Paretsky's character V.I. makes "the jump from words on a page to celluloid."

Penzler, Otto, ed. *Murder for Love*. London: Orion, 1996. Print. Anthology includes Paretsky's short story "Heartbreak House."

Pepper, Andrew. *The Contemporary American Crime Novel: Race, Ethnicity, Gender, Class*. Edinburgh: Edinburgh UP, 2000. Print. Discusses Paretsky's *Burn Marks* in relation to identity politics; judges it fails sufficiently to acknowledge "difference" in female identities.

_____. "The 'Hard-Boiled' Genre." Rzepka and Horsley 140–51. Essay argues that "hard-boiled writing is always inflected with political assumptions, even where these assumptions are unclear or indeed contested" (141); claims the hard-boiled is not "a fixed category ... but a fluid, open-ended term" (141).

_____. "Policing the Globe: State Sovereignty and the International in the Post-9/11 Crime Novel." *Modern Fiction Studies* 57.3 (2011): 401–24. Print. Critical/theoretical article discusses "the crime novel as a vehicle for exploring the complex nature of the post–9/11 security environment" (404). Refers to Paretsky's *Blacklist* as "indicative of the more general limitations of the crime novel when trying to map the fault lines of contemporary geopolitics" (404).

Perkins, Bethany. "Sara Paretsky: An Annotated Bibliography." *Bulletin of Bibliography* 4 Dec. 1999: 225–33. Print. Comprehensive survey of critical work up to 1999 on author and her detective series. Lists novels, short stories, biographical and autobiographical sources, and critical essays.

Pether, Penelope. "Trouble with Iphigenia: Feminist Critiques of Feminist Crime Fiction and the Case Against Sara Paretsky." *Australian Journal of Law and Society* 9 (1993): 3–18. Print. Article challenges "feminist critics of the genre" such as Anne Cranny-Francis and Ann Blake who criticize the work of Paretsky and others for tending to reinscribe the patriarchal order. Pether assembles textual evidence from the novels that she argues has been overlooked and that makes a difference to the argument.

Phillips, Gary, and Andrea Gibbons, eds. *Send My Love and a Molotov Cocktail*. Oakland, CA: PM P, 2011. A collection of gritty futuristic stories with examples of crime fiction and sci-fi. Anthology includes Paretsky's short story "Poster Child."

Phipps, Sam. "She Gets Beaten Up for Me." *The Herald* 18 Mar. 2006: 4. Print. Feature article on author who "broke the crime fiction mold."

Pinto-Bailey, Cristina Ferreira. "'From V. I. Warshawski to Dora Diamante': Sonia Coutinho and the Gendered Crime Fiction in Brazil." Minardi and Byron 87–99. Essay outlines work of Brazilian author Coutinho who wrote about Paretsky in the 1994 monograph *Queens of Crime* and whose own detective figure was inspired by V. I. Warshawski.

Plain, Gill. *Twentieth-Century Crime Fiction: Gender, Sexuality and the Body*. Edinburgh: Edinburgh UP, 2001. Print. Critical study uses theories of gender and sexuality to explore the notion of crime fiction as a conservative genre. Discusses Paretsky's novels as "walk[ing] a tightrope between hard-boiled reinscription and feminist revision" (93) and judges them as "a fairy tale of feminist agency ... ultimately torn apart by structural contradictions" (ibid).

Pope, Rebecca A. "'Friends Is a Weak Word for It': Female Friendship and the Spectre of Lesbianism in Sara Paretsky." *Feminism in Women's Detective Fiction*. Ed. Glenwood Irons. Toronto: U of Toronto P, 1995. 157–70. Print. Explores the nature of V.I.'s close female friendships, especially with Lotty, suggesting mother/daughter label or sexual label are inadequate descriptors for the deep bonds between the women.

Porsdam, Helle. "Embedding Rights Within Relationships: Gender, Law, and Sara Paretsky." *American Studies* 39.3 (1998): 131–51. Print. Scholarly article draws on gender and feminist theoretical perspectives to analyze and "illuminate main character V. I. Warshawski's development from autonomous selfhood to a selfhood embedded within relationships." Treats series to date as a "female *Bildungsroman*."

Preiss, Byron, ed. *Raymond Chandler's Philip Marlowe: A Centennial Celebration*. New York: Knopf, 1988. Print. Anthology includes Paretsky's short story "Dealer's Choice," an homage to Chandler, on pp. 119–33.

Price, Stuart. "Sara Paretsky." *The Independent* (London) 5 Aug. 2000:17. Print. Short review of *Hard Time* finds it "a complex and accomplished tale of industrial espionage."

Prichard, Ann. "A Winner among Women Behind Bars." *USA Today* 16 Sept. 1999: 7D. Print. Short review of *Hard Time* states, "It's hard not to like *Hard Time*, with its offbeat characters, fine local color and straightforward handling of the 'women-in-prison' issue so often exploited in TV dramas."

Priestman, Martin. *Crime Fiction from Poe to the Present*. Plymouth, UK: Northcote House, 1998. Print. Short historical and critical introduction to the traditions of the classic whodunit, the thriller, and the private-eye novel. Mentions Paretsky, Gillian Slovo, and Sarah Dunant as writers who "provide their sleuths with ample networks of friends, relatives, and sometimes even male partners, who offer emotional support" (59).

Quinn, Anthony. "No Smoke without Fire; Books." *Sunday Times* (London) 27 May 1990: H7a. Print. Perceptive review of *Burn Marks* praises novel's "expose of corporate rottenness" and detective's "courage and moral rectitude."

Rader, Barbara S., and Howard G. Zettler, eds. *The Sleuth and the Scholar: Origins, Evolution, and Current Trends in Detective Fiction*. New York: Greenwood, 1988. Print. Contributions to the Study of Popular Culture, No. 19. Collection of papers from an early academic symposium on detective fiction.

Randisi, Robert J., ed. *The Eyes Have It: The First Private Eye Writers of America Anthology*. New York: Mysterious P, 1984. Print. Anthology includes Paretsky's short story "Three-Dot Po."

_____. *Mean Streets: The Second Private Eye Writers of America Anthology*. New York: Mysterious P, 1986. Print. Anthology includes Paretsky's short story "At the Old Swimming Hole."

Randisi, Robert J., and Marilyn Wallace, eds. *Deadly Allies: Private Eye Writers of America/Sisters in Crime Collaborative Anthology*. New York: Doubleday, 1992. Print. Anthology includes Paretsky's short story "Strung Out."

Reaves, Jessica. "Blog's Readers Enjoy a Good Whodunit." *New York Times* 18 July 2010: A23B. Print. Article explores dynamics of a Chicago-based authors' blogging group: "The Outfit, an online consortium of local mystery and thriller writers who ... share the burden of blogging and benefit from the built-in audience of one another's fans..." Paretsky "retired from the collective blog in 2009," telling Reaves, "I wasn't getting the personal feedback that I get from my own blog."

Reddy, Maureen. "The Female Detective from Nancy Drew to Sue Grafton." *Mystery and Suspense Writers: The Literature of Crime, Detection, and Espionage*. Vol. II. Ed. Robin W. Winks and Maureen Corrigan. New York: Scribner, 1998. 1047–67. Print. Essay gives overview of the twentieth-century female detective figure and outlines significant developments in the depiction of amateur sleuths, policewoman detectives, private-eyes citing authors such as Paretsky, Amanda Cross, Katherine V. Forrest, and Barbara Neely.

_____. "The Feminist Counter-Tradition in Crime: Cross, Grafton, Paretsky, and Wilson." *The Cunning Craft: Original Essays on Detective Fiction and Contemporary Literary Theory*. Ed. Ronald G. Walker and June M. Frazer. Macomb: Western Illinois UP, 1990. 174–87. Print. Important essay outlining features of feminist counter tradition in genre of crime and mystery writing, and assessing current variations in four established series by writers (including Paretsky) who have been "singled out for critical attention and praise in both the popular and the academic press" (174).

_____. "Sara Paretsky." Herbert et al. 324. Biographical author entry describes novels as "intricately plotted but intensely character-driven, elegantly written, and thematically rich."

_____. *Sisters in Crime: Feminism and the Crime Novel*. New York: Continuum, 1988. Print. An important early contribution to the project of documenting the emerging relationship between feminism(s) and the crime/mystery novel. Identifies a cluster, including Paretsky, of "women writers borrowing familiar features of detective fiction in order to turn them upside down and inside out."

Reed, Cheryl L. "I Spy Myself." *Chicago Sun-Times Books* 22 Apr. 1997: 11–12B. Print. Review of Paretsky's memoir *Writing in an Age of Silence*, in which the author details "an oppressive childhood in rural Kansas where she was raised in a violent, hyper-intellectual Jewish family."

Reese, Jennifer. Rev. of *Bleeding Kansas*. *Entertainment Weekly* 21 Dec. 2007: 83. Print. Short review calls *Bleeding Kansas* an "unruly melodrama."

Rhee, Jooyeon. "Are You My Friend or Enemy? Female Friendship at the Crossroads of Class, Race, and Gender in Sara Paretsky's and Natsuo Kirino's Detective Fictions." Minardi and Byron 101–15. Print. Essay compares how both writers create "cross-generational and interracial female friendships" in their fiction that are "formed by socioeconomic and political factors" (103) in their different backgrounds.

Rich, B. Ruby. "Private Instigator." *Mirabella* July 1991: 36–37. Print. Lengthy author interview anticipates release of V. I. the film; Rich wonders "whether Hollywood can possibly get it right."

Richards, Linda L. "January Interview Sara Paretsky." Nov. 2001. Web. http://www.januarymagazine.com/profiles/paretsky.html Lengthy profile and Q&A with author on publication of *Total Recall* finds that "over a quiet lunch … both Paretsky's humor and compassion seem never far from the surface."

Riggs, Cynthia. "Paretsky Ventures into New Territory." *First Person BookPage*. June 1998. Web. http://www.bookpage.com/9806bp/sara_paretsky.html Review of *Ghost Country* and author interview finds "the twists and turns of *Ghost Country* entertaining and thought provoking."

Robinson, Peter, ed. *The Penguin Book of Crime Stories*. New York: Penguin, 2008. Print. The anthology includes Paretsky's short story "Lily and the Sockeyes" (152–72).

Robshaw, Brandon. "Paperback Review: *Breakdown*, by Sara Paretsky." *The Independent* (London) 5 May 2013: 56–57. Print. States that novel is "a stylish, intelligent thriller which wears its liberal heart on its sleeve."

Rombeck, Terry. "In a State of Belief." *Lawrence Journal-World* 24 Jan. 2008: 6B. Print. Interview on publication of *Bleeding Kansas* explores author's childhood in Lawrence and notes after her move to Chicago, "a soft place in her heart remained for Kansas."

Rothschild, Matthew. "Sara Paretsky." *The Progressive* Mar. 2008: 31–34. Print. Editor's interview with author leaves him impressed about "how engaged she is politically."

Ross, Jean W. "Paretsky, Sara." *Contemporary Authors* Vol. 129. Ed. Susan M. Trosky. Detroit: Gale, 1990. 334–38. Print. Author profile quotes writer as struggling to gain the "kind of confidence" necessary to take her own writing seriously.

Ross, Michele. "Louise Penny, Ruth Rendell and Christopher Fowler Deliver Top-Drawer Mysteries." *Cleveland Plain Dealer* 4 Oct. 2010. Web. http://www.cleveland.com/books/index.ssf/2010/10/louise_penny_ruth_rendell_and.html Brief note on *Body Work* describes it as "a little sluggish but still offers the pleasures of catching up with old friends."

Rousseau, Caryn. "Paretsky Kindly Stops Adding Years to V. I." *Chicago Sun-Times* 12 Sept. 2010: D21. Print. Interview on publication of *Body Work* quotes author saying V.I.'s personality "used to be much more distinctive than mine but with time the two got merged."

Rowland, S. A. "Sara Paretsky: Overview." *Contemporary Popular Writers*. Ed. Dave Mote. Detroit: St. James P, 1997. 316–17. Print. Short overview of V. I. series through *Tunnel Vision* (1994) states, "[R]ealistic depictions of working America are infused with feminist passion and humor."

Royal, J. "V. I. Warshawski's Chicago." http://www.communitywalk.com/vi_warshawskis_chicago#00047Eln Interactive map of Chicago locations referred to in Paretsky's works.

Rozan, S. J. "Sara Paretsky: A Gun of One's Own." *Publishers Weekly* 25 Oct. 1999: 44–45. Print. Lengthy author interview by fellow crime writer following publication of *Hard Time* notes that novel "like all Paretsky's books, grew out of a deeply felt anger at social injustice."

Rubin, Hanna. "Our Kind of Private Eye." *Glamour* Aug. 1991: 78. Print. Short feature describes the forthcoming debut of Paretsky's famous detective on screen in V.I. Warshawski film based on several Paretsky novels and starring Kathleen Turner. Also mentions new short story collection *A Woman's Eye* edited by Paretsky.

Rubins, Josh. *New York Times Book Review* 8 Oct. 1995: 24. Print. Brief review of *Windy City Blues* finds collection "a letdown," although it notes that "the mystery short story is a notoriously difficult form."

Rubio, Steven Penner. "Killer Eyes, Killer Legs, Killer Instincts: An Evolution of the American Hard-Boiled Detective Novel." PhD diss., U of California, Berkeley, 1997. Web. Proquest document ID: 304345926. Discusses Paretsky's "complicated and even contradictory body of work which questions the basic assumptions of heroic individualism while simultaneously handing the powers of that ... individualism to her own heroine" (160).

Rule, Vera. "Paperbacks: Non-Fiction: *Writing in an Age of Silence*, by Sara Paretsky." *Guardian* (London) 11 July 2009: 19. Print. Brief review of "surprising series of essays [linking] her personal life with public politics in the Bush interregnum."

Ryan, Laura T. "Sara Paretsky." *The Post-Standard* 30 Apr. 2006: 4–6. Print. Interview with author on occasion of Paretsky delivering final talk in Syracuse's Rosamund Gifford Lecture series. Traces similarities between author and her famous character, and Paretsky's career path as a writer. Notes author's candor in admitting that "writing remains a struggle.... [S]uccess does not bring her a comfort zone" (6).

Rzepka, Charles J. *Detective Fiction*. Malden, MA: Polity P, 2005. Print. Brief discussion of "alternative detection today" refers to V. I. Warshawski as "probably the toughest of the feminist hard-boiled detectives" (240). Says Paretsky's male villains "approach the flat monstrosity of melodrama" (240–41).

Rzepka, Charles, and Lee Horsley, eds. *A Companion to Crime Fiction*. Chichester, UK: Wiley-Blackwell, 2010. Print. Guide to selected significant authors and topics in history of crime fiction. Short author essay on Paretsky's oeuvre to date (523–30); further references to her work in entry on "Feminist Crime Fiction and Female Sleuths" (258–69) and entry on "From Sherlock Holmes to the Present" (28–42).

Sale, Jonathan. "'We went at our own pace': An Education in the Life of Sara Paretsky." *The Independent on Sunday* (London) 22 Apr. 2010: 2, 3. Print. Interview quotes Paretsky's memories of her own education from primary school through graduate studies at the U of Chicago, where "because of my department's relentless misogyny, I was the only one of 13 women starting the US history programme who returned for our second year."

Sandburg, Carl. *Chicago Poems*. New York: Holt, 1916: 3. Print. Collection includes famous poem describing early-twentieth-century Chicago as "proud to be alive and coarse and strong and cunning."

Sandels, Robert. "It Was a Man's World." *Armchair Detective* 22 (1989): 388–96. Print. Essay surveys current developments in the genre with a focus on innovations by women writers, but is dismissive of Paretsky's work, describing Warshawski as "a Frankenstein monster put together from the bodies of male detectives long dead and a few female shoppers."

"Sara Paretsky." *Behind the Mystery*. Ed. Stuart Kaminsky. Cohasset, MA: Hot House P, 2005. 188–99. Print. Interview with Paretsky.

Saricks, Joyce. "Bleeding Kansas." *Booklist* 15 Oct. 2007: 4–5. Print. Short article on *Bleeding Kansas* describes story as "character-centered" and "issue-driven."

Saunders, Kate. "A Passion for Peril; Books." *Sunday Times* (London) 10 July 1994: 14. Print. A comprehensive review of *Tunnel Vision* praises the author for originality in providing "a dry crackle of wit and a deep emotional sympathy with her characters, which never tips into slushiness."

Scaggs, John. *Crime Fiction*. New York: Routledge. 2005. Print. Concise history of crime fiction including key subgenres and contemporary TV series. Outlines critical concepts central to study of crime and mystery fiction. Uses Paretsky as example of feminist appropriation of private eye traditions.

Schaffer, Rachel. "V.I. Talks Back: Sara Paretsky's Unlikable Characters as Foes and Foils." *Clues: A Journal of Detection* 25.2 (2007): 31–42. Print. Essay discusses functions served by a range of secondary characters in the V. I. series.

Schmich, Mary T. "The Case of the Curious Mystery Writer." *Chicago Tribune* 16 July 1987, sec. 5: 1, 5. Print. Author profile discusses Paretsky's experiences at CNA writing "very erudite speeches" for the company's executive officers, and her struggle to create the V.I. character.

Seaman, Donna. "Breakdown." *Booklist* 1 Dec. 2011: 25. Print. Enthusiastic review of novel finds "both Paretsky and her sharp-tongued justice-seeker, V.I. Warshawski, remain formidable in the masterfully suspenseful fifteenth novel in this superb and adored Chicago-set series."

Shane, Alice. "Crime/Mystery; In Short: Fiction."

*New York Times Book Review* 20 Oct. 1991: 36. Print. Brief review of *A Woman's Eye* edited by Paretsky notes that the "collection of 21 short stories by an international coterie of mystery writers that celebrates women who solve and commit crimes" is "a relaxing, breezy entertainment for mystery fans."

Shapiro, Laura. "The Lady Is a Gumshoe." *Newsweek* 13 July 1987: 64. Print. Short appreciative piece on author and character concludes the detective is "the most engaging woman in detective fiction since Dorothy Sayers's Harriet Vane."

_____. "Sara Paretsky." *Ms Magazine* Jan. 1988: 66–67, 92–93. Print. Comprehensive profile feature on author on occasion of being named a *Ms* Woman of the Year "for bringing a woman detective and feminist themes to murder mysteries, and for championing women writers in this mostly male genre."

_____. "The Skill of Houdini." *Newsweek* 14 May 1990: 67. Print. Enthusiastic review of *Burn Marks* enjoys novel because "V.I. tackles corruption and murder in Chicago's construction industry, but Paretsky also probes her heroine's stubborn independence ... [V. I.'s] deepest loyalties ... survive assaults and indignities."

_____. "V. I. Does It Her Way." *Newsweek* 4 July 1994: 67. Print. Short review of *Tunnel Vision* notes that by the end of the novel "unfinished business-both romantic and psychological-has piled up all over her life."

Sharoff, Robert. "Sara Paretsky." *Crain's Chicago Business* 7 June 2004: W72. Print.

Shaw, Marion. "The New Avengers; Books." *Sunday Times* (London) 12 Mar. 1995: 8. Print. Discusses expansion of crime lists by Virago and the Women's Press, noting that "feminist sleuthing is feeding a very healthy appetite."

Shepherdson, Nancy. "The Writer behind Warshawski." *Writer's Digest* Sept. 1992: 38–40. Print. Sympathetic profile of Paretsky includes author's explanation of her creative practice.

Sherwood, Juanita. *Journal-Gazette Times Courier* (Matoon, IL) 5 Feb. 2008. Print. Review of *Bleeding Kansas* notes that story is framed by "conflicts of various kinds" including generational, religious, neighborly, marital, financial.

Shiffman, Stuart. *Bookreporter.com*. July 31, 2008. http://www.bookreporter.com Web. Review of *Bleeding Kansas* says novel "represents a noteworthy change of style" for the author.

Six, Beverley G. "Breaking the Silence: Sara Paretsky's Seizure of Ideology and Discourse in Blacklist." *South Central Review* 27.1/2 (2010): 144–58. Print. Long theoretical essay discusses *Blacklist* as an example of "protest literature"; argues novel belongs to American tradition of "literature of dissent" by writers who "illuminate the ills of society."

Smiley, Robin H. "Collecting Sara Paretsky." *Firsts* June 1991: 24–28. Print. Comprehensive overview of Paretsky oeuvre through *Guardian Angel* provides a checklist of her first editions to date.

Smith, Joan. "Daring to Be Different." *Sunday Times* (London) 3 Nov. 2013: 46. Print. Review of *Critical Mass* applauds novel as "a career-crowning triumph."

_____. Rev. of *Killing Orders. New Statesman* 25 Apr. 1986: 27. Print. Review observes that the novel "restores politics to its rightful place in the mainstream private eye novel, and in doing so revitalizes the tradition."

_____. "On Chicago's Mean Streets." *Sunday Times* (London) 19 Mar. 2006: 54. Print. Laudatory review of *Fire Sale* states, "Paretsky has always been at her best when describing blue-collar America. Paretsky's grasp of industrial architecture, the barren wastelands in which factories and warehouses dwarf the humans who toil inside them, is without parallel in contemporary crime fiction."

_____. "Something Rotten." *Sunday Times* (London) 17 Apr. 2011: 52. Print. Review of *Body Work* notes it is "one of the most memorable novels in this fine series ... a heartfelt commentary on her country's involvement in the Iraq war."

Smith, Marie, ed. *Ms Murder*. London: Xanadu Publ., 1989. Print. Anthology includes Paretsky's short story "Three-Dot Po."

Solimini, Cheryl. "Playing Hardball." *Mystery Scene* 112 (2009): 16–19. Print. Lengthy cover story/ interview with author on occasion of publication of *Hardball*, which delves "into a 40-year-old disappearance connected perhaps to the murder of a black activist during the [1966] riots [and] digs up another dirty chapter of the city's past that some would like to keep buried."

Squier, Susan Merrill, ed. Introduction. *Women Writers and the City*. Knoxville: U of Tennessee P, 1984: 3–10. Print. A collection of critical essays exploring "women writers' literary treatment of the city" (6). Essays look at, for example, Virginia Woolf, Katherine Mansfield, George Eliot, and Chicago author Elia Peattie and how each writer negotiates "the culturally enshrined opposition between domestic, natural, female labor and public, cultural, male labor" (5).

Stasio, Marilyn. "Crime." *New York Times Book Review* 12 June 1994: 42. Print. Review of *Tunnel Vision* notes that "V.I. sticks out her jaw and goes it alone on this dirty, complicated fraud case."

_____. "Crime." *New York Times Book Review* 3

Oct. 1999: 24. Print. Brief review of *Hard Time* praises "the tough prison scenes and frontal-assault action that make this book her best" and the "high-minded (and hot-tempered) Chicago private eye [who] stops to help an accident victim and is railroaded on a manslaughter charge."

_____. "Crime." *New York Times Book Review* 23 Sept. 2001: 23. Print. Short review of *Total Recall* "featuring V.I. Warshawski, a female private eye with the sharpest tongue and hardest head in Chicago" comments that "Paretsky tends to lose her story in the details ... but her expertise in financial crime is tightly linked to her convictions on human rights."

_____. "Crime." *New York Times Book Review* 19 Oct. 2003: 25. Print. Review of *Blacklist* notices it plays on V.I.'s "worst nightmare—of being deprived of the right to sound off—by drawing grim parallels between the repressive political climate of the McCarthy era and present-day threats to First Amendment freedoms in the name of national security."

_____. "The Firebrand Grits Her Teeth." *New York Times Book Review* 9 Oct. 1988: 22. Print. Review of *Blood Shot* notes that detective "has a temper that could bend cutlery."

_____. "Flight or Fright." *New York Times Book Review* 2 Aug. 2015:25. Appreciative review of *Brush Back* describes V.I.'s latest case that takes her back to "the seedy streets she once called home ... in an effort to vindicate her cousin's [Boom-Boom] memory."

_____. "Lady Gumshoes: Boiled Less Hard." *New York Times Book Review* 28 Apr. 1985: 1, 38–40. Print. Lengthy feature article on cluster of new female detectives highlights Paretsky, "the Chicago writer whose name always makes the top of the list when people talk about the new female operatives." Article notes that new breed of private eyes also known for "emphasizing humanist values in the hard-boiled world of crime fiction."

_____. "Loathe Thy Neighbor." *New York Times Book Review* 13 Jan. 2008: 24. Print. Short review of *Bleeding Kansas* highlights theme of "religious intolerance" and notes "the multi-generational narrative bristles with the kind of prickly social issues that give substance to Paretsky's detective stories."

_____. "My Flesh Is Your Canvas." *New York Times Book Review* 5 Sept. 2010: 2. Print. Review of *Body Work* notes that "the role played by private security contractors in the Gulf wars is the weightiest topic, sensitively embodied in the back story of that stressed-out vet." Stasio writes "her subplots are loaded with provocative ideas"; the story of the Body Artist and her erotically charged act raises the question of "how society perceives the female body and how those perceptions can inspire both contempt for and violence toward women."

_____. "Mystery Alley." *Cleveland Plain Dealer* 25 Mar. 1984. Print. Brief review of *Deadlock* refers to "a fast-action adventure involving sabotage and murder in the Great Lakes shipping industry." Paretsky "illustrates ... how an intelligent and energetic woman can maneuver with ease in hardboiled detective fiction."

_____. "Politics as Blood Sport." *New York Times Book Review* 8 Jan. 2012: 22. Print. Review of *Breakdown* describes Paretsky's underlying "crime-behind-the-crime" theme about the loss of "a venerable newspaper that was once the pride of Chicago" when it is bought up by the "right-wing news operation called the Global Entertainment Network." It makes both author and detective "fighting mad."

_____. "Summer of '66." *New York Times Book Review* 20 Sept. 2009: 22. Print. Review of *Hardball* notes "Chicago's legacy of police brutality and political corruption is a never-ending source of material" and says it is "a distinct pleasure to hear her un-apologetically strident voice once again."

_____. "Without a Trace." *New York Times Book Review* 15 Nov. 2013: 23. Print. Review of *Critical Mass* says novel "hits a nerve with its historical back story about a Viennese atomic physicist ... a character inspired by the brilliant but unsung Austrian physicist Marietta Blau."

*States News Service* press release 15 June 2013. Print. Announces the American Library Association Public Programs Office's program LIVE! Reading Stage at 2013 ALA Annual Conference in Chicago. Paretsky participates in live stage event on Sunday, 30 June 2013.

*States News Service* press release 31 Oct. 2013. Print. Announces Paretsky's return to the Library of Congress on 15 Nov. 2013 to discuss *Critical Mass*, her 16th V. I. Warshawski novel. Free event sponsored by the LOC's Humanities and Social Sciences Division.

Steinberg, Sybil. "Burn Marks." *Publishers Weekly* 26 Jan. 1990: 406. Brief review notes although "everyone else in this complicated ... plot urges her toward traditional female paths, V.I. resolutely forges her own trail, maintaining the spunk and humor that have earned her a large, devoted following."

Storrar, William. "William Storrar." *Commonweal* 7 Dec. 2007: 35. Print. Brief mention of *Writing in an Age of Silence* in book review column notes that Paretsky's detective "has a deep sense of outrage at the violation and silencing of ordinary people, especially women, by powerful institutions with no public accountability ... a constant theme in the novels and in the story of Paretsky's own life."

Sullivan, Catey. "Best-Selling Author Tells Success Story." *The Lisle Sun* 16 Dec. 1994: 3A + 7. Print. Article covering an author appearance at Lisle Library on 15 Dec. 1994.

Sullivan, Jane. "A Life of Crime." *The Age* (Melbourne) 5 Mar. 1994: 7. Print. Lengthy interview with author on tour to promote *Tunnel Vision*. Author tells Sullivan that V.I. acquired "her creator's own flaws: anger and sloth." Paretsky says, "My flaws are not adorable, and neither are V. I.'s.... People are reacting to her emotionally as if she's a real person and it's a compliment to me that she gets on their nerves."

Szuberla, Guy. "Paretsky, Turow, and the Importance of Symbolic Ethnicity." *Midamerica XVIII*. Ed. David D. Anderson. East Lansing, MI: Midwestern P, 1991: 124–35. Print. Lengthy essay discusses two famous Chicago authors in terms of how their fiction is "pervasively shaped by a rhetoric of ethnicity" (124). Argues that Paretsky's construction of V.I.'s ethnicity, based on her immigrant parents, is complex; the character's "identity rests on her ethnic bonds, and, paradoxically, upon her rejection of ethnicity" (134).

———. "The Ties That Bind: V. I. Warshawski and the Burdens of Family." *Armchair Detective* Spr. 1994: 146–53. Print. Essay explores paradoxes of V. I.'s relationship to her ethnic background. Although she is proud of the Polish Catholic and Italian Jewish mix, she also feels "a sense of suffocation among her aunts, uncles, and relatives from South Chicago."

Tannen, Ricki Lewis. "The Fictive Female Sleuth: Mirror, Myth, and Metaphor." PhD diss. Carpinteria, CA: Pacifica Graduate Inst., 2003. Web. Proquest document ID: 305234396. Dissertation explores the psychological significance in the collective consciousness of readers who are hungry for "imaginings of women as resourceful, independent, strong, smart, and reflective of the diversity found in the reader's (sic) lives" (11). Makes considerable reference to Paretsky's oeuvre to date.

Taylor, Andrew. "Recent Crime Novels." *Spectator* 30 Jan. 2010: 36. Print. Review of *Hardball* notes it is "a strong, well-constructed novel, firmly grounded in Chicago and its politics, past and present."

Taylor, Elizabeth. "Editor's Choice." *Chicago Tribune* 9 June 2007. Print. Short review of *Writing in an Age of Silence* notes Paretsky's appearance at the Harold Washington Library "as part of the Printers Row Book Fair," an annual event in Chicago.

Thompson, Elizabeth. "'Turning Toward the Things That Make You Afraid': Growing Pains in Sara Paretsky's Feminist Hard-Boiled Fiction." Minardi and Byron 51–65. Print. Essay discusses the physical and emotional suffering that V. I. experiences in the novels, arguing the "pain is purposeful" as Paretsky seeks to find "a language for women's pain" (57).

Thomson, Liz. "Shooting from the Hip and the Lip." *Dillons News* May/June 1992: 4. Print. Interview with Paretsky as *Guardian Angel* is published in the United Kingdom. Paretsky tells Thomson, "V. I. shares my politics.... You have to live with a character for a long time so you have to have an empathy with them."

Toepfer, Susan. Rev. of *Guardian Angel. People* 16 Mar. 1992: 23–24. Web. Review states, "The case ... is so difficult to follow, and intrinsically dull, that readers must be engaged by merits beyond (or beneath) a traditional whodunit. Fortunately, Paretsky—and her cranky but commendable female detective, Warshawski—has [sic] plenty else to offer."

———. "Picks and Pans." *People Weekly* 9 Sept. 1991. n.pag. Short review of *A Woman's Eye* anthology notes "victims' voices at last resound."

Rev. of *Total Recall*, by Sara Paretsky. *Publishers Weekly* 16 July 2001: 161. Says novel explores its Holocaust victims and themes with "compelling, terrible clarity and inevitability."

Rev. of *Total Recall*, by Sara Paretsky. *Kirkus Reviews* 1 July 2001. Web. https://www.kirkusreviews.com/book-reviews/sara-paretsky/total-recall/ Notes author "loves to bite off more than she can chew ... her furious energy keeps the final pages still churning."

Rev. of *Total Recall*, by Sara Paretsky. "Smokin' Reads; New Thrillers." *The Economist* (USA). 15 Dec. 2001: 68. Print. Review notes that "Lotty's traumatic experiences in the past ... provide some important leads for V.I. in [this] case" and says Paretsky "brings an admirable lightness of touch to what might otherwise have been a sentimental story."

Tran, Christine. "*Brush Back.*" *Booklist Online* 1 June 2015. Web. http://www.booklistonline.com/Brush-Back-Sara-Paretsky/pid=7509601 Enthusiastic review finds V. I. "as intrepid and tenacious" as ever as she "battles the circled wagons of the tight-knit South Side Chicago neighborhood in which she grew up."

Trembley, Elizabeth A. "Sara Paretsky." *Great Women Mystery Writers: Classic to Contemporary*. Ed. Kathleen Gregory Klein. Westport, CT: Greenwood, 1994. 266–69. Print. Short biographical entry notes that the novels to date (eight) all "indict patriarchal society by placing traditionally respected, authoritative institutions at the center of whatever evil V.I. probes."

Trosky, Susan M. (ed). "Sara Paretsky." *Contemporary Authors: A Bio-Bibliographical Guide* Vol. 129. Detroit: Gale, 1990. 334–337. Author entry provides biographical profile of author and bibliographical information to date.

Tuite, Cornelia Honchar. "A Very Happy Marriage." *Chicago Times* Nov./Dec. 1989: 78–82. Print. Article on Paretsky marriage to Courtenay Wright.

Rev. of *Tunnel Vision*, by Sara Paretsky. *Publishers Weekly* 11 Apr. 1994: 57. Print. "As prickly and principled as ever, Chicago's preeminent female PI, V. I. Warshawski, forcefully unravels several knotted mysteries."

Rev. of *Tunnel Vision*, by Sara Paretsky. *Kirkus Reviews* 1 Apr. 1994. Web. https://www.kirkusreviews.com/book-reviews/sara-paretsky/tunnel-vision/ Review criticizes novel as an "overstuffed saga."

Rev. of *Tunnel Vision*, by Sara Paretsky. "Thrilling Women." *The Economist* 9 July 1994: 87. Print. Complains that novel is "preachy to a fault and far too complicated."

Turner, Jenny. "Right-Ons." *London Review of Books* 24 Oct. 1991: 22–23. Print. Column assessing recent mysteries includes short review of *Burn Marks* with praise for the detective who "knows her city's bent cops, corrupt politicians, leaky journalists and criminal real-estate developers" (23).

Vanacker, Sabine. "V. I. Warshawski, Kinsey Millhone and Kay Scarpetta: Creating a Feminist Detective Hero." *Criminal Proceedings: The Contemporary American Crime Novel*. Ed. Peter Messent. London: Pluto P, 1997. 62–86. Print. Lengthy essay explores how the three novelists are "redirecting the genre" along loosely defined feminist/"feminine" lines (63).

Virshup, Amy. "Newly Released." *New York Times* 17 Jan. 2008: E8. Print. Review of *Bleeding Kansas* notes that author "reimagines the violent clashes between pro-and antislavery forces of the 1850s on a contemporary stage."

Vretos, Linda A. "Hard Time: A V. I. Warshawski Novel." *School Library Journal* Mar. 2000: 265. Print. Review describes novel as a "suspenseful thriller" that kicks off when Vic swerves to avoid the victim of a hit-and-run accident in a dark street in Chicago. The "tough, stubborn, passionate" detective has to clear her own name.

Wade, Robert. "Spadework." *The San Diego Union Books* 7 Mar. 1982: 3. Print. Brief review of *Indemnity Only* notes author "shows enough raw talent to lead us to expect that, once she finds her own style, she'll be a worthwhile addition to the field."

Wallace, Marilyn, ed. *The Best of Sisters in Crime.* New York: Berkley, 1997. Print. Anthology includes Paretsky's short story "The Maltese Cat."

_____, ed. *Sisters in Crime.* 1989. London: Allison, 1990. Print. Anthology includes Paretsky's short story "The Case of the Pietro Andromache."

_____, ed. *Sisters in Crime #3.* New York: Berkley, 1990. Print. Anthology includes Paretsky's short story "The Maltese Cat."

Walker, Ronald G., and June M. Frazer, eds. *The Cunning Craft: Original Essays on Detective Fiction and Contemporary Literary Theory.* Macomb: Western Illinois UP, 1990. Important collection of critical/theoretical essays exploring continuing appeal of detective fiction as the form broadens to include, e.g., post-modernist and feminist subversions of formulaic conventions. Contributors include Robin Winks, George N. Dove, Maureen T. Reddy and others.

Walmsley, Heather. "Crime Thriller." *The List* 29 Nov. 2001: 104. Print. Short review of *Total Recall* praises Paretsky's ability to entwine "seemingly random strands of a local Chicago story into an international crime that stretches back to Switzerland and Germany and binds small financial claims to the brutal horrors of war and genocide ... jumping between different character perspectives, and taunting with tiny half-truths."

Walsh, Ray. "Books." *Lansing State Journal.* 26 Oct. 2003: 9D. Print. Short review of *Blacklist* describes novel as "disappointing, despite strong characterization and unusual plot[s] ... [a] wordy, atmospheric effort."

Walton, Priscilla. "Form and Forum: The Agency of Detectives and the Venue of the Short Story." *Narrative* 6.2 (1998): 123–39. Print. Article discusses contemporary short story anthologies of, e.g., Sisters in Crime as providing "a mainstream venue for women's writings [and] open[ing] a crucial forum for new authors ... and more established writers" (131).

_____. "Paretsky's V. I. as P.I.: Revising the Script and Recasting the Dick." *LIT: Literature Interpretation Theory* 4.3 (1993): 203–13. Print. Essay draws on postcolonial theory to discuss ways in which Paretsky's work can be seen to decenter and "question the assumptions and the elisions" (203) embedded in canonical hard-boiled fiction.

Walton, Priscilla L., and Manina Jones. *Detective Agency: Women Rewriting the Hard-Boiled Tradition.* Berkeley: U of California P, 1999. Print. A carefully detailed discussion of the ways in which Paretsky and others are using the conventions of the "hard-boiled" genre and transforming the masculinist ideologies of that tradition. Important critical and historical analysis of the ways in which contemporary women are rewriting the subgenre.

Washington, Betty. "This Sleuth Is a Woman.... But a Lady, She's Not." *Chicago Sun-Times* 5 Mar. 1984: 33. Print. Early feature article with sidebar on author and detective at point when Paretsky was still working "in the automation division of CNA Insurance." Describes Warshawski as "crafty, brash, cynical—...Warshawski packs muscle."

Waugh, Harriet. Rev. of *Deadlock. Spectator* 5 Jan. 1985: 21. Print. Review finds detective "convincingly tough."

_____. "Recent Crime Fiction." *Spectator* 9 Sept. 2006. Web. *Literature Resource Center*. Review of *Fire Sale* notes the novel "moves fast with many twists and turns."

Weaver, William. "Crime." *Financial Times* (London) 8 Mar. 1986: 16. Print. Short review of *Killing Orders* praises detective figure as "a prickly but essentially human character."

Webb, Betty. "*Hardball* by Sara Paretsky." *Mystery Scene* 2010. Web. http://mysteryscenemag.com/26-reviews/books/344-Hardball Rev. praises novel as "deeply satisfying ... for its heart-tugging history lesson."

Weissmann, Dan. "Spine Tingler. (The Business of Life)." *Crain's Chicago Business* 8 Aug. 2005: 38. Print. Brief article on author.

Wells, Linda S. "Popular Literature and Postmodernism: Sara Paretsky's Hard-Boiled Feminist." *Proteus: A Journal of Ideas* 6.1 (1989): 51–56. Print. Article identifies Paretsky's popular literature as providing female readers with vicarious assurance that V. I.'s imagined life, informed by feminist politics, female friendships and a quick wit, is possible.

Welsh, Louise. "Tough Guys, Hard Cases." *The Independent* (London) 31 Oct. 2003: 26. Print. Review of *Blacklist* finds V.I. "love-sick, and chronically tired, for most of the novel."

Wetzel, Eric. "Sara Paretsky: There's a Light in the Attic: It's the Bright and Funny (But Tortured) Creator of Private Eye V. I. Warshawski." *Book* 30 (Sept.–Oct. 2003): 30. Print. Interview with author on eve of publication of *Blacklist* took place in her attic office and includes photographs of items in the study such as family photos, V. I. book covers, a Chicago Bulls cap accompanied by Paretsky's explanations of their meaning to her.

White, Jean M. Rev. of *Blood Shot. Washington Post Book World* 18 Sept. 1988: 6. Print. Review notes the novel is "tough, tender, gritty and scary."

_____. Rev. of *Indemnity Only. Washington Post Book World* 21 Feb. 1982: 10. Print. Review praises author for writing "with assurance about a milieu that she knows well."

Wilkinson, Joanne. Rev. of *Body Work. Booklist* 1 July 2010: 5. Print. Review notes "as always, the city of Chicago, from its gentrified lofts to its working-class bars, is given a starring role."

Willett, Ralph. *Hard-Boiled Detective Fiction*. Halifax, UK: Ryburn, 1992. Print. BAAS Pamphlets in American Studies 23. Pamphlet essay traces the emergence of the American hard-boiled detective novel and explores its flexibility as new developments introduce different perspectives of gender, race, and class.

_____. *The Naked City: Urban Crime Fiction in the USA*. Manchester, UK: Manchester UP, 1996. Print. Discusses representations of the city in range of contemporary American authors, including Paretsky's portrayal of Chicago.

Williams, John. *Into the Badlands*. London: Paladin, 1991. Print. Chronicles a series of interviews conducted on author's trans-American roadtrip. Chapter on Paretsky and Chicago based on the driving tour Paretsky gives Williams, taking in the city locations used by her. Author discusses Chicago's reputation for graft and corruption: "[T]his is a city where it doesn't really matter what you do" (161).

Willis, Chris. "'Blacklist' by Sara Paretsky." *Mystery Women* Dec. 2003: 8. Print. Review praises book as "gripping, fascinating and disturbing, both as a crime novel and as a reflection of the increasingly repressive society in which we live."

Wilson, Ann. "The Female Dick and the Crisis of Heterosexuality." *Feminism in Women's Detective Fiction*. Ed. Glenwood Irons. Toronto: U of Toronto P, 1995. 148–55. Print. Essay discusses appeal of the hard-boiled heroine "a woman who is self-reliant and independent, a prototype of a feminist ideal" (149); concludes "female hard-boiled fiction offers a mild challenge to the dominant social order but not a radical assault on it" (155).

Wilson, Laurel A. "*Ghost Country.*" *Library Journal* 15 Apr. 1998: 115. Print. Review states that the novel "isn't for everyone ... but open-minded readers will savor it."

Rev. of *Windy City Blues*, by Sara Paretsky. *Publishers' Weekly* 28 Aug. 1995: 106. Print. Contributor prefers "broader canvases" of Paretsky's novels to the "slight" short stories in this collection.

Windrath, Helen, ed. *Reader, I Murdered Him, Too*. London: The Women's Press, 1997. Print. Anthology includes Paretsky's short story "The Man Who Loved Life."

Winks, Robin. "Mysteries." *New Republic* 13 Mar. 1982: 38. Print. Brief review of *Indemnity Only* notes that author "weaves a thoroughly convincing, and gritty tale about V. I. Warshawski, a tough and attractive Chicago private detective who is a woman."

Winks, Robin, and Maureen Corrigan, eds. *Mystery and Suspense Writers, The Literature of Crime, Detection, and Espionage.* Vols. 1 and 2. New York: Scribner, 1998. Print. Two-volume collection of lengthy essays on influential writers in the genre and on themes such as "The Ethnic Detective" and "The Police Procedural." Paretsky's work is discussed in an author essay (Vol. 2) and theme essay "The Female Detective" (Vol. 2).

Wisniewski, Mary. "Paretsky Paints Wry Portraits in 'Body Work.'" *Chicago Sun-Times* 12 Sept. 2010: D21. Print. Praises novel with its "wry observations about greed and sexism" and V. I.'s character as "a cranky, vulnerable woman with a messy life, but a superhuman willingness to put herself in harm's way for the sake of justice."

_____. "Paretsky Lets PI Get Vulnerable." *Chicago Sun-Times* 4 Oct. 2009: D8. Review praises *Hardball* as a "touching, gripping story, showing Warshawski at her most vulnerable ... the perfect detective for Chicago—she's tough but sentimental, and both savvy and paranoid enough to know that if something looks crooked, it probably is."

Rev. of *A Woman's Eye*, ed. Sara Paretsky. *Publishers Weekly* 2 Aug. 1991: 65. Print. Short review praises author Antonia Fraser's detective Jemima Shore "in one of the collection's best stories."

Rev. of *Women on the Case*, ed. Sara Paretsky. *Publishers Weekly* 29 Apr. 1996: 54. Print. Describes anthology of 26 stories by women crime writers as a "purposeful collection" that "endorses good politics at least as much as good storytelling."

Woodhead, Cameron. "Fiction." *The Age* (Melbourne). 7 Nov. 2009: 26. Print. Short review of *Hardball* says story takes detective "into Chicago's racially charged history, and into her own family secrets." Notes the appearance of "young cousin Petra, a woman as privileged, soft and charming as V. I. is unvarnished, cynical and streetwise."

Woodrell, Kathy. "Moving to the Page: Author Sara Paretsky Delivers Judith Austin Lecture." *Library of Congress Information Bulletin* May 2001: 105. Report on Paretsky's 3 Apr. 2001 lecture delivered in memory of Judith Austin, "head of the Main Reading Room at the time of her death in 1997." Woodrell writes, "Paretsky's spirited and articulate lecture ... declared truths that many do not have the courage to address—about a meanness of spirit that per-

vades society, about the travesty of denying girls a destiny expected of boys."

Rev. of *Writing in an Age of Silence*, by Sara Paretsky. *Kirkus Reviews* 1 Mar. 2007: 212. Print. Brief review notes that "Paretsky links different kinds of oppression in compelling ways."

Rev. of *Writing in an Age of Silence*, by Sara Paretsky. *Publishers Weekly* 15 Jan. 2007: 38. Print. Review praises the "brief, potent memoir [which portrays] an engaged intellectual looking to make a substantive and life-affirming mark on society."

Wyrick, Laura. "Sara Paretsky: Overview." *Reference Guide to American Literature.* 3rd ed. Ed Jim Kamp. Detroit: St. James P, 1994. Print. Short summary of author's career and oeuvre through *Guardian Angel* (1992). Notes that, although "Paretsky's books were reviewed positively, they have been criticized for displaying [a] political agenda too ostentatiously ... however, critics have long recognized Paretsky's work as well-written and an important update to popular detective fiction."

Yager, Susanna. "Murder, Deceit, Swindle." *The Sunday Telegraph* (London) 18 Nov. 2001: 18. Print. Short review of *Total Recall* finds it "a gripping read by one of the best writers of PI fiction around."

Yondorf, Lisa. "Paretsky and Paschke: The Art of Crime." [Northwestern] *University College Alumni Newsmagazine* Win. 1998/Spr. 1999: 3. Print. Short article on Paretsky's appearance at an evening of Conversations sponsored by the Block Museum of Art and the Center for the Writing Arts at Northwestern U. Event takes place Oct. 1998 during semester that Paretsky is teaching the writing seminar "Moving to the Page" at Northwestern.

Zahara, Irene, ed. *The Third WomanSleuth Anthology.* New York: Crossing P, 1990. Print. Anthology includes Paretsky's story "Lily and the Sockeyes."

Zappia, Susan A. "Writers on Writing: Collected Essays from the *New York Times.*" *Library Journal* 15 Mar. 2001: 83. Print. Review of NYT editor John Darnton's compilation of essays on authorship by writers such as Saul Bellow, Alice Walker, and Sara Paretsky praises the "intimate, chatty collection ... [giving] a sense of the mysterious way in which fiction chooses those with not merely good stories to tell but dedication to the physical act of writing itself."

Zheutlin, Barbara. "Distaff Detective Is Down by Law." *In These Times* 24–30 Jan. 1990: 18. Print. Insightful analysis of Paretsky's contribution to the "new genre within a genre—the female detective novel."

Zvirin, Stephanie. Rev. of *Blacklist. Booklist* Aug. 2003: 1927. Print. Describes novel as "a tightly woven and thoughtful thriller, this enticing mix of history and mystery showcases sharp, clever, vulnerable V. I. at her best."

_____. Rev. of *Critical Mass. Booklist* 1 Sept. 2013: 46. Print. Says "V. I. [is] at her stubborn, reckless, compassionate best in this complicated page-turner."

_____. Rev. of *Hardball. Booklist* July 2009: 7. Review notes "another stellar performance from a storyteller as dedicated to entertainment as to exposing humankind's treachery."

_____. Rev. of *Total Recall. Booklist* July 2001: 1952. Print. Review notes that "as usual, the Chicago backdrop is vividly imagined, and V.I. comes across as smart and appealing."

## Web Sites and Other Online Sources

Sara Paretsky Web site. http://www.saraparetsky.com/http://www.saraparetsky.com/

Online interviews with Paretsky:

- Claire Armistead interview with Paretsky regarding *Hardball*. The *Guardian* 12 Mar. 2010. Podcast. http://theguardian.com
- Steve Bertrand interview with Paretsky on *Critical Mass*. WGN Radio. 7 Dec. 2013. Web. http://wgnradio.com/2013/12/07/sara-paretsky-critical-mass/
- Bob Cornwell interview with Paretsky. Tangled Web UK CrimeScene 06. n.d. Web. http://www.twbooks.co.uk/crimescene/Sara-Paretsky-An-interview-by-Bob-Cornwell.htm
- Hodder interview with Paretsky on V. I. Warshawski series. n.d. Web. https://soundcloud.com/hodderbooks/interview-sara-paretsky-on-the-vi-warshawski-series
- Donna Seaman discusses *Bleeding Kansas* and *Writing in an Age of Silence* with Paretsky. *Open Books Radio*. ca. 2008. Web. http://www.openbooksradio.org/interviews.htm#
- *Saturday Live*. BBC Radio 4. 19 Mar. 2011. Web. https://soundcloud.com/saturday-live/satlive-19-march-2011
- Studs Terkel interview with Paretsky about *Guardian Angel*. 29 Jan. 1992. Studs Terkel Radio Archive, WFMT Radio Network/Chicago History Museum. Web. http://studsterkel.org/

"Book Club of the Air." *Talk of the Nation*. Natl. Public Radio. 21 Jan. 1999. Web. http://www.npr.org/templates/story/story.php?storyId=1010013 Peter Wolfe, Walter Mosley, and Sara Paretsky discuss Raymond Chandler's books and his style of writing with Ray Suarez.

"Chanson des Femmes." *The Early Music Show*.

BBC Radio 3. 27 Mar. 2011. Web. http://www.bbc.co.uk/programmes/b00zt5t6 Paretsky discusses music in *Body Work*.

Chicago Public Media, WBEZ:

- "Author Sara Paretsky Tours Chicago for Her Next Crime Scene." *Eight Forty-Eight*. 24 Aug. 2011. Web. http://www.wbez.org/episode/eight-forty-eight-82411 Twelve-minute tour of Chicago settings used in V. I. stories.
- Randy Cohen Interview with Paretsky. *Person, Place, Thing*. WAMC Northeast Public Radio. 8 Jan. 2014. Web. http://personplacething.org/person-place-thing-episode-57-sara-paretsky
- *Critical Mass* Author Sara Paretsky. 11 Nov. 2013. Web. https://soundcloud.com/afternoonshiftwbez/critical-mass-author-sara
- "Diving into the Dark and Gritty World of Chicago Noir," 4 Dec. 2014. Web. https://soundcloud.com/afternoonshiftwbez/diving-into-the-dark-and-gritty-world-of-chicago-noir
- *Chicago Tribune*'s Rick Kogan Interview with Paretsky. Harold Washington Lib. Ctr. 14 Mar. 2012. Web. http://www.wbez.org/story/sara-paretsky-day-97379
- On Paretsky's *Indemnity Only*. *Afternoon Shift*. Web. https://soundcloud.com/afternoonshiftwbez/detective-novel-indemnity-only-tells-the-story-of-female-private-investigator-vi-warshawski
- Printers Row Book Fair. 12 June 2010. Web. http://www.wbez.org/episode-segments/printers-row-book-fair-sara-paretsky

*Fear No Art*. WTTW TV. 29 Oct. 2011. Web. http://thedinnerparty.tv/v-i-warshawskis-sara-paretsky/ Paretsky talks about Chicago poet Gwendolyn Brooks.

*The Food Programme*. BBC Radio 4. 18 Aug. 2013. Paretsky talks about V. I. and food.

*Interesting People*. Ed Sutkowski talks to Sara Paretsky. WTVP. 28 May 2009. Web. http://wtvp.org/programming/Ipeo/1–406.asp

*Open Book*. BBC Radio 4. 9 Dec. 2001. Paretsky and audience discuss *Total Recall*.

"Paretsky on Her Best-Selling Chicago PI and Diversity in Mystery Writing." Illinois Public Media. 30 Jul. 2015. Web. https://www.popuparchive.com/collections/1468/items/41782 Paretsky talks about *Brush Back*.

Paretsky, Sara. "*Fire Sale*" [An event commemorating V. I. Warshawski's 25th anniversary]. Lib. of Congress Center for the Book. Jan. 2007. Web. https://youtu.be/ikBfYY82Dp0

_____. "My Quest for Heroes," John Hersey Memorial Address, Key West FL Literary Festival, 9 Jan. 2014, http://www.kwls.org/podcasts/sara-paretsky-2/

_____. "Safe and Free." Print and TV campaign. American Civil Liberties Union. Aimed at educating the public about the dangers of the Patriot Act. http://www.aclu.org

_____. "Sara Paretsky on *Critical Mass*," Lib. of Congress. 15 Nov. 2013. Web. https://www.youtube.com/watch?v=Jlpu-82Jiqs

_____. "Sara Paretsky: My First Car." *Chicago Tribune.* 6 Feb. 2014. Web. http://www.chicagotribune.com/chi-sara-paretsky-on-her-first-car-20140207-story.html

_____. "Sara Paretsky: 2011 National Book Festival." Lib. of Congress. 24 Sept. 2011. Web. https://youtu.be/M-pjk0oCVHM

_____. *Sweet Folk, Chicago.* WFMT. 21 Dec. 2013. Rebroadcast 24 May 2014. Web. http://www.sweetfolkchicago.org/swf20131221.htm Paretsky serves as guest DJ.

_____. *Sweet Folk, Chicago.* WFMT. 7 Mar. 2015. Web. http://www.sweetfolkchicago.org/swf20150307.htm Paretsky serves as guest DJ.

_____. Third Annual Judith Austin Memorial Lecture. Lib. of Congress. 3 Apr. 2001. Web. http://www.loc.gov/

_____. "I Love Libraries" Campaign. Amer. Lib. Assn. 18 May 2013. Web. http://www.ilovelibraries.org/ourauthors/ourauthorsouradvocates/authorpage/sparetsky

"Paretsky's PI Uncovers Murder in Chicago. *Talk of the Nation.* Natl. Public Radio. 31 Aug. 2010.

Web. http://www.npr.org/templates/story/story.php?storyId=129555599 Paretsky discusses *Body Work.*

*Private Passions.* BBC Radio 3. 3 Sept. 2006. Web. Paretsky chooses favorite music tracks.

"Sara Paretsky." Wikipedia author entry. Web. http://en.wikipedia.org/wiki/Sara_Paretsky

*Science Friday.* Natl. Public Radio. 7 Feb. 2014. Web. http://www.sciencefriday.com/person/sara-paretsky/ Paretsky talks about science themes in *Critical Mass.*

Sisters in Crime. http://sistersincrime.org

*Start the Week.* BBC Radio 4. 6 Mar. 2006. Web. http://www.bbc.co.uk/radio4/factual/starttheweek_20060306.shtml Paretsky discusses religious faith and the modern world with Andrew Marr, Moazzam Begg, Charles Allen, and Rod Liddle.

*Woman's Hour.* BBC Radio 4. 8 Aug. 2000. Paretsky discusses *Hard Time.*

_____. BBC Radio 4. 25 Mar. 2008. Web. http://www.bbc.co.uk/programmes/b009j28b Paretsky discusses *Bleeding Kansas.*

_____. BBC Radio 4. 15 Jul. 2015. Web. http://www.bbc.co.uk/programmes/b062kqzq Paretsky discusses *Brush Back.*

YouTube clips, including Gwendolyn Brooks dedication event on 20 Oct. 2011. Web. http://www.youtube.com

# Index